Welcome All Wonders

Welcome All Wonders

A Composer's Journey

J. A. C. Redford

Baker Books

A Division of Baker Book House Co
Grand Rapids, Michigan 49516

Published by Baker Books
a division of Baker Book House Company
P.O. Box 6287, Grand Rapids, MI 49516-6287

Printed in the United States of America

Library of Congress Cataloging-in-Publication Data

Redford, J. A. C.
    Welcome all wonders : a composer's journey / J. A. C. Redford.
      p. cm.
    Includes discography, worklist, and bibliographical references.
    ISBN 0-8010-1120-5
    1. Redford, J. A. C. 2. Composers—United States—Biography. 3. Ex–church members—Mormon Church—Biography. 4. Evangelicalism—United States. 5. Mormon Church—Controversial literature. 6. Church of Jesus Christ of Latter-Day Saints—Controversial literature. I. Title.
    ML410.R2397A3 1997
    780′.92—dc21

                                                                    97–19487

For Jessica, Jerusha, Jonathan, and Ian, and for their children to come:

⎯⎯➤●◄⎯⎯

For this reason, I bow my knees before the Father,
from whom every family in heaven and on earth derives its name,
that He would grant you, according to the riches of His glory,
to be strengthened with power through His Spirit in the inner man;
so that Christ may dwell in your hearts through faith;
and that you, being rooted and grounded in love,
may be able to comprehend with all the saints
what is the breadth and length and height and depth,
and to know the love of Christ which surpasses knowledge,
that you may be filled up to all the fulness of God.

—Ephesians 3:14–19 NASB

⎯⎯➤●◄⎯⎯

Contents

Acknowledgments

*B*ecause this is a book about my life, there are many to whom I owe a debt of gratitude beyond the scope of the work itself. No list could ever adequately credit or thank them all. The following, however, are those who directly impacted the writing and to whom I am most deeply grateful for its completion:

First and foremost, to my Lord and Savior, Jesus Christ, for enduring the pain and humiliation of death on the cross for my sake, and telling yet another tale of His amazing grace through the events of my life.

To my wife, LeAnn, for thirty-one years of friendship and twenty-two years of marriage; for her constant love, support, encouragement, and prayers; for listening and editing, sometimes under duress; and for having the courage to tell me things I didn't want to hear, but needed to hear anyway.

To my children, Jessica, Jerusha, Jonathan, and Ian, for their patience with me as I labored over the book between professional assignments. It was often their time that was sacrificed, and I hope they will be repaid in some small measure by the love they find between these pages.

To Bruce Lockerbie and Jim Sire, inspired and inspiring authors and mentors, for awakening me to the possibility that my story might indeed be a book after all; for reading the manuscript at various stages and offering constructive criticism, encouragement, and in the end, their endorsements.

To Ron Haynes, for shepherding the project through the publishing process, and to his wife, Carolyn, for her encouragement and prayers. Also to Baker Books, for committing its resources to a story I never imagined would have a life beyond the circle of my own family and friends.

To Erika Hill, the "book piranha," and Joy Parker, both uniquely gifted and delightful friends and colleagues, for innumerable hours of editing, hand-holding, buoying up, and toning down. Also to Maria denBoer, my editor at Baker, for believing in the book, polishing details, and answering last-minute questions; and to Deborah Gibbs and Carol Gibson for much needed help in typing and editing.

To Janice Rossen for long-suffering friendship that manifested itself through inspiration, prayers, and pages of invaluable suggestions and comments.

To David Dominguez, Mark and Marcia Ensminger, Alan Grant, Dan Greene, Jeanie Johnson, Jenni Key, Pat Lampman, Scott and Sara McKinney, Rick Rivette, Jon Strain, and Danny Webb for reading the manuscript, cheering me on, and keeping me honest by alerting me to errors, weaknesses, and potential misunderstandings. Those that remain are my own fault, not theirs.

To Michael Card, Stephanie Edwards, Earl Henslin, Gary Richmond, and Howie Stevenson for their friendship and endorsements.

To Carl and Chris Arrington, Dale and Becky Burke, Marcus Hummon, Jac and Jackie LaTour, Michael and Lori Shanebeck, John Vigran, and Fred and Linda Wevodau for reading the manuscript, offering kind words of support, and spurring me to stay with the task at key points in the process.

To the Joint Heirs, especially Bob and Melanie Byde, Don and Jan Frank, Pete and Diane Freeman, Jim and Jenni Key, and Don and Mary Pedrick for their prayers.

To Chuck Swindoll and R.C. Sproul, for timely letters of encouragement.

To my mother, Patricia Dawson, my father, H.E.D. Redford, my stepfather, Jack Dawson, my dear grandparents, Al and Ruth Clawson, and my uncles and aunts, Gene and Sue Smith and Jay and Toni Jensen, for raising me with love, faith, and a deep sense of honor and values. Also to my brother, Rick, for his loyalty and love.

Finally, to all those I mention in the following chapters, who gave much of themselves to enrich my life and teach me what it means to be human. If there are any I have inadvertently omitted, I ask your forgiveness.

Overture: A New Song

I waited patiently for the LORD; and he inclined unto me, and heard my cry. He brought me up also out of an horrible pit, out of the miry clay, and set my feet upon a rock, and established my goings. And he hath put a new song in my mouth, even praise unto our God: many shall see it, and fear, and shall trust in the LORD.

—Psalm 40:1–3

In the introduction to his luminous spiritual memoir, *The Sacred Journey*, Frederick Buechner writes that "God speaks into or out of the thick of our days . . . not just through the sounds we hear . . . but through events in all their complexity and variety, through the harmonies and dishar-monies and counterpoint of all that happens." Hence, Buech-ner thinks of his life, "and of the lives of everyone who has ever lived, or will ever live, as not just journeys through time but as sacred journeys." He tells of trying to "listen back" to certain key moments of his life to find "whatever of meaning, of holiness, of God, there may be in it to hear."[1]

I love the tales God spins in the lives of the people He has made. Each one is unique as an autumn leaf or an ocean wave, yet all bear the unmistakable imprint of their Maker, the con-summate artist of whose work our greatest flights of imagina-tion are mere reflections. This book is the story of my sacred journey. In telling it I have endeavored to listen back through the sometimes cacophonous circumstances of my own life for hints of God's voice, hoping to identify and understand the themes and fragments of themes He wove together while lead-ing me on this spiritual odyssey. It is the story of what a friend of mine has called "the appalling strangeness of the mercy of God."

Buechner speaks of life in terms of music: harmony, disharmony, and counterpoint. I am a composer by trade—and by vocation—and these metaphors resonate deeply within me, particularly the idea of counterpoint. In music, counterpoint occurs when two or more independent melodies sound together, producing an effect that is greater than the sum of the individual parts. While good counterpoint seems natural and inevitable to the listener, the composer must create it, line upon line, with painstaking care. The process begins with a single theme, which then becomes the basis for all the music that follows. This fundamental theme is called the "cantus firmus."

Mormonism provided a kind of cantus firmus for my life from the beginning. I was born into a close-knit, Latter-day Saint family with Mormon heritage extending back at least five generations on each side. As a young man, I was an active member of the Church. My involvement extended well beyond mere activity, however: I was a true believer. I read extensively from LDS literature and had many profound spiritual experiences that convinced me of the truthfulness of Mormon doctrine and the exclusive authority of Church founder Joseph Smith and his successors. At the appropriate times I underwent all the rites of passage common to dedicated young Mormon men: receiving the priesthood, serving on a proselytizing mission, and marrying in the temple. Faith, family, and personal goals seemed to blend together into one seamless, harmonious whole.

As I grew older, however, and confronted the challenges and ambiguities of adulthood, I began to experience increasing dissonance and the gnawing sense that my understanding of the world was somehow out of tune and out of rhythm with what was real and true. For a long time, I thought the problem was strictly my own fault. In part, this was the case. I was certainly hearing the false notes sounded by my own failures and immaturity. Still, this did not account for everything. Gradually, I came to believe that reality itself was something different than I had supposed. I concluded that I had the wrong fundamental theme.

In the spring of 1984, my wife LeAnn and I left the Mormon Church after a long and painful process; but, by the grace of God, we did not find darkness and despair on the other side. "In the juvescence of the year came Christ the tiger."[2] At just the right time, Jesus seized hold of us, challenged our cherished assumptions, and then, through the sheer surprise of His mercy, created in us a brand-new life. Despite the fact that the term "born again" has become a popular pejorative in some circles, this is the best way to describe our experience. Following Jesus out of Mormonism meant the joyous discovery of a new song, a cantus firmus with which our counterpoint finally made sense, created with unforced authenticity and purpose. My sacred journey has not been without distance or destination, but a journey into grace.

This book began as a letter of explanation to my family and Mormon friends. It has since grown well beyond the scope of its original intent and has passed through several incarnations, finally arriving at its present state via circumstances that can well be called circuitous. The writing has been therapeutic for me, the work itself becoming part of the journey. In some ways, leaving Mormonism has been like coming to grips with a personal tragedy—I have traveled through passages of denial, anger, and grief, and finally found, I hope, some measure of understanding. Now I am twelve years farther down the road from the first draft of my original letter, crossing the shell-pocked terrain of midlife. I still want my family to hear and understand why I left their church, but this goal has been overshadowed by the desire simply to tell my story, one more tale to add to the collected works of God's astonishing intervention in human lives. Midlife is a time of reflection and assessment, and I feel an almost visceral impulse to gather together the loose strands of my life, to find coherence and meaning in the disparate threads.

When LeAnn and I left the LDS Church, some of our loved ones responded as if we had rejected them personally. Although this reaction was probably unavoidable, it was not what we intended by our decision. We did not feel that we had rejected our families and friends; in fact, now more than ever, we want them to know that we love and respect them in spite of our differences. We continue to honor the fundamental human values our families taught by precept and example. Nevertheless, we did choose to leave because we genuinely no longer believe that Mormonism presents a true picture of reality. Throughout the process of writing this book, I've struggled to find language to communicate this conviction in a clear and courteous way. For readers who are not Mormons and know little of the history and beliefs of the LDS Church, I've also taken pains to explain its basic tenets as fairly and straightforwardly as I can so that my story can be seen in its full and proper context.

In the course of writing this book, three prominent themes emerge repeatedly: faith, family, and artistic expression, manifest particularly through music. I believe these three elements are really facets of a single theme, tributary streams flowing into a larger river. The centrality of faith and family is of obvious importance to me; likewise, the circumstances of my growth and development as a composer. The reasons behind my inclusion of so many widely variegated outside influences, however, may not be as clear. Assembling and making sense of the music, art, books, and films that have shaped my life has been one of the major challenges of this book. Nevertheless, they are integral to my experience, part of the main current of the journey, and their variety is part of their significance. God has used music and art to speak directly to my life and touch me in a unique and personal way, sometimes with even greater force and clarity than through my contemplation of His Word. This is how He made me. I feel compelled to include this aspect of my nature in a discussion of my spiritual development.

When composing his sacred music, J.S. Bach wrote the letters "JJ" at the beginning of his scores and "SDG" at the end. "JJ" stands for *Jesu Juva* or "Jesus, help" and "SDG" for *Soli Deo Gloria* or "To God alone the glory." These statements anchored his music like two points plotted on a graph—he knew where to start and he knew where to finish. While I do not imagine myself for an instant to be in Bach's league, I nevertheless crave that sense of vulnerability and consecration in my own work, whether it be writing music or this book.

And so I set out to listen to the music of my sacred journey. This journey is a river. And the river is a bloodstream that flows from the heart of Christ. It flows from grace into grace.

Jesu Juva!

1

I, . . . having been born of goodly parents, therefore I was taught somewhat in all the learning of my father.

—*Book of Mormon:* 1 Nephi 1:1

*A*s I listen for the distant music of my childhood, a chorus of voices wells up. The oldest and deepest are those of family—mother and father, grandparents, great-grandparents, and great-great-grandparents—a vast, interlocking chain of relationships that, according to Mormon teaching, stretches back into eternity.

The Mormon Church, popular appellation for The Church of Jesus Christ of Latter-day Saints, was founded in 1830 by Joseph Smith in a region of western New York State so intensely agitated by religious fervor that it came to be called the "Burned-over District." Latter-day Saints believed Mormonism to be a restoration of the authority and pristine teachings of Jesus Christ, which Joseph Smith taught had perished in a universal apostasy after the death of the original twelve apostles. Joseph Smith claimed to be a prophet and produced three new "standard works" of scripture, which are considered by Mormons to be equal in authority to the Bible: the *Book of Mormon,* the *Doctrine and Covenants,* and the *Pearl of Great Price.*

Mormonism was controversial from its inception, and the Latter-day Saints were driven west from state to state, finally settling in Illinois, where Joseph Smith was murdered by an angry mob in 1844. Brigham Young succeeded him in leadership and led a faithful contingent of Mormon pioneers across the plains to establish the Latter-day Saints in the western territory of Utah. Utah eventually achieved statehood and the LDS Church has since become part of the American mainstream, currently claiming almost ten million members worldwide. From its beginnings, it has asserted its exclusive authority to teach the truth about God and perform the ordinances necessary for the salvation of mankind. Mormons consequently believe theirs to be "the only true and living church upon the face of the whole earth" (D&C 1:30).

My family has been solidly Latter-day Saint since the earliest days of the Church. Some of my forbears became leaders in Brigham Young's Great Basin Kingdom, as Utah was sometimes called. One maternal great-great-grandfather, Hiram Bradley Clawson, served as a bishop in Salt Lake City for twenty-two years. He was also a notable actor, the impresario of Utah's first theater; a colonel in the Utah Militia; a builder, designing Salt Lake City's famous Eagle Gate monument and supervising construction of the first LDS Church office building; a merchant, owning and operating several successful businesses; and a statesman, serving in the territorial legislature and frequently as Church emissary to Washington. Finally, but surely not least, he was a family man with four wives and forty-four children—truly a Mormon-style Renaissance man.

Many of my progenitors made enormous sacrifices for their faith. Some were forced to leave their homes, suffering violent persecution at the hands of mobs, and eventually escaping across the plains, burying husbands, wives, and children as they went. The story of Lettice Eckersall Redford, a paternal great-great-grandmother, is typical of the sort of tales I heard repeatedly as a young Mormon boy. In the 1860s, Lettice lived in England with her parents and a baby daughter from a former marriage. Her father had forbidden her to join the Mormon Church. When he found out that she had converted, he took her to the door of the house and demanded that she choose between her home and daughter and the Church. Despite his threats, her faith in Mormonism was so strong that she couldn't give it up.

"What about my baby?" she asked. "Can't I take her with me?"

"No," shouted her father angrily. "You shall never see her or us again."[1]

And she never did. In 1868, Lettice emigrated to Utah, where she remarried and settled in a small community in Cache Valley north of Salt Lake City. Her son, Robert Eckersall Redford, was my great-grandfather.

This story is illustrative of the heavy cost many Mormons have paid for their faith. It helps explain why they now find it hard even to imagine questioning its truth. Such doubts feel like a rude slap in the face to those with loved ones who gave up their lives for it. The connective tissue holding Mormons to the Church and undergirding their personal sacrifices, however, ultimately lies deeper, in the realm of the supernatural.

In my family, the veil between this world and the next often seemed very thin indeed. Writing his family history, Robert Eckersall Redford remembered an incident during the winter of 1871 when he and his brother John were working in a cabinet shop, making chairs, bedsteads, and cupboards for fifty cents a day. After a trip across Cache Valley to collect a bill, John returned home late one bitterly cold night. When he came in the door, his hands, nose, and feet were frozen solid and his footsteps sounded like rocks hitting the floor. "Boys, I'm frozen," he said, and fell over unconscious. His feet were in such bad shape that his brother and friends had to cut off his shoes, and he eventually lost all his toes but the big toe of his right foot. After they had thawed him out, he told this story: he had fallen from his horse twice during his journey and his father, who had been dead for three years, had appeared and lifted him onto his feet each time to start him on his way again.[2]

One maternal great-great aunt, Ella Jensen, was restored to life after perishing at the age of nineteen from scarlet fever. Early one morning, after weeks of illness, she called out excitedly, asking for a comb, brush, and scissors. She explained that she wanted to get ready because her deceased Uncle Hans had visited her and told her that messengers would be coming at ten o'clock to conduct her into the spirit world. Her parents suspected delirium; nevertheless, the family was gathered together and Ella said goodbye. At about ten o'clock, her pulse stopped as her father Jacob was holding her hand.

Shortly thereafter, Jacob hitched up his wagon and drove south to the Brigham City tabernacle where Lorenzo Snow, fifth president of the LDS Church, was speaking. President Snow quickly excused himself and, along with Rudger Clawson (a great-grand uncle, then president of the LDS Council of Twelve Apostles), accompanied Jacob back to the Jensen farm, arriving some two hours after Ella's death. To the family's surprise, President Snow asked President Clawson to anoint Ella with oil, then laid hands on her head and blessed her, saying, "Come back, Ella, come back. Your work upon the earth is not yet completed, come back." More than an hour later, Ella opened her eyes and gave a long and detailed account of her experiences in the "spirit world," including accurate descriptions of deceased relatives she had never met. She even specified the clothes her Uncle Hans had been wearing the night he drowned in the Snake River eight years earlier.[3]

This incident became part of the family lore and appeared not only to confirm the truth of the Mormon worldview but to underscore our special sense of "blessedness" as well. We are a visionary family and stories like these are frequent among us. I never heard anyone question the assumption that such experiences came from God.

My family history is bound up with the history of Mormon polygamy, the doctrine that permitted a worthy LDS man to marry multiple wives. Joseph Smith had introduced "the principle" as early as 1831. In reality, only a small percentage of loyal Church members actually engaged in the practice, some wearing it as a badge of honor, a symbol of their devotion, others with anguished tears, as it tore at the fabric of their moral upbringing. Polygamy created great animosity between the Mormons and their neighbors and eventually with the U.S. government, which passed several laws making it illegal.

Rudger Clawson was prominent among the thirteen hundred Mormons who were jailed for "unlawful cohabitation" under the Edmunds Act of 1882. In 1884, he was indicted by a grand jury for polygamy, arrested, and released on $3,000 bail. His case came before Judge Charles S. Zane, who viewed the Mormon plural marriage system as immoral, but was lenient toward those who would abandon it. Nevertheless, Rudger Clawson would not plead guilty. When asked why judgment should not be pronounced, he retorted, "I very much regret that the laws of my country should come in conflict with the laws of God, but whenever they do I shall invariably choose the latter." This fiery declaration resulted in a stiff sentence of three and one-half years in prison and a $500 fine for polygamy, plus an additional six months and $300 for unlawful cohabitation.[4]

Even those who did not enter into plural marriages suffered the consequences of its practice. At one point, the government sent out deputized spies to search for polygamists. When found, they were taken and, without trial, thrown into prison. One night, Robert Eckersall Redford visited a neighboring home only to find a government deputy there taking information from the owner. Robert saw the deputy and reported it to the Bishop, for which the owner of the house vowed "to get that Redford." From then on, Robert had to hide out on the border of his farm whenever spies were in the area. "Often," he wrote, "in the middle of the night there would be a knock on the window and someone would whisper, 'Uncle Robert, the Deputies are here,' or 'Brother Redford, the Deputies are in town.' I would jump out of bed and hurry up to the farm. My neighbors were very faithful in informing anyone whose name was on the list. Then my dear wife would have to manage alone until I was able to return home."[5]

Despite these trials—or perhaps because of them—the family remained close. Robert's daughter remembers the warmth and happiness of the "family nights" they shared. "Father and Mother would tell us of their childhood experiences, teach us songs and poems, and the evening would always close with family prayer, kneeling around chairs placed in a circle. Those were the happiest and most remembered times of our childhood. Father always had one of us on his knee whenever he was in the house and not reading. He loved his children greatly and they loved him."[6]

My family takes a great deal of pride in this pioneer heritage—occasionally to a fault. In fact, Latter-day Saints sometimes talk as if no one else's predecessors had tales to tell of sacrifice and devotion. Being Mormon is not simply a matter of faith, but of family honor and loyalty, honed by persecution, exalted to heroic proportions, and confirmed with mystical experience. However, the ties that bind can bind both for good and for ill. In leaving Mormonism, did I betray my heritage? Or did I recreate it in some sense by following the voice of God though it meant breaking faith with my fathers, just as they had done?

When I was a boy, I was closest to my grandparents on my mother's side. My grandfather, Dr. Thomas Alfred Clawson Jr.—Poppie—was a prominent medical doctor in Salt Lake City. A man of great kindness and integrity, he was truly the patriarch of the family. I often picture him in one of the favorite haunts of his later years: sitting in a lawn chair by the pool, book in hand, skin brown and wrinkled as tree bark from spending hours under the hot summer sun.

Grandma Ruth Clawson was a free spirit, a singer, actress, and wonderful cook, a warm and nurturing presence. She had worked on Broadway in the twenties and was always involved in something new and unusual, such as teaching yoga to hefty Salt Lake City matrons during the late fifties or taking up painting in her seventies. Grandma was the kind of person who had a powerful effect on people. She was a civilizing force, a symbol of culture and grace for her community, and many sought her wisdom and counsel over the years. Poppie loved to hear her sing, which she often did, either publicly in musical theater productions and performances of works such as Handel's *Messiah* with the Utah Symphony, or privately in meetings of her music clubs or at family soirées.

My grandparents were proud of their Mormon faith and always ready to talk about it. They were also close friends with many leaders in the upper echelons of the LDS hierarchy, leaders known in the Church as General Authorities. I often heard Poppie and Grandma relate anecdotes about their experiences with these friends and members of their families. In the aristocracy of Mormonism, my grandparents were nobility.

My mother Patricia was the elder of their two daughters. A highly intelligent child, she skipped two grades and entered the University of Utah early. Like my grandmother, she was gifted with a beautiful singing voice and gravitated to the performing arts. My father, H.E.D. Redford, came from Logan, a small town in Cache Valley. He had also skipped a grade and graduated from Logan High School in 1942. After a year of college, he joined the Marine paratroops, eventually serving in the South Pacific. Returning from the war, he majored in theater at Utah State University and then took a job as a teaching assistant in the theater department at the University of Utah.

My parents met during a production of Kurt Weill's *Lady in the Dark* in which my grandmother starred. They were married in the Salt Lake Temple in August 1950 and spent the first few months of their marriage touring the Midwest in the cast of a theatrical revue. Following this, Dad did postgraduate work for two quarters at the University of Minnesota before returning to Utah in the summer of 1951. Then, in September, they moved to southern California, where Dad hoped to build a career as an actor in films and television. Life, however, has a way of unexpectedly altering plans, and within two years Mom and Dad were greeted with a surprise that would radically change their course—a surprise in the shape of a baby boy.

I am a child of God, and he has sent me here,
Has given me an earthly home with parents kind and dear.
Lead me, guide me, walk beside me, help me find the way.
Teach me all that I must do to live with him someday.

—LDS Children's Song[1]

I was born in Los Angeles, California, on July 14, 1953—
Bastille Day. My parents named me Jonathan Alfred
Clawson Redford, and called me Jac for short. About two
weeks later, my father stood with a circle of elders and blessed
me before the San Fernando Ward of the LDS Church in the
beautiful priesthood ceremony that marks every Mormon
infant's entry into the world. At that time, Dad was serving in
the ward as the Gospel Doctrine teacher and president of the
elders quorum.

Faced with the realities of new fatherhood and the lack of
prospects for employment in Hollywood, Dad soon became
frustrated and moved the family back to Salt Lake City in 1954.
We lived in my grandparents' basement while he worked again
as a teaching assistant at the University of Utah. The following
year he took a job teaching theater at Weber State College, north
of Salt Lake. Dad commuted to work that year, after which we
moved into a duplex in Ogden until my parents were able to buy
a house in a little suburban community called Roy in the spring
of 1958. My brother Rick was born the following April. In the fall
of 1959, Dad landed a full teaching position in the theater
department at the University of Utah, and we moved into a
home on 12th Avenue in Salt Lake City.

Sometime after my parents' return to Utah, Dad renounced
the LDS Church. As I was so young, I don't remember being greatly

affected by his decision at the time, although I began to feel the consequences a few years later, when I grew old enough to be aware of his absence at Church meetings and activities that other boys attended with their dads. Nevertheless, the strength of the rest of my family's commitment to Mormonism was more than enough to offset any sense of disruption I may have experienced. We rarely discussed Dad's decision and, despite his personal convictions, he didn't place obstacles in the way of my growth and development in the Church.

Music was an essential part of my life from the very beginning. Many of Dad's theatrical roles required him to sing, and Mom was a member of the Mormon Tabernacle Choir. She often played recordings on the hi fi when I was a toddler, and favored the great nineteenth-century operas. She sang along in her clear, sweet soprano, and I sat in front of the speakers, mesmerized. Apparently, I could even repeat portions of the libretti by the time I was three-and-a-half. Speaking with Mom at my nursery school one afternoon, a classmate's mother said with a chuckle, "If I didn't know better, I'd swear this child was singing the toreador song from *Carmen!*" In fact, I was—it was one of the strongest tunes in my repertoire.

One of my favorite recordings was Igor Stravinsky's *Firebird Suite,* on a set of old 78s, complete with one side of commentary by Deems Taylor. I was fascinated by the strange story of the brave young prince, the enigmatic Firebird, the evil Kastchei, and the magic egg that casketed his soul. Bernstein and Sondheim's *West Side Story* also captured my imagination. I used to sing along with the score: "Could be! Who knows? It's only just out of reach, down the block, on a beach, under a tree . . . I got a feeling there's a miracle due, gonna come true, coming to me!"[2] All of this music was seeded deep into my heart, creating a vocabulary of melody, harmony, and rhythm with which my ear still resonates.

My childhood memories are rich with warm family experiences, many of which unfolded at my grandparents' home. They owned a stately, red-brick house on 11th Avenue that, because it was situated on the hill overlooking Salt Lake City from the northeast, provided a breathtaking view of the Salt Lake Valley, especially at night when the streets were festooned with rows of multicolored lights.

Our summers were spent in and around their pool. I learned to swim late, because I had a terrible fear of drowning. This fear ended one afternoon when I was bouncing around in the shallow end and suddenly slipped and floated "out to sea." The moment I realized the water would hold me up, I began to swim like an otter and was soon diving off the board into the deep end with reckless abandon.

We often swam all day with cousins and friends, eventually gathering on the south porch at twilight to watch the sun set and to gorge ourselves on Grandma's juicy hamburgers. In some odd fashion, my grandmother's hamburgers were like a sacrament to me, a symbol of the warmth of her love and my sense of utter belonging. In her home, my heart was completely at rest and filled with unclouded joy.

Christmas was always an extraordinary time, and Grandma decorated the house exquisitely every year. Her Christmas trees left my young senses awestruck, like the giant tree in productions of Tchaikovsky's *Nutcracker,* which we attended every year at Kingsbury Hall on the University of Utah campus. Grandma's holiday feasts were also legendary. She set a huge table so aunts and uncles and cousins could join us, as well as other guests who didn't have anywhere else to go. Poppie always prayed eloquently before the meal. Whatever I know of hospitality, I saw modeled in my grandparents' generous life.

When I was eight years old, Poppie baptized me in the old baptismal font at the Salt Lake Tabernacle. I have vivid memories of that event: the dim, yellow-green light and musty smell in the room, the feel of the tepid water as it closed over my head, the white clothes clinging to my legs and chest, and the slap of my bare feet on the cold tile of the changing room floor. I was confirmed the next day with the laying on of Poppie's hands, becoming an official member of the Mormon Church and receiving "the gift of the Holy Ghost" as the Church teaches. In addition, Poppie blessed me, making several declarations that spoke to my family's fondest dreams for my future. The text of this blessing, as transcribed by my mother, is as follows:

> Brother Jonathan Alfred Clawson Redford, in the authority of the Holy Melchizedek Priesthood vested in us, and in the name of the Lord, Jesus Christ, we lay our hands upon your head and confirm you a member of the Church of Jesus Christ of Latter Day Saints and say unto you, receive ye the Holy Ghost.
>
> We bless you at this time with faith in the Lord Jesus Christ, faith in the principles of the Gospel, the plan of salvation. We bless you with the spirit of the Lord, that it will be round about you at all times—

guiding your life, guiding your actions, teaching you truth, confirming your testimony of the truthfulness of the Gospel here upon the earth, and helping you to live righteous in the sight of our Heavenly Father.

And, our Father, we ask Thee in humility, that Thou wouldst let Thy Holy Spirit be round about this Thy Son [sic], guiding him and let him feel its very presence, that he will know that Thou are mindful of him and anxious to have him follow in the footsteps of truth and righteousness and return unto Thee again in due time.

Our Father, we ask Thee to bless him that as he reads Thy scriptures, that he will have a feeling within his heart that these things are true, and inasmuch as he has already started reading that sacred book, the Book of Mormon, bear this record unto him of its truthfulness.

Now JAC, we feel to give you an extra blessing, in the name of the Lord Jesus Christ we bless you that you will grow in integrity, and in due time you will receive the holy Priesthood, and that you will grow in stature in the Priesthood, and eventually fill a mission to the people of the world and then go into the house of the Lord and be sealed for time and eternity.

We bless you, JAC, that this will come about, and we say unto you, seek always the spirit of the Lord and listen to His voice, which will prompt you, because this will be so, and you will be blessed, and that mind of yours will become great in the teachings of the Gospel of Jesus Christ.

We seal these blessings upon your head and with the blessings of life, health and strength, and we do this in the authority of the holy Melchizedek Priesthood vested in us and in the name of the Lord Jesus Christ, Amen.[3]

This was an important moment for me and my family. I was already a chosen child, the repository of their hopes and treasures. With this blessing, I felt a strong sense of God's favor and a clarity about His specific will for my life. In fact, my path seemed to have been laid out before me in some detail. More subtly, however, the message that my family and the Church had great expectations for me had also been reinforced, and the unquestioning presumption of the truth of Mormonism underscored through powerful ritual experience.

Poppie blessed me many times in my life, not only at watershed moments such as these, but also when I was sick or needed strength to accomplish a difficult task. These blessings were a tangible expression of his love for me and a significant thread in the fabric of my life. These and other such experiences ultimately released forces that kept me in the Church long after my mind could no longer assent nor my heart believe.

My first four grade school years were spent at Ensign School in Salt Lake City. I enjoyed classes as well as activities such as the Cub Scouts, which was sponsored by the LDS Church. I moved to Morningside School for the fifth and sixth grades after my parents purchased what was to become our family home in the Holladay area of Salt Lake at the feet of Mount Olympus. There I was fortunate to have kind and dedicated teachers who really encouraged me to stretch my mind and to take joy in learning. During the summers I played Little League baseball, covering second base and pitching (not very well) for a team called the Aces.

I liked working by myself on creative projects from the time I was very young. By the age of seven, I was spending hours drawing cartoon characters, war scenes, and complicated mechanical contraptions, and designing elaborate houses and self-sustaining country estates. My artistic career peaked in the sixth grade when I won the school's Caldecott Award for an original illustrated short story called "Millionaires Are Funny People," featuring Bullwinkle-style characters in top hats and tails.

One of my favorite activities was playing archaeologist. My mother's cousin had participated in several archaeological expeditions to Central America, and I was captivated by his tales of adventure and discovery. He gave me some archaeology books, and I stashed them in my backpack along with some trowels and brushes to explore the backyard looking for artifacts. Though I never pursued any formal studies in archaeology, my interests later flowered into a passion to learn the truth about purported empirical evidence for the *Book of Mormon.*

These elementary school years were extremely important to my aesthetic development. Because Dad was directing and acting in stage productions at the University of Utah, I had the opportunity to work with him in several plays. I appeared in a melancholy little play about Mormon polygamy called *The Wife of the Winter,* in which Dad played the polygamist and I played his son. I also played Patrick Dennis in *Auntie Mame* and took the role of Whitney in *Life with Father.* The latter was especially fun (and slightly daring) because I had to grow my hair long and dye it red for the part, much to the amazement of my classmates. That same year I portrayed Scrooge in our school's ambitious production of *A Christmas Carol.*

Mom was also actively involved in the theater. She and a friend performed entire Broadway shows, such as *West Side Story* and *Guys and Dolls,* for social clubs and Church groups, dividing the parts and songs between them, using clever props to identify the characters and suggest the scenery.

The "roar of the greasepaint" was loudly heard around our dining room table. Mom and Dad threw regular dinner parties for a select group of university theater students they called the "Lost Boys." I enjoyed these evenings tremendously and listened in awe to their stage tales, gasping appreciatively at their exploits and laughing heartily at their jokes. Some of the Lost Boys were Mormons but most were not—one was flamboyantly homosexual and wore a black cape that he flipped dramatically when he entered our home.

Every year the University of Utah theater department put on its Summer Festival, mounting productions of one musical and one opera in the football stadium. I loved bundling up in blankets under the cool night sky, watching classic Broadway shows spring to life before my eyes, thoroughly kindling my imagination. We wore out the original cast recordings of Rodgers and Hammerstein's *Oklahoma, South Pacific,* and *The Sound of Music,* as well as those of the great Lerner and Loewe musicals *My Fair Lady* and *Camelot.* I was even on familiar terms with Anthony Newley and Leslie Bricusse's offbeat *Stop the World I Wanna Get Off.* I'm convinced that much of what I understand now about dramatic musical form is rooted in these formative experiences.

My first inclinations to compose dramatic music were born in a rather unexpected way. I liked to lay out elaborate jungle terrains for my toy soldiers on the floor of my room, gluing together cardboard elevations, cutting out blue felt lakes, and distributing Easter egg grass for foliage. My soldiers generally squared off against prehistoric monsters rather than against one another—the principal challenge was "man versus nature gone berserk." My favorite character was a cameraman, an observer. He was not equipped with a gun and had to survive only by his wits, which he always did even when his well-armed companions were destroyed by the ravening beasts. I accompanied their exploits with music, which I hummed aloud but heard fully orchestrated in my head. As a child, I thought as easily with music as most people think with words. At the time this didn't strike me as peculiar because I assumed it happened to everyone.

An abiding love for Christmas music began at this stage of my life. I delighted in the carols, of course, but also treasured seasonal classics like the *Nutcracker,* Handel's *Messiah,* and Menotti's *Amahl and the Night Visitors.* I remember my father singing "O Holy Night" at the top of his lungs one evening in his bedroom. He had a powerful tenor voice and when he belted out the high notes, I felt that nothing could go wrong as long there was music like that in the world.

I picked up the trombone in the third grade, mainly because I liked pumping the slide. By the last two years of elementary school, I was a mainstay in the school orchestra, though I earned only mediocre grades for my efforts. Despite the fact that playing the trombone always felt a little like wrestling to me, I stuck with it for nearly twenty years.

One day when I was ten or eleven years old, I heard organist E. Power Biggs and a brass ensemble performing the "Prince of Denmark March" on an LP. Something about the music pierced my heart. For the first time, I was aware of feeling both pain and joy simultaneously as the direct result of an encounter with a work of art. I burst into tears and ran upstairs to express this overpowering and complicated feeling to my mother. She was delighted at first, but when I couldn't stop crying, she told me to pull myself together. Feeling dejected, I walked back downstairs, having learned two transforming things: that while I was hearing the music, I had felt more fully alive than I ever had before, and that this sort of experience was ultimately impossible to share, though I would spend the rest of my life trying to do just that.

While I had my share of difficult times, my early years were basically happy ones. My life was essentially one of privilege, and I was a dedicated consumer of experience. I moved through my days with the sort of self-absorption that assumed that God was on my side and that He was actively interested in my having a very good time.

The LDS Church was the hub around which everything else revolved. It was the grid through which my family observed and understood the world. It provided a cosmology, a community, a moral framework, and a sense of purpose that we accepted implicitly. Because of this, I grew up with a strong sense of values, fundamental principles that I still affirm today. With the clarity of hindsight, three of these values stand out most significantly.

The first is faith. Stated most simply, I was brought up to believe in God. Despite the disagreements we now have about who this God really is—and I do believe that who He is matters—I'm profoundly grateful to my family for making the idea of having faith at all credible to me from my earliest years. I feel this gratitude most when I talk with those who were raised without faith, who have only themselves to rely on when hard times come or when they feel overwhelmed by the enormity of the evil in the world. They have to travel so far to begin believing in God at all, let alone in His goodness and love.

The second value is that of reason. I was taught that truth was objective, absolute, and universal, and that I could actually know something about it. I learned early that reason and faith were not enemies but complemented one another.

The third value is integrity. I understood that my life ought to be consistent with the things I believed and that I had an obligation to stand up for my convictions, no matter the cost. I learned that faith must not be passive, but must express itself actively and authentically in the world. I grew up with the belief that lying and artificiality were shameful.

I have my family to thank for this, and I do thank them—with all of my heart. In the end, I left Mormonism because of these values, not in spite of them.

Of Time and Innocence

[Time] starts at whatever moment it is at which the unthinking and timeless childhood of innocence ends, which may be either a dramatic moment . . . or a moment or series of moments so subtle and undramatic that we scarcely recognize them.

—Frederick Buechner, *The Sacred Journey*[1]

My twelfth birthday in the summer of 1965 heralded the beginning of a new season in my life, a sometimes painful season of change and development. Things seemed to begin well enough—eleven days after my birthday, Poppie ordained me a deacon in the LDS Aaronic Priesthood. This is an important honor and rite of passage for all worthy Mormon boys, and it marks the beginning of the climb up the ladder of priesthood responsibility that ultimately leads to higher positions of authority in the Church.

One of the central concepts of Mormonism is that of the priesthood. It would be difficult to exaggerate its importance, since it is defined in terms far loftier than those merely sacerdotal. To Latter-day Saints, the priesthood, in its broadest sense, is the eternal power and authority of God, by which the world was created and is currently governed. The priesthood has been delegated to man on earth so that he may act in God's name. This authority is exercised in the Church through a strictly organized hierarchy, staffed by lay men—women are not permitted to hold the priesthood. There are two major orders: the Melchizedek Priesthood and the Aaronic Priesthood. The Melchizedek Priesthood is the greater of the two, and all other authorities or offices in the Church are appendages to it.

The offices of the Aaronic Priesthood are, from lesser to greater, deacon, teacher, and priest. Mormon boys may be ordained deacons at the age of twelve, teachers at fourteen, and priests at sixteen. The offices of the Melchizedek Priesthood are elder, seventy, and high priest. The leadership of local Mormon congregations is drawn from among men holding these offices, although the seventies have been discontinued at the local level. The General Authorities of the Church, its only full-time paid clergy, are officers of the Melchizedek Priesthood. Foremost among the General Authorities are the First Presidency (made up of three presiding high priests, including the president, also known as the Prophet, and two counselors) and the Twelve Apostles.

Mormons believe the priesthood is essential to the salvation of man. Without it, the Church could not have been restored, nor could the true doctrine of God be revealed, the gospel preached, or the ordinances of salvation, such as baptism and "the laying on of hands" for the gift of the Holy Ghost, be performed with God's approval. Possession of the priesthood is therefore considered a cardinal distinguishing feature of the true church.

As a deacon in the Aaronic Priesthood, I became part of this noble inheritance and could now serve by passing the sacrament (the bread and water Mormons use to observe the Lord's Supper) during Sunday services, as well as attend the exclusive priesthood meetings, at which women and children were not allowed. I could also join the Mormon-sponsored Boy Scouts and participate in the Church's Wednesday night youth program called MIA (Mutual Improvement Association). I felt like a whole new world was opening up to me and I was happy to be on track with the Church.

Mormon congregations are organized geographically into wards and stakes, roughly analogous to Catholic parishes and dioceses. I belonged to the Holladay 13th Ward, which met in a large LDS stake center on 45th South in Salt Lake City. Our stake center had one prominent distinguishing feature: a huge sloping copper roof that glinted impressively in the sun. It had been designed by my best friend's father and we called it "the pagoda." Sometimes during sacrament meeting, while everyone was gathered in the chapel, I would slip out (on the pretext of getting a drink of water or using the lavatory) and walk determinedly down the long empty hallways, listening to my hard black shoes clack and echo in the silence. The church building felt thoroughly familiar and I was completely at home there.

In the fall, I entered the seventh grade at Churchill Junior High School and promptly had cold water thrown all over my confidence. Whereas I had been on top of the world in elementary school—a successful actor, artist, and student—I now found myself at the bottom of a huge heap of pubescent zombies, all clawing to get to the top where they would presumably be rewarded with unlimited popularity and the admiration of the opposite sex. My sense of alienation was especially acute in that none of my new peers seemed to value the strengths that were the source of my self-esteem in elementary school.

Despite my efforts, both popularity and admiration eluded me that year. It appeared that I was doomed to remain an outsider. Worse still, I experienced a slump in my own creative pursuits—nothing fired my imagination like it used to. Had it not been for friends and activities at church, I would have pined away in utter despair (to the accompaniment of tiny violins).

It was in the seventh grade, however, that I first met LeAnn Allred, the girl who would become my wife. I noticed her because she was bright and witty, much more interesting than the other girls. She had been born on the Prophet Joseph Smith's birthday (December 23) in 1952, the first child of a young couple serving Uncle Sam in San Antonio, Texas, during the Korean War. Her parents hailed from the tiny adjacent communities of Delta and Hinckley in the central Utah desert. When LeAnn was two years old, the family returned home to Utah, eventually taking up residence in Salt Lake City.

Her great-great grandparents had also been in the wagon trains and handcart companies of the Mormon pioneers. One had been Joseph Smith's bodyguard and another the seamstress who made the first LDS temple garment under the prophet's direction. Two of our great-great-grandfathers had even served together in the bishopric in Delta. LeAnn had been a devout Mormon from the time she was very little, and loved going to church each Sunday. We became friends that year, though not particularly close ones. Little did we suspect that this acquaintance would later become the most important human relationship of our lives.

The summer I turned thirteen, Mom and Dad were divorced. There had been tensions in their marriage for a long time, especially with regard to Mormonism. They had almost separated the year before, but when it came to it, Dad had been unable to leave. He sat for a long time in the driveway in our ancient blue Volkswagen bug with all of his things packed inside. The only time I ever saw Dad cry, except on stage, was when he slowly came walking back to the house and into my mother's arms.

Mom tried to make him promise he would give the Church another chance, but it was a futile exercise. Deep inside, Dad didn't believe in Mormonism anymore, and once the spell was broken he could no more recover his faith than call back his youth. When he left the second time, it was for good.

My relationship with Dad had been a rocky one. We didn't have the sort of intimate connection that made it safe to be affectionate or vulnerable with one another—Dad wasn't that kind of man. On the positive side, we enjoyed working in the theater together, and he often took me fishing or to basketball games. Occasionally, he allowed me into the inner sanctum he called his "den," and together we would pore over our stamp albums. Sometimes on Sunday mornings, my brother and I were allowed to skip church and drive with Dad to his sister's home, where she cooked us a fabulous breakfast of bacon and eggs and we played cards for hours.

Dad, however, was a perfectionist—a hard man to live with—and this quality had a profound impact on me. Praise for success or good behavior was in short supply. Discipline for wrongdoing could be severe, whether it was administered physically or took the form of withering criticism. Dad didn't like to observe birthdays and holidays or attend school functions. I honestly felt more relieved than hurt when he moved out. I wouldn't become aware of the hole his departure left in the center of my chest until much later.

Soon after Dad left, Mom moved the family to Farmington, New Mexico, so she could be near her sister, Sue. I think she needed to get away from Salt Lake and the hurtful memories the divorce had left in its wake. We all needed time to heal in a safe place.

Farmington turned out to be just such an oasis. Eighth grade was a year of coming out for me. I became friends with two popular brothers in my ward, and because of their acceptance and influence I was invited to many parties. My confidence soared. I suddenly discovered the opposite sex and loved to dance and play "spin the bottle." When our church MIA group went roller skating, I felt myself flush with excitement as I sped around the rink, hand-in-hand with a girl. My friends and I often got together for "bike hikes" on Saturdays and sometimes we talked older friends who drove into taking us cruising for tacquitos, *American Graffiti*-style, at the twin A&W drive-ins perched at either end of Farmington's main street.

I read J.R.R. Tolkien's *The Hobbit* and *The Lord of the Rings* for the first time in the eighth grade, and I loved them passionately. Given the experiences of my childhood, I was already predisposed to a romantic worldview; now that perspective was beginning to manifest itself seriously, and the Tolkien books abundantly nourished it. Another influence that spurred my budding romanticism was the television series, *The Twilight Zone*. These strange and beautiful tales of humanity tested in alien circumstances captivated me. From my insulated environment, I looked out on a world of heroes and villains, treasure and dross with no in-between. Life was a great quest with daring deeds to do, vile monsters to vanquish, and a destiny to achieve.

I listened to a great deal of music that year. I fell in love with the inventive music and lyrics of the Beatles' *Sgt. Pepper's Lonely Hearts Club Band,* though George Martin's unique arrangements and production arrested my attention as much as the songs themselves: the surrealistic "Lucy in the Sky with Diamonds," the string quartet and harp that accompanied "She's Leaving Home," the glorious chaos of calliopes on "Mr. Kite," the amusing trio of clarinets on "When I'm Sixty-Four," and the devastating symphonic crescendo of "A Day in the Life." I didn't know popular music could sound like this, and I vowed that someday I would do something similar.

The Beach Boys provided another revelation. I was spellbound by the timeless beauty of "God Only Knows," the innocent sexual yearning of "Wouldn't It Be Nice," but especially the magnificently eccentric "Good Vibrations." I loved the sophisticated vocals of The Association and the raw earthy edge of Buffalo Springfield. I first heard the Doors at an LDS Church youth dance. We all became suddenly awkward and unsure of ourselves when that alien and seductive music began to slither from the sound system.

I started picking out popular tunes on the piano and soon found that I had an aptitude for playing by ear. Within a short time, I started a rock 'n' roll band with three schoolmates. We couldn't think of a proper name, so we resorted to the dictionary and arbitrarily came up with "The Spectres." I played the organ and sang lead, although my voice hadn't changed yet. It must have been absurdly comical to hear a boy soprano singing "The House of the Rising Sun" with absolutely no concept of what the words meant.

When I was fourteen, my Uncle Gene ordained me a teacher in the Aaronic Priesthood, the next step up in priesthood responsibility. This office allowed me to prepare the bread and water for the sacrament. Soon thereafter we moved back to Salt Lake, but not into our family home. My mother had rented it out while we were in Farmington and the tenants wanted to stay another year, so we moved into Poppie and Grandma's basement again, and I commuted across the valley to school at Churchill until we were able to return.

My new-found confidence stuck with me through the move and I quite enjoyed my ninth-grade year. I had a minor singing role in the school musical, started a new rock 'n' roll band with my best friend, and played trombone in the Utah Youth Symphony under the direction of the fiery tympanist and conductor, Robert Lentz. My creative interests seemed to be expanding in several directions at once. I had survived my emotional slump, the blows to my self-esteem, and the divorce of my parents, and had finished junior high school with a new sense of who I was. By the end of my ninth-grade year, I was ready to move into high school with ambitious enthusiasm.

Your Young Men Shall See Visions

And it shall come to pass afterward, that I will pour out my spirit
upon all flesh; and your sons and your daughters shall prophesy,
your old men shall dream dreams, your young men shall see
visions.

—Joel 2:28

I attended the relatively affluent Skyline High School in
Salt Lake City from 1968 to 1971. My time there unfolded
against the backdrop of the Vietnam War and the cultural
upheaval of the sixties. In some respects, Salt Lake was a land
that time forgot, leaping directly from the fifties into the seventies. Some of us, though, were determined to savor the decade
of revolution despite the opposition of the "establishment."

News of the outside world filtered into my experience via the
hypnotic blue-green glow of a television tube. Every night Vietnam burst across the screen like renegade flak from a John
Wayne movie. From our sofa I witnessed the death and mutila-
tion of scores of American boys not much older than I was.

My only direct contact with the war occurred one evening at
MIA. One of the older fellows in our ward had just returned from
Vietnam and a few of us, "compelled by calamity's magnet," gathered in a corner of the gym to hear his war stories. At first his conversation was filled with the macho bravado of the young soldier; but his tone soon changed to one of haunted desperation
and barely suppressed rage as he told us how his jeep had been
blasted, killing all of his buddies and leaving him inexplicably
alive. We listened with silent horror, suddenly realizing that there
was a vast gulf between us, a chasm between life and death that
he had crossed and we had not—nor would we ever understand

it as he did. He became an apparition before us—Banquo's grim nephew sent as a harbinger of some terrible judgment to come.

The draft for military service was handled by lottery in those days. Every young man was required to register with the draft board by his eighteenth birthday. Each day of the year was randomly assigned a number from one to 365. Those with low numbers were conscripted and most were sent to Vietnam while the war lasted.

As my eighteenth birthday approached in the summer of 1971, I became more and more strident in my opposition to the war, even though it was winding down. I was also scared stiff. I seriously investigated the possibility of obtaining conscientious objector status, but the chances were almost nil in Utah, where the boards were staffed with active Mormons, most of them Republican hawks who were encouraged in their jingoism by the General Authorities of the Church. I even toyed briefly with the idea of fleeing to Canada. My family was appalled that I would even consider such an option.

Ultimately, I was neutralized; hamstrung by the ambiguities, I simply did nothing but wait for my number to come up. When it finally did, and I was assigned a 305, I fell on my knees and thanked God more fervently than I ever had before. My mother was working as a bank teller at the time. When I called the bank to give her the good news, she broke down, gasping, "Thank God! Thank God!" I was struck by the contrast between her obvious relief and the position she had maintained so strongly in our discussions about the war.

My evolution as a student "radical" was slow but steady. Like most Mormons, my family had been Republican for many years. Poppie delighted to recount the tale of Franklin Delano Roosevelt's visit to Salt Lake City and then LDS President Heber J. Grant's private pronouncement that he was "an evil man." I don't remember ever even meeting a Democrat—the word itself had a slightly malevolent ring to it—but I was beginning to feel more sympathy for the peace movement than for the Republican Party.

As a junior, I ran for class president and astonishingly won against two far more popular candidates. Perhaps it had something to do with a stunt I pulled during the campaign. A special assembly had been called for the hopefuls to deliver their speeches. I began mine by declaring, "I'm running for office because I'm desperately hungry for power." Then I exclaimed, "Wait a minute! This isn't my speech!"

and handed my notes to one of the other candidates. His campaign never recovered. I ran on a platform of policy change: open campus, unrestricted library privileges, and so forth. Little did I realize that the office was bereft of the slightest power to implement or even demand such improvements. My principal assignment would be planning the junior prom, and at this I failed miserably.

By this time, I was becoming somewhat distrustful of institutions in general, including even some aspects of the LDS Church. The Church's support for the government contributed to this attitude, as did a few encounters I had with authoritarian Mormon leadership. My bishop had a strong point of view about the authority of the Church. In fact, one year when our stake sponsored a family recreation day at a local amusement park, the bishop announced in sacrament meeting that "the Lord Jesus Christ" expected us all to be there. I had to wonder at the time whether the Lord Jesus Christ expected me to ride the Rockets or the Wild Mouse. I wore my hair relatively long and my bishop told me that in so doing I was in "open rebellion against the kingdom of God." This incident did nothing to encourage my confidence in the system—or to motivate me to cut my hair.

On television, I saw disturbing scenes of violent protest in other parts of the country and watched the youth movement unfold with all of its "sex, drugs, and rock 'n' roll." Most of this painful unrest seemed foreign to me and to my LDS friends, but the era's cry for educational reform was one crack in the wall through which some ideas were able to penetrate even our conservative community. I wrote pages of polemic about the ills of our educational system, and contributed turgid social criticism to an underground newspaper.

My own radicalism, though, was rather tame in comparison with the turmoil that had exploded across the rest of the country. There were many in Salt Lake who sampled the smorgasbord of experience that was the sixties to a far greater degree than I ever did. My little revolution was heartfelt, nevertheless, and represented an important step toward my intellectual independence.

My friendship with LeAnn deepened significantly during our high school years. She, too, became somewhat radicalized, joining the Debate Club (a nest of student dissenters) and attending conferences on educational reform. She was the only member of the Pep Club to wear a black arm band to school when Nixon invaded Cambodia. The following day the remainder of the Pep Clubbers wore red, white, and blue arm bands to assert their patriotism. I admired LeAnn for taking such a courageous stance.

LeAnn and I were also linked by our passion for learning and by the breadth of our reading. She was the one girl with whom I felt I could converse about anything. My dating experiences were not so successful. Once I inadvisedly tried to tell a girl about *The Lord of the Rings.* LeAnn later told me I was the object of derision among the Pep Club crowd at school the next day, with all my bizarre talk about elves and dwarves.

I read passionately throughout high school, though not necessarily the books that were assigned in my English classes. Early on I discovered Ayn Rand, and read *The Fountainhead* and *Atlas Shrugged.* I was challenged by Erich Fromm's *The Art of Loving,* though I found much there that overlapped my Mormon worldview. St. Exupery's *The Little Prince* and the poetry of e e cummings appealed to my romantic nature. Following my enthusiasm for Tolkien, I went on to C.S. Lewis's *The Chronicles of Narnia* with much rejoicing.

I began writing poetry in high school, initially with my mother's help and encouragement. With a nod to the counterculture, I read my first major poem aloud to my sophomore English class, barefoot and dressed in ragged jeans, accompanied by the Moody Blues' "Legend of a Mind" and the pungent odor of burning incense.

Films began to play an important role in my life during high school. I loved westerns and biblical epics such as *Ben Hur,* but it was *2001: A Space Odyssey* that really piqued my interest. I was fascinated by this work of "theology on celluloid" and my imagination spun off innumerable permutations of the ideas it incarnated. I was deeply disturbed by Fellini's *Satyricon,* finding its intense sensuality almost suffocating. After I'd seen it, I felt terribly guilty, as if I had entered the domain of some dark and perilous beast.

Perhaps I had. In my final year of school, I fell head-over-heels in love with a beautiful flautist two years my junior. The sexual attraction I felt for her was so powerful that I was desperately frightened that I would end up betraying my family and my faith, so I cruelly broke up with her without much explanation. I regretted deeply how much I had hurt her, but I hadn't the slightest idea how to handle my sexual feelings and abruptly cutting off the relationship seemed the only safe course of action open to me.

Family relationships were primary. Though my brother Rick and I had declared sibling warfare as soon as he was old enough to annoy me and to interfere with my adolescent plans, we shared a genuine affection nonetheless, which has blossomed in the years since into a true and abiding friendship. My rapport with my mother was strong and deep. We were good friends as well as having a mutually respectful parent/child relationship. I often had long discussions with Mom about art or religion or politics—even science, a topic neither of us knew much about. It was hard for her to be a divorced Mormon mother raising two sons by herself. She sacrificed many of her own dreams, including that of a professional singing career, for our sake. This she did willingly, however, with courage and humor. Now I can only imagine how impoverished my life might have been without the strength of her dedicated and unselfish love undergirding my successes.

The greater family still assembled frequently for meals, swim parties, and musical evenings. One of the most potent images I have of our family gatherings from this period is of Mom and Grandma singing together. Their voices blended perfectly and were uncannily beautiful. They used to sing a duet called "Homing": "All things come home at eventide, like birds that weary of their roaming. And I would hasten to thy side, homing."[1] By this time, Grandma and Poppie had been compelled to sell their home and move to an apartment, because of their advancing age and Poppie's ill health. The move was a great blow to me and I felt as if my roots had been torn out. This is one of the reasons that the poignant words of "Homing" always took hold of my heart with a deep ache for settledness, for rest and peace—for heaven. In fact, the LDS concept of heaven is an extension of family life, an endless succession of moments such as these. Whatever there was of the bohemian lurking in my soul, it was offset by the warmth and security implicit in these family scenes. It was at these gatherings that Mormonism carved its deepest furrow.

I had started high school with the intention of becoming a doctor like my grandfather and uncle before me, feeling that I needed a stable career that would bring in some money—unlike music or the theater. Initially, I selected science classes that I thought would advance me toward this goal, but something happened that altered the course of my life forever: during my sophomore year, I discovered jazz.

Hearing Skyline's jazz ensemble ignited a fire in me. The music was fast and loud with huge complicated chords, jutting rhythms, and improvisational solos that sounded wild and free—I *had* to be in that band! I was playing trombone in the concert band at the time and its director also led the jazz ensemble. He was a wise, inspiring teacher who recognized the eagerness in my eyes and encouraged me to try out. I made the cut for the following year.

During the summer, I attended a week-long jazz clinic at the University of Utah and became immersed in this new world. The program was staffed by a plethora of jazz heroes. Through the influence of a brilliant local trombonist, I started listening to jazz/rock crossover bands such as Blood, Sweat, and Tears and Chicago Transit Authority. Later I broadened my tastes to include purer forms of jazz and was especially drawn to albums that featured unusual rhythms and irregular meters, such as Dave Brubek's *Take Five* and Don Ellis's *Turkish Bath*.

My junior year was a great success. The Skyline Lab Band boasted some real talent and we even recorded an album for posterity, featuring some difficult arrangements, such as the famed Buddy Rich *West Side Story* suite. I formed a new rock 'n' roll band called The Going Concern with some of the best players from the Lab Band, and we began playing LDS Church dances (for scant compensation) on the weekends. It was a large group, with two trumpets, two saxes, a trombone, guitar, keyboards, bass, and drums. I played keyboards and covered most of the lead vocals. I also played flute and recorders, learning the instruments on my own from fingering charts and method books.

We needed music, so I started transcribing popular tunes from the radio and arranging them for the group. I had a good ear and writing seemed to come naturally to me. I just plunged in and began learning the craft by trial and error. I wrote my first original instrumental work for this group: a three-movement jazz suite I called *Silverlode* after Tolkien—the Silverlode was the stream at the east gate of Moria in which Durin, father of the dwarves, saw his destiny reflected. By the time I finished this piece, I knew my destiny as well: I would be a composer.

That year the Lab Band was prevented from attending the Reno Jazz Festival, a popular national conference of high school jazz bands, because school policy only permitted this trip every other year. In spite of this policy, some of us were able to persuade the administration to let The Going Concern attend. We played *Silverlode* there and won a First Division Award.

By the time I was a senior, I was playing lead trombone with the Lab Band and The Going Concern was working regular gigs around Salt Lake City. My class schedule, which included five music classes, along with Latin and English, reflected the certainty I felt about my vocation. I adapted *Silverlode* for the Lab Band and wrote several other new arrangements for this ensemble as well, including a transcription of Frank Zappa's arcane and thorny "Dog Breath, In the Year of the Plague." Zappa influenced me significantly; his sardonic music fed my interests in composition, politics, and social criticism, as well as my insurgent adolescent attitude.

Another important musical influence developed during my high school years. I became a great fan of the music of Joni Mitchell on the sunlit morning in 1968 when I first heard "Night in the City" on my grandma's old console stereo. I loved the bell-like purity of her voice, the way the complexity of her melodic and harmonic language contrasted with the simplicity of her arrangements, but especially the vulnerability of her lyrics. Inspired by her music to write some songs of my own, I borrowed my grandmother's gut-string guitar and began working up chords and picking patterns that reminded me of hers, with subtle dissonances and passing tones pervading the texture. Lines from her early songs still haunt and inspire me even today.

My interest in Joni Mitchell and other folk-oriented artists such as James Taylor and Simon and Garfunkel led me inevitably to one of their common influences: the traditional music of England and Ireland. At first I listened to rock/traditional crossover bands such as Fairport Convention and Steeleye Span, but soon friends introduced me to serious traditional groups like the Chieftains. I was entranced by their soaring, heart-wrenching melodies and the raw, undomesticated sound of the pipes and whistles. Something about this music called forth an answering voice from the depths of my soul.

I rediscovered my classical roots in high school through the encouragement of a classmate who loved choral music and was studying Brahms' *German Requiem.* One evening he sat at the piano with LeAnn and me and another close friend and took us through the first movement. The beauty of classical form and harmony opened up for me again—LeAnn and I immersed ourselves in Brahms after that, plunging with great fervor into his symphonies, especially the first and the third, as well as his piano compositions. I took a basic music theory class, taught by Skyline's enterprising and dedicated choral teacher. This class laid the groundwork for my composition technique. As soon as I was out of high school, I wrote my first sacred song to a text from the *Doctrine and Covenants* using the new tools I had acquired.

Through all of these adventures, however, Mormonism was still the central verity of my life, the gravity that held me in orbit no matter how far out into space I sailed. Poppie ordained me a priest when I turned sixteen. This meant I could bless (consecrate) the sacrament. That summer I also earned my "Duty to God" award for consistent attendance and service in the Aaronic Priesthood over the previous four years. In Utah, high school students were allowed a period of "released time" in order to attend seminary, a special class in which LDS students are trained in Mormonism. I had trouble with the person who was teaching the course during my junior year—my independent attitude collided with his iron rule—and I was kicked out of class. Since there were no other junior seminary classes available in that time slot, I was transferred into a class of seniors studying Mormon Church history and was ultimately allowed to graduate, despite this minor stain on my record.

My relationship to the Church went much deeper than institutional activity, however. Ironically, the year of my trouble in seminary was the year I became even more serious about Mormon doctrine, largely due to the influence of LeAnn's next door neighbor and fellow Skyline classmate, Mark. He was completely given over to Mormonism with an intensity I had never before witnessed in anyone else. This single-mindedness bore fruit in a variety of extraordinary behaviors that I found more reminiscent of the unpredictable characters of early Mormon history than the safe conservatism of the present-day Church. For example, Mark frequently skipped classes in order to read LDS books in the open court at school. I was intrigued and impressed by his dedication, and sometimes I joined him in long and earnest talks. I, too, began to read LDS classics voraciously, such as *Teachings of the Prophet Joseph Smith* and *Orson Pratt's Works,* as well as the uniquely Mormon scriptures: the *Book of Mormon,* the *Doctrine and Covenants,* and the *Pearl of Great Price.*

Ultimately, it was my association with these works that fueled my political idealism. The Prophet Joseph Smith was a firebrand when it came to politics, running for president of the United States in 1844 on a fairly radical platform of reform. Apostle Orson Pratt unambiguously wrote:

> The kingdom of God is an order of government established by divine authority. It is the only legal government that can exist in any part of the universe. All other governments are illegal and unauthorized. God, having made all beings and worlds, has the supreme right to govern them by His own laws, and by officers of His own appointment. Any people attempting to govern themselves by laws of their own making, and by officers of their own appointment, are in direct rebellion against the kingdom of God.[2]

Ideas like these tended to have a deleterious effect on my confidence in any human institution, including, sometimes, even the LDS Church. I was observant enough to recognize that the Church had its problems and occasionally seemed to operate with less than divine motives. Nevertheless, I still genuinely believed that it was the kingdom of God on earth. Any resemblance it bore to a flawed human institution, I reasoned, must be the fault of the people, not the Church.

A close group of friends formed, linked by a radical, visionary commitment to Mormonism. LeAnn and I were a part of this group. We liked to spend our free evenings attending lectures or seminars featuring leading LDS writers such as Truman Madsen, Hugh Nibley, and Stephen Covey. We took voluminous notes and had intense discussions for days afterward about the issues that were raised and their implications. I occasionally skipped school at Skyline to sit in on the philosophy classes of a professor named Hagen at the University of Utah. He was a self-styled "testimony buster," and I took pride in my ability to absorb all the venom he could dish out and not only remain faithful, but even take the offensive against what I thought were glaring holes in his reasoning.

The summer following my graduation, LeAnn and I attended a course on comparative religions at the LDS Institute of Religion on the University of Utah campus. Several representatives of other faiths addressed our class. I particularly remember the Sikh who spoke. I am ashamed to admit that we received him rather rudely, barely containing our childish laughter at his strict regimen and peculiar-sounding scripture. It was abundantly clear to us that his religion couldn't hold a candle to ours. Absent during this course was any representative of evangelical Christianity.

That summer, however, I did come face to face with some actual evangelicals. Two female missionaries from a local Baptist church rang our doorbell one morning. I happily invited them in and then aggressively turned the tables, attempting to persuade them that Mormonism was true. They appeared somewhat flustered by my behavior and asked if I would permit their pastor to contact me. I said that would be fine, little knowing that I would soon be visited by a notorious local anti-Mormon. My mother must have been appalled when he pulled up in front of our house, brandishing a loaded briefcase.

He and I sat talking on the back porch for over an hour. I don't remember anything he said, but he did leave a manuscript copy of his book. Though I managed to read it without flinching much—it struck me as so much shabby nit-picking at the corners of what I believed to be a great tapestry of truth—one issue troubled me enough to stick: he claimed that there were over three thousand changes in the text of the *Book of Mormon*. I had never heard such a thing before. On the contrary, I had been taught that Joseph Smith dictated the text word for word to his scribes. Obviously, there shouldn't be changes in a work of pure revelation. When I called my bishop with this question, he cheerfully informed me that there were indeed changes, but that they were largely grammatical in nature and that this was a matter of common knowledge. At the time, I was perfectly satisfied by his response, and it never occurred to me to ask why God should need His grammar corrected.

Apart from these minor instances, my faith remained largely unchallenged. Although my confidence in Mormonism was essentially unassailable, there was one thing I yet lacked: a "testimony." This is the word Latter-day Saints use to describe a special spiritual confirmation of the truth of Mormonism, usually manifested by a powerful feeling LDS scripture describes as a "burning in the bosom." Mormons believe that the right to this personal revelation from God belongs to all worthy members of the one true church. A testimony is often expressed as a kind of Mormon mantra: "I know that Jesus is the Christ; I know that Joseph Smith was a prophet of God; I know this Church is true." As a child, I had often said these words—and meant them—but despite this and all my experiences as a young Mormon, I still sought for that one unique and conclusive spiritual witness.

I can still vividly recall the day I got my testimony. LeAnn and I had gone to the airport to see a friend off on his proselyting mission. Before he boarded the plane, he bore witness to us of the truthfulness of the Mormon gospel in eloquent terms. In fact, he claimed to have seen Jesus Christ in a vision. As we listened, I was overcome with a rush of feeling that seemed to catch up my entire being, body and soul, with fire. This feeling confirmed that Mormonism and all that went along with it was absolutely true. There was no room left for doubt. I consciously recommitted myself to a lifetime of serious study and total dedication to the LDS Church. LeAnn had received a similarly powerful witness and recommitted herself as well. The sharing of this important moment bonded us even closer together as friends.

Since our leaving the Church, some have speculated that LeAnn and I never had real testimonies. This is simply untrue; we most certainly did. A better question would be: having had such testimonies, how then could we leave? I have since learned that one cannot rely on overwhelming emotional sensations to determine what is ultimately true. I now know by sad experience how deceptive the heart can be. To my young mind, however, things all seemed so marvelous and clear, and I lived for these ineffable moments of radiance, for each random spark of seemingly divine favor.

With my testimony as a model and a guide, I began to have more frequent and varied spiritual experiences. The following summer, while on vacation in Farmington, New Mexico, I was overcome with a sense of guilt for my sins—the usual teenage preoccupations with lust and lack of discipline. I hiked up onto a bluff overlooking my aunt's house and prayed intensely, begging God to forgive me and set me back on track. As I was praying, a cool and gentle wind began to caress my face and my *Book of Mormon* fell open to this passage:

> And if men come unto me I will show unto them their weakness. I give unto men weakness that they may be humble; and my grace is sufficient for all men that humble themselves before me; for if they humble themselves before me, and have faith in me, then will I make weak things become strong unto them. (Ether 12:27)

I was overjoyed. God had spoken and I was forgiven. All was right with the world.

Priesthood blessings continued to be an important part of my spiritual life throughout high school. Three of them stand out in my mind: one deadly serious, one rather amusing, and one prophetic.

I received the first of these in my sophomore year. As part of a Church-sponsored activity, I spent a weekend snowmobiling with a group of boys from my ward. We had a great time, skimming over the crystalline snow at breakneck pace, recklessly leaping moguls rising like lumps in a billowing white blanket. At one point, riding in tandem, a friend and I sped toward what appeared to be a mild depression in the terrain, intending to jump over it. It was actually a sunken creek bed, obscured by drifts along its banks. We flew over, ramming the other side just shy of the top, and slid down backwards, laughing uproariously. Dragging the snowmobile back up the bank was a good deal more difficult than sliding down had been, but we managed it with some effort. After entertaining our companions with the tale, I didn't think much more about it until several weeks later when a dull ache developed in my upper left arm.

At first, Poppie diagnosed it as a muscle strain connected with the accident, but it wouldn't go away and the pain steadily increased. Finally, he arranged for X-rays. When the results came in, they were sent directly to his office. He called me in and, without explanation, he laid his hands on my head and confidently blessed me with healing. Then he scheduled me for a biopsy. The X-rays had revealed a lump in my arm about half the size of a golf ball. There was a good chance that I had Ewing's sarcoma, a virulent form of bone cancer that is nearly always fatal. Even knowing this, Poppie had blessed me with recovery.

On the morning of the operation, I awoke to the specter of a three hundred pound orderly with a patch over one eye, stropping a large straight razor next to my bed. He was there to shave me for the biopsy. At this macabre sight, I lost all dignity and began to blubber uncontrollably. Nevertheless, the preparations proceeded, and I was then drugged, transferred to a wobbling gurney, and wheeled down several brightly lit corridors to the operating room where Poppie and my Uncle Gene were waiting along with the doctor who was to perform the operation. I was given an anesthetic and asked to count backward from a hundred. I never made ninety-seven.

The operation was successful. The only difficulty that arose was excessive bleeding. A tourniquet was recommended, but Poppie, a pioneer in the use of medical hypnotism, stepped in and hypnotized me while I was still under the anesthetic, instructing my subconscious mind not only to control the bleeding, but also the nausea often experienced in recovering from anesthetics. Poppie's suggestions worked spectacularly. The bleeding stopped, the operation was successfully concluded, and I awoke with a ravenous appetite. Best of all, the lump was benign. Healing quickly, I was soon back in school without any long-term physical effects. I and everyone else in the family regarded this incident as a miraculous deliverance from the jaws of death through the power of the Mormon priesthood.

The second of the priesthood blessings I remember was also one of healing, though for a condition considerably less serious. It was given by a neighbor who served as our family's "home teacher." In LDS wards, home teachers are assigned to visit each family at least once a month to deliver a general message from the First Presidency and monitor any special needs the family might have. One evening, about an hour before I was to perform for a Church dance, I fell desperately ill with nausea so severe that I couldn't stand on my feet, let alone perform. Mom called our home teacher and he promptly came over and laid his hands on my head. With the power of the priesthood, he commanded the sickness to leave my body, and I immediately threw up all over the floor. Though still "green around the gills," I felt well enough to go to work after this blessing and managed to get through the evening without further unpleasantness.

The most significant of all the priesthood blessings I received as a Mormon was my patriarchal blessing, a special prophetic revelation given to members of the LDS Church by stake patriarchs, ordained specifically to the task. I became eligible for this blessing as I neared my sixteenth birthday. If my confirmation laid the groundwork for my future as a Mormon, my patriarchal blessing was the capstone. It was recorded and transcribed by the patriarch's staff as follows:

Dear Brother Jonathan Alfred Clawson Redford:

Pursuant to your desires, in this sacred hour we seek the inspiration of our Heavenly Father as I humbly lay my hands upon your head, by virtue of my office and calling in the holy priesthood, and bestow your Patriarchal Blessing upon you.

The Lord is pleased with your life thus far and is cognizant of your problems. He has spared you and has been kind and merciful, and is preparing the way for you to complete your mortal appointment. Because of your valiance in the spirit world, the time of your mortal probation was set for the dispensation of the fulness of time, when the strongest, most worthy and capable of His spirit children are clothed with a body and called forth to spread the gospel message throughout the nations of the world for the last time. Unto this labor you have been appointed. Utilize whatever means at your disposal to fill this assignment. Never refrain nor fear to raise your voice in defense of gospel principles. You will be buoyed up and sustained, endowed with the spirit. Remember the key—the spirit of God is the medium through which you and your fellow man communicate; this alone is the witness that will come.

Now, as a descendant of Ephraim, of believing blood, the tribe designated to preach the gospel unto the House of Israel, you are an heir to all the rights, gifts and blessings that have been promised the worthy. Chief among these is the priesthood, which is after the order of the Son of God. If you are obedient to the principles and the order of the priesthood, in its exercise and acceptance, these elements will empower you to rise high in the order, that you may become more perfect, greater in the service of your Eternal Father, and esteemed in the eyes of your fellow men.

I bless you with desires to exercise all the gifts with which you have been endowed, especially that of music. The Lord himself has declared that the humble, righteous song of the heart is a prayer unto Him. Let your compositions be patterned after Him—pure and holy, filled with love and inspiration to lift the heart of man, to give encouragement and to feed his soul.

I bless you with powers of discernment, that you may be qualified to judge properly between right and wrong and not be deceived, but that through the power of the Holy Ghost, which gift you possess, the course you are to follow will be made known to you. Let your mind dwell on the spiritual, of which you are also a steward. You will be held accountable for the manner in which you develop your gifts and endowments. Seek after those qualities and elements that will outlast this existence. Build upon those things which have been pronounced by the Almighty as permanent.

In your efforts to prepare yourself for your ministry, study the holy scriptures; for from these you will determine the eternal nature of the gospel, which is the same now as anciently. Upon these fundamental, underlying facts, you may structure your eternal life.

I bless you with fulfillment of all the purposes of your mortal existence. In the time appointed may you select a companion worthy of temple marriage, sealed to your posterity, and have joy in the establishment of your own household under the influence of the priesthood. Always be mindful of those who have contributed to your success and welfare, who have given much of themselves for your personal advancement.

I bless you that as you conclude your mortal days you will be lifted up, empowered to restore your body to immortality, to be glorified, redeemed, to receive your inheritance of all the blessings promised the faithful. As a king and priest, you will be privileged to rule and reign over your own household together with all your loved ones.

I bless you with the powers to endure unto the end, even though you will be called upon to endure trials and tribulations; for you will witness iniquities that will cause your heart to mourn, and you will weep bitter tears over prevailing conditions. Contrarily, you will also witness the hand of God made manifest as you participate in the establishment of the new Zion where the saints of God who have been appointed unto that high and holy calling may dwell in peace. You will witness the fulfillment of many of the prophecies concerning the Lord's church and the devotion of those appointed to accomplish the labors to which they were fore-ordained.

These blessings I seal upon you, the realization of which is dependent upon your worthiness, in the name of Jesus Christ. Amen.[3]

I rejoiced to hear that God was pleased with me and aware of my problems. Though my life was rich with interests and opportunities passionately pursued, I often felt insecure and unable to live up to my potential. Sometimes I felt that my sins and shortcomings doomed me to fail. With this blessing, I realized that God knew all of this and was planning to do something about it. He had a purpose for me—"to spread the gospel message throughout the nations of the world for the last time"—and I was proud to be numbered among the valiant, "the strongest, most worthy and capable of His spirit children." I took the words "He has spared you" to refer specifically to my deliverance from cancer. The emphasis on "the spirit" encouraged me further in seeking spiritual witnesses and experiences.

One important purpose of the patriarchal blessing is to reveal to which tribe of Israel the one being blessed belongs. Mormons believe that upon reception of the gift of the Holy Ghost, one is adopted into the House of Israel. Joseph Smith taught that this involved a literal blood change:

> . . . the effect of the Holy Ghost upon a Gentile, is to purge out the old blood, and make him actually of the seed of Abraham. That man that has none of the blood of Abraham (naturally) must have a new creation by the Holy Ghost.[4]

Mormonism emphasizes the leadership role of the tribe of Ephraim and most white Anglo-Saxon Latter-day Saints are pronounced members of this tribe. Again, I was proud to be set apart from the world and singled out for special power and position. The thought that I might "rise high in the order" filled me with hope and ambition.

I was amazed that the patriarch spoke of music, particularly composition, as I had written only a few pieces prior to receiving the patriarchal blessing. His words sanctified my drive to compose and affirmed my vocation as a musician. I treasured being given the gift of discernment as well. I had a deep desire to be right, to avoid deception and illusion, and it seemed that God acknowledged and confirmed my passion for the truth.

Like Poppie's sacred words at my confirmation, this blessing emphasized missionary work, marriage in the temple, the importance of the scriptures, and the influence of the Holy Ghost. The language was even more exalted, speaking of my being "lifted up, . . . glorified, and redeemed," eventually to become "a king and priest" to "rule and reign" over my household with all my loved ones. I took a romantic and naive satisfaction in the prediction of "trials and tribulations" and I had already wept many "bitter tears over prevailing conditions."

Finally, the promise of participation in the establishment of Zion compensated for any fear I may have found in those words. Zion is the LDS Utopia, wherein all the hopes of Mormonism are realized on earth in a theocentric society of perfectly balanced order and freedom. In the city of Zion, everything is held in common. No money is exchanged; each contributes to the community in the area of his own strength and is compensated with the resources he needs. Christ is the head and the local leadership positions are administered by the Prophet and the other General Authorities. John Taylor, the successor to Brigham Young, had described it as a culture that would be the envy of the world in education, science, government, the arts, and every other endeavor. I yearned to go there as one of God's minstrels. With this blessing I felt I had His guarantee that I would, and I wanted to shout with joy. My head swam with anticipation every time I read those words.

And so the hook was set. It was inconceivable that I would ever renounce Mormonism or leave the LDS Church in light of these grand promises. A bright light illuminated my path and all I had to do was walk in it. That was all. Just that. Merely that.

In retrospect, I now recognize in my patriarchal blessing a potent and seductive appeal to pride that was completely hidden from me at the time—I was too giddy with the wine of my own potential. One of its key concepts is personal empowerment: power to rise high in the order of the priesthood, power to structure my own eternal life, power to restore my body to immortality, to be glorified, to receive my inheritance of all the blessings promised the faithful, power to endure to the end. By contrast, the person and grace of Jesus Christ are conspicuous in their absence. There is no hint of unmerited favor here, only endowments of power contingent upon my worthiness. The struggle to be worthy soon became a dominating theme in my life.

The Glory of God Is Intelligence

5

The glory of God is intelligence, or, in other words, light and truth.

—Doctrine and Covenants 93:36

*O*n each side of the main entrance to the campus of Brigham Young University, a slogan appears: one side reads, "Enter to learn, go forth to serve," and the other, "The world is our campus." Cynical students used to reverse these: "Enter to serve, go forth to learn" and "The campus is our world."

I had long planned to attend BYU. As important as music had become to me during high school, my faith was more important still, and it was for reasons of faith that I finally made the decision. Oddly enough, no one among my family or friends ever encouraged me to consider a music school such as Julliard or Eastman.

I applied for the coveted presidential scholarship, named for the sitting president of the LDS Church and open in those days only to young men of exceptional quality. I hoped to be included among these.

I wasn't awarded the scholarship, however. My grades were good, but not exceptional, and perhaps I was also too "risky" for the honor. My personal record bore the occasional indication of latent rebelliousness and I was too willing to express my own opinions during the interview. Moreover, I was a jazz musician. My hair, even though it had been trimmed for the occasion, refused to stay in one place for more than twenty minutes. All in all, I just did not fit the profile of the ideal young LDS men the Church wanted as its representatives. Instead, I was offered a small scholarship, which I accepted gratefully. Then I began addressing the many details of my first move away from home into the environment of academia, or "academania," as I was then fond of calling it.

That autumn, I moved into an apartment just southeast of campus named for that most genteel of rebels, Robert E. Lee. These were spartan digs with paper-thin walls and matchstick furnishings. The apartment was built for four and was divided in two by a common kitchen and sitting room. Each side had a small bedroom with two single beds, a bathroom, and a wood veneer study cubicle featuring a built-in desk with bookshelves above it.

I roomed with Scott Abbott, a friend whose family we had grown close to in Farmington, New Mexico. A senior majoring in German literature, Scott was an exceptional man: handsome, brilliant, piercingly honest, stoic, and tending toward the mystical. I trusted him and looked up to him like a big brother. He made it possible for me, a lowly freshman, to live enviably off-campus.

On the other side of the apartment lived Mark and Jim, two students I had never met before and whom I rarely saw or spoke with. I don't remember much about Mark, but Jim was a bulky upperclassman from Boise, Idaho, who once astounded the rest of us with his remarkable ability to shave with a razor-sharp machete. Down the hall lived another foursome, one of whom would have a lasting impact on my life. Sterling Van Wagenen was an actor/director studying philosophy and aspiring to work in film. His street clothes production of *Hamlet,* in which he played the title role, still occupies a place in my mind as a prime example of scalding intensity and truthfulness. Sterling became one of my closest friends, later going on to produce the film *The Trip to Bountiful,* for which I wrote the score.

Life at BYU soon became a routine of classes and meals, a continuum of rising up and lying down, coming and going, bleary-eyed early morning showers and late-night cramming. Having no car, I walked everywhere, and these walks proved one of the highlights of my college experience. BYU is nestled in the lap of the Wasatch range of the Rocky Mountains, and just east of campus is a wonderful craggy rock face that took on a personal character as I considered it each day. I began to see it as a man sees a woman with whom he lives for a long time, in all lights and disguises: gentle, angry, stern, warm, nourishing, simultaneously full of judgment and grace.

My schedule included a hodgepodge of general education, honors, music, and religion classes. BYU required all students to take religion, and freshmen had to study the *Book of Mormon*. I had an honors *Book of Mormon* class from a stern and dedicated teacher named Chauncey Riddle, who inspired me with the depth of his insight and the strength of his commitment. What I remember most is his rigorous insistence on the necessity of ongoing personal revelation and the high level of daily worthiness required to receive it. He once told us that we shouldn't even put on a shoe in the morning without revelation. How could we know there wasn't a scorpion lurking within? I also remember the wry smile that crept over the face of his son—a classmate—when I audaciously asked him what it was like to live with such a spiritual giant. I soaked up Dr. Riddle's ideas without question, little understanding how they would later come to haunt me with despair.

I took an honors class in political science from another teacher, Ray Hillam, who, unlike Dr. Riddle, seemed to have a high tolerance for ambiguity. This class was held in the afternoon and I often struggled to keep my eyes open, not so much because the good doctor was dull, but because of my own lack of discipline and interest in the subject. Despite my political action in high school, I had surprisingly little patience for studying the labyrinthian machinations of real politics. I didn't put much effort into this class. When the time came to write a paper, I began one entitled "A Subjective Analysis of the Vietnam War" in which I tried, without success, to pour out all the bile and fear of my high school activism. I never finished the paper. I handed in a few angry pages, ready to accept the consequences. I was shocked when I was given a C in the course—surely an act of kindness or pity on Dr. Hillam's part.

One of my favorite courses was about film. It was in this class that I first saw Jean Renoir's *Grand Illusion,* John Ford's *Cheyenne Autumn,* and Elia Kazan's *On the Waterfront* with its brilliant and moving score by Leonard Bernstein. When the instructor asked us to write a paper in this class, I again took the subjective approach, this time attempting to define "art." The style of my paper was heavily influenced by e e cummings' *i six nonlectures* which were originally delivered as part of the 1952–1953 Charles Eliot Norton series at Harvard. I wrote that the world was best understood through music and poetry—logic and precision killed the spirit. I genuinely believed Rilke's advice to the young poet:

> Works of art are of an infinite loneliness and with nothing so little to be reached as with criticism. Consider yourself and your feeling right every time with regard to every such argumentation, discussion or introduction; if you are wrong after all, the natural growth of your inner life will lead you slowly and with time to other insights.[1]

In this class I elevated my thinking about film, learning to understand it as an art form and opening the door to the possibility of my working in the field.

The bulk of my classes were music classes. In one of the first sessions of my composition class, we were all asked what we were going to do when we graduated. Many students weren't sure and some were practical, planning for careers as music teachers. I responded, somewhat arrogantly I suppose, that I was a composer already— true, an untrained, inexperienced one, but a composer nonetheless. My identity as such was a state of being as far as I was concerned. This statement was met with a bemused response from the team of teachers who were present that day. They didn't seem to believe me—or in me. Perhaps they had heard this sort of bluster before and had seen it wane in the glare of the harsh realities of the years that followed; or maybe they smiled in memory of the same impulse within themselves when they were fresh out of high school and as boldly naive as I was then.

In any event, the school was not well suited to handle someone with my ambitions. I was funneled into the general music program, ironically titled "Expanding Musicianship," along with music students of every conceivable stripe and stature. Although I didn't like the program and was terribly frustrated, if the truth be known, I was undisciplined and found the work tedious. My problem was not just laziness, however. It is very difficult to foster the development of genuine musical disciplines within the vacuum of institutional prerogatives. The BYU program highlighted this problem in spades.

For example, ear training was required, not in the context of real music, but via tapes featuring pitches created by piercing electronic beeps. Everyone grew to hate these beeps, mind-numbing exercises that bred hostility rather than appreciation for the important ability to hear the basic building blocks of music: pitch, intervals, harmony, and rhythm. In their effort to reduce these elements to a fundamental, teachable system, the creators of "Expanding Musicianship" had sucked the life out of the music.

One memorable event stands out from my composition class, involving another student composer named Helge, who was a confirmed modernist. I had already made my mind up about anything smacking of serialism or atonality, twentieth-century compositional approaches that create dissonances which are off-putting to many listeners. I didn't like it and wasn't afraid to say so. To my shame I had even tarred Bartok with this broad brush of bias. Early Stravinsky was good, late Stravinsky was bad. I was an unapologetic tonalist who loved the ordered forms of Bach and Mozart, the romanticism of Beethoven, and the exquisite balance of the Apollonian and Dionysian sensibilities of Brahms. I didn't mind dissonance per se; I just could not appreciate it outside the scope of traditional forms and harmony.

Helge was an eccentric collection of paradoxes, arrogant and oddly humble at the same time. As much as I despised his modernist tastes and predilection for making dogmatic pronouncements in class, I found myself drawn to these very characteristics. In any event, one afternoon he loaned me an LP of *Utrenja: The Entombment of Christ*, a work by the twentieth-century Polish composer Krzysztof Penderecki, which I promptly took back to my apartment and put on the turntable, expecting to hate it. As I had anticipated, the piece was harshly dissonant and the form seemed chaotic and impossible to follow; but there was also an amazing emotional power in this music that overwhelmed my preconceptions, especially a solo for male voice that rises out of the texture, becoming a falsetto scream. Listening to this piece was a turning point for me. I never again heard or wrote music as I had done before.

Apart from the customary class assignments and exercises, I composed two new pieces of chamber music while at BYU: a prelude for organ and a second sacred song, based on a *Book of Mormon* text and dedicated to two of my BYU "sisters" who performed it in sacrament meeting one afternoon. I also wrote a single-movement string quartet that was premiered at the University of Utah the following summer.

By far the most important hour of my schedule at BYU was devoted to the jazz ensemble. Synthesis, as the band was called, was led by a gifted and generous teacher, Newell Dayley, who had spotted me in the Skyline band and made a point of encouraging me to pursue my playing and writing. He and the BYU band had even performed *Silverlode* in concert while I was still in high school, an unusual honor. Newell continued to provide me with opportunities to develop at BYU. I played in the trombone section of Synthesis and had many chances to improvise solos, which was both a freeing and frustrating experience for me. There's nothing quite like the feeling of standing in front of a sizzling jazz band with nothing but the driving rhythms and shifting chord changes bearing you along—it's the aural equivalent of surfing. While improvising a jazz solo, I was free to play anything I could imagine, but I was frustrated with the chasm between what I could imagine and what I could actually play. My technique lagged well behind my ideas.

I did some writing for the band that year. The most significant work of this period was a piece I called *Rebirth*. Newell was committed to the expression of the spiritual dimension through the medium of jazz and I shared his agenda without hesitation. *Rebirth* didn't employ traditional jazz idioms but was more symphonic in character, adding French horns and woodwinds to the saxes, trumpets, trombones, and rhythm section that traditionally make up a jazz ensemble. The work was programmatic, a musical fable about a soul struggling through the chaos of worldly voices for self-definition and transcendence. *Rebirth* began with individual members of the band reading selections from random philosophical texts, the daily newspaper, and various other sources, building from a single declamatory voice to a cacophonous chorus of shouting. Out of this tumultuous mêlée of competing ideas rose a solo trombone in an a capella improvised solo, representing the individual soul. The soloist journeys through a series of encounters with various sections of the band. The turning point of the piece hinged on the regeneration of the soul through a gracious act of divine initiative. In part, this idea rose from the symbols and metaphors of my Mormon faith; but there was another element that mirrored a spiritual struggle in my own heart and the aching desire for a redemption that I intuitively began to suspect I could not bring about through any act of my own.

I rarely dated and engaged in few extracurricular activities while at BYU. LeAnn was attending the University of Utah, and, while we remained close friends, we saw each other only on the weekends. I never attended any sporting events or joined any clubs. Rather, I spent hours at the KBYU radio station listening to music—KBYU was the only place I could find obscure recordings such as Steeleye Span's "Please to See the King." I also listened to Joni Mitchell's *Blue*, Cat Stevens' *Tea for the Tillerman* and *The Teaser and the Firecat*, and Judy Collins' *Wildflowers* and *Whales and Nightingales*.

At the station, I met Brian Capener, an announcer who became one of my dearest friends. Brian hosted a classical music program and read liner notes with a mellifluous voice as if they had sprung to mind spontaneously from an unimaginably vast wealth of knowledge. He was also an aspiring filmmaker, a fact that would later alter the course of my life considerably when he hired me to score his documentaries.

I also met David Koralewski, the host of my favorite progressive music program, "Crosscurrents." "Crosscurrents" introduced me to many eclectic artists and ensembles, such as the Paul Winter Consort, which later became staples of my listening diet. Dave allowed me to put together an aural montage for his show. My subject was "home" and I drew material from a wide range of sources, including a recording of e e cummings' *i six nonlectures* which contained a poignant tribute to the poet's parents, and Frank Zappa's "Mama" from the classic Mothers of Invention album, *We're Only in It for the Money*. This montage was an exercise in form and content that I remember principally for the emotional resonance that the subject held for me. I was mortified the night it was broadcast, however, because of a couple of technical errors that got by without my noticing. Just as when I played music, I couldn't seem to perform without mistakes. This is one of the reasons I have always felt more comfortable composing than performing. Writing became a refuge where I could make my mistakes privately.

Two contemporary jazz artists really caught my attention that year. LeAnn and I discovered Paul Horn at a macrobiotic dinner that was hosted in a dank Salt Lake basement apartment decorated with beaded curtains, packing crate bookshelves, plants, and tree stumps that served as chairs. Incense hung so thick in the air, it felt as if we were underwater. We drank miso soup from wooden bowls, an appetizer powerful enough to cleanse the sinuses more efficiently than a whiff of ammonia. The cook boasted of the age of his fermented soybean mash as if it were a vintage wine. Throughout the evening, Paul Horn's *Inside* album, recorded in the Taj Mahal, provided the musical accompaniment. The album was entirely solo flute, except for the natural sounds of bells and chanted prayers in the background. The tone was rich and pungent, and the notes seemed to hang suspended in the air of the Taj Mahal, weighty as little planets. This music certainly spoke to the mystic in me.

The other jazz musician who captured my ear was English guitarist John McLaughlin. His album *The Inner Mounting Flame* exploded into my world from the very first notes of "Meetings of the Spirit," in which McLaughlin's virtuosic flights of piercingly intense electric guitar became a new metaphor for the spiritual search. The album was full of treasures, from the unexpected time changes of "The Dance of Maya" to the impossibly beautiful "Lotus on Irish Streams." I wanted desperately to write music with this kind of power, power that would make "the wicked stop their ears and run for the doors and the righteous leap to their feet with hallelujahs." Again, there was a strong Eastern influence in this music. Never shy about sharing *his* faith, McLaughlin included in the LP an insert with the words of his guru, which I devoured hungrily. It is significant that I never sensed any conflict between this spiritual adventurism and the content of my Mormon faith.

I read three books that year that were particularly influential. My roommate Scott introduced me to Rainer Maria Rilke's *Letters to a Young Poet,* and Rilke's words seemed to be addressed specifically to me. Frank Herbert's *Dune* contained a maxim that remained lodged in my mind: "Fear is the mind killer." I also read *Dove,* the story of Robin Lee Graham's solo sail around the world when he was sixteen. The sheer chutzpah of this adventure greatly fired my imagination. I was surprisingly tolerant in my own mind of a sexual relationship he had with Patti, a girl he met on the journey who later became his wife. Despite the many injunctions in Mormonism against sexual sin, deeper still was my belief that the feelings of one's heart were the ultimate arbiters of right and wrong, of truth and falsehood. In other words, if two people were really in love, sex without a wedding ceremony might be permitted in some corner of the universe, just as polygamy was among my forebears.

Religious life at BYU was well organized, as one would expect from the Mormons, given their keen interest in authority and structure. In a microcosm of the Church at large, students were organized into wards and stakes based on the location of their housing. Faculty members and other mature Mormons from the area were called to serve as bishops and stake presidents, while older students manned the lesser positions. It was not unusual for a BYU professor to act as a student's teacher on Friday and "confessor" on Sunday. The student wards were further subdivided into mock "families" with a male student as "father," a female student as "mother," and four or five others as "brothers and sisters." This practice of creating artificial families has been discontinued since I left BYU, in part, I'm told, because a few "fathers" and "mothers" took their roles too literally.

I attended campus church meetings faithfully. How we rejoiced when a "nonmember" was "loved into the Church" and baptized while a student there. On one hand, the routine was all perfectly familiar—life seemed to be the same everywhere, a seamless cloth unfolding, for the most part, without a hitch just as Mormonism had taught me that it would.

On the other hand, unexpected wrinkles began to appear in my relationship with the Church. It was at BYU that I first became conscious of how uncomfortable my comments made others in Sunday school classes feel. My thoughts about art and spirituality, politics and the corruptibility of institutions seemed somehow vaguely dangerous, hovering on the edge of respectability. I could sense a veiled disapproval like a hum in the air. My response to this unspoken censure ran the gamut from "Nuts to them" to mental self-flagellation at my inability to fall in line.

The locus of my spiritual expression at BYU was less my student ward, however, than it was my involvement with an idealistic group of Mormon artists and musicians, caught up in the first stirrings of what we believed would be a renaissance of Mormon arts. We felt as if we stood at the headwaters of a great movement in the Church. LeAnn and I discovered this group at an informal concert of LDS folk and rock musicians held in the auditorium at Provo High School.

By now, it ought to be obvious that I lived for "peak" experiences. In fact, I leaped from peak to peak, barely clearing the valleys in between. This particular evening was the biggest high yet, not counting the day I got my testimony. The songs spoke to my deepest hopes and the sensation of the presence of God was as imminent as a thunderstorm that raises the hair on the arms with each crack of lightning. LeAnn and I were caught up together in the intensity of the moment, intoxicated with passion, destiny, triumph, vindication, redemption, and glory. We introduced ourselves to everyone we could that night, discovering several kindred spirits all at once. It was the beginning of many important friendships.

The whole experience felt like a foretaste of the Mormon utopian dream of Zion. In Zion we would all be of one mind; peace and love would reign supreme, as it did that night. Our group's yearning for the establishment of God's culture dove-tailed with our countercultural bent in a uniquely Mormon way. Like me, the other musicians LeAnn and I met that night dreamed of becoming minstrels in Zion.

The characters in this theater of the spirit were a ragtag collection of eccentrics and visionaries. There was Marvin Payne, the square-jawed iconoclastic troubadour who took his guitar and went door to door selling his records all over the Provo/Orem area. His songs combined esoteric LDS theology with personal insights and experiences. Always reaching, he frequently scaled the mystic spiritual heights that had become a touchstone of true sanctification for me. The sharing of these experiences was how many of us came to identify our spirit kinfolk.

There was Debbie Au, an LDS "Janis Joplin," whose songs had a country-rock flavor. She looked like an angel disguised as an earth mother, and she could work up tremendous intensity on stage with her "whiskey voice" or deliver a ballad with crystalline purity.

Alan Cherry was a black Mormon in an era when it was assumed that being black and Mormon was an oxymoron. Since the days of Joseph Smith, the LDS Church had taught that blacks could not hold the priesthood or participate in the temple ceremonies. This effectively shut them out of the ordinances that were necessary for exaltation in the celestial kingdom of God. Amazingly, Alan believed the Church was true in spite of all this. He had published his conversion story in a book that Mormons liked to offer in those days as evidence of their egalitarianism. Philosophical and given to optimism and grand designs, he wrote lyrics that he wanted turned into funk tunes.

These three were united by their association with a small record company called Trilogy Arts run by Gerald Pearson, a blond man of big vision and gentle speech. Gerald was the sort of manager who seemed able to pull together and market a stable of artists without compromising the idealism that lay at the root of their beliefs. Marvin and Debbie had released albums with Trilogy, and the company had published Alan's book. Gerald's wife, Carol Lynn, was a successful poet and playwright in the LDS community, and some of her works had become Mormon cultural icons. The Pearsons were a formidable couple and gave encouragement and help to many of us.

The most conspicuous member of our group was Joseph Germaine. He was tall and thin with thick brown hair, perfectly straight, falling down to the middle of his back, and a foot-long beard. His moustache hairs were as thick as wires and they completely obscured his wry and ubiquitous half-smile. He never wore anything except denim and often sported large and interesting hats from which his hair cascaded like sheets of water off a mill wheel. Joe worked at a record store in an old building on Provo's Main Street called the Union Block. Also housed there were craft and health food shops. This was the haven of Provo's counterculture and the air was always redolent with psychedelic music and patchouli oil.

My role in the movement began with Free Agency, Mormonism's only bona fide professional rock 'n' roll band. Originally known as the Sons of Mosiah, after characters from the *Book of Mormon,* it had been founded by David Zandanotti, former member of San Francisco's Moby Grape. A bassist extraordinaire, David wrote many of the band's songs, and his style was characterized by unusual chord progressions and tuneful McCartneyesque bass lines. He was joined by a rock-solid drummer, Randy Guzcman, who also had a brilliant high voice. Lead guitar was covered by Dennis Meese, blond and tan as a California surfer with a nervous manner that carried over into the short percussive riffs that characterized his solos. Dennis MacGregor was fourth man, playing fiddle and rhythm guitar. They all sang, sometimes with tight four-part harmony a la Crosby, Stills, Nash, and Young. The night I first heard them at Provo High, they ended the concert with one of David's songs based on the 88th section of the *Doctrine and Covenants:*

> Behold, that which you hear is as the voice of one crying in the wilderness—in the wilderness, because you cannot see him—my voice, because my voice is Spirit; my Spirit is truth; truth abideth and hath no end; and if it be in you it shall abound. And if your eye be single to my glory, your whole bodies shall be filled with light, and there shall be no darkness in you; and that body which is filled with light comprehendeth all things. (D&C 88:66–67)

I was profoundly moved by this combination of the power of rock anthem with the LDS scripture.

I met David following the concert. Not long afterward, he asked me to join the band. I played keyboard (principally organ), flute, and occasionally bass when David switched to acoustic guitar. I also sang some high harmony. I really flourished working with them. My flute technique improved tremendously, and I loved improvising extended unaccompanied organ solos that allowed me to express myself spiritually as well as musically. It was a grand time, creatively.

With Free Agency I experienced to a greater degree than I had known before that unique brotherhood found among musicians. We did a number of concerts on the road. After every concert, people would come up and share their struggles or their experiences with God. It seemed that what I had felt at the concert in Provo was part of a much broader spiritual hunger among the youth of the Church, and we were heartened by signs of the revolution of spirit we were sure was coming. It seemed we were collecting new brothers and sisters wherever we would go. We also had a lot of fun, a few disagreements, and some genuinely outrageous times.

Many weekends, I packed up my dirty laundry in a pillowcase and hitch-hiked home to Salt Lake. LeAnn and I spent most of these weekends together. Behind her house there was an elementary school with a huge swing set from which we could look west across the Salt Lake Valley, splayed out like a glistening carpet of light. There we talked about our dreams, our faith, and the books we had read. We would linger for hours, laughing and swinging as high as we could. If only we could swing right around the top bar, we thought, we could achieve what we jokingly called "nirvana."

About midway through the school year, I realized I was beginning to fall in love with LeAnn. I began to feel strange emotions when I was with her. My face flushed, I couldn't breathe, and I felt a little ball in the pit of my stomach. I wanted to take care of her, spend money that I didn't have on her, make love to her. I couldn't imagine spending the rest of my life without her.

Of course, I wanted to tell her all of this, but I was afraid that if I confessed, somehow our friendship would end. So I kept these feelings to myself, not knowing how to break the ice. Besides, I thought LeAnn had plans to marry someone else. For some time she had been involved with a mutual friend, until he left on his mission. Then she had dated a sturdy, steady, unassuming young man, radically different from me. I didn't think I had much chance and I despaired.

After one of our weekend evening swings, I was overtaken with an irresistible desire to broach the subject, come what may. I couldn't wear a mask any longer. I asked her rather timidly, "Have you ever thought about what it would be like to be married to me?" I lobbed the question like a pebble into the middle of a still pond and waited for the ripples. I was utterly shocked when she laughed lightly and said, "Oh yes, thousands of times." I didn't know what to say next. I just sat there dumbfounded, jaw gaping, wondering how to follow up this statement. Finally, I said something idiotic like, "I'm so relieved. I had no idea." Nevertheless, my question had the desired effect, opening up new dimensions of conversation between us. We began to exchange a few tentative ideas about our relationship and the possibility of marriage. A few weeks later, we decided to read one another's patriarchal blessings.

To a Mormon adolescent this is a very intimate thing to do. To read the prophecies that have been uttered over someone else's head is to open up a vulnerability that's very unusual—not a decision to be taken lightly. We decided to fast from all food and drink one Sunday in anticipation of the event. That night we met together, prayed, and then traded blessings. While LeAnn was reading my blessing, she had a mystical experience, a revelation: reading one of the lines about my future wife, she was overcome with a strong impression that it referred to her. She suddenly knew that she was supposed to marry me. But how could she tell me? I had barely begun to express any romantic inclinations, and we hadn't so much as held hands.

Finally, after several days of soul-searching, LeAnn decided that she had to make a special trip down to Provo to tell me the news. We went on a long walk through one of the parks near my apartment and talked over her revelation, typically analytical at first. We never actually touched one another until the following weekend, when we attended a dance together at a local stake center. That night LeAnn was wearing a white turtleneck and white jeans. When we tentatively walked onto the dance floor and put our arms around each other, I was undone. All my nerve endings became sparklers and I felt as if I were holding a shard of eternity in my hands. I felt unworthy and sanctified, wounded and healed—breathless, as if I had just been born.

After the dance we drove to the parking lot of our old junior high school and tried to kiss for the first time, but I was so hamstrung by uncertainty about what kind of physical contact would be appropriate that LeAnn finally took the lead, pressing her lips to mine with an intensity and passion that was overpowering. I don't know how we avoided more intimate contact during those days, but we did. With all that intensity we should have incinerated like matchheads; but there was a strong pull from the Church that kept us from going the full way to expressing our physical passion for one another. We were prohibited by our principles from consummating our love until we were married.

We were officially engaged on February 20, 1972. Together we went to a jeweler's shop and chose a tiny diamond costing $150, a small fortune! The strength of LeAnn's commitment was evident when she had "Redford" added to her name as it was engraved on her leather-bound scriptures. We began making plans: first, I would serve a two-year proselyting mission for the Church and LeAnn would wait for me. There was never any question about the imperative of my going on a mission—all worthy young LDS men were expected to do so and LeAnn would never marry anyone but a worthy returned missionary. We would marry in the temple as soon as I came back, buy land in an outlying rural community called Wallsburg, build a home consecrated to God, raise twelve faithful children, and make music, laughter, and love for time and the rest of eternity. No one could have accused us of setting our sights too low!

In the spring of 1972, before school was out, I applied to become a proselyting missionary for the Church of Jesus Christ of Latter-day

Saints. As I waited for my call, the summer months were filled with preparations for the missionfield. LeAnn was well equipped to help me prepare both mentally and spiritually. During the summer following our graduation from high school, she had been one of two female members of a study group made up of a dozen friends committed to going on missions for the Church. They read the *Book of Mormon,* and two important books by Mormon Apostle James E. Talmage, *Jesus the Christ* and *The Articles of Faith.* She had hoped at that time that she would serve a mission as well, although, unlike young men who were generally called at age nineteen, young women were not permitted to serve until they were twenty-one. Over the eight subsequent months, most of her friends had left, and she had supported them in their preparations and sent them off with her prayers. Now LeAnn realized that God had called her, not on a proselyting mission, but to marry me; and she began to envision supporting her husband-to-be as her own "mission." She knew this commitment was not limited to theological support, but included intellectual and emotional support as well. As part of our preparation, LeAnn and I read C.S. Lewis's *The Lion, the Witch, and the Wardrobe* aloud to one another.

For my part, I vowed not to make the mistake I had seen one of my closest friends make. When he left on his mission, he packed his suitcase with the works of Kierkegaard. I was disturbed that he had included this obviously non-Mormon material. A mission was supposed to be a time of single-minded focus on the basics of Mormonism; personal interests had to be set aside. The books seemed a symbol of my friend's misunderstanding of the depth of the sacrifice that he was called to make. Sure enough, he abandoned his mission and returned home only a few weeks after leaving. My sadness and shame were deep. His failure strengthened my resolve to prepare well and to be willing to give up what was necessary. There was a lot at stake. Now I look back and feel sympathy for my friend. I had no idea how difficult the next couple of years were going to be.

Two days after my nineteenth birthday, I was ordained an elder in the Melchizedek Priesthood through the laying on of hands by my grandfather in the Holladay 13th Ward. I could trace the lineage of my priesthood authority from Poppie back through Joseph Smith and the apostles, Peter, James, and John, to Jesus. I was given a chart that filled in the names showing the links.

On July 18, I went through the Provo Temple for the first time to receive my "endowments." The temple ritual is set apart from the weekly Sunday meetings in LDS ward and stake buildings. The "endowment" refers to the actual temple ceremony, an ordinance of salvation required for exaltation in the highest degree of the celestial kingdom. One goes through the temple the first time for oneself. Thereafter, one goes through in proxy for someone else who died without receiving this vital ordinance.

Mormons are not taught that nonbelievers go to hell, but to a "spirit prison" where they are ministered to by Latter-day Saints who have passed on and serve as spirit missionaries. If deceased individuals embrace Mormonism, they have to remain in spirit prison until a living Mormon performs the essential ritual ordinances for them. Only then are they free to cross over into Paradise, the flip side of spirit prison, a kind of lobby for the righteous dead until final judgment assigns them to kingdoms of glory. Mormons do their well-known genealogy work in order to cull names from the past so they can do their "temple work" for them, which, according to LDS teaching, the dead are then free to accept or reject. The Latter-day Saints' goal is to give everyone who has ever lived this opportunity. Without it, no one can be "saved."

I was nervous about going through the temple for the first time. I had heard hushed references about the ceremony but only in oblique terms, as everyone is sworn to secrecy during the ritual itself. Some of my friends tried to defuse this anxiety by telling me that it was okay if parts of the ceremony seemed a little strange. "Everyone feels that way at first," they said. "You'll learn something new every time you go." It was assumed there would be many subsequent visits—worthy Mormons are encouraged to attend as frequently as possible.

Upon entering the Provo Temple, I came first to a desk where I rented some special temple clothing. I was then led to a locker room where I was instructed to remove all my clothes and don a hospital gown-like "shield" that hung pancho-style over my front and back. The first portion of the ceremony was known as "initiatory work." I stepped into a small cubicle where an elderly man symbolically washed me with water, reaching under my shield and lightly touching various areas of my body with his fingertips, in order that I might be "clean of the blood and sins of this generation." I was then similarly anointed with oil that I might become "a King and Priest unto the Most High God."

Following this, I was told to put on a special undergarment similar to light cotton long johns, a version of the underclothes all temple-going Mormons are expected to wear throughout their lives. The garment was marked with four small symbolic slits—one over each breast, as well as slits above the navel and knee—to remind me always of the temple covenants I was about to make for the first time.

I was led to a small curtained room where a "new name" was whispered into my ear. This was my sacred temple name that I was never to reveal to anyone, not even to my own wife. I thought the new name was going to be in an angelic tongue, unrecognizable to me. When it turned out to be a familiar biblical name I was only mildly disappointed. It was a reasonable compromise between English and the language of heaven. At that time, I didn't know that every male receiving his endowments that day was given the same name.

After receiving my new name, I returned to the locker room and dressed in white shirt and pants, socks and slippers. Carrying a small packet that held a robe, a cap, a sash, and a green apron, I was led to a chapel with an altar at the front. Everyone was seated in gold fabric-covered, theater-style chairs, the men on the right and the women on the left facing forward. The women all looked like brides, wearing veils on their heads which they would pull down over their faces later in the ceremony.

The main body of the ceremony took the form of a dramatic presentation set in several locales and featuring a varied cast of characters, both human and supernatural, from Adam and Peter, James, and John, to God, Jesus, and Satan. In older temples, temple patrons (as the celebrants are called) would move from room to room as the scenes changed and live temple workers would perform the roles, but in newer temples such as the one I was in, these shifts were accomplished through the medium of film.

The film began with a "Creation" scene, in which Elohim (God the Father) commissions Jehovah and Michael (Jesus and Adam) to actualize His creative blueprint for the earth. This section was roughly analogous to the first two chapters of Genesis, only more repetitious—every command was repeated right after God had spoken it and again immediately following its execution. This was followed by a scene in the "Garden of Eden," starring Adam and Eve, private parts modestly covered by the surrounding foliage. Here they were persuaded to eat the forbidden fruit and then were driven out into the "Lone and Dreary World." A major player in these scenes was Satan, who answered prayer, dialogued with God, and even articulated Mormon doctrines. At one point he hired a minister to "preach" to Adam and Eve. The substance of the sermon was a mocking presentation of orthodox Christian doctrine, leaving temple patrons with no doubt about the diabolical source of the historic Catholic or Protestant creeds. This was the only point in the ceremony where people laughed. The rest of it was all quite sober. Adam and Eve eventually ascended through their faithfulness to the "Terrestrial World."

At various points, the film was interrupted by live ritual segments involving the patrons in oath-like covenants to be obedient, to sacrifice everything for the kingdom of God, to avoid "light-mindedness, loud laughter and evil speaking of the Lord's anointed," to remain chaste, and to consecrate everything to the Church. These covenants were accompanied by handshakes called tokens, as well as special names, signs, and penalties. Represented by various symbolic hand and arm gestures, the penalties we acted out were gruesome modes of death to which we would be willing to submit rather than reveal the secrets of the temple.

At the end of the ceremony, selected patrons stood in a circle around the altar and reenacted all the tokens with their names, signs, and penalties, then engaged in a prayer of supplication called the "true order of prayer" for people whose names had been submitted by concerned patrons and placed in packets on the altar. We then stood in front of a large room-length curtain called a veil, with slits in it corresponding to the marks on our garments and were tested on our memory of the tokens and names we had just been taught. Our responses were given to a temple worker who represented God and stood on the other side of the veil. Following this ceremony, we were allowed to enter the "Celestial Room," the presence of God where we could ask questions, pray, or meditate and seek inspiration or answers to problems.

As strange as this experience was, I was determined not to be like those who had found it disturbing. The temple was the highest articulation of the Mormon worldview, and I was prepared to accept and even revel in it without question. There was no way I was going to allow anything to hinder my complete immersion in the Church's way. I truly believed that this is what the Savior expected of me.

Deep in my heart lay the single most important aspect of faith that united LeAnn and me: our common fascination with Jesus Christ. From the time we were small, it seemed that we were the ones in our classes who brought Him regularly into the discussion. We often felt He wasn't getting the emphasis that He deserved. Jesus was our ultimate hero, the perfect man, the man who was a God. My thoughts about Jesus coalesced in a sonnet I composed that summer:

> We, conceived of Earth and Sky, by Sea were born
> And darkness veiled our waking. Over tide,
> Over sand and stone our paths were traced, so worn
> Our light, that when the final glimmer died
> The stars wore black and all the seabirds cried.
>
> But as we sadly lay our late selves down, He came
> To call us from our graves; all life was His to bear
> And in His eyes no death, no fear had claim
> To victory, His countenance so free and fair
> That all our being burned within His presence there.
>
> For Fathering our second birth, He struck our light
> Anew, while Eastern Sun burst on the fleeing night.
> Then strode we off across the Sea, no more alone,
> But following our Brother, turning home.

At the time, I really thought I knew Jesus, but this was a knowledge grounded in my own dreams and my own efforts—the focus was always on my striving rather than His provision. Years later, I would discover how little I really did know of Him, of His work, and of His glory.

I was so full of fire and motion in those days. I experienced powerful spiritual manifestations that confirmed my faith, explored the intellectual world of Mormonism with diligence and delight, and believed that Joseph Smith was a great prophet and a latter-day hero.

I hungered for the day when Zion would at last be established on the earth. Perhaps, as some have since suggested, I was setting myself up for a fall. At the time, though, I felt I was basking in the glory of all God had to offer a believing young man.

But there was a dark side to all of this enthusiasm. The Church made it abundantly clear what God required of me, and I earnestly desired His blessings, but I was unable to live up to the standards set out for me. In the first place, there were simply too many commandments. Regular attendance at meetings, consistent scripture study, fasting and prayer, tithing, family home evenings, home teaching, food storage, welfare service, temple work, missionary work, et cetera, et cetera ad infinitum, were all emphasized as being critical to my worthiness. It seemed that I would never be able to keep all these bases covered. In addition to these sins of omission, I struggled with my behavior and my thoughts, with selfishness, light-mindedness and loud laughter, laziness, and a host of other petty sins. I also felt guilty about my sexual feelings. I often felt condemned in my heart because of my failure to improve myself and I experienced deep depression.

I had read the *Doctrine and Covenants* in which God was reported to have said: "I, the Lord am bound when ye do what I say; but when ye do not what I say, ye have no promise" (D&C 82:10). I understood this in the light of a Bible passage from the epistle of James: "For whosoever shall keep the whole law, and yet offend in one point, he is guilty of all" (James 2:10). Repentance provided little comfort as it was merely a postponement of the inevitable return of sin: the *Doctrine and Covenants* also stated that "unto that soul who sinneth shall the former sins return" (D&C 82:7). At one point in the temple ceremony, Satan turns to the patrons and declares that "if they do not walk up to every covenant they make at these altars in this temple this day, they will be in my power." How could I possibly live up to this standard? When would I begin in earnest that steady ascent that was supposed to characterize my eternal progression? I began to feel that I was ultimately unworthy of the things I desired most.

I spent my late teenage years on the horns of this dilemma, believing on the one hand that I was a "god in embryo" as the Church taught, destined someday to rule my own planet, even as God ruled this one, and fearing on the other hand that I was ultimately doomed to betray my potential.

And They Shall Go Forth

And the voice of warning shall be unto all people, by the mouths of my disciples, whom I have chosen in these last days. And they shall go forth and none shall stay them, for I the Lord have commanded them.

—Doctrine and Covenants 1:4–5

In the summer of 1972, I received my call from President Harold B. Lee to serve in the Northern Italian Mission of the Church of Jesus Christ of Latter-day Saints. At that time, I believed that all missionary applications were personally considered, prayed over, and sorted on the Prophet's desk, and that my call was the result of a direct revelation from God. Sometimes missionary calls made sense: those who studied Spanish went to Spain, those who studied French went to France. On other occasions, there were absurd ironies, such as in the case of one friend who studied Spanish and ended up in Japan. The fact that there wasn't always a rhyme or a reason to these calls only served to underscore in our minds their special revelatory aspect.

Missionaries and their families were expected to bear the expense of the mission. Since I hadn't saved any money—the little that I had earned as a musician had gone for college and other expenses—my family, especially my uncles, stepped in to provide for my financial support. I was humbled and grateful that they were willing and able to make this sacrifice for me and for our faith.

I felt reasonably prepared for the intellectual demands of the missionfield. I had studied Latin in high school and had an aptitude for languages, so I was comfortable with the prospect of learning Italian sufficiently to communicate with the Italian people. Furthermore, with the exception of the Old Testament, I had studied all the standard works of the Church in some detail and had made extensive cross-references in the margins of my scriptures. I was familiar with all the essential Mormon doctrines and able to explain them. Moreover, I had gained some experience in thinking and speaking on my feet, even while under fire. All of this made me feel, perhaps somewhat overconfidently, that I would indeed be able to accomplish the daunting task that lay before me.

On the other hand, I had characteristically romanticized prose-lyting work. Mine was a distinctly nineteenth-century vision: in my daydreams, I saw myself riding on horseback from one rural community to another, preaching Mormonism persuasively from soap-boxes in public parks, engaging my listeners with articulate explications of Mormon doctrine, and seeing them press forward en masse for the privilege of joining what I had just incontrovertibly proven to them was the one true church. While I recognized that the details of this scenario were an anachronistic exaggeration, still the emotional content rang with transparent truth in my callow heart.

No one helped me get a grip on reality more than my friend, Dennis MacGregor, with whom I had worked in Free Agency. He was the only person who tried to tell me the whole story: about how hard missionary work was; that there was boredom as well as excitement, disappointment as well as fulfillment; about the rules and those who kept them—as well as those who broke them. I was very grateful to Dennis for discussing these things with me. I felt that I had been adequately forewarned.

After all the waiting and preparation, the time finally arrived for me to speak in church prior to my leaving for the Mission Home. When a Mormon missionary leaves, an entire sacrament meeting service, known as a missionary farewell, is devoted to him. Members of his family are given the opportunity to speak or perform music. The bishop also offers his counsel and faithful friends give testimonials and encouragement. Afterwards, the family holds an open house, featuring food and talk, jokes and tears, back slapping goodbyes from buddies and kisses from girlfriends past, present, and future—a community gathering for a hero's send-off.

My mother sang at my farewell and a friend played the Brahms Intermezzo in A major, op. 118 no. 2 for piano, a work that held particular meaning for LeAnn and me. My string quartet and sacred songs were also performed. Poppie, the principal speaker, spoke of Nietzsche and the contrast between his declaration that God was dead and our faith that God lived, a truth I was going to be carrying to the world. He said some encouraging and supportive things, but ultimately his talk was philosophical and, as a consequence, somewhat impersonal. He could have been speaking to any departing missionary. I felt a little let down—I suppose I was looking for some special torch to be passed.

I chose to speak on the subject of salvation by grace, although my conception of both salvation and grace was certainly different from the definitions one normally associates with these words in Protestant Christian communities. In Mormonism, the grace of God referred primarily to the opportunity to *earn* one's salvation.

A week later, on August 19, I checked into the Mission Home in Salt Lake City, which served as locus for a three-day orientation period for new missionaries. Before I entered, I got the regulation haircut—trimmed above the ears and collar—and had my picture taken. LeAnn cut my hair herself and I have to say it looked pretty awful. In the picture, I have a rather foolish grin on my face.

In those days, the Mission Home was an old, dark brick building near Temple Square in Salt Lake City. There we would be transformed from worldly-minded adolescent boys into godly young men on fire with the passion of sharing the Mormon gospel with the people of the world. Prior to entering the Mission Home, the missionaries were required to complete a psychological examination, including such questions as "Have you ever thought about killing yourself?" and "Have you ever wanted to kill your mother?" Naively literal, I thought, "Well, who hasn't thought about doing these things at one time or another?" The first day of a mission for God seemed a bad time to be even slightly dishonest, so I answered most of the questions "Yes." This decision was to come back to haunt me in a few hours.

Upon arrival, I took my bags upstairs to the dorm, which looked like a military barracks with rows of bunks stretching down the length of the room. After stowing our gear, we met in a huge conference room to begin our training. The first thing I noticed when I walked in was a huge banner with the letters "PMA" emblazoned on it. When I asked what it meant, I was told it stood for "Positive Mental Attitude." My only contact with that term, at this point in my life, had left me with the impression that it was an artificial sales trick, a manipulative pretense, something that had more to do with selling used cars than the Spirit of God. What, I wondered, did we need with self-help aphorisms or promotional gimmicks borrowed from the world of advertising if we were truly directed and empowered by the Holy Ghost?

That evening's meeting was the first of many long seminars featuring motivational speeches by various mission leaders and General Authorities. In one way, it resembled a business conference, and in another, a pep rally. We were to learn to be "good salesmen" of the gospel. I endured these meetings in the way a person would endure a session with thumbscrews, amazed that there wasn't more focus on God.

I look back on this attitude with mixed feelings. In one sense I was right: there should have been more emphasis on spirituality in our preparation for the missionfield. On the other hand, I had such a high-minded view of things that I was completely unable to comprehend the practical necessities of carrying on a missionary program that had to service the entire world using thousands of young men from differing backgrounds, most with no experience whatsoever and some with no certainty that Mormonism was even true.

I expected that the high point of the Mission Home experience would be an afternoon at the Salt Lake Temple. We were to attend one session, then have an audience with the Prophet in an upper room where we could ask him questions about the temple ceremony. Many parts of the ceremony were obscure and difficult for me to understand, so I was anxious to hear President Lee address our questions and unfold the deeper meaning of some of the symbols. Subsequently, we would go through the ceremony again, this time in light of the Prophet's elucidation. It was a unique opportunity I looked forward to with anticipation. After the first session, when the time finally arrived for questions, I raised my hand and, to my great excitement, the Prophet called on me. Eclipsed by what was about to happen, I can't recall the content of my question, but the gist of President Lee's response was clear and unforgettable: "You shouldn't ask a question like that. That's not the right sort of question." I was aghast. Not only did he avoid answering my question, but he made me feel like a fool for having asked it! My sense of shame rose up like a flood.

Not long after this, prior to the second temple session, several missionaries, including me, were called back to the Mission Home. Despite the Prophet's dismissal, I was thinking, "Maybe I'm going to be chosen for a leadership position." Hadn't my patriarchal blessing mentioned "rising high in the order" of the priesthood? Instead, I was informed that those missionaries whose answers on the psychological examination had raised red flags would be spending the remainder of the afternoon taking a new five hundred-question test. This added more insult to my already painful injury. I wanted to go through the temple again, even more now that I needed to find out what I had gotten so wrong. I felt depressed and discouraged. In the course of only a few hours, I had been rebuked by the Prophet of God and was now suspected of being mentally and emotionally unfit for service! Part of it was my own fault—I should have seen between the lines of the questionnaire and acted in a more politic manner. But I was a very serious-minded young man and I really believed in the sanctity of my calling. I did not doubt that God was going to speak to us and direct us in our training. I trusted that the Church was led by God and not by man.

After answering a few questions on the new test, I couldn't stand it any longer—the anger burned like an elixir in my throat and I stormed into the office of the resident psychologist, railing at him for calling us out of the temple early and subjecting us to secular testing when we were training for spiritual service. In fact, one of the questions inquired, "Do you consider yourself a special emissary of God?" Presumably, in a secular arena, only a lunatic would answer that question affirmatively. Yet we missionaries were all supposedly special emissaries of God. I wondered how the others were answering that question. I refused to finish the test.

The doctor remained calm, and even seemed slightly amused in the face of these hysterics. He asked me a few follow-up questions of his own and, apparently satisfied that I wasn't completely insane, sent me on my way without further hindrance.

That night, in a spectacular breach of regulations, I called LeAnn and spilled out all of my fears, discouragement, and disappointment. She spoke many comforting words and managed to settle me down and rekindle the hope that I could suffer these "slings and arrows" and complete my mission honorably. She didn't tell me about the fear that suddenly gripped her own heart, even as she heard the sound of my voice. What would become of her if I didn't persevere? Of course, she couldn't marry me under those circumstances. I had to succeed—there was no alternative, at least none that either of us could live with.

A few days later, all the missionaries were piled into buses and driven south to the town of Provo, home of the Language Training Mission, or LTM, as it was called. The LTM was divided into sections, grouped by language and subdivided by mission. All the missionaries heading to Italy, either north or south, were housed in an old, ramshackle white home called the Iona House, situated just below the BYU campus.

We studied there for two months, undergoing long sessions of repetitive language training. Sometimes our exercises took on a mechanized atmosphere during which the instructor hurled questions and snapped his fingers to keep up the pace. It seemed a lot like brainwashing, and perhaps it was in a sense. Though grueling, the study was also satisfying as we began to master our new language. In addition, we received instruction in Mormon doctrine and proselyting techniques, which included the memorization of six "discussions," or lesson plans formatted as dialogues, all in Italian. Our independent study hours were filled with the sound of our own voices, intoning the lines of the discussions over and over again, as if we were actors preparing for a role.

Often during lulls in class, I found myself doodling, drawing pictures of cardboard missionaries with x's for eyes and blank expressions. They stood in rows, propped up by two-by-fours, each with a bubble overhead in which the same words appeared. In one sketch I drew a mustachioed old man with a tear coming out of one eye. In these drawings I intuitively revealed feelings I couldn't express to anyone, not even to myself. Acknowledging these emotions would have undermined the purpose for my being there and the joy that I was supposed to be experiencing as I prepared for God's work.

At the LTM we were assigned "companions." One of the fundamental rules of Mormon proselyting is that a missionary must never work alone. Missionaries live and teach in pairs and one's colleague is called a companion, or "comp" for short. Companions were not to introduce or address each other by their first names, not even privately. Instead, we were called by our ecclesiastical title, "elder," combined with our last names. I was known as Elder Redford.

My first companion in the LTM loved literature, wrote poetry, and listened to the music of Jethro Tull in his former life. As a consequence, our conversation went deeper than ordinary chit chat or even the details of a shared spiritual vocation. He also had a girl waiting for him. They had a very serious relationship, and knowing this somehow gave me hope that LeAnn and I would be able to live through the ordeal of a two-year separation. I felt very fortunate to have a companion with whom I could communicate and share some understanding. This was not always the case among the missionaries.

There were a number of other interesting characters at the LTM. One elder was adept at imitating the sounds of animals or vehicles, which he often did, to our great amusement, in moments of frustration or triumph. Missionaries developed many coping mechanisms to help them deal with the harrowing regimen. Some seemed to approach the experience as a technical challenge, with little emotion, as if missionary work were simply another skill to be mastered, like mathematics. Others tackled it like a sport. Our group was a microcosm of many different personality types, all blended together in an environment where we had to learn to help each other, very much as if we were new military recruits. While this situation could sometimes be quite maddening, it also had its rewards. I have always enjoyed the peculiar tensions that are created when people are thrown together by fate—or sovereignty.

While I was at the LTM, LeAnn attended school at BYU, having transferred there from the University of Utah to pursue studies in early childhood education. She often drove by the Iona House. I would watch longingly as her Toyota disappeared down the street. Occasionally, she would stop and leave a letter, but we were never allowed to speak to one another. My zone leader told me to forget about her. She probably wouldn't wait for me anyway, he said, and caring for her so much would only get in the way of my work. I told him that he didn't know LeAnn, that she *was* going to wait, and that there was no way on God's green earth that I would be able to forget about her. In fact, I needed her love and support to finish this task for God.

After two long months we completed our course of study at the LTM, and were taken to Salt Lake City International Airport. Our families and friends were allowed to meet us there and there were many hugs and kisses. Though I was glad to see my family, and especially LeAnn, I couldn't help but feel distracted. My heart and my mind were already far away in Italy, anticipating my new life with a mixture of trepidation and enthusiasm, hoping that I would soon be baptizing many new converts into the one true church.

The flight to Italy was the longest I had ever taken. Prior to this, I had never been farther east than Durango, Colorado. There was a plane change at Kennedy Airport before we boarded the flight to our final destination, Malpensa Airport, north of Milano. I was charmed by the pert European stewardesses, but politely demurred their continuous offers of coffee or tea. This was the first time either had ever been offered to me. Even without caffeine, I didn't sleep much and was bleary-eyed by the time we landed.

Upon arrival we took a bus into the city. It was a gray day with a light drizzle of rain. I watched the unfamiliar Italian landscape flicker past the window like scenes from a riffled deck of cards. As we drew closer to Milano, I began to notice small clumps of people, mostly women, standing along the roadside near smoking bonfires made with piles of old tires. Someone told me that the women were prostitutes and that the bonfires were for advertisement as well as for warmth. Appalled and titillated by this revelation, I stared dumbly at the plain-looking women and their nervous clients. My naive and idealistic universe simply didn't contain a slot for acts so brazen and desperate.

The bus trip lasted about an hour, and then we were taken by car to the headquarters of the Northern Italian Mission. The office was located on a tiny back street not far from the famed opera house, La Scala. There I was introduced to several elders, including the one who was to be my companion. As new elders, or "greenies," we were the butt of many jokes, mostly having to do with how long we had left in our two-year stint—"If I had as many months left as you do, I'd slit my wrists!" The teasing was good-natured, however, and intended to initiate us into a kind of men's club. Soon we would be fully a part of the tight knit group and ribbing new greenies ourselves.

One of the older elders was just leaving for home and had a bicycle to sell—the Mormon missionary's best friend! This one was a rusted but sturdy five-speed with short, straight handlebars unlike any I had ever seen in the United States. He was asking fifteen "mill"—fifteen thousand lire in the parlance of the missionaries. Unaccustomed to the value of Italian money (around six hundred lire to the dollar in those days), this sounded like an immense amount to me, but I paid it anyway. I needed a bicycle and didn't know where else to get one.

The first order of business was transporting my luggage to our apartment. I had one suitcase, limited by mission mandate to forty pounds, but it felt as if it weighed a ton as my "comp" and I hiked to the nearest cable car stop and hoisted it on board a bright orange "tram" for the ride across town, leaving our bicycles at the office to be collected later. It was rush hour, and I was compacted between several sweat-drenched bodies, barely able to breathe the pungent air, as the tram stuttered forward to the clamorous accompaniment of wildly ringing bells and the demonic buzz of arcing electricity. We dropped off the luggage and immediately headed back to the office for our bicycles.

Before this, it had been sprinkling, but now it had begun to rain in earnest. Visibility was low, and the cobblestones were slick. The bike ride back to our apartment outstripped Mr. Toad's wild ride. We dodged careening Fiats with blaring horns, glimpsing behind each windshield the shadowy silhouette of a maniacally gesticulating Italian. We were nearly flattened by trams on oily streets that garishly reflected an absurd circus of neon signs, hawking bizarre products with untranslatable idiomatic names. Slipping and sliding, we nearly fell a dozen times. The tram tracks had a groove down the center exactly the width of a bicycle tire and when our tires entered that groove, they suddenly locked into place, shaking both bicycle and rider back and forth like a plucked rubber band. Keeping one's balance was like walking a tightrope in a high wind.

By the time we got back to the apartment, I was thoroughly terrified. Only now was I able to take in our lodgings for the first time—one room about twelve by twelve feet with bunk beds along one wall and a detached closet along another. There was one window, a sink, and a shelf with a portable heating device, much like the ones that had asphyxiated elders all over the world in the nightmarish news stories that haunted the horizon of my adolescent memories. The room was quite humid and moss was growing on the wall nearest the window. When I climbed up to the top bunk, I saw that the mattress was dank green and stained with the wet dreams of many missionaries past. This was the last straw. I collapsed in utter despair and wept openly like a lost little child.

Our apartment was located in the Ticinese district of Milano, an area characterized by old Italian apartment houses called "palazzi" with small, family-owned shops on the ground floors, the sort that Italian women frequented daily to buy meat, bread, and pasta. Upstairs were lower-class apartments like ours, many of them without bathrooms. Our bathroom was located down the hall and was shared in common by the entire floor. It contained a Turkish toilet— basically a hole in the floor covered by ceramic with two corrugated foot positions, and a handle mounted on the back of the door. One could close the door and lean back, holding the handle. We called it the "bomb chute." Given the sanitary conditions in these apartments, I was actually grateful for a toilet I didn't have to sit on.

Our street ran parallel to an open canal that gave forth a horrifying stench, especially at night—it seemed to function as a kind of sewer. The water was green and dense, filled with the detritus of contemporary "civilization": plastic cups, paper sacks, and worse. In the evening, certain street corners in our district boasted gaggles of female impersonators and male prostitutes who alternately hailed and cursed us as we rode by on our bicycles in the steaming Italian dusk. The smell of the canal, the sexual innuendoes, the hoarse scatology of the prostitutes, and the motion of our bikes made a pungent mix for a wet-behind-the-ears American Mormon boy.

Our zone leaders, who lived near our apartment on Via Gola, literally "Throat Street," told farfetched tales of the local fauna. One sweltering night, they left their windows open and one of the elders awoke to find two gargantuan rats sporting themselves on his feet above the sheets. Once we went to visit these elders and were offered banana bread pancakes. They were out of money and banana bread mix sent from home was the only food they had left to serve. Lacking eggs, they had ended up with banana bread pancakes that were a thin crust, flat and hard. Lacking syrup as well, they poured root beer extract over the sad mess. I was horrified, but they seemed to revel in their degradation.

Missionary life was rigorous, focused, and spartan. Always excelling in organizational techniques, the Church had divided the missionaries into districts of four to six elders, which were then organized into zones, ultimately coming under the leadership of the mission president, a mature, married man who was called by the Church to serve in this capacity. He was assisted by a couple of experienced elders known as assistants to the president. Missionaries were moved around quite a bit, serving from a few days to several months in a given district. Transfers were frequent from district to district and from city to city, but never outside the Northern Italian Mission. In the course of my mission, I served in Brescia, Varese, Genova, and Lugano, Switzerland, in addition to Milano.

There were many rules, all detailed in a missionary handbook that we were enjoined to follow religiously, covering everything from moral imperatives, such as not getting intimately involved with women, to the practical problems of daily life. The rules varied somewhat from mission to mission, although they were enforced as absolutes in each one. For example, in northern Italy, we were never allowed to remove our jackets. The mission president was a banker and felt that taking off our jackets would undermine our image as serious, well-groomed young men. At one point, we were also told to eliminate the phrase "you bet" from our English vocabulary, because of its reference to gambling.

Our weekly schedule was sharply defined. We were expected to work sixty hours over a seven-day period. One half day was set aside to write letters home, do our laundry, and attend to various other practical tasks. When I began my mission, this was known as D-Day, or Diversion Day, but when the expression came to the attention of the authorities, it was altered to P-Day, or Preparation Day, to emphasize preparation for the following week rather than relaxation. Heaven forbid that anyone should relax!

Occasionally, this weekly schedule would be broken up by a zone or mission conference during which we would meet with other elders to discuss proselyting techniques and to motivate each other. We looked forward to these breaks because we could share testimonies or trade stories and jokes about mission experiences.

Proselyting goals were strictly determined as well. Each week we were to "place" a certain number of copies of the *Book of Mormon* and conduct a certain number of discussions, as well as achieve on several other levels. At the end of the week, we filled out reports indicating our progress. These were submitted to our district leaders, then given to our zone leaders, summarized, passed on to the assistants, and ultimately reviewed by the president. There was accountability from bottom to top. I felt as if we had failed when we succeeded in working only fifty hours in a given week or when our *Book of Mormon* placement rate fell below the required number.

The average missionary day began early with an hour of personal prayer and study, followed by a time of language, scripture, or discussion study with one's companion. Breakfast was somehow thrown in too. In Milano, we took showers at a local bathhouse once or twice a week. These facilities were not at all like the image conjured up by the words here in the United States, and were used by many in the community who lacked plumbing in their homes. Sometimes we got pretty ripe between showers, especially after a few hot days of bike-riding in our jackets!

We tried to get out the door by nine to begin our daily activities, which consisted mainly of "tracting," a verb derived from the act of distributing tracts. We would select a populous area in our district and, starting at the top floor of one of the palazzi, would work our way down to the bottom, going from door to door. Then we would go on to the next palazzo and begin again. We kept notebooks containing complete records of each building that we tracted and the response we received at each door. These notebooks were passed on to the elders who succeeded us when we were transferred so that continuity could be maintained. Tracting books achieved the level of folk literature, with many humorous asides penned by the missionaries describing the reactions to our "door approaches."

Tracting was actually rather ineffective. We faced many of the same challenges and discouragements that a door-to-door salesman would—perhaps the Mission Home had it right in this respect. We were instructed by our leaders to try to contact the fathers in each family. Most of the fathers worked during the day, however, as did many mothers, so the grandmothers were often the only ones left at home watching the preschool children. Our knock was often answered by the distinctive click of an opening peephole and an aged, cracking voice that queried "*Chi e?*" "Who is it?"

We were directed not to identify ourselves as missionaries at that point, but to say, "We're a couple of Americans here to talk with you about the family." We used a survey we had prepared about family life as a door opener. This survey served no other practical purpose, however—no tally was ever kept of the results and we simply threw away the sheets at the end of the day. "*Non c'e nessuno!*" "No one is home!" was the most common reply to our announcement. If we were feeling especially peevish, we might then ask, "What about you? You're home, aren't you?" This rarely got us any closer to entry, but a little humor sometimes helped assuage the sting of rejection.

So it went, from door to door, with the responses often so predictable that we had standard abbreviations for them in the tracting book. Occasionally, someone would let us in and talk with us. Sometimes we were actually able to complete the survey at which stage we would introduce ourselves as Mormon elders. There was no Italian word for the term, "elder," as defined in an ecclesiastical context, so the word we used was "anziano," or literally, "old one." It must have sounded silly to the Italians for a couple of nineteen-year-olds to refer to themselves as "old ones." Most of the time, after finding out who we were, they would say they weren't interested and we would leave.

Sometimes the discussion would veer from the family to politics. Italians are passionate about politics, and we tried to avoid the subject because it was so chaotic. During the two years I served in Italy, the government changed several times—I could never figure out how it worked, if in fact it did. There appeared to be much evidence to the contrary and Italians were rarely shy about pointing that out.

Political discussions were often dominated by issues raised by the Communists. The Italian Communist Party, though quite different in character from its counterpart in the Soviet Union, shared its antipathy for all things American. The missionaries had to be cautious in word and deed. Once, while we were working in the Piazza del Duomo, the square was suddenly filled with a hundred thousand chanting Communists. It was not a safe place for Americans, so we beat a hasty retreat.

Sometimes, conversations actually turned to the topic of religion. In such cases, Italians often used us as sounding boards to express their disappointment or skepticism concerning the Catholic Church and its leadership or doctrine. One family was scathing in its accusations that Pope Paul VI was a flagrant and notorious homosexual. As their hyperbole about the pope's alleged misdeeds escalated, we reacted with disbelief. Nobody could be this bad, we thought, not even the pope. Only rarely were we able to talk seriously about Mormonism with an Italian family. We were surprised to find that, in a predominantly Catholic country, our primary obstacle was not Catholicism, but profound apathy and even antagonism where any religious faith was concerned.

After a morning of tracting, we rode back to the apartment for an hour to eat lunch, which usually consisted of either a bowl of pasta or a sandwich made with fresh "panini" and sliced meat we bought during our weekly shopping runs. We found it hard to break the American habit of shopping weekly and usually bought our food on P-Day, riding our bikes to the nearest supermarket and returning with four to six plastic shopping bags hanging across our handlebars.

In the afternoon, we either continued tracting or opted for another proselyting technique, such as approaching people in a park or working a street board. The street board was a kind of religious billboard set up in a busy piazza. We would stand next to it, handing out tracts or copies of the *Book of Mormon*, or simply engaging passersby in conversation. In Milano, our street board was located in the Piazza del Duomo, between the great cathedral and Mussolini's Galleria. We shared that location with missionaries from other churches and cults; encyclopedia salesmen; booths selling trinkets, gelato, and postcards to tourists; con men and prostitutes. One day we interrupted a man negotiating with a prostitute. We stood with our arms folded, clicking our tongues in the international symbol for disapproval. To her great anger, the prostitute's embarrassed client abandoned the deal.

At one point, our district decided to make a new street board for the Piazza del Duomo. The old one took a rather sensationalistic approach. It was filled with words like "fear," "crime," and "hatred," surrounded by flame-colored shapes like little explosions. "What is the solution to these problems?" one side of the street board demanded. The other side proposed that the answer was to be found in the *Book of Mormon* or a program of Mormonism such as the Family Home Evening. Our district felt that this approach was too negative, so we spent an entire week working on a more positive one. Our district leader was a talented artist and, with his supervision, we built a new street board with one side covered with images of nature, lush foliage, and animal life. Christ was symbolically featured at the center. We wanted to attract interest with images of life, rather than images of death and fear.

Confined to our apartment, as we worked together on the new street board, we listened continuously to three tapes: one was Joni Mitchell's *For the Roses,* another was Jethro Tull's *Thick as a Brick,* and the third was Marvin Payne's *Utah.* They provided lubrication as well as inspiration for the long hours. Our musical diet was a bit on the controversial side: missionaries were discouraged from listening to music other than the Mormon Tabernacle Choir and classical music, though we were ultimately allowed some personal freedom in the matter.

It was a great disappointment when, a few days after we had inaugurated our new street board, the mission president strolled into the Piazza del Duomo, took a look at our work, and said, "You know, elders, I think we need a new street board." We were crushed. Not long after that, following a communist demonstration, we found that the place where we kept the street board hidden at night had been discovered. "*Quanto vi pagano?*" had been carved into it with a knife: "How much do they pay you?" So the mission president's wishes soon had to be respected anyway, simply because of our street board's defacement.

Sometimes during the day, there was business to do that couldn't wait for P-Day: a visit to the office to pick up new materials, urgent repairs to the apartment, errands to run, and service to local church members. Anything that fell within the category of proselyting, however loosely defined, contributed to our sixty hours. The quest to meet that elusive goal yielded some creative, even comic results: a tract left in a doctor's waiting room transformed a routine bout with the flu into an hour of proselyting on the weekly report, travel time included. It was very difficult to put in sixty solid hours of pure proselyting work and we found ourselves constantly playing catch-up. That might have been the idea—an idle mind, after all, is the devil's playground.

Unless we had a conference to attend, or one of us became ill, this routine continued day after day, month after month. Our mission president even expected us to go tracting on Christmas Day, reasoning that we would find more fathers at home. While this was true, we were the last people these fathers wanted to see. The year we tried it, my companion and I gave up rather quickly when it became obvious that no one was going to let us in.

Apart from tracting and working the street board, there were few other options available to us to round up new contacts. The LDS Church is small in Italy. We urged Church members to provide us with contacts among their friends and business associates because it was far more likely that a contact would lead to a meeting when we were on friendly ground with a potential convert before we began. But it was often difficult for the members to summon up the courage to this. They had much at stake: their jobs, family relationships, and reputations in the community. Mormonism was generally perceived as a kind of cult by the Italians.

In the evening, we would return to our apartment for an hour to eat dinner before going on to our late meetings. All of our efforts at making contacts were dedicated to this end: to persuade people to meet with us and investigate the Church via a series of lessons, the six discussions we had memorized in the LTM. The ultimate aim of these discussions was baptism.

The standard missionary discussions were formatted like scripts with lines of dialogue assigned to each missionary as well as to the "investigator," which was the term we used for someone who studied with us. The missionary dialogue was mainly organized into digestible blocks of information followed by leading questions. The logic was directed to elicit a particular response from the investigator, though we frequently had to reword the questions again and again until we got it. Even minor courtesies and expressions of encouragement were programmed. These discussions could sound embarrassingly wooden, especially if the missionary had difficulty with the language. A skillful missionary could disguise the fact that the dialogue was scripted and make the conversation seem natural. Some even used the technique of admitting that we were working from a script and apologizing for it, drawing people in by virtue of their sincerity. The most comical presentations occurred when a missionary attempted to maintain the pretense that the lines were occurring to him spontaneously. One missionary from southern Utah spoke his lines with a drawl, sounding a little like John Wayne speaking Italian. This never failed to evoke giggles from the Italians, until they got to know him. They soon realized that he was just a good-hearted American boy who couldn't manage the accent.

Beginning with the first discussion, the dialogues contained frequent challenges for the investigator to be baptized: "When you come to know what we're telling you is true, will you be baptized? Let's set a date now, in anticipation that you will soon know it is true." The *Book of Mormon* contained the key verse we used to help investigators get a testimony:

> And when ye shall receive these things, I would exhort you that ye would ask God, the Eternal Father, in the name of Christ, if these things are not true; and if ye shall ask with a sincere heart, with real intent, having faith in Christ, he will manifest the truth of it unto you, by the power of the Holy Ghost. And by the power of the Holy Ghost ye may know the truth of all things. (Moroni 10:4–5)

This method was guaranteed to work if investigators had "a sincere heart" and "real intent." If they didn't receive a confirming testimony, it was because they lacked a sincere desire or sufficient faith for God to reveal the truth to them. The deck was stacked—if they failed, it was their own fault, not ours, and certainly not God's.

We rarely had the opportunity to talk with an entire Italian family at once, though this was our objective. I did have this experience in Milano with a family that seemed to comprise just the sort of people we hoped would take us seriously, an ideal situation known among the missionaries as a "golden contact." The family members were loving with one another and gracious to us—I felt intuitively that their roots went deep. As my companion and I gave our initial presentation, they listened closely and understood what we were saying, yet they courteously declined to accept our message. There was something about them that made me feel that they didn't need it, and this intuition filled me with vague, unsettling fears. If I dared suppose that there was a soul in the world that didn't need Mormonism, it would completely undermine my worldview, so I tried to quench the feeling as quickly as it bubbled up inside of me.

As we were leaving, the father took me aside. He said, "You're young and you believe these things very strongly now. But in ten years you're going to believe something very different." I said, "No, I'm not. I know the Church is true. I'm never going to believe anything different than that." When the time came that I did begin to wonder whether Mormonism was true, however, his words came back to me. It was indeed about ten years later that I seriously began to question whether I still held the same beliefs as I had held in 1973.

Obviously, there wasn't much time for any kind of personal life in the missionfield. What little there was manifested itself primarily in my letters home. I kept a journal in the form of over six hundred pages of letters to LeAnn. I also spent many hours in as private a place as I could find—in the hall, on the porch, sometimes even in the bomb chute—making audiotapes to send home. LeAnn wrote to me regularly as well, and sent many tapes and poems—anything to keep me connected and to encourage me in my work.

While I was in Italy, LeAnn studied at BYU and worked part-time. Committed to spiritually maturing apace with me, she found friendship in a club called Shomrah Kiyel, made up of about seventy young women who were either engaged to missionaries or had promised to wait for them. Club members were committed to supporting their young men in the missionfield, rather than detracting from their focus, as a popular LDS stereotype suggested. The group was also dedicated to spiritual service in other areas, as well as to comforting and encouraging one another during the long months of waiting. In her second year, LeAnn became the club's president, organizing its weekly meetings, socials, and service projects, including a trip to the Provo Temple to perform baptisms for the dead.

Our correspondence was like food and air to me. Despite our efforts to focus positively on the work at hand, however, it always reminded me of how much time remained until LeAnn and I would be reunited. In part, this awareness was fed by the unremitting loneliness of missionary life. Even though I was never alone, I often felt terribly alone because I was cut off from so much that defined me as a person. Perhaps the lack of solitude itself contributed to my sense of loneliness. Time was also a factor. It seemed subject to different laws of physics in the missionfield. Hours dragged on interminably when no one would talk with us, or sped by when we were engaged. I measured my days from meal to meal, my weeks from report to report, and was constantly aware of the ratio of months I had been out against those that remained. "Hump Day" was the term missionaries used to describe the midway point at which they had exactly one year left to go.

Gratefully, however, the tide of time also left an inevitable acclimation in its wake. As I adjusted to missionary life, I also adjusted to life in Italy and learned to love the unique ways of the Italians. They are exceptionally warm people, generous and hospitable, passionate and prone to argue. Music is bound up with the deepest roots of the Italian soul. I often heard blue-collar workers singing arias from Verdi or Puccini operas as they dug trenches or hauled refuse.

On the other hand, Italian life could be frustrating. Bureaucracy was omnipresent. Upon our arrival in Italy, we were required to register with the police via an instrument known as the *carta bollata,* a special form that could only be purchased at certain stores. We had to fill it out and have it stamped by the requisite authorities every time we were transferred to a new city. The spirit of bureaucracy seemed to trickle down to the grassroots as well—it was harder to get things done there than it was in America. Even the simplest activities seemed to require many steps and the permission of multiple authorities, each of whom seemed anxious to pass the responsibility for approval on to someone else.

I was shocked by Italian attitudes toward sexuality, even though I had learned something about them from books and movies. One young man, barely past puberty, insisted that if he was still a virgin at age fourteen, he would be considered gravely deviant by his peers. When we taught a young woman in her twenties about the necessity of refraining from sexual intercourse as an unmarried Mormon, she gasped audibly and claimed that this was not possible—she understood that it was a commandment, but how could one possibly be expected to keep it?

In spite of these caveats, however, I enjoyed living in Italy and of all the finest things Italian, I fell most in love with the food. Every day at supper time the air was pervaded by the deliciously pungent aromas emanating from a host of Italian kitchens. We were frequently invited, to our great delight, to dine with Church members, who apparently felt it was their solemn duty to fatten us up. The meals were large and sumptuous, just the sort of thing a hard-working American boy could appreciate after a long day of largely frustrating activity. Food became more than a meal to me—it was a relationship, a religious affirmation, a cry of hope in the dark. In Italy, I was reminded of the close connection between food and nurturing, the sacramental bond I had first experienced in my grandmother's kitchen.

Even food purchased on the street seemed extraordinarily flavorful. In Milano, during stints at the street board, we would often walk to a small Pugliese bakery behind the Galleria and buy enormous panzerotti, deep fried scones filled with mushrooms, Italian ham, mozzarella cheese, oregano, and basil. On wintry days they steamed in the cold while we devoured them. We also savored minipies filled with sweet ricotta cheese and surrounded by a perfect pastry crust. In Genova, we enjoyed focaccia, a salty pizza dough baked flat and brushed with butter and garlic or herbs. Dairy products were also exceptional. Swiss yogurt was so rich and fresh that we paid our zone leaders to bring boxes of it back with them when they visited the elders serving in the Italian-speaking zone of Switzerland. Pasta, of course, was the mainstay and almost always excellent, especially when served homestyle in a family-owned trattoria. Each region of Italy boasted its own distinctive style of cuisine, and we were able to sample a wide range of culinary delights simply by eating at the local trattorie run by families hailing from other provinces.

We also experienced a variety of foods at the homes of local Church members. The mother of one of the members in Genova served us fresh mushrooms taken directly from her garden, cooked only in fresh olive oil with basil. They were bursting with dark, dusky flavor and called to my mind images of Farmer Maggot's mushrooms in the *Lord of the Rings*. At the home of one Mormon family in the country south of Torino, we sampled homemade goat cheese, made by curdling a vat of milk with a goat's esophagus. The parents were incredibly poor and lived with their several children in a farmhouse without heat, electricity, running water, or a telephone. We visited them once a month, always unannounced since we couldn't phone them in advance. Strangely, they always seemed to sense when we were going to visit—just before we would arrive they would buy extra pasta. We attributed this foreknowledge to God. Things like it seemed to happen regularly, at least in the mythology of the Italian mission.

I met a number of intriguing and eccentric people on my mission, some of whom I baptized into Mormonism: Brother Aprile, a gentle-hearted businessman and amateur actor to whom I gave my first stumbling discussion in Italian; a convert from the Jehovah's Witnesses with such bad arthritis that it took several of us to lower her into the water at her baptism; a disturbed artist who painted powerful, expressionistic images of Munch-like screaming faces; a woman who read a copy of the *Book of Mormon* that we had tossed into her apartment in desperation just as her husband was slamming the door in our faces; and a young man who had learned to speak English by listening to Neil Young and Eagles records, and who later went on to play bass in an internationally known Italian bluegrass band.

Some of my fellow missionaries were also remarkable. One was a kindred spirit; we secretly called each other by our first names when we switched off with our comps. He and I visited an old castle in the hills above Genova one afternoon to write letters, wander through the ruins, talk quietly, and think in silence—he was the sort who would permit that. Silence was a luxury many missionaries seemed to find uncomfortable.

One of my companions was simply not cut out to be a missionary because he was so painfully shy. While out tracting, when it was his turn to knock on the door, he would stand there paralyzed and silent. No amount of coaxing would persuade him to speak, so I had to do the talking at every door. Later, I heard that he had been appointed the mission handyman, maintaining missionary apartments all over the mission. It was a wise move on the part of the mission president to recognize both his weakness and his gift and design a way in which he could serve honorably.

One of the most unusual people I worked with joined my companion and me as a temporary partner while he was awaiting reassignment, and for a while we worked as a threesome. I had to sympathize with the Italians, who must have regarded our appearance on their doorstep as a posthumous visit from the Three Stooges. Our new companion carried tools with him, hanging from little cloth loops inside his suit jacket. One of his most prominent achievements was the construction of a makeshift blowgun, which he used in order to shoot rats with homemade darts.

The art in Italy was overwhelming. I was constantly surrounded by reminders of its history and former glory. Milano was especially rich with culture. Despite the fact that it had been constructed by what we considered an apostate religion, the Duomo was impressive, topped by a huge, golden Madonna. Da Vinci's *Last Supper* was deeply moving to me. Even in its corrupted state, it seemed to stand out in relief from the wall, illuminated by an inner light of its own. I also had the good fortune to attend two operas at La Scala: Donizetti's *Norma* and Debussy's *Pelleas et Melisande*. Tickets were expensive and my companion and I had to stand for the duration, but it was worth it. Though neither opera was a favorite of mine, it was exhilarating just being there, soaking up the atmosphere where so many classic works had been performed.

In most of the cities were I served, I found a way to borrow a guitar and wrote a number of songs. Lyrics occurred to me while I was riding my bike or walking and I'd set them to music late at night. Sometimes I also wrote free-verse poems. In Lugano, I gave a concert of my original songs at the church as a kind of proselyting experiment. We encouraged members to invite their friends and distributed leaflets throughout the city, but hardly anyone showed up except the few Mormons who knew me.

Sometimes on P-Day I visited a Catholic church or cathedral and asked permission from the priest to play the organ. While in Genova, I played an organ that had been built before Columbus sailed for America, and before Bach began composing. I played for an hour and a half, improvising and trying out all the stops. It was a wonderful, refreshing experience.

In Milano, I met a jazz musician in the Ricordi Music Store just off the Piazza del Duomo and he invited me and my companion to come over for a jam session one evening. When I arrived with my flute, I found an improbable cast of characters sitting cross-legged on the floor playing free and dissonant jazz, fully improvisational without accompaniment. Soon I was surrounded by the croaks and gutturals that have become part of the standard vocabulary of jazz since John Coltrane. My technique wasn't anywhere near their level. I found myself playing the simple, pure melodies of several LDS hymns above the fray, in my own way making a statement that faith would ultimately triumph over the chaos of the human condition without God.

In Milano, I also discovered the Vaughn-Williams' *Symphony No. 5*, which has since become a staple that I often listen to when my soul needs nourishment. It contains all the elements that I love about Vaughn-Williams' music: earthy English folk themes, weighty climaxes, colorful orchestrations, poignant yearning melodies, and an overall texture unique to English impressionism. This symphony was a touchstone of sanity for me during this time. Two books that I purchased at an English bookstore similarly became important to me: one was a collection of the poems of William Wordsworth and the other, *Colossus,* was a book of poems by Sylvia Plath. These authors seemed an unlikely combination for a Mormon missionary, but each fed a different part of my soul.

I served in Milano from October 24, 1972, to March 24, 1973. Then I was transferred to Brescia, north of Milano. The thing I remember most about Brescia is the sun, warm and generous after the bone-biting Milano winter. Moving to Brescia in the spring was an awakening for me. Life was definitely more comfortable there, since I lived with my companion and four other elders in a penthouse apartment with a terrace. We spent most of our time tracting door to door or talking to people in the ruins of a castle situated on a hill in the middle of town. At the castle, we sometimes felt free to identify ourselves as missionaries right from the beginning of a conversation.

In Brescia, the mission rule about wearing our jackets at all times became particularly onerous. As summer approached, it grew very warm, and when we rode long distances to get to the outer edges of the city, large dark circles of sweat formed under our armpits. To my mind, this was less professional-looking than shirt sleeves, but the mission president's word was law, so we gritted our teeth and complied.

The other elders living in the apartment were a mixed group. One had a record player and two LPs that he alternated incessantly whenever we were at home. One album was Neil Diamond's *Hot August Night* and the other was by the rock 'n' roll band, Deep Purple. I sometimes sat out on the terrace at night, listening to the strains of "Smoke on the Water" or "Space Truckin'," looking up at the stars and wondering how it all fit together.

On July 13, 1973, I was transferred to Varese, near the Swiss border, where I spent a little over a month. In Varese, the community of Mormons was so small that the living room of our apartment was used for church meetings on Sundays.

One Sunday after church, while I was playing my guitar, the district leader walked into my room and demanded, "What are you doing, playing your guitar on the Sabbath?" He claimed that I was contravening a mission rule and ordered me to stop. This seemed like a clear-cut abuse of power to me and I flatly refused to obey.

Once we were invited into a house by a woman who said, "My husband is eating his dinner, but you can come in and talk to him." She ushered us into a long shadowy dining room with a large Italian marble table set in the middle. At the opposite end, a man was eating a raw steak swimming in olive oil. He claimed to have eaten a steak like this every night of his life for thirty years. I was impressed. He appeared to be in pretty good shape, although he did have the ruddy cheeks laced with capillaries that are characteristic of so many rural Italians.

On August 31, I returned to Milano, the period that became the dark night of my soul. I had a series of companions, most of whom were going home soon. This meant that, over and over again, I had to go through all of the pining and preparation that happens at the end of a two-year stint, albeit vicariously. It was very hard to keep my sense of balance and focus as a missionary and I felt homesick.

We had no heater, and our studio apartment became incredibly cold as winter approached. The assistants to the president, however, had heard about a number of coal-burning stoves for sale and thought they'd be a great way to provide cheap heat for missionaries who couldn't afford to buy the standard asphyxiator units. So we acquired one. The first night, we couldn't light it. The next night, we finally got it going, but it got so hot in the room that we took off all our blankets and slept practically naked on top of our beds, sweating rivers. We even had to open the window, because there was no other way to control the heat! Of course, by morning the coal had burned out, we'd fallen asleep, and the sweat had nearly frozen on our bodies. I was miserable.

During this period, I was made president of a small branch of the Church in Milano. A branch is the missionfield counterpart of the ward in LDS Church organizational structure, but generally lacks adequate membership to staff all the usual ward positions. Therefore, missionaries are called upon to fulfill some of the responsibilities. As president, I was in charge of the administration of the branch. I also had to counsel members with their personal problems, sometimes even hearing their confessions—a heavy burden for a twenty-year-old.

After serving in this capacity for a short time, I was told by the mission president that he was looking for new mission leaders. He thought I had potential, if only I would buy a new pair of shoes. I currently wore informal, brushed leather footwear, which he felt was the chief obstacle that stood between me and a leadership position. He encouraged me very strongly to buy a new pair of hard shoes, and I bought some that could actually be shined. It may have been this decision that resulted in my transfer to Genova on December 6.

If my second stint in Milano had been a spiritual and emotional trough, Genova was a renaissance. I got along well with my new companion, and the only fellow missionary I knew on a first-name basis was also one of our apartment mates. My new shoes had garnered me the position of one of two zone leaders. As a consequence, my companion and I had the use of a car. There was also a great deal more variety in our work. For example, our duties included switching off with elders working in various cities of the zone in order to observe how they were doing, to spot any potential problems, and to offer suggestions about how they might improve their work. Our observations were then reported to the assistants, who passed them on to the president. What this all boiled down to was less tracting and more travel, a change of pace I welcomed enthusiastically.

On one trip, we traveled to a small country village called Varese Ligure, located in the hills north of La Spezia on the Ligurian coast. There we spent the afternoon attending the funeral of the mother of Brother Ottoboni, a member of the Church in his seventies who had spent most of his life in Argentina. Before the funeral, we had lunch with Brother Ottoboni and his uncle, Brother Giannini, who was in his nineties. It was a revelation to converse with these two old men whose life experience had been so utterly different from mine. Their lives were such full cups that mine seemed empty by comparison. As I listened to them tell their stories, I felt as if I were somehow being mentored. As was the custom with many Italian funerals, especially in small towns, the body was laid out in black on her own bed for viewing beforehand. It was a poignant sight to see that old woman sleeping her final sleep in the room where she had spent so many nights while alive.

Since Brother Ottoboni's mother had been Catholic, a priest conducted the service in the local cathedral. In those days, I was ill-equipped to appreciate a non-Mormon funeral. Catholics were unbelievers, as far as I was concerned, at best, prospective investigators. What value could their liturgy hold for me? Wasn't it an expression of false faith, the hope of things that were *not* true? In spite of my prejudices, however, something about this funeral connected with me on a deep level. Maybe it was the old men and their stories that prepared my heart, or perhaps the richness of the symbolism. At any rate, while I was resisting Catholicism on the surface, underneath I was touched by its ritual and traditions.

Another trip took us to Portofino, a beautiful coastal town with sparkling beaches south of Genova. In most missions, elders were forbidden to swim or even travel by boat because of a revelation Joseph Smith produced decreeing that "the destroyer rideth upon the face" of the waters (D&C 61:18–19). We must have tempted fate in Portofino because we all went wading. Fortunately, everyone returned in one piece, greatly refreshed for having cooled their heels in the ocean on a lovely spring day.

On May 23, 1974, I was transferred to the last city of my mission, Lugano, located in the Italian-speaking zone of Switzerland. Situated on the shores of Lake Lugano, it is one of the most gorgeous spots in the world. The late spring and summer weather was perfect, and we tried to avoid tracting as often as possible, working outdoors in the park instead, just as I had done in Brescia. Once we were walking through the park at a point where a stream flowed into the lake. An adolescent boy was fishing off a bridge over the stream with a bare hook. He would throw his line down and snag the fish expertly by the gills. He was having more success than we were as fishers of men.

I was a senior companion for the first time in Lugano. The work was hard and we had very few contacts. We taught only one discussion in the three months I was there, to a young woman who was a lapsed Jehovah's Witness. She was single and lonely, and I believe that what little interest she may have had in Mormonism was eclipsed by her interest in the two young American men who visited her apartment once a week. Though she continued to ask us back, we finally had to stop going. She really wasn't spiritually curious at all. The lack of response to our message in Lugano was even greater than it had been in Italy, if that were possible, and we battled discouragement.

Throughout my mission, I struggled with the same emotional peaks and valleys I had experienced at home. Depression was a frequent, though unwelcome guest. At one point, I thought I found an answer, at least in part, to the problem. An elder in the Brescia district loaned me a cassette tape on which an LDS woman taught that, if we just did our very best, God would accept us and overlook our sins. For a time, this idea encouraged me tremendously—I needed desperately to believe that God was still pleased with my life. I found that I could let go and be more at ease with myself and others while I believed in this idea.

Soon, though, cracks began to appear in the wall. Central to my faith as a Mormon was the idea of ultimate human perfection. The "do your best and God does the rest" concept seemed to lower God's standard rather than empower me to attain it. Furthermore, at the bottom line, this philosophy struck me as being unscriptural—the *Doctrine and Covenants* taught that God could not "look upon sin with the least degree of allowance" (D&C 1:31).

I found out later that the teacher on the tape had been excommunicated from the Church for having an affair with a missionary. In the Mormon mind, one's ideas can be discredited by moral failure. It is an ad hominem argument that runs deep in the community. This was the mind-set with which I received the news of her excommunication. Nevertheless, it was a painful blow because her material had helped me keep my discouragement at bay for a time. Would I ever find a permanent solution, I wondered, a lasting peace to still the dark currents that roiled about the roots of my soul?

Earlier in my mission, I had written a poem that expressed my feelings on this subject.

however hunger deep my spirit gnaws
or thirst drags broken longing to my lips
my heat remains indifferent in my jaws
my life remains oblivious to its steams

days and nights will not deny their just revolving
nor seasons quit their rightful cyclic station
but I, like some disgusting drunkard, reeling,
stumble through this quiet wonder of creation

a captive of mortality, my shame
to watch the gods from steel-shod windows
and bear my oddly human ball and chain

the times I've thought
to flee my fleshy prison
and rocket to the stars
even if I burned to nothing for the speed
one moment rushing freedom
one moment to be clean
would drive to wildness my joy
and consummation in the brightness
of my intense young flame

watching for the Liberator through the filthy glass
I await the breaking of the wicked walls at last
and bursting light, more than a thousand silver suns surpass

By the time my mission release date arrived in August 1974, I was mentally, emotionally, and spiritually exhausted and ready to go home. I felt wrung-out, like an old sponge. Most of the time, the thought of returning to LeAnn and my family, my music, and the rest of my life filled me with excitement and pleasure. I couldn't wait to get married, start a family, and get on with it.

At the same time, however, I began to sense an overcast of anxiety, hovering at the horizon of my mind. LeAnn had taken a job as a real estate agent and used her commission to buy a house in Orem, Utah, about an hour's drive south of Salt Lake City near BYU. She had also bought a car. Before I left Italy, I knew that a wife, car payments, and a mortgage were all waiting for me. I had no job prospects and no skills aside from my music, and I was petrified whenever I considered the tenuousness of my position. I wanted to get married as soon as possible, but what did I know about making a living—or even about marriage, for that matter?

The weeks that preceded my homecoming took on an atmosphere of unreality. If the transition to Italy was difficult, it was at least expected. The returning transition was just as tough and thoroughly unexpected. I suddenly found myself obsessing about little things such as not remembering how to kiss. I imagined stepping off the airplane, falling over my feet as I walked toward LeAnn, moving to kiss her, and sucking on her nose instead! Foolish scenes like that gave rise to a nebulous uneasiness.

I finished my mission with some ambivalence. I had served honorably and with success, baptizing more than the mission average. I had survived the discomforts and distractions of mission life and learned that I could make my way in the world, an important rite of passage that had left me feeling older and wiser. I had grown spiritually as well: my journal was filled with pages of commentary on scriptural passages and reflections on my spiritual experiences. While these experiences were perhaps not as spectacular as the ones prior to my mission, I believed, nonetheless, that I had seen God at work in my mission, the overarching designer behind many fortuitous circumstances. If I hadn't conquered my tendency toward depression, at least I had kept it from destroying or neutralizing me.

Still, I had the nagging sense that there was something left undone, and this feeling tugged at my legs like a dark, chilling undertow. My mission hadn't turned out the way I thought it would. Perhaps the discouragement of those final months in Lugano, despite the glorious surroundings, contributed to the feeling that somehow, something was missing. Whatever the explanation, my mission didn't end with a bang, but something more akin to a whimper.

Coming home held out the hope of some sort of redemption for me. I was not yet aware of how much my longing for inner peace was invested in the altering of my outer circumstances. This realization would be a hard-won lesson, long in the learning.

For Time and All Eternity

And again, verily I say unto you, if a man marry a wife, and make a covenant with her for time and for all eternity, if that covenant is not by me or by my word, which is my law, and is not sealed by the Holy Spirit of promise, through him whom I have anointed and appointed unto this power, then it is not valid neither of force when they are out of the world, because they are not joined by me, saith the Lord.

—Doctrine and Covenants 132:18

Friday, August 16, 1974, was a typically warm summer night in Salt Lake City. The air was humming. I stepped off the plane into a dream, the kind in which everything moves in slow motion and voices sound close and dry, without reverberation. There was no jetway and from the top of the stairs, I could see my mother and brother waiting for me across the tarmac, as if I were staring at them through the large end of a telescope. My brother was twice as tall as I remembered. I felt curiously numb. There was a hole burning in the center of my chest. I moved forward and in a moment I was in their arms and the night was full of tears and congratulations and welcomes home.

The illumination in the terminal shone out through the gate like klieg lights. A jostling crowd of family and friends was framed there, everyone beaming with smiles of love and pride. It reminded me of a scene from the LDS proselyting film *Man's Search for Happiness* in which a kindly old grandfather enters heaven and is reunited with all his loved ones. LeAnn had waited inside, and as I walked through the door, she was suddenly there, dressed in a long, slinky maroon dress, luminous as a vision. At last the long wait was over! Why did I feel that I was outside of my body, watching myself embrace her tenderly? It wasn't until we were in the car on the way to Poppie and Grandma's apartment that I overcame my fears and we kissed for the first time in almost two years. I hadn't forgotten how after all!

The equivalent of a Nantucket sleighride began less than twelve hours later when reality breached like a harpooned whale. LeAnn had scheduled a photo session for our wedding announcements early the next morning, so I was awakened, groggy and uncomprehending, and hustled into a shirt borrowed from my brother. I felt like a refugee from a Salvador Dali painting—only the crutches and melting watches were missing. Tired as I was, a more starry-eyed couple than we were would have been difficult to find. For us, marriage was the culmination of a lifelong pursuit, our most cherished dream, the stuff of fairy tales. Though we would have denied it at the time, we essentially expected to live happily ever after. Despite the bags under my eyes in the photo, our faces are full of anticipation and the unquestioned presumption that what we were doing was a genuine cosmic imperative, that everything we held in principle was about to work out in practice. The golden treasure was ours, the Prince was to marry the Princess, Pinocchio was about to become a real boy.

We scheduled our marriage for Monday, September 9, in the Salt Lake Temple, just three weeks after my return. The days in between were congested with activity. There was simply no time to entertain the worries that had troubled me in the final weeks of my mission. The myriad preparations for the wedding combined with the details of my reentry into the mainstream of life to keep us careening forward in high gear most of the time. We moved all my belongings into our little green house in Orem. Aside from the activity, what stands out most in my mind about these weeks is the ever-increasing challenge of self-restraint. LeAnn and I really wanted to be married as virgins, both for our own sake and for that of the Church; but we ached for each other intensely, viscerally. We knew that we had to deny ourselves virtually any physical intimacy or we simply wouldn't be able to hold out. So we forbore, threw our energies into the wedding logistics as if we were Spartans, gritted our teeth, and bided our time.

Mormon values associated with marriage and family are widely known and respected outside the Mormon community, at least among those with a conservative bent. It's a rare American who didn't notice the LDS "Families Are Forever" bumper stickers or wasn't

touched, however unwillingly, by the sentimental Mormon television commercials encouraging positive family relationships. Mormons believe in premarital chastity, marital fidelity, lifetime commitment, and involved parenting. They stand against divorce,
promiscuity, abortion, and most forms of birth control. More than
this, however, they believe that couples whose marriages are sol-
emnized in LDS temples by the requisite priesthood authority are
"sealed for time and for all eternity." In other words, these marriages
are supposed to continue eternally in the hereafter. Children born
to these couples are "born in the covenant," automatically sealed to
their parents for eternity as well. So the catchphrase "families are
forever" is less metaphoric than descriptive.

There are many lesser-known but equally powerful corollaries that
attend this central premise. For example, it is axiomatic that if the
proper priesthood authority is necessary to seal marriages for "eternity," all other marriages not so sealed are for "time" only, halfway
measures doomed to end with mortal life. Indeed, the words "'til death
do you part" have an ominous ring for Mormons, weighted with the
emotional devastation of separation from those most loved. Mormons
look at non-LDS marriages with a twinge of sadness and pity.

Even so, it is not guaranteed that all temple marriages will last forever. Everything is predicated upon the worthiness of the individual in living up to the high standards of perfection, as taught in Mormonism. As a young man, I was solemnly warned that tepid
Latter-day Saints, assuming their marriages would last merely
because of the ritual, would be sadly surprised on the day of judgment when confronted with their own lack of dedication. The righteous wives of men in this unfortunate condition would be given in
marriage to other, more deserving men, while righteous husbands
of less than devout women would have many more pious wives to
assuage their loss. Those poor souls left behind would be their servants forever in the courts on high.

The Mormon "heaven" is divided into three kingdoms of glory:
the celestial kingdom, home of God, Jesus, and all righteous Mormons; the terrestrial kingdom, where honorable people who rejected
Mormonism on earth, but afterwards received it in the spirit world
will dwell; and the telestial kingdom, for liars, sorcerers, adulterers,
and other assorted sinners. The celestial kingdom is further subdi-

vided into three levels. Only the most worthy Latter-day Saints, whose marriages have been sealed in the temple for eternity, rise to the highest of these three levels, and those in the lower two act as their ministering servants. This prospect alone was terrifying enough to drive many of my attempts at personal holiness.

Furthermore, temple divorces are possible. A sealing can be dissolved by the same authority that performed it. My mother and father, for example, were divorced civilly first, for "time," and were granted a temple divorce fifteen years later, to enable my mother to marry my stepfather for "eternity."

Situations like these create ambiguities that provide the grist for much speculation about who belongs to whom and in what order after this life; nor are these issues purely theoretical. My own family provides several concrete examples of this dilemma. To whom are the children sealed in the case of a temple divorce? Will my brother and I be sealed to our stepfather or our maternal grandfather in the hereafter? Perhaps we remain in the Redford line, claimed by one of Dad's older brothers according to the custom of ancient Israel. What happens when someone breaks the chain by rejecting Mormonism? Are these families still "forever"? Multiple wives can be accounted for by polygamy which continues in Mormonism as a principle if not a practice; but what of multiple husbands such as in the case of my beloved Grandma, who remarried late in life and proceeded to annoy the family by coyly wondering aloud to whom she would belong afterward? While most Mormons categorize these things as mysteries that will be resolved by a loving God, the questions still retain the power to sting the heart in the unguarded moment.

Fundamentally, however, it is crucial to know that in Mormonism eternal marriage is required for exaltation, the word Latter-day Saints use to describe ultimate salvation in the highest degree of God's celestial kingdom. Worthy Mormons married in this way may themselves become gods, bearing spirit children and populating their own worlds throughout the eternities. The people of these worlds in turn worship them as God, and the worthiest among them become gods themselves, thereby continuing the cycle. And so on and on it goes forever.

Much is expected from Mormon marriages in this world as well. LeAnn and I were not unusual among the Mormons in making our union the repository of so many of our hopes and dreams. A large measure of our self-worth was invested in the success of this relationship. LDS teaching on marriage nourished the idea that spouses were somehow responsible to fulfill one another personally. Much of a woman's value in Mormonism is derived through her husband and his priesthood. Even her relationship with God depends significantly upon her husband, a fact unambiguously underscored in the temple ritual. Eternal marriage is the great prize in the LDS worldview, the thing that was to answer our longings and heal our wounds, the great ball of gold in the sky. This is the sort of marriage for which LeAnn and I dreamed and strove.

There was also a lighter side to all of these weighty expectations. The LDS concept of eternal marriage appealed to our imagination as well. LeAnn and I often amused ourselves with speculations about our life as gods beyond the grave. Our favorite daydream involved a picnic on one of our unpeopled worlds that looked a lot like Hawaii. Divine skinnydipping took on a whole new aura when combined with the prospect of being able to fly.

Most LDS women go through the temple for the first time shortly before their weddings, frequently on that very day. In addition to receiving their endowments, there is a special ritual that anticipates the marriage ceremony. Instead of giving her new name through the veil to an anonymous temple worker, along with the other names and tokens, the prospective bride enacts this ritual with her husband-to-be standing in the place of God. At this time, he learns her new name, the name by which Mormons believe he will call her from the grave in the resurrection. Though the husband must know his wife's new name, it is strictly forbidden for him to reveal his own new name to her. There is an odd kind of folklore that surrounds the new name. Nightmarish stories are told of weak-willed husbands, pestered by their avid wives to reveal their temple names, only to reap dire, if seemingly unrelated, consequences later in life.

LeAnn went through the Salt Lake Temple for the first time on Thursday, September 5, four days before we were to be married. When we arrived at the veil, she gave me her new name, but she mispronounced it. Because of this, we had to redo the new name ritual at the veil just prior to our wedding the following Monday. LeAnn was deeply chagrined at failing at one of the key moments of her life.

What if I called her by the wrong name at the resurrection? Would she be left behind? Or would some other woman by that name rise up and take her place? These kinds of details can drive analytically minded Mormons crazy; but beyond the paranoia, it's significant that something as minor as the mispronunciation of a name would be taken so seriously.

Our wedding day finally arrived, and I awoke early. My daily routines, showering, shaving, and grooming, all seemed like sacraments that day. I dressed in the pale gray-green corduroy suit I had purchased in Switzerland, picked LeAnn up at her parents' home, and we drove to the temple together in our new little red Chevy Vega.

Our families and a few close friends met us there. One of the most visible differences between LDS temple weddings and those of Catholics and Protestants is that only worthy adult temple recommend holders are permitted to enter the temple to witness the actual wedding ceremony. A church sanctuary filled with witnesses and well-wishers, believers and nonbelievers alike, is missing in Mormonism. In our case, our brothers and sisters were not allowed to attend because they were too young to hold a recommend. My father couldn't be there because he wasn't deemed worthy by the Church, though it must be said that this form of validation held no importance for him.

We all met in one of the sealing rooms where the ceremony was to take place. It was rectangular and had a couple of large windows. The walls were white and the floor was covered with beige plush carpeting. A few dozen chairs stood on three sides and there was an altar in the center of the room. The chairs and altar were upholstered with gold velvet. No traditional Christian symbols, such as the cross or the fish, were in evidence, nor are they to be found anywhere within or without the Salt Lake Temple. There was, however, a Bible laying on the altar along with the LDS scriptures, all of which remained unopened for the duration of the ceremony. The most memorable aspect of the room was also an interesting study in applied theology: two of the opposing walls were covered with enormous full-length mirrors. As LeAnn and I knelt facing each other across the altar, we could see ourselves reflected and multiplied ad infinitum in both directions.

Mormon General Authority S. Dilworth Young, a distant relative on my mother's side, performed the wedding. The ceremony consisted of some extemporaneous advice and a specific prayer of sealing, the wording predetermined by Church canon. I can't recall a single thing the officiator said. Both of us felt that the ceremony was somewhat anticlimactic, given the intensity of the buildup. My chief recollection of the experience is the return of that feeling of distance I had at the airport, as if the wedding ceremony was happening to my body while I stood outside watching. All that day, I felt as if I were wandering about in a fog. Brooding about this later, I was troubled that I had felt so dissociated during these supremely important events. This was a new feeling for me and it frightened me the more I thought about it.

After the ceremony, LeAnn and I and the whole family, including brothers and sisters, stood on the stairs and in the niches on the east side of the temple to have our pictures taken. The atmosphere was as festive now as it had been solemn just a few minutes before. We all felt a great sense of accomplishment, like a party of mountain climbers who have just reached the summit. Our wedding banquet was held shortly afterward at the Lion House, Brigham Young's pioneer home, just a block away. LeAnn and I had contrived with my dad to sneak off to his apartment after the banquet so that we could make love for the first time. We were completely inexperienced and fumbled about awkwardly, but we were deeply in love and knew that we would grow together over the years. That afternoon tryst was our little secret and my dad's sly wedding gift to us.

Our reception was held that evening at LeAnn's parents' home, which had been beautifully renovated for the occasion. Friends sang and played guitars, and a string quartet performed. For hours we stood in line greeting family, friends, and ward members. By the time it was all over and we had driven to our house in Orem, we staggered, thoroughly exhausted, into bed and fell immediately asleep.

Our honeymoon was a disaster. We were under the mistaken impression that we would be making love night and day for the duration. We didn't think we had to travel anywhere special for that, so we just stayed in Orem. It soon became obvious that we really *did* need to do something other than remain in bed. Unfortunately, we weren't in a location where there was anything particularly new and exciting to do, nor did we have any money. The "high point" of our honeymoon became a night out at the movies to see Barbra Streisand in *For Pete's Sake,* an abysmally bad film that didn't make for much of a celebration. Our honeymoon didn't even have a proper end. It just faded into the routines of daily living.

And so our life together began. In addition to her real estate work, LeAnn had taken a second job selling shoes at a local department store, hoping to augment our income in a manner not subject to the vagaries of commissions. I learned of an opening for a bass player and singer with Manna, one of the busiest bands in Salt Lake City. Although I'd never played the bass, I had some experience with guitar, a good head for theory, and a lot of confidence. Dad gave me some money and I bought a Fender Jazz bass at a pawn shop, practiced for a few days, auditioned, and got the job. Because the band worked primarily on weekends, I was free to take other work during the week, either arranging or recording. I could also work on my own compositions. This arrangement seemed ideal—until the sky fell.

Sometime during those first few weeks, LeAnn became pregnant. It was "contrary to the teachings of the Church artificially to curtail or prevent the birth of children." The position of the First Presidency was that "those who practice birth control will reap disappointment by and by" and they enjoined "self-control" in deference to conserving a mother's "health and strength."[1] In consequence of these teachings, LeAnn and I hadn't taken any steps to prevent a pregnancy. Besides, our Wallsburg dream was all about family. We wanted children—twelve of them, to be precise. So we were surprised and scared, but also excited. Believing it was God's will for us, our fear of becoming new parents so suddenly was mostly swallowed up by joy. Then severe "morning" sickness set in. Within a few weeks LeAnn began to vomit, morning, noon, *and* night—not just light regurgitation, but a deep, violent retching. Anything could provoke it: the smell of soap, the smell of the furnace, the smell of my body. She could hardly stand to be near me. We drastically revised our plan to have twelve children.

The nausea continued steadily for the next seven months. There was nothing the doctor could do, and no drug seemed to help. LeAnn dwindled to less than a hundred pounds. She was so sick, she couldn't continue to work. She tried to hold down a few part-time jobs in the course of her pregnancy, but was no more successful at that than she was in trying to hold down her dinners. Soon I was left with total responsibility for the house and car payments and all of our living expenses. Within a few months of my return from Italy, I had become the sole provider for a new wife and soon-to-be-first-born daughter.

Jessica Lee Redford was born on June 23, 1975, exactly nine months and two weeks after our wedding day—and she was a week late! The whole birthing experience was stunningly new for me, to say nothing of its effect on LeAnn. For many hours, she endured an incredibly exhausting and painful labor while I tried to coach her with the marginally effective Lamaze methods that we had dutifully practiced beforehand. Our doctor was on vacation at the time and the obstetrician on call was a crusty, stone-faced Utah conservative who talked politics throughout the delivery. Sympathetic with the John Birch Society, he railed about how the country was going to the dogs unless people who thought as he did stepped in to save it. This, even as Jessica emerged from the birth canal!

Nothing he said, however, could diminish the wonder of the moment. We both burst spontaneously into tears of joy and relief at Jessica's appearance. She was absolutely beautiful, perhaps the most beautiful thing either of us had ever seen—only a parent could say this about a red, squalling newborn. LeAnn and I were proud as punch when the doctor announced that her Apgar score was a perfect ten.

Afterward, LeAnn's face glowed like a torch. Pure delight coupled with the sudden release of hundreds of hormones gave her a shining aura. I was thrilled as well, but I was also dazed. For the third time in a year, I felt that sense of distance intrude. As soon as LeAnn was comfortably situated, I kissed her goodnight and drove to Sambo's, a local twenty-four-hour cafe, for something to eat. For a long time I sat at the counter with some truck drivers and tried to comprehend what had just happened.

A couple of weeks later, I stood in a circle of elders at the front of the Orem 8th Ward and blessed my new baby daughter, just as my father had blessed me as an infant. I flung out our hopes and dreams for her like nets and prayed that God would make her life fruitful and good.

Throughout the term of LeAnn's pregnancy, our life was magnetized about the twin poles of work and church service. Where the

Church was concerned, our roles were relatively well defined. All that was required was that we live out our faith in the daily duties of the dedicated Mormon, keeping the commandments and serving others in ways that were considered valid among the Latter-day Saints.

Primarily, this meant regular attendance at weekly Church meetings. It also meant accepting "callings" to work in positions of responsibility at the ward or stake level in the Church organization. Mormons are taught both by precept and cultural mandate that it is wrong to turn down a Church calling. Callings are believed to come from the Lord via revelation through the local Church leadership. As such, all personal life circumstances must, by definition, have already been taken into account, thus rendering an individual's refusal an automatic expression of faithlessness. Mormons don't quit or retire from these callings but continue in them until formally released. Despite her illness, LeAnn served as a leader in the young women's program. I was called to work with the young men as well as serving as a home teacher.

LDS home teachers, like missionaries, worked in pairs. Our principal duty was to visit assigned families in the ward at least once a month in order to maintain an active line of personal contact between them and the ward leadership. We were to find out if they needed any material help and deliver a short spiritual message, which derived its content from Church publications. Each month, we were also expected to hold Personal Priesthood Interviews with the fathers of these families. These PPIs were intended to undergird the father's authority and provide an opportunity for more intimate discussion of his family's needs. We were instructed to ask each father questions about his family relationships and encourage him to talk with us frankly about his problems. It was stressed that we ought not allow these visits to become routine, but instead that we should learn to care genuinely for each family member. Of course, reports were to be filled out and submitted to our priesthood leaders following each visit. They, in turn, reported to the bishop. Thus, through the Home Teaching and PPI programs, the bishop was theoretically kept apprised of the spiritual and material needs of each member of his ward.

Some of the men in our ward laughed and rolled their eyes when Personal Priesthood Interviews were introduced. It was yet another duty to be heaped on an already great host. The older home teachers also appeared to express a natural reluctance to such prescribed intimacy. They seemed to have heard it all before. But I was young and idealistic. Having just returned from the missionfield where each day was fully planned for two years, home teaching and PPIs constituted a fairly straightforward obligation. I could see some value in the programs and was convinced that with the right attitude, I would be able to make the most of them. So I threw myself into the work and ignored those who appeared to be less serious about it than I thought I was.

I confidently presumed that my experience as a missionary qualified me to do well as a home teacher. After all, I had served in several different leadership positions in Italy and had counseled many, Italians and missionaries alike, from radically different backgrounds; but I hadn't recognized at the time that there was an inherent unreality in those situations, born of the fact that I was essentially a stranger to each of those people, impermanent, without any real stake in their future. I could afford to play at solving their problems and absolving their sins and they could afford to go along with it. Here at home, however, my neighbors were confronting issues that camped in my own backyard and refused go away. I found that I was suddenly helpless, unable even to connect with my charges. I was too young and inexperienced with life to truly empathize with them, let alone suggest solutions to their problems. I could only offer the standard Church panaceas: prayer, fasting, and scripture study. They viewed me, not as a friend in whom they could really confide, but as a Church representative doing my job, which indeed I was. Nor did some of them want to maintain this kind of intimate contact with the Church. They seemed to find it oppressive. I was painfully aware of the artificiality of the situation. Fulfilling this calling became an uphill struggle that no amount of prayer or hard work would ameliorate. I found myself wondering if this is what service in the Church would be like for the rest of my life.

While LeAnn was still pregnant, the stake asked our ward to increase its temple attendance. She and I tried to attend once a week, doing two sessions in a row each time, but it was very difficult with LeAnn as sick as she was. One night we arrived home after a session and she couldn't even make it into the house. She fell on her knees in the front yard and threw up on the grass like a dog. I was absolutely horrified that she had to go through this, and I felt completely powerless to help her. I also have to admit to feeling disgust. This was not the life that I had planned.

Sometime during this period I had an unusual experience that affected me profoundly. I was in the temple doing initiatory work when, for the fourth time in my life, I felt as if I traveled outside myself for a fraction of an instant. The fog that had accompanied this feeling each time before was absent, however, and I suddenly saw myself with a great burst of clarity and objectivity. An almost audible voice came into my mind saying, "What are you doing here?" There was nothing condemnatory about the voice, yet it cut me to the quick. I wasn't sure what the answer was, but I knew that something was terribly wrong. This was the same sort of revelatory spiritual experience that had given me my testimony that the Church was true, yet now it called into question the Church's most profound ritual. From that moment on, the spell of the temple was broken for me. I could never regain my faith in it, though I tried.

Yet all was not bleakness and frustration. There were sweet experiences too, when genuine human connection occurred. No institution can program or prevent such things. Perhaps the sweetest transpired, paradoxically, when a neighbor contracted a particularly virulent cancer. There was no doubt that he was going to die. One evening LeAnn and I went to visit him in the hospital. I took Poppie's mandolin, and, together at his bedside, we sang for him that most poignant of pioneer folk songs, "A Poor Wayfaring Man of Grief." We all wept and he asked us to sing the song at his funeral. LeAnn and I did so a few weeks later, new life straining at the seams of her dress even as he lay lifeless in his casket.

It would be hard to overstate the personal upheaval created by this first year of our marriage. There were so many changes in so short a time; yet, on the inside, I was still the same person with the same propensity for melancholy. I had returned from my mission with such an intense focus on getting married that, for the short term, I was able to keep the darkness at bay. Indeed, I thought that being married would change me. Once the marriage was made, however, the old patterns of guilt and depression soon reasserted themselves with even greater force. As early as two weeks after our wedding, I wrote a poem that illustrates this:

I speak a word to heal a wound and leave a wound instead
I give my heart to wake a man and leave his spirit dead
I lift my hand to dry a tear and leave the sockets blind
For what I would not, that I do and scars are left behind
And scars are left behind

I had thought I was ready for real life. I had married my true love and best friend in God's holy temple for time and all eternity. I was ready to find a deep sense of contentment in my marriage and through my service in the Lord's kingdom. Why did I feel instead a pervading undertow of despair and emptiness?

LeAnn was crushed. She took my depression as a personal failure. Why was she unable to make me happy? Wasn't she good enough for me? Why wasn't Mormonism a stronger source of peace in the midst of this struggle? It had to be our fault. We just needed to try harder.

At the time, we knew of no tools to help us deal with these issues, no forum in which we could even discuss them. There were certainly no Church-sponsored support groups where we could give vent to the ways we were beginning to fail one another, nor was such expression welcome in most circumstances. We could barely admit it to ourselves, intuitively knowing that we might open a Pandora's box of hidden fears that would perhaps even reflect negatively on the Church in some way, raising a host of questions that must never be asked. So we just kept quiet and tried to work our problems out alone in our private tears and prayers.

While LeAnn was sick and unable to work, it quickly became clear that I was going to have to make more money, but my single-minded focus as a composer prevented me from seriously considering extra-musical work. Being a composer is not simply a choice of careers. It is more like a vocation in the religious sense, that is, a calling, a divine vision, a burden that is placed upon the heart. Many composers have described the necessity of composition, the feeling that they write because they must, because they cannot "not write." The need to create music is a deep emotional current, flowing inexorably from the inner self. From the time I wrote my first piece at sixteen, I knew without a doubt that I was a composer. It was not merely something I wanted to do when I grew up; it was a state of being. There is an invisible boundary between work that fits this call and work that does not, and this line is discerned intuitively. Somehow, I knew in those early days of our marriage that I must not take a steady job outside of music.

Ill as she was, LeAnn was nevertheless completely supportive of this risky proposition. Throughout our marriage, she has believed in me even when I found it hard to believe in myself. In hindsight, this time was a critical juncture in our marriage, although we didn't fully recognize it as such. If I had taken a steady job, my life's work may have been sidetracked or even derailed in the crush of earning a living. That LeAnn was not tempted to insist on this is indicative of her own faith in my vocation. This attitude is characteristic of the sacrifices, many of them unconscious, that she has made to advance it through the years.

Nonetheless, bills had to be paid and lucrative music-related opportunities were rare in Utah. I took whatever jobs I could to keep us afloat. In addition to my work with the band on the weekends, I began a professional recording career. I made $20 on my first session, playing trombone and flute for another local composer. I taught for a week at Nephi High School in central Utah for the Artists in Schools program under the auspices of the National Endowment for the Arts. As a freelance arranger and orchestrator, I worked on a number of projects more notable for their variety and eccentricity than their visibility. Once I orchestrated a cantata for a festival celebrating the arcane history of Kanab, Utah. On another occasion, I arranged music for a family of trumpeters who called themselves the Brunson Burners. Many arrangements were done for local amateur songwriters who wanted to record demonstration tapes of their songs. I made package deals with them and frequently played most of the instruments myself.

I also worked for LDS recording artists Marvin Payne and Debbie Au, prominent figures in the Mormon arts renaissance movement I had been a part of prior to my mission. I loved their music and enjoyed working for them, but the movement had changed significantly in the time that I was gone. The life seemed to have gone out of it. Some negative comments from General Authorities, both public and private, had a discouraging effect on the artists themselves and undermined the possibility of whole-hearted support from the LDS audience. The primary culprit, I believe, was a resistance to the challenging aspects of experimentation and widening expression in the arts. This attitude is found throughout American culture in general and amplified in subcultures such as Mormonism. We are slow to embrace what is new and different because it requires us to stretch and change, which can be inconvenient, uncomfortable, and even painful. At any rate, by the time I returned from Italy, the creative community had largely dispersed, leaving individual artists to carve out their own paths in a severely straitened landscape.

Several months into our marriage, I felt that I should return to school. It was not lost on me that most concert music composers are associated in some manner with universities. I feared that my music would never be taken seriously unless I had a series of degrees behind my name. Furthermore, I keenly felt my lack of technique. I wanted to study traditional harmony and counterpoint to deepen my craft. Hoping my former disgust with the academic environment had been primarily a matter of immaturity, I decided to return to BYU.

Within a semester I knew that the university route was not for me and bade it farewell, without doubt or regret, resolving to continue my education through private study. While at BYU, however, I did have a number of opportunities to write, largely through the generosity of my friend and teacher of years before, Newell Dayley. With his encouragement, I wrote some new jazz pieces for the BYU jazz ensemble as well as arrangements for the theater and dance departments and touring entertainment groups.

Newell also put me in contact with a producer working for the Utah State Board of Education and I scored a number of educational films with such unlikely titles as *Minerals, Metric World,* and *Are You Drinking, Charlie?* About the same time, I was hired to score some documentaries for the BYU television and film departments, working with Brian Capener, whom I had first met at KBYU prior to my mission. Brian had become a gifted director—his films were ripe with subtext that required not only my technical skills, but the resources of my soul as well.

These documentaries and the Board of Education films became my training ground, providing seminal experience in the field of film music. Through them, I began to learn and develop the craft of composition for the cinema, dealing with all of the special challenges that film composers have had to face since the advent of the sound-track: synchronization, the delicate balance between writing music that stands on its own and writing music that enhances a scene without overwhelming it, and perhaps most pointedly, the tyranny of the deadline. The great ones have left behind a legacy that is truly an art form. I was beginning to walk gingerly in their footsteps and found that I had an aptitude for it.

Nor did I neglect my stage roots. Newell recommended me to Carol Lynn Pearson, who was writing the book and lyrics for a musical based on *Aesop's Fables* for Robert Redford's Sundance Summer theater. Other commitments had prevented Newell from writing the music for the songs himself, and only a few days remained before rehearsals were to begin. So I took a tape recorder into my studio and in three days' time wrote and arranged fourteen songs that were incorporated immediately into the show. This was a terrific experience for me, requiring that I apply the principles of musical theater I had absorbed as a child, and giving me a chance to observe first-hand how they worked out in practice on the stage.

Another opportunity to compose music for the theater was offered by James Arrington, son of the LDS Church historian, Leonard Arrington. James, an accomplished local actor, was writing a one-man show based on the life and letters of Mormon prophet Brigham Young. The requirements were rather different from those of my work with Carol Lynn, involving incidental music only, without songs or texts. I composed and recorded an original fanfare and several arrangements of early Mormon hymns and folk tunes for brass quintet. *Here's Brother Brigham* achieved remarkable success in the LDS community.

The closest I ever came to holding a nine-to-five job was working part-time with LDS music publisher Sonos Music as a music typist. In those precomputer days, the music had to be laid out by hand, typed on a music typewriter equipped with musical notation instead of the alphabet, and inked, again by hand, prior to publishing. Errors were difficult to correct. It was painstaking, detailed work but highly instructive for an enterprising young composer. The atmosphere was lightened considerably by the omnipresence of good music issuing from the office stereo. Tastes were eclectic among the employees, but they all favored quality, whatever the style.

It was a co-worker at Sonos who introduced me to Vaughn-Williams' *Five Mystical Songs,* a work that has since become one of the most important influences in my musical and spiritual life. The music is elegant and soulful, flavored with the loamy richness of English folk song, as is the same composer's *Symphony No. 5.* The five texts are poems by the English Renaissance poet George Herbert. They are replete with memorable images, but none more than those of the third song, which awakened a yearning deep within my heart, though I didn't then fully understand why.

> Love bade me welcome; yet my soul drew back,
>   Guilty of dust and sin.
> But quick-eyed Love, observing me grow slack
>   From my first entrance in,
> Drew nearer to me, sweetly questioning
>   If I lacked anything.
>
> 'A guest,' I answered, 'worthy to be here.'
>   Love said, 'You shall be he.'
> 'I, the unkind, ungrateful? Ah, my dear,
>   I cannot look on thee.'
> Love took my hand, and smiling did reply,
>   'Who made the eyes but I?'
>
> 'Truth, Lord, but I have marred them; let my shame
>   Go where it doth deserve.'
> 'And know you not,' says Love, 'who bore the blame?'
>   'My dear, then I will serve.'
> 'You must sit down,' says Love, 'and taste my meat,
>   So I did sit and eat.[2]

I found my secret thoughts laid bare in these words, revealed as excuses, subtle ways of resisting God; but serving God was the only ground I knew on which to build my relationship with Him. I had been taught that proving worthy was the path to His approval, and failure to do well resulted in the withdrawal of His Spirit; yet in the deep places of my heart, I felt so weary of striving and ached to hear those words, "you must sit down."

Another composer who had a profound impact on me at this time was Samuel Barber. I loved *Adagio for Strings* and *Hermit Songs,* but it was *Knoxville: Summer of 1915* that spoke to me most deeply through the combination of Barber's eloquent lyricism and James Agee's poignant, unflinching text. Where the *Five Mystical Songs* broke my heart with respect to my relationship with God, *Knoxville* did so with respect to my family. I, too, was "one familiar and well-beloved" in my home, but I wept at Agee's declaration that, despite their care for me, my loved ones "will not ever tell me who I am."[3] I knew the truth of those words deep in the core of my being. There are some truths that can only be discovered alone.

During this period I was also introduced to Leonard Bernstein's *Chichester Psalms*. From these I learned that the music of faith didn't always have to be "reverent." Full of angular rhythms, brimming with life and passion, the *Chichester Psalms* painted an aural picture of the sort of muscular faith that I wanted—not a dead, routine faith, but a faith full of surprise and motion. For similar reasons, I began to appreciate Beethoven's fifth, seventh, and ninth symphonies on a deeper level. I felt that I could hear the angry voice of Beethoven speaking directly to me through them. I also discovered Aaron Copland's dance music, especially *Appalachian Spring*, Ravel's *String Quartet in F,* and Bela Bartok's *Concerto for Orchestra*. I loved these twentieth-century works and was fascinated by their counterpoint, brilliant coloration, and subtle dissonances. As a freshman in college, I hadn't been ready to appreciate how important dissonance was as part of the musical vocabulary. Now I began to understand it and crave contemporary works incorporating it, often to the exclusion of other earlier works.

The first concert work I composed following my return from Italy reflects this new-won sensibility—a song cycle based on five sonnets by the twentieth-century American poet e e cummings. I wrote them for my mother, whose voice is the instrument I know best in all the world. I think the sound of her singing must have entered my soul while I was still in her womb, and I believe that if there is anything lyrical or heartfelt about my music, I owe a great part of it to my mother's voice. To my great surprise and delight, the cummings cycle won second prize and $200 in the classical division of the Utah Composers Guild contest in 1976. It was a real feather in my cap and served as a great encouragement as well as a confirmation of my vocation as a composer.

The combination of these listening and composing experiences engendered within me an abiding love for the marriage of music and text. I most enjoyed the work of poets who created a visceral rhythm with their language. The poetry of Gerard Manley Hopkins, for example, began to exert a powerful influence on me in this regard. I liked the challenge of setting such poems to music that would preserve the natural spoken rhythms of the words and reveal underlying meanings through dramatic shading and color, the tension between consonance and dissonance, counterpoint, and other musical techniques. The early days of our marriage marked the beginning of my inevitable pull toward the composition of large-scale choral works, a genre that now looms large in my oeuvre.

I was also simultaneously engaged with popular culture on many fronts. I listened to Jackson Browne, Tower of Power, and Oregon (a breakoff from the Paul Winter Consort); discovered the Broadway musicals *A Chorus Line* and Stephen Sondheim's *Company;* and read Ursula LeGuin's *Earthsea* trilogy and Richard Adams' *Watership Down.* Important films of the period for me were *A Man for All Seasons* and Stanley Kubrick's *Barry Lyndon,* mostly for its evocative Irish soundtrack performed by the Chieftains. On television LeAnn and I watched Ingmar Bergman's devastating series, *Scenes from a Marriage,* and rarely missed an episode of *Monty Python's Flying Circus.*

In general, the mundane details of our life as young marrieds in Orem unfolded just as they did for millions of others in small suburban communities across America. The logistics of shopping and banking, home and car maintenance, medical appointments, and errand running are universal and devour more time than anyone likes. Despite the slogan, "Things are happening in Orem," community life apart from the Church didn't offer a lot of stimulation. For cultural enrichment, one needed either to attend functions at BYU or drive to Salt Lake City. Our free evenings were spent most often with friends, themselves young parents, with whom we shared our new experiences with babies, our faith, and our immersion in the arts. Our special treat was eating lunch out together at Shakey's Pizza Parlor. The all-you-can-eat luncheon special cost only $2.99 in those days and was a veritable feast for a financially strapped young couple.

Relationships with our families were good, although altered, as one would expect, from the days when we lived at home. Both LeAnn's parents and my mother were closely involved in our life, and our families were frequent visitors in our home. LeAnn threw a dinner party there for her parents' twenty-fifth wedding anniversary. My dad, however, was not the sort to get involved. At this stage of my life, I began to grieve his absence as a wound and took the first steps in pursuit of a deeper relationship with him.

For my own part, I took to fathering more naturally than I could have anticipated. Jessie was an easy child to love: sweet, intelligent, and affectionate. I felt a deep satisfaction when I rocked and sang her to sleep in my arms at bedtime, or when I found her standing up in her crib in the morning, crowing with delight. Later, when she began to call me "Daddy" and toddle after me while I worked around the house, my heart was filled with joy. Of course, LeAnn and I had to adjust to the loss of freedom—we couldn't just take off and go anytime we liked anymore. Because my work as a freelance musician often required exactly that, LeAnn felt the tensions of remaining housebound. For me, the hardest thing about being a father was fearing that I might not be able to provide for my family.

Soon after Jessica was born, LeAnn was able to work again, though her choice of jobs was limited to those that allowed her to take care of the baby. She had learned to copy music, largely by copying parts for my pieces, and thus was able to get a job with a local music preparation company. It was good work because she could do it at home. Within a few months, however, we learned that she was pregnant again. At first, this was a real blow—we couldn't face the thought of months of her being ill again and the accompanying loss of income that would almost certainly result. Besides this, we were just getting used to the new challenges that being parents of one child brought into our life. How could we ever manage with two?

LeAnn's second pregnancy precipitated a serious ongoing discussion about the idea of our leaving Utah. My professional options there were limited. If I was going to make a living in music, we had to move to a place where that was a real possibility. Furthermore, I wanted to test myself in the real world, to see if I really had what it takes to make it. That meant New York City or Los Angeles. Westerners down to the bone, we couldn't imagine living in New York, so our thoughts inevitably turned to the West Coast. One of my jazz compositions for BYU had won a prize at the Orange Coast Jazz Festival, which we thought we could parlay into some opportunities. We made the move a matter of much thought and prayer.

We had essentially made up our minds and were simply waiting for the right moment when I was approached by a Mormon bandleader from Los Angeles with the offer of a job playing guitar in clubs and at LDS Church dances throughout southern California. This was the sign we had been waiting for! To secure the job, I had to leave almost immediately. I arranged for temporary lodging with some friends in La Canada, a few miles northeast of Los Angeles. LeAnn planned to stay behind with Jessica, sell our house, and then join me in California. On July 4, 1976, I stepped out the front door of our home and played the "Star Spangled Banner" on my trombone, a "swan song" for our life in Utah and, as it turned out, a farewell to the world as we had known it.

8

But 'tis a common proof,
That lowliness is young ambition's ladder..

—William Shakespeare, *Julius Caesar*[1]

Southern California in 1976 looked like the promised land to me, the land of milk and honey. It was the place I would either make my fortune or learn to settle for something considerably less than my dreams. I had heard of a few Utah musicians who had moved there before me. Some had given up after a couple of years of struggling and returned, discouraged and resigned. I believed they had simply thrown in the towel too soon. So, in an uncharacteristic burst of pragmatism, I concluded that making it in the music business was going to require a lot more time. LeAnn agreed and together we resolved to give ourselves ten years. If we weren't reasonably successful by the end of that period, I wouldn't stop composing, but I would have to find something other than music to provide for our family.

This ten-year commitment proved to be another of the watershed decisions of our life, though we didn't realize its full significance at the time. Had we known how difficult the years ahead would be, I don't know if we could have proceeded with our plan; but we were young, naive, and flexible, willing to gamble with our security and to risk stepping out into the unknown.

And a great unknown it was. We didn't know whether I would find work in films or with the record industry. Would I be an artist in my own right or play a supporting role to someone else's lead? Not having any real contacts to mine, I would have to start from scratch. We decided just to close our eyes and leap.

The band for which I had been hired to play was called the Justus Brothers and, as Manna had been in Salt Lake City, it was well established and successful in the southern California LDS community. We would be performing for Church youth dances as well as adult formals called Gold and Green Balls. There was also the promise of steady work at a club near Pasadena. I was guaranteed $200 a week, which seemed a fabulous sum to us at the time. Between this and my independent composing and arranging projects, I felt that LeAnn and I could establish a financial foothold in the Los Angeles area.

The plan looked good on paper, but soon proved to be another sharp reminder of the difference between wishes and horses. The gig at the club was a total disaster. We were awarded the contract without an audition, owing principally to the reputation of the band. This reputation, however, had been built by its former personnel. I was one of three new members. Only the bandleader remained from the earlier lineup and he turned out to be unfocused, an entrepreneur who divided his time between the band and a number of other projects. Rehearsals were irregular and inefficient, and we were woefully unprepared when work finally began at the club.

We were actually fired on opening night. Not only did we perform atrociously, but we didn't have a clue about how to behave in a club. Our jokes were too corny, our breaks were too long, and we didn't hobnob appropriately with the clientele. My $200 a week quickly evaporated in the low-hanging smoke and smell of stale beer. I was disappointed—this was a genuine setback—but I was also a little relieved at escaping the oppressive atmosphere.

The Justus Brothers continued to play Church dances every weekend, however. That brought in a little money and gave me a crash course in the geography of my new environment. After a few months of this routine, the bandleader announced that we would be expected to participate in some combination dance and "fireside" gigs. A fireside is an informal social gathering of Mormons in a home or at the church, usually featuring a special speaker who addresses the group on a topic of particular interest to the LDS community. Given the fascination people had for anyone even peripherally involved in the entertainment business, the bandleader felt that he could make package deals for a combination Saturday night dance and Sunday evening fireside at which we would speak and give our testimonies.

I felt intensely uncomfortable with the idea, despite the fact that I had taken part in similar gigs with Free Agency. This seemed different to me somehow. In part, it was the contrast of musical styles: to my mind, our versions of "top forty" songs were less conducive to testimony bearing than Free Agency's original, spiritually rooted rock anthems. Beyond this, though, the ethics seemed blurred—I felt I was being asked to market my testimony for the Justus Brothers, converting it into a commodity. Moreover, I didn't share the bandleader's particular way of looking at Mormonism and didn't want to endorse it.

When I told him I wouldn't participate in the firesides, he told me he would dock my pay and suggested that my testimony must be in trouble. That tore it for me. Under these circumstances, I couldn't continue working regularly with the band. I left the Justus Brothers within a few months of my hiring, although I still occasionally accepted calls from the band to fill in on a per-gig basis.

In the meantime, LeAnn had been able to sell our Orem house within two weeks, and she and Jessie joined me in southern California in mid-August. The family with whom I was living had graciously offered to allow all three of us to stay there until we found a place of our own. We planned to rent a house or apartment. Afterward, I would return to Orem, load our things into a truck, and drive back to Los Angeles. Once again, this proved easier to plan than it was to carry out.

We had hoped to find a house for between $250 and $300 a month, arriving at this dubious figure by adding thirty percent to our Orem house payment; but we couldn't find a chicken coop that fell within these parameters! Some of the houses we visited were positively terrifying. One was so close to the freeway that bottles and other trash jettisoned by passing motorists had formed a small museum of urban detritus in the backyard. The rooms of that house were so small that we couldn't imagine getting our bodies to fit in them, let alone our furniture. Things were very discouraging, to say the least.

Finally, after weeks of scouring the classified ads, we came across a house in Whittier. It was more expensive than we had budgeted, and farther from Los Angeles, but it was roughly the right size. I had heard of Whittier before—Newell Dayley had lived there and had spoken well of it. That was enough for us. We immediately called and set up an appointment with the owners.

The home was clean and well kept. A unique feature was the owners' dichondra lawn, a delicate variety of grass that they cherished and nurtured like a pet. They were asking $350 a month. We didn't know how we were going to come up with that much money, but, taking a deep breath, LeAnn and I agreed to their terms. Shortly thereafter, I returned to Orem, where my brother Rick and I packed all our belongings into a U-Haul. Together we drove without air conditioning through the sweltering desert to my new home.

For me, this drive was a pioneer journey of sorts. The last of my life in Utah was now tightly crammed into the back of the truck behind us, the contemporary equivalent of the Mormon handcart. There was no going back. The road stretched out beyond the vanishing point before me, not just the road to California, but the road into my future. I have driven that stretch a hundred times since and never once have I failed to feel an odd sense of suspension, of anticipation, as if anything could happen to me there. I marvel at the harsh beauty of the desert and the hardy eccentrics who populate it, clinging to the surface of this patch of earth like sage clings to sand or rock, without visible means of support. At night the sky is enormous and vibrant with stars that can't shine past the streetlights of our cities. The desert solitude is palpable and grand. It is during these drives that I feel most quintessentially a son of the American West.

Not long after we settled, LeAnn gave birth to our second daughter, Jerusha Ann. LeAnn's second pregnancy was considerably easier than her first, but it lasted longer. When it had stretched two weeks beyond her due date, the doctor recommended that LeAnn's labor be induced. So on the morning of November 8, 1976, we checked into Whittier Presbyterian Intercommunity Hospital, and LeAnn was set up with an intravenous pitocin drip. Nothing happened. We talked and read to each other. Still nothing. We played a complete game of Scrabble. Then cards. After several hours, there was still no imminent sign of a baby, so I left LeAnn and walked across the street to get a bite to eat at Marie Callendar's.

No sooner had my order arrived than the phone rang and someone called out, "Is there a J.A.C. Redford here? Your wife's having the baby!" Leaving my food, I dashed across the street and arrived just in time to don my hospital garb and see Jerusha born. Whatever anxiety we felt about becoming parents again melted in the joy of seeing our healthy and beautiful new baby girl. LeAnn and I were twenty-three years old. We felt like veterans. And now we were four.

The next few years were the career-building equivalent of climbing a sheer rock face, supported only by a jerry-rigged system of ropes and grommets. The basic landscape looked much the same as it had in Utah: I was playing for various bands and singers, arranging demos for hopeful songwriters, and scoring the occasional documentary or educational film through the contacts that I still maintained there. I taught another week for the NEA's Artists in Schools program, this time at Cedar City High School in southern Utah, and wrote a second musical with Carol Lynn, based on the Grimm fairy tales. Although there were more opportunities in California, the cost of living was higher, and we were barely able to make ends meet. Among musicians, this sort of thing is called "paying your dues."

The bands I worked with throughout this period were mostly LDS groups, plugged into the reliable Mormon youth dance circuit. I was a founding member of one of these, called Sportin' Life, formed some months after I left the Justus Brothers. The star of the group was our lead guitarist, Jon Woodhead, whose credits included work with Leon Russell and a band called Ace. I played a Fender Rhodes electric piano and rhythm guitar, and sang songs as diverse as "Disco Inferno" and "The Sultans of Swing."

Sportin' Life's calendar was somewhat haphazard, not unusual for a new group, and eventually I left them to play bass and sing with a band called Hourglass. Well-managed and well-connected, Hourglass could generally provide me with a couple of hundred dollars a week.

I loved playing rock 'n' roll. It was fun and physical, my only real form of exercise. The music wasn't difficult and I liked working the audience with stunts, like leaping from the drum riser and landing on the stage precisely on a big downbeat. On the negative side, I was away from home every Friday and Saturday night from five or six o'clock in the evening until about three in the morning. This took a toll on our marriage: LeAnn and I didn't have many special evenings out together while I was performing regularly. The schedule also left me exhausted, and it became harder and harder to get up and go to church on Sunday morning.

While all of this was going on, I kept trying to find ways to break into the record business. Songwriting was one avenue, and, since music was my strong suit, I looked for opportunities to collaborate with lyricists. I accompanied one chanteuse who premiered three of my songs at McCabe's, the famed Santa Monica guitar shop. It didn't turn out quite as we had hoped, however. McCabe's is a t-shirt and jeans sort of venue, and the singer emulated Streisand, appearing in a long black gown and pearls. Needless to say, her performance was not well received. She broke down in tears afterward. She had focused so much on getting her big break that she failed to recognize how inappropriate the setting was for her.

This story is almost archetypal in Los Angeles. The city is filled with hungry dreamers, each one hoping to be the next hot ticket, all trying to climb to the top of a heap, most without any clear idea of what the heap is and where the ladder lies. In my own way, I was one of them. It was hard sometimes to imagine how I would ever rise out of that milieu and achieve anything of real value.

The world of film and television music was a world unto itself, governed by its own laws and populated by its own characters. Producers and directors shopped for composers as consumers shop for automobiles, labeling and categorizing them according to function and style. The composers ran the gamut from battle-hardened veterans of proven abilities to untested unknowns like myself, from solid craftsmen who had labored for years and achieved modest success to golden boys with star quality who shot immediately to the top of the game. Agents acted as liaisons between the composers and the producers, trafficking in cassettes and persuasion. Credits and connections were money in the bank. Deals went down continuously by phone, during lunches, and at parties. An army of orchestrators, copyists, music editors, and other support personnel served in the trenches to help the composers accomplish the herculean task of preparing hours of music for recording, and a body of world class musicians—deep enough to staff several fine orchestras simultaneously—performed daily on sound stages and in recording studios to bring their scores to life. The musicians' union jockeyed for advantage and the performance rights organizations, ASCAP and BMI, kept composer royalties flowing in once their work hit the airwaves. Egos inflated and values deflated in the mad scramble for a golden statuette. Through it all, a perpetual Hollywood buzz elevated the hot and debased the not with unquestioned authority.

I developed a strategy for making some inroads into the film and television business. I took arranging classes at the Dick Grove School of Music and studied orchestration privately with Albert Harris. I joined the union and cultivated a relationship with the west coast representatives of ASCAP, Michael Gorfaine and Sam Schwartz, who were later to play a crucial role in the development of my career. I knew that many composers had gotten their start in television, so I began there, watching a lot of TV programs and noting the names of those who scored them. I listened carefully to their work, trying to absorb the craft through observation. Some I telephoned, explaining that I was a young composer trying to break into the business and asking to meet with them. I wanted to be disabused of my illusions and learn the lay of the land from those who had been there before me. The most fruitful of these calls was to Bruce Broughton, a composer whose scores I greatly admired. He became a mentor and friend, willing to set aside his own time to talk and study scores with me. I will always be grateful for his help.

Another of those who agreed to meet with me was Lalo Schifrin, composer of the *Mission Impossible* theme. I played a tape for him containing my e e cummings song cycle and selected cues from my documentary scores. He was very encouraging as well. Just before I left, he said, "The ones who make it in this business are not necessarily the most talented, or even the best connected. The ones who make it are the ones who learn to endure." This bit of wisdom has since sustained me through many arduous writing marathons.

My first big break came about by sheer serendipity. On one of my occasional trips back to Salt Lake City, I spent an afternoon with composer and conductor James Prigmore, a friend of the family and a professor at the University of Utah. Jim had been commuting several times a year to Los Angeles to score episodes of the television series *Starsky and Hutch*. He said that he was growing tired of the increasing demands the producers were making on him, particularly in the area of style. They wanted his music to sound more like popular music, to be "funkier." Jim's forte was opera and symphonic music; funky was not in his musical vocabulary. He knew that my experience had included both rock 'n' roll and orchestral work. That afternoon, out of the blue, he asked me if I would be willing to collaborate with him and his partner, Murray MacLeod, to inject a note of "funkiness" into their scores for *Starsky and Hutch.*

My first effort for Jim and Murray in the fall of 1976 involved the orchestration of their cues, the term used to describe the segments of music in a film. As orchestrator, my job was to flesh out the sketch, which was written on two staves like piano music, for all the instruments of the small orchestra we had hired. In most cases the instrumental assignments were already indicated in the sketch, though in some I had to make creative decisions of my own. In addition, I was asked to compose a few source cues, that is, music that proceeds from a source visible on the screen, such as a radio or a marching band.

This job was my first experience with a Hollywood deadline. In practical terms, this meant finishing the score no matter how late I had to stay up, whether I was inspired or not. The principal difference between this deadline and the ones I had faced before was that the stakes were higher. "Screw this up," as the aphorism goes, "and you'll never work in this town again!" The score was a success, however, and soon we were offered another episode.

Before the writing began, Murray and I were called into the office of one of the producers of *Starsky and Hutch.* He wanted to explain to us how he wanted a particular scene treated. He sat behind his desk, searching for the right words to communicate what he was looking for. "I think this scene needs . . . ," he ruminated aloud, ". . . a tenor sax!" Bingo! Having now scored the scene, at least in his own mind, he leaned back in his chair, put his hands behind his head and his feet on the desk, and dismissed us to what little work he apparently thought we had left. It remained for us to decipher what mood had taken him on that fateful night when, in the corner of some dark, ash-acrid watering hole, with a few drinks behind him, he heard the tenor sax that defined the moment in this week's episode—because, of course, it was that feeling he really wanted in the scene, not just the presence of a generic "tenor sax."

For this episode, I composed several dramatic cues of my own and was asked to conduct them at the recording session. The first time I stood in front of an orchestra in Los Angeles, I was terrified. I had requested musicians whose names were familiar to me from credits on the backs of albums I admired: Victor Feldman was there, keyboard and percussionist extraordinaire from Steely Dan's *Asia*, as was Max Bennett, bassist for the L.A. Express, the band that had accompanied Joni Mitchell on *Miles of Aisles*, along with several other notable Los Angeles session men. I felt completely intimidated.

Furthermore, we were working at a recording studio where the orchestra set-up was rather awkward. The conductor's podium seemed to stand half a football field away from the musicians. They were all surrounded by "baffles," soundproof screens with plastic windows allowing them to see, while at the same time preventing the sounds of their instruments from "bleeding" into each other's microphones. This enabled the music engineer to mix the overall balance of the instruments in the control room. It also meant that none of them could hear me unless I was yelling at the top of my lungs. I was simply not prepared to holler at my heroes and when I gave my first downbeat, nobody played. In fact, the musicians were still talking amongst themselves and hadn't even noticed that I was starting the cue.

I recognized a watershed moment unfolding. I felt that I had two options: (a) I could run screaming from the room, hurl myself through the window to the ground below, and end the humiliation then and there, or (b) I could grit my teeth and continue the session. There were bars across the windows at this particular studio, no doubt to prevent such eventualities, so I opted for (b).

Surprisingly, the session finished smoothly. The musicians were gracious, helpful, and encouraging and actually seemed to enjoy playing a few of the more challenging cues. My great-great grandfather had once written that "great men are courteous and can often be reached easier than half-great men."[2] Some of the finest musicians in Los Angeles taught me the truth of these words that day. And thus began my association with the musicians of Los Angeles, a wonderful group of extraordinarily gifted instrumentalists who continue to surprise and impress me each time it is my privilege to work with them.

On the heels of *Starsky and Hutch*, Murray and I worked on another series called *James at 15*. Jim Prigmore had opted out, owing again to the emphasis on popular music. We were to score the first episode on Tuesday after Thanksgiving in 1977. LeAnn and I, along with our girls, spent the holiday with her parents in Utah and drove home that night. As soon as we returned, I fell into bed for a nap. I woke up with a sharp pain in my abdomen. It soon became so unbearable that LeAnn had to drive me to the emergency room. The doctor on call diagnosed appendicitis and an emergency appendectomy was scheduled immediately. This was a terrible blow—I couldn't afford to lose the work. Somehow I had to finish the score on time. Fortunately, the surgery was successful, and I ended up composing cues in my bed afterward. I checked out of the hospital on Monday and recorded the score on Tuesday, according to plan.

James at 15 was my first steady television gig. Murray and I composed a second score for the show before it fulfilled its partial season commitment of six episodes, after which it was renewed for another six and rechristened *James at 16*. We continued working on the series until it was canceled after the second set of episodes. Following this, Murray and I were hired to score a vile little car chase movie called *Stingray,* my first feature film. As awful as this movie was, it was still a rush to see my credit flash across the big screen. I hoped it revealed the shape of things to come.

By the spring of 1978, LeAnn and I were ready to look for a home of our own. Our landlords had been deeply disappointed by our failure to care adequately for their pet lawn. Dichondra wasn't at all like the grass we had grown up with: Utah lawns never had to be watered in the winter, for one thing. Within a few months, the dichondra had died, and we had replaced it with a hardier variety of grass. Nevertheless, the owners stepped up surveillance on their investment as a result. At one point, a colony of bees built a hive in the rafters of the house. One afternoon, we found one of the owners spraying some kind of insecticide, without informing us, into the walls just outside the bedroom in which our children were taking their naps. This incident provoked a confrontation that confirmed for us that it was time to move.

With a few credits garnishing my resume, things were looking up. It appeared that we would now be able to afford the monthly obligations of home ownership. The only problem was that we couldn't come up with a down payment. The money we had made on the sale of our home in Orem had been used to pay off debts, and we hadn't been able to save anything since. In an extraordinary expression of generosity, my partner Murray and his wife, television personality

Stephanie Edwards, loaned us enough to buy a home that LeAnn and I found on the east side of Whittier. In April we moved in.

Soon afterward, I was contracted to orchestrate the songs from *Saturday's Warrior*, a stage musical that had been composed by Lex de Azevedo, of King Family fame. A dramatization of the struggles of a teenage boy in an LDS family, the show struck a nerve in the Mormon community and achieved enormous monetary success. The original cast recording had been made with a small instrumental ensemble. I was asked to create a fully orchestrated version, including chorus and soloists, which was to be recorded in London. English orchestras are popular with producers of lower-budget projects because, while costs per musician are less than those set by the American Federation of Musicians, the quality of the performances remains uncompromised.

LeAnn was also slated to go along on the trip in order to read score for the recording engineer while I conducted. Her task was to cue him at the entrances of the various instruments so he could balance them properly as they were being recorded. The girls would stay with LeAnn's parents. We looked forward with great anticipation to our first trip to the land of Vaughn-Williams and Monty Python, and we were not disappointed. For lodgings, Murray had referred us to a woman in Hammersmith, on the outskirts of London, under the mistaken impression that she ran a bed and breakfast. She didn't. We didn't discover this until after we arrived, however, because when we called ahead to ask if we could stay with her, she simply answered, "Yes." She was a delightful eccentric of decidedly English character, a birdwatcher who gave us a bed in her guest room and grilled tomatoes for breakfast.

We recorded at the venerable Pye Studios near the Marble Arch. The recording sessions went exceptionally well and the English musicians performed magnificently. With this experience, my confidence soared. If I could lead an orchestra successfully this far from home, I felt I could do it anywhere.

LeAnn and I were able to carve out time for a little sightseeing once the sessions were concluded. One afternoon we took a train out to Stratford upon Avon on a pilgrimage to Shakespeare's childhood home. On the way back to London, we found a copy of the *Herald Tribune* lying open between the seats. Our eyes were immediately drawn to an article announcing that the Mormon Church had just extended the priesthood to African Americans.

This news was both a shock and a great relief. For years Mormonism had maintained that African Americans could not hold the priesthood. The doctrine was grounded in Mormon scripture.[3] One LDS General Authority, Bruce R. McConkie, had gone so far as to say that "the gospel message of salvation is not carried affirmatively to them."[4] Many Mormons, including us, had been severely distressed by this position and craved the day it would change, though few expected it would happen in their lifetime. Now it was a reality, and LeAnn and I were thrilled, barely noticing the slight tug of perplexity we felt at the reversal of such a long-standing Church doctrine. Was it no longer true, or had times changed? Elder McConkie was unfazed and unapologetic, saying, "It doesn't make a particle of difference what anybody ever said about the Negro matter before the first day of June of this year."[5]

With all of my emphasis on career building in the late seventies, my family continued to counterbalance the scales for me. LeAnn and I saw ourselves as a team: my career belonged to both of us, and together we worked hard to advance it. This unified focus created both benefits and tensions in our marriage, but either way, our relationship definitely occupied center stage. Jessica and Jerusha were delightful children and they owned their daddy's heart. Jessie was already showing signs of a fine, analytical intelligence and Rusha, equally bright, was our free spirit, never walking anywhere when she could skip or dance. I loved playing Irish music on the stereo and improvising makeshift jigs with my girls all around the living room.

Between junkets for work, holidays, and vacations, we were often in Utah, visiting our greater family. Changes were occurring there as well. Poppie and Grandma were growing older and Poppie's health was failing. Every visit with him was treasured since it might be the last. As my brother Rick became a young man, Mom had greater freedom to pursue her passion for singing. While he was still in high school, she toured with the Roger Wagner Chorale, occasionally appearing as a soloist. After Rick graduated, Mom moved out of our family home and into a condo located in the small community of Centreville, north of Salt Lake City. Rick spent a couple of semesters at BYU before being called on a mission to Alberta, Canada, in May 1978.

Early in 1979, we learned that LeAnn was pregnant again. As we geared up for another new addition, however, we suffered a tragic loss: Poppie died on March 21. His death was not entirely unexpected, since he had been gravely ill for some time; but no matter how much one prepares for such events, it is never quite enough to staunch the flood of grief. Poppie was the cornerstone of our family and I loved him very much. We would all miss him terribly. One of the greatest regrets of my life is that I couldn't go to his funeral— I was desperately trying to meet another deadline at the time. My friend and collaborator, Carol Lynn Pearson, once wrote: "this world has more of coming and going than I can bear."[6] This seemed especially true for our family that year.

Chief among the comings was our son, Jonathan Thomas, who was born on October 19, seven months after Poppie's death. He was a breech baby, but was not delivered by Caesarean. He leapt into the world feet first, like a parachutist. The doctor held him up high as evidence to all that he was indeed a manchild. We cheered and later the family made jokes about Poppie and Jonathan somehow passing each other along the way, Poppie heaven-bound, Jonathan approaching this vale of tears.

Another notable coming occurred between Poppie's death and Jonathan's birth. On one of my mother's singing engagements in northern California, she was introduced to a suave and dashing widower by the name of Jack Dawson. They fell deeply in love and were married in September. Mom glowed with happiness and the family was thrilled with the match. Jack had two children of his own, a daughter and a son, who were added to our circle. From the beginning, he treated Rick and me as if we were his own children. I have never met a more generous, big-hearted man. Mom packed up her things again and moved into his spacious home in Los Altos Hills, south of San Francisco.

LeAnn and I soon faced new challenges as our children grew old enough to begin their formal education. We had vowed to provide them with a better education than we had received. All three of them were curious and eager to learn, and we were concerned that they not have the love of learning "educated" right out of them. Choosing a school became a major preoccupation for us. After a great deal of research, we finally settled on a nearby Montessori school with a philosophy of learning we could support and several excellent, nurturing teachers.

Meanwhile, Murray and I continued to work together, scoring television episodes and pilots and whatever else we could scare up. We had an agent working for us as well. Late in 1979, I felt the need to pursue further formal musical training. School was not an option, so I made connections with a private teacher named Harold V. Johnson and began lessons. This was soon to prove a fortuitous decision.

In 1980, the American Federation of Musicians called a strike that resulted in a virtual shutdown of film and television recording in America. At the time, it seemed like a disaster. Many producers took their business overseas or found other more imaginative means of making up for the loss. The strike seriously damaged the industry and was the biggest test of our resolve to stick it out in the music business for ten years. At one point, LeAnn and I had to sell all the living room furniture that my grandmother had given us just to pay one month's bills. The possibility of our going under was very real. We would have done so, had not my mother and new stepfather graciously supported us throughout the year of the strike.

I used the down time to focus on my private studies, turning a season that began with despair into one of the most fruitful of my life, preparing me as nothing else could have for the level of work that lay ahead, just beyond the sight line. My experience so far in the film scoring business had shown me that I needed to improve my craft significantly. Although I was already a professional, I had to be able to work faster, and I needed deeper resources of technique upon which to draw when inspiration flagged. Beethoven once remarked that in his early works, one could tell where the inspiration left off and the craft took over, but that in his later works it was impossible to tell. In practical terms, I needed that kind of skill in order to survive.

I also needed something else: to deepen my roots as an artist. This was really a question of content. I was acutely aware of the gap between what I wanted to say and what I was able to say with my music. I simply lacked the vocabulary. I knew, however, that the answer lay in further study of harmony and counterpoint, the basic intellectual disciplines of music—and that meant studying Bach. The works of J.S. Bach are the composer's Bible. Virtually anything one needs to know about composition, at least in the context of Western civilization, can be found there, executed with the highest degree of quality.

Throughout the months of the strike, I took three sets of lessons, all scheduled on Monday so I would only be required to commute to Los Angeles once a week. The first of these were my composition lessons with Hal Johnson. Hal was a composer who had a firm grasp of counterpoint and a clear method for teaching it, but who also had worked in the film business and understood its particular demands. Together we went through the Bach two- and three-part inventions, chorale preludes, and fugues. My assignments were to write my own pieces in imitation of the forms we were studying. As I did, certain musical elements began to rub off on me, both consciously and unconsciously. My music began to change, although at first my gains were subtle. Ideas sprang more quickly to mind and, when they did, they were more transparent, easier to transcribe, and more sophisticated, lending themselves with greater facility for development. I found that I feared the blank page less.

Following my lesson with Hal, I had a conducting lesson with Frederick Zweig. Now in his eighties, Zweig had been an apprentice of the great European conductor Bruno Walter before fleeing Germany at the outbreak of World War II. What an amazing man he was! There was no conducting to recordings with him; he insisted on playing every score at the piano, including extremely difficult twentieth-century works such as Stravinsky's *Soldier's Tale.* We studied Haydn's *Symphony No. 104,* portions of Mozart's *The Magic Flute,* Mendelssohn's *Hebrides Overture,* and the fourth symphonies of Beethoven and Schumann. He taught me the transpositions of obscure instruments in Wagnerian opera scores and compelled me to sight-read Bach chorales in four different clefs, regardless of the fact that I wasn't a pianist. It was an extraordinary privilege to be taught by one who embodied the living legacy of the great nineteenth-century masters. I knew I would never absorb a hundredth part of what he knew, but my music was forever changed by my work with him.

My third set of lessons was a Monday evening master class in the art of film composition, offered through the UCLA extension program. Walter Scharf was the teacher, a film composer one generation removed from those who invented the genre. A legendary figure, he had actually composed the "Burning of Atlanta" sequence in *Gone with the Wind.* Apparently Max Steiner, faced with what originally amounted to over forty reels of film to score, farmed out scenes to just about every composer in town. Max's style was so well known that there was no problem maintaining continuity. Walter was one of the young guns who got a shot at a few reels. Here was another unique opportunity to learn from a master. From Walter, I received a sense of the legacy of film composition, confirming my belief in the integrity of the art form and the necessity of never abandoning the quest for excellence in every detail. He never allowed me to settle for second-best in my writing assignments.

Perhaps the most important contribution he made to my work was to wean me from the "click track," a type of metronome that aids in synchronizing music to film. While the click has its uses, especially in recording cues with quick tempi and many precise hit points, it can also render the music heartless and mechanical. Walter gave me confidence that I could conduct many scenes without the click, allowing the music greater freedom to ebb and flow, room to breathe.

Inspired by these lessons, I sought to further expand my musical vocabulary independently. My explorations covered the waterfront from Mozart's *Jupiter Symphony,* through the Mahler symphonies, to Carl Chavez's *Sinfonia India.* My love for English music grew to include Vaughn-Williams' *The Lark Ascending,* as well as his first four symphonies; Benjamin Britten's *Serenade for Tenor, Horn and Strings;* and William Walton's *Variations on a Theme by Hindemith.*

In the area of musical theater, LeAnn and I were captivated by the work of Stephen Sondheim. *A Little Night Music* and *Pacific Overtures* were among our favorites, but the most influential of Sondheim's musicals for us was *Sweeney Todd.* The music and libretto of this hybrid form of opera and musical theater were excellent, but what ultimately stuck with us was the unblinking portrait of characters completely lost and driven by their personal demons. We didn't recognize it at the time, but it was a potent illustration of the classic Christian doctrine of original sin. I suspect Sondheim didn't intend this, but even if he were a theologian, he couldn't have constructed a more powerful case for man's utter depravity.

Significant films for me during this period were Woody Allen's *Annie Hall* and *Manhattan.* I became enamored of Peter Weir's films,

The Last Wave and *Picnic at Hanging Rock,* with their uniquely Australian version of magical realism. The adventurous male panache of John Milius's *The Wind and the Lion* and John Huston's *The Man Who Would Be King* captured my imagination, as did the psychological undercurrents in Hitchcock's *Vertigo* and the rough beauty of Ireland in John Ford's *The Quiet Man.* LeAnn and I loved Louis Malle's *My Dinner with André,* and the issues it raised connected profoundly with us. It was a movie that opened up our vision of the world, making it larger and more humane.

I also threw myself into listening to as many great film scores as I could. I was introduced to the film music of Bernard Herrmann and became a great fan of his music for the classic Hitchcock films, *Psycho, Vertigo,* and *North by Northwest,* as well as *Citizen Kane, The Ghost and Mrs. Muir, The Day the Earth Stood Still, Journey to the Center of the Earth,* and *The Seventh Voyage of Sinbad.* Many other classic scores made my 'A' list, such as Hugo Friedhoffer's *The Best Years of Our Lives;* Richard Rodney Bennett's *Murder on the Orient Express* and *Nicholas and Alexandra;* Erich Korngold's *King's Row;* Miklos Rozsa's *Ben Hur, Quo Vadis,* and *Providence;* Franz Waxmans' *Hemingway's Adventures of a Young Man;* and Victor Young's *The Quiet Man.*

Two contemporary film composers whose work I admired were John Williams and Jerry Goldsmith. Jerry Goldsmith's scores for *The Wind in the Lion* and *Planet of the Apes* were highly influential, as were John Williams' scores for *Jaws, Close Encounters,* and *Star Wars.* LeAnn and I saw *Star Wars* within a few days of its opening at Mann's Chinese theater in Hollywood. The audience was a clearly an industry crowd that cheered every dissolve and wipe, every cinematic trick. What a kick!

So, in the end, inspiration and creative growth were the hallmarks of the strike season for me. As a result, I composed three new works that reflected the dynamics of these eclectic influences: *Valse Triste,* a duo for 'celli that owed its inspiration to the Bach inventions; a cinematic, Coplandesque orchestral divertimento called *October Overtures,* which was premiered by the Pasadena Chamber Orchestra the following year; and *The Dance,* an LDS-oriented musical I collaborated on with Carol Lynn Pearson.

When the strike ended, I had no trouble getting back to work. In the spring of 1981, Murray MacLeod and I were hired to score my first movie for television, *The Long Summer of George Adams* starring James Garner, and went on to resume our other activities, composing for various television pilots and episodes, among them *Fame* and *American Dream*. A contact at the Sundance Summer Theater led to my writing scores for *A Midsummer Night's Dream* and *Macbeth* at the Sherwood Shakespeare Festival in Oxnard, California. That summer, my friend, Sterling Van Wagenen, brought me on board as music consultant with Robert Redford's fledgling Sundance Film Institute. That work led to an opportunity to attend the Eugene O'Neill Theatre Center in Connecticut for an opera and musical workshop later that summer.

Murray and I were disheartened during the strike when our agent "fired" us as part of what he called a "stable cleaning," but we had the last laugh in 1981, when we were asked by one of Murray's old friends, Stuart Margolin, to write the music for James Garner's new television series, *Bret Maverick*. *Maverick* provided many interesting opportunities to combine folk-oriented acoustic guitars with Coplandesque orchestrations. The show was canceled after one season and James Garner, gentleman that he was, sent gifts and called everyone personally to thank them for their contribution to the show.

Work for the series lasted into the spring of 1982, after which I composed two more new chamber works: *Dream Dances*, a duo for violin and harp, based on themes I had written for the Sherwood Shakespeare Festival; and *Five Songs for Flute and French Horn*, a duo commissioned by two friends in Los Angeles, which they went on to record for Crystal Records. In August, I wrote the incidental music for the first West Coast production of Harold Pinter's *Betrayal* at the Matrix Theater, an equity waiver theater in Los Angeles. The director was Sam Weisman, a friend I had met at the Sherwood festival.

In 1982, I began to get offers to do film and television work on my own. Bodie Chandler, the music supervisor for Lorimar, was one of the first to show some interest in me. While I was still writing with Murray for *Bret Maverick*, Bodie hired me to score some episodes of *King's Crossing* and *Knot's Landing* on my own. By fall, I was ready to take a leap of faith and begin writing without a partner. Murray and I talked it over and parted ways amicably. We both had known it would come to this someday—that's how apprenticeship works. Still, there was a lot of emotion attached to this step for me. We had been through some great experiences together and I was deeply grateful for his help and friendship.

About this time, Mike Gorfaine and Sam Schwartz, two friends from ASCAP (the American Society of Composers, Authors, and Publishers), an organization that collects and distributes composers' performance royalties, were starting a new agency to represent film composers and expressed a desire to include me on their first client list. This turned out to be an incredible blessing.

One of my new agents' first transactions was to arrange for me to meet with the producers of a new medical series called *St. Elsewhere*. They were looking for a young, fresh face, a relative unknown who could create a unique sound for their show. I met with the associate producer first and, after getting the green light from her, was scheduled for a meeting with the creators of the show, including Bruce Paltrow, the executive producer.

I clearly remember walking into the office on the day of our appointment, and seeing them draped about the room on sofas and chairs, waiting to be "blown away." Bruce had heard that I wrote "classical" music and had asked me in advance to bring to the meeting a recording of my favorite piece among the concert or chamber works I had written. That was my cummings song cycle, but something told me that they weren't quite going to relate to that, so on side two, I included a recording of the premiere of *October Overtures* by the Pasadena Chamber Orchestra. Sure enough, after hearing the first few bars of the song cycle, Bruce stopped me and said, "That's not really what we're looking for. Do you have anything else?" I flipped the tape over and the bright rhythms and cheerful harmony of *October Overtures* filled the room.

"So you're the real thing," Bruce said, as if somewhat surprised.

"Yes, sir," I answered. I composed the scores for *St. Elsewhere* for the next six years—not without a wrinkle, however. Originally, I was slated to write the theme music as well. Finding a single melody that sustains the weight of an entire series is a tricky procedure. After several stabs at it, I finally came up with one they liked. Bruce must have had second thoughts, however, and he consulted with Arthur Price, then president of MTM, the company that produced *St. Else-*

where. "How can I be sure JAC's theme is really good?" I was later told Bruce had asked. Arthur was a friend of veteran film composer Dave Grusin. "Hire Dave to write the theme," he told Bruce, "then you'll know." So they hired Dave Grusin, who wrote an excellent theme and also scored the first episode. This experience could have been a setback for me, but it turned into a blessing. Dave and I became acquainted. He liked my music and was later instrumental in my getting other work.

St. Elsewhere made my career. It was a well-constructed, entertaining, and thought-provoking series that provided me with long-term employment and a reputation that attracted more work along the way. My relationships with the producers were good and I enjoyed working for them. I grew to love the characters as if they were members of my own family; they often seemed as real. I had many opportunities to score scenes written with wit, heart, and wisdom. *St. Elsewhere* was a textbook for cinematic compositional challenges. There were chases, love scenes, and suspense cues. I composed source music in the styles of Beethoven, Mozart, Vivaldi, and Handel, as well as rock 'n' roll, jazz, musical theater, and Christmas music. In short, my six years with the series yielded some of the finest, most satisfying experiences of my creative life. Furthermore, the financial boon was augmented by the fact that LeAnn and I were able to work together and thus to keep the orchestration money in the family: building on her copying experience, she learned to transfer my sketches to full score. For many of the recording sessions, she helped by reading score in the booth.

The capstone of these successful years was 1983. I composed a ballet for children, *Clementina's Cactus,* which was premiered in New York and performed at the Kennedy Center the following year as part of the "Imagination Celebration" (the National Festival of Children's Arts). I wrote incidental music for two more plays at the Matrix, Percy Granger's *Eminent Domain* and the world premiere of Lyle Kessler's *Orphans;* a couple of TV movies, including *Helen Keller: The Miracle Continues;* and several episodes of television series in addition to *St. Elsewhere.*

No matter how successful I became, however, no matter how many wonderful discoveries or peak experiences I chalked up, my struggles with depression would not go away. Feelings of guilt and despair sometimes became unbearable, and bouts with depression could last for days. Gradually, I came to realize that I was severely damaging myself and LeAnn and I felt that I had no right to do this. So one day I decided, "I'm going crazy and I don't really have to! I can be happy. I just need to let go and stop worrying about things so much!" By a sheer act of will, I made a conscious decision to adopt this attitude, and it really seemed to work, just as a similar way of looking at things had worked for a short time during my mission. This time, however, the inoculation seemed to take. I convinced myself that moderation and a healthy acceptance of ambiguity was the secret to a mature outlook. To the degree that I was successful in thinking this way, I found that I was able to take myself, including my faith, less seriously.

Nevertheless, I felt exhausted. I tried to give one hundred percent to all of my jobs, but it was impossible. I felt like a circus performer who frequently appeared on the Ed Sullivan Show. His talent was to set plates spinning on large dowels. He'd start with one, then add another, then another. Within moments he had a stageful. Once this was achieved, he spent the remainder of his time running back and forth from plate to plate to keep them all going. By the end of his act, he was rampaging all over the stage. That is how I felt.

Perhaps I should have paid closer attention to these warning signs, taken them *more* seriously, and been less willing to rationalize my way out of them. Somewhere inside I was aware that my success had a dark side. Music had become a kind of idol to me. The more involved I became in my music, the more it took me over, filling the abyss that with increasing frequency seemed to open up beneath me.

With so much emphasis on film at this stage of my life, it is not surprising that powerful images from four films broke through and challenged my thinking in ways I couldn't ignore. One of these was *Jesus of Nazareth*. The scene that held the most potency for me was that in which Jesus sits at dinner in Matthew's house among the publicans and prostitutes, telling the story of the prodigal son. Peter is listening outside the door because he won't defile himself by entering the home of a tax collector. As the weight of the story settles on Peter, he wrestles in the doorway with the implications, finally bolting in terror and seeking safety in the comfortable familiarity of his boat. But there is no security for him there any longer. Though he doesn't yet know it, the words of Jesus have already made the backward glance impossible. The struggle is visible on his face. Finally, he returns to Matthew's house and staggers across the threshold, leaving his old life behind. The first time I watched that scene, I wept like a child. Instinctively, I sensed there would be a threshold that I would have to cross someday, an old life that I would have to leave behind for a new one.

Another film that challenged my thinking was Horton Foote's *Tender Mercies*, a beautiful parable of the healing grace of Christ in a man's life. The baptism of Mac Sledge was profoundly moving to me. There was something simple and genuine about it that I couldn't resist. As a Mormon, I had been taught that only Mormon baptisms were performed with the authority of God, and that all other baptisms were invalid. I had never seen a Christian baptism, but the image in my mind was of a hollow, impotent ritual. The straightforward depiction of the baptism in *Tender Mercies*, reflective of a true change of heart, made my LDS assumptions seem arrogant and shallow.

A third influential film was the documentary about the history of gospel music, *Say Amen, Somebody*. Full of life and joy, the faith of its subjects was infectious. In some respects, I envied them the palpable passion that they felt for their God. When our daughter Jessica was baptized in the LDS Church in 1983, LeAnn and I played the soundtrack to *Say Amen, Somebody* at the open house afterward, raising a few eyebrows among our Mormon friends, especially the bishop.

Finally, there was *Gandhi*. After seeing this picture, LeAnn and I sat in our car talking and crying. *Gandhi* reminded me that in my search for relief from my chronic despair, I had lost the sense of something central in my life that was worth dying—or living—for. I missed that depth of dedication. That night, LeAnn and I vowed to recover it, whatever the cost.

These four films all spoke to a gnawing hunger that was in the center of my soul. I couldn't put a name to that hunger, but I knew it was there and I also knew that someday I would have to reckon with it.

Things fall apart; the centre cannot hold;
Mere anarchy is loosed upon the world,
The blood-dimmed tide is loosed, and everywhere
The ceremony of innocence is drowned.

—W.B. Yeats, "The Second Coming"[1]

The emotional tensions that accompanied the growth of my career between 1976 and 1984 were symptomatic of a deeper reality. A gradual dissembling of my Mormon worldview was taking place. I was not aware of it at first, and probably would have denied it vigorously if pressed, but it was happening nonetheless, with an inevitable momentum. If I couldn't consciously admit it, even to myself, I certainly sensed along the way that I was losing my passion for my faith. That was the price of the treaty I had made with my despair.

Music rushed in to fill the vacuum, with all its ancillary ambitions and activities, influences and experiences. Nevertheless, while music is a wonderful gift, it makes a very poor god. It can sing of redemption, but it can't provide it. Despite all that I had invested in my art, there was still a hollow place inside of me that wouldn't be filled. In the midst of my success, I felt out of sync with life. The inner turmoil resulting from this dilemma fueled the tensions I experienced throughout those years. Boiled down to their simplest expression, the stresses coalesced in an aching hole in the pit of my stomach.

Mormonism was ill equipped to handle the powerful, visceral challenge of my growing anxiety. After all, my feelings were supposed to be the medium through which I would receive personal revelation, the manifestation of God's will in my life. It is axiomatic among the Latter-day Saints that the Holy Ghost speaks to the heart through a "burning in the bosom." What was I to make of the continuing sense of emptiness I felt? In the rigid terms of my faith, I could only conclude that I must have failed in some significant way and grieved the Holy Ghost. The diagnosis was unworthiness and the prescription was to try harder. Consequently, Mormonism not only failed to assuage my pain and answer the central nagging questions of my life, but it provided further grist for despair in my failure to measure up. I sometimes felt like a hapless insect under the hot glass of a wanton boy. So are we to the gods, I thought in my darkest moments—"they kill us for their sport."[2]

The emotional terrain was not the only ground on which my worldview was challenged, however. During this period of my life, I felt the heat of battle on virtually every other front. Intellectually, I was assaulted by information that cast doubt on the veracity of the Church's history and scriptures. Morally, I was deeply disturbed to learn of the occultism and exploitative sexual practices of early Church leaders. Spiritually, I was hungry—the spiritual experiences I had relied upon were less and less nourishing to me, nor was I satisfied with the answers to my questions regarding Church doctrine. Experientially, I was discouraged by the failure of Church principles and policies to answer the cry of basic human need as sin fractured my own life and the lives of my friends. My once invincible lines of defense felt the force of this sustained battering and the shape of my faith had to change.

I suppose one could interpret my story in light of the clichéd tale of the boy who moves to the big city and is seduced into straying from the values of his fathers. This stereotype haunted me because there was a kernel of truth in it: you really can't "keep 'em down on the farm after they've seen Paree."

In my own frame of reference, "Paree" took the form of people who lived apparently meaningful lives without Mormonism. The diversity of lifestyles was astonishing: various manifestations of Judaism and Christianity, Eastern mysticism, New Age paganism, and secular humanism all had enthusiastic proponents among my friends and colleagues. In the company of this welter of worldviews, Mormonism began to dwindle in its ability to explain all of what I observed and experienced. Even at its most persuasive, however, an accommodation to religious pluralism was not sufficient to dislodge me from my own place at the smorgasbord. If Mormonism was not the only true choice, my faith was at least as good as anyone else's.

I don't remember the precise moment when I became aware that I was losing my faith altogether. In some respects, retracing the steps of my journey from belief to unbelief is like tracking a fugitive through a forest of memories. There are plenty of signs to observe—footprints and bent twigs, bits of cloth in the brush, even a few crimson-tinted leaves—but it is difficult, in retrospect, to put events back in order.

Soon after our move to Whittier, LeAnn and I had become immersed in the activities of the Whittier 6th Ward. I served for a time as a Sunday school teacher. My thirteen-year-old students, gangly and awkward, reminded me of my own early adolescence. Unlike me, though, they seemed to lack a basic curiosity about their faith. Was this a generational difference? I tried to make the lessons spicier, sometimes by dubious means. On one occasion I led a discussion based on the movie *Star Wars,* suggesting that "the Force" was analogous to the power of the Mormon priesthood. It is significant to me now that I was unable to discern that this pantheistic idea was antithetical to the teachings of Jesus.

Working late on Friday and Saturday nights and striving to meet marathon deadlines eventually interfered with my Sunday morning church attendance. Many times, LeAnn found herself taking the children to church alone. I grew reluctant to accept new callings because I didn't want to commit myself to responsibilities I would not be able to fulfill consistently. I actually began feeling some relief at the prospect of being without a Church job. I told myself I needed a break, a hiatus after years of intense effort and focus. Without even realizing it, I subtly began to drift into what Mormons call "inactivity."

Despite my less frequent appearances at church, however, Mormonism still defined my worldview. At this point, I still believed the teachings of the Church painted a true picture of reality. This conviction found expression most often in conversations with LeAnn, members of my family, or our LDS friends. We discussed Mormonism frequently and intensely, with all of its multihued facets.

Occasionally, in talks with friends, guarded complaints about the Church would arise. Such criticism was usually veiled unless we all knew we were among those with whom it was "safe" to talk about such things. In Mormonism, there is no tradition of constructive dissent. In fact, in the temple ceremony, faithful Latter-day Saints vow to "refrain from all evil speaking of the Lord's anointed." This interdiction refers specifically to Church leaders and, by extension, to the programs they sponsor. Thus, virtually any criticism of the Church can be interpreted as falling under the ban. Furthermore, the *Book of Mormon* teaches that "contention is of the devil." Contention is extrapolated to refer to any sort of dialogue, argument, or debate in which opposition to the Church is expressed. Perhaps owing to the persecutions suffered in their past, Mormons are particularly sensitive to criticism, from within or from without, and are suspicious of concerns that stray across the border into fault-finding or doubt. Still, every community has its problems and the Latter-day Saints are not immune. Most often, however, problems in Mormonism are attributed to "the people" rather than to "the gospel," meaning that breakdowns are not the fault of LDS leaders or programs per se, but rather the failure of individuals to live up to their commitments. This distinction helps Mormons maintain confidence in their leadership, which exercises an authority tantamount to infallibility.

When LeAnn and I moved in 1978, our new home fell within the boundaries of the Whittier 3rd Ward and the locus of our relationship with the Church changed. We made new friends and found new avenues of service there. I eventually accepted a call to teach in the elders quorum. LeAnn taught the Laurels, a group of high school senior girls.

Some things didn't change with our move to the new ward. Mormon meetings, for instance, were universally organized into three-hour blocks, in which an hour each was devoted to priesthood meeting, Sunday school, and sacrament meeting. While the young men of the Aaronic Priesthood met in their deacons, teachers, and priests quorums, the young women of corresponding ages met in groups called Beehives, MIA Maids, and Laurels. Wives attended Relief Society while their husbands holding the Melchizedek Priesthood met in the elders and high priests quorums. Children were enrolled in Primary for the priesthood and Sunday school hours.

The most significant new opportunity for the expression of our faith opened up when LeAnn and I were invited to join a study group constituted of ward members, most of them serving in leadership positions. These fellow readers soon became good friends. The group's literary agenda was divided into thirds, including fiction, nonfiction, and writings on Mormonism. LeAnn and I had always felt that study and discussion were important avenues for confirming and deepening our faith. The study group provided a unique forum to pursue this activity in community with other like-minded adults. We often felt that our monthly meetings were the high point of our spiritual life.

At the suggestion of one of the study group members, we began regularly reading the Mormon intellectual journals, *Sunstone* and *Dialogue*. Although their circulation was small, these magazines had a notorious reputation among Latter-day Saints for being too "liberal," that is, they didn't always toe the party line. Indeed, they were maverick publications that operated outside the perimeter of official Church sanction. Nevertheless, LeAnn and I felt that truth had nothing to fear—we were intrigued by the unorthodox approach of these journals and impressed by the credentials and attitude of the contributors, primarily LDS writers, scholars, and historians. Their research appeared thorough and accurate, and they had access to all kinds of historical documents and other resources to which I had never been exposed. While some of this information raised questions about the fundamental assumptions of Mormonism, the writers invariably included efforts to harmonize the ambiguities within the framework of active LDS faith. In so doing, they seemed to have a maturity and balance that I envied.

A number of the *Sunstone* and *Dialogue* articles we read, however, contained well-documented evidence demonstrating that crucial historical events of Mormonism could not have actually taken place as the Church taught. This discovery was especially unsettling for me in light of the two years I had spent in Italy, testifying that the propositional truth of these events was an absolute. Other articles examined textual difficulties within LDS scriptures or problematic aspects of Mormon doctrine. A few raised moral questions concerning the character of Joseph Smith. Even in articles such as these, however, the writers suggested that there was some kind of overarching truth that could somehow encompass the disparities. Whatever this "truth" was, it was not a truth I recognized from the teachings of my youth. I began to learn what it meant to consciously live with conflicting beliefs, a state known as "cognitive dissonance." For a while, I assured myself that this ambivalence was a healthy part of growing up.

Examples of the sort of historical difficulties I encountered in my reading are provided by two key events from LDS Church history: Joseph Smith's "First Vision" and "the restoration of the priesthood."

In his 1838 history, a portion of which was later canonized as scripture by the Church, Joseph Smith related the story of an 1820 vision in which he said God the Father and Jesus Christ appeared to him in response to a fervent prayer he offered up in the woods near his home. During this vision, Joseph was told that all of the Christian sects of his day were "wrong," that their creeds were an "abomination" in the sight of God, and that their professors were all "corrupt."[3] This story is commonly known among the Mormons as the First Vision. As an LDS missionary, it was the first thing I taught potential converts as evidence of the prophetic calling and authority of Joseph Smith. The First Vision also served to illustrate the fundamental Church doctrines that God has a physical body and that the Father and the Son are two separate and distinct beings. Underscoring the importance of the First Vision, current Church President Gordon B. Hinckley once said: "Without it as a foundation stone for our faith and organization, we have nothing. With it we have everything."[4]

I was truly shocked to find in my reading that there were four different accounts of the First Vision. I had been told of only one. The earliest of the four, and the only one in Joseph Smith's own handwriting, was a personal history written in 1832. The other three were dictated to scribes, including the canonized version of 1838. There are significant discrepancies among the four accounts, involving major points of the story such as the date, the purpose of Joseph's prayer, the number and identity of the beings who appeared, and the content of the divine message. The variances are sufficiently glaring to cast a shadow of doubt over the entire story. The most serious conflict, however, involves who is supposed to have appeared: in 1832, Joseph Smith reported seeing Jesus alone, while in the 1838 version, both Father and Son are said to have been present.[5] To me, it looked a lot like the tale had grown in the telling.

A further problem was Joseph Smith's description of the historical context in which this vision supposedly occurred. He claimed that it took place during a period of intense religious revival in his neighborhood, with churches warring against one another in a fierce competition for converts that extended even to members of his own family. Extensive research in local church and community records, however, reported no such revivals in the vicinity of the Smith home at the time in question.[6] This portion of the story also seemed to have undergone some kind of exaggeration or embellishment.

Similar problems plagued Joseph Smith's claims regarding the restoration of the priesthood. Latter-day Saints believe that the priesthood must be objectively transmitted through the laying on of hands by one who already holds the authority. Since, according to Mormonism, this authority passed away with the original apostles, it had to be restored again via the appointed ordinance as administered by those who last held it, even though they were long dead. In his 1838 history, Joseph Smith claimed to have received the lesser Aaronic Priesthood from John the Baptist in an epiphany dated May 15, 1829. The LDS Church teaches that sometime later, the greater Melchizedek Priesthood was restored under the hands of Peter, James, and John when they appeared to Joseph in another vision.[7]

Curiously, there is no definite date for the restoration of the Melchizedek Priesthood in any of the annals of the Church.[8] It seems almost incomprehensible that a date of such surpassing importance would be forgotten or ignored by Joseph Smith, his family, and every other early Mormon chronicler. The problems do not end there, however. LDS doctrine clearly states that the office of elder falls under the authority of the Melchizedek Priesthood—a man cannot be set apart as an elder without first having been ordained to the high priesthood. Yet the *History of the Church* recounts that "the authority of the Melchizedek Priesthood was manifested and conferred for the first time upon several of the Elders," including Joseph Smith himself, at a conference in June 1831, sans any supernatural apostolic appearance.[9] This discrepancy also appears in a number of other independent sources.[10] Given that the Church was formally organized on April 6, 1830, it seems this was accomplished without the authority of the Melchizedek Priesthood.

To make matters worse, early references to the restoration of the priesthood found in current editions of the *Doctrine and Covenants*, the canonized compilation of Joseph Smith's revelations, were inserted into the original texts between the time of their first publication in 1833 and their second in 1835.[11] In short, the writings were doctored. This fact did not go unnoticed by at least one early Latter-day Saint. David Whitmer, one of the key "three witnesses" of the *Book of Mormon*, separated himself from the Church partly because Joseph had "changed the revelations from the way they were first given."[12]

These are only a few examples of the many contradictions that surfaced during the course of my study. These discrepancies presented me with an enormous problem. It was as if my parents could produce no evidence of their wedding: no witnesses, no records, no pictures, only conflicting stories about who married them and who was in attendance, even disparate accounts of the date and venue of the ceremony. Common sense told me that something was desperately wrong.

I had believed all my life that the official version of Church history was absolutely true. Learning of these variant, incompatible accounts created a state of cognitive dissonance between the historical facts and the Church's teachings. Which was I to believe? What was really true? In light of the evidence, could Joseph Smith's story really be trusted? These were questions that were beginning to affect the central core of my faith, not just the periphery.

In the late seventies and early eighties, such problems with Mormon history were largely unknown to the general membership of the Church. Discussions of difficulties with the official Church story were mainly the province of "anti-Mormon" polemicists and a small circle of LDS historians writing for esoteric scholarly journals like *BYU Studies* and the *Journal of Mormon History*, as well as for *Sunstone* and *Dialogue*. LDS historical archives had been effectively shut for many years, owing to the restrictive policies of Joseph Fielding Smith, the apostle and longtime Church historian who eventually became President in 1970. After his death in 1972, the archives were made available to scholars, in part to provide source material for a definitive, multivolume history of Mormonism. As researchers burrowed into these and other records, they opened a veritable Pandora's box of problematic historical documents that soon began to receive wider recognition.

It was an intense and exciting period for those passionate about Mormon history. Many were shaken by the implications of the material that came to light. New discoveries lined up like 747s waiting to land. The Church tried to suppress the most damaging of the documents. The atmosphere was highly charged, and it was easy for an opportunist like Mark Hoffmann to take cruel advantage of the situation with frauds like the notorious "Salamander" letter.[13] He could never have fooled so many historians if the basic content of his forgeries had not already been found in other documents known to be genuine. Eventually, access to the archives was strictly limited again. The focus of my study, however, took place while the window of opportunity was still open.

I felt a strong desire to talk about the concerns raised in my reading, to get the information out into the open. Perhaps in part it grew from a kind of "fear of the dark"—the monsters might be less frightening if brought into the bright light of day. If the First Vision and the restoration of the priesthood were instances of genuine divine revelation, shouldn't we discuss any apparent problems openly with an eye to finding some answers? I hoped that in facing the issues head-on, I could discover some resolution for my own encroaching anxieties. This was the assumption I brought to my job as an elders quorum instructor. I devoted some class time to the First Vision and included material on the four different versions. I was careful to conclude with the harmonization that had been offered by LDS historians. Soon thereafter, I was asked to "tone down" my lessons—I was disturbing the testimonies of some who were, as the elders' quorum president put it, "weaker in the faith" than I was.

Gentle as this reprimand had been, it only served to amplify my concerns. I resigned my position, feeling both that I had no right to undermine anyone's testimony, and that I couldn't continue to lead the group if I wasn't allowed to tell the whole story about the subjects I taught. To me, this was not simply a historical issue, but also one of censorship, the willful suppression of information. I didn't want to be party to a cover-up—America had forced a president to resign over that sort of thing.

Serious as they were, conflicting accounts of LDS Church history were not the only source of dissonance uncovered in my reading. In addition to the altering of Joseph Smith's revelations as published in the *Doctrine and Covenants*, there were also significant problems associated with the other Mormon standard works, the *Book of Mormon* and the *Pearl of Great Price*.

Latter-day Saints believe that the *Book of Mormon* is a sacred and historical record of ancient America. It is primarily concerned with the descendants of a prophet named Lehi, who leaves Jerusalem and migrates to the New World with his family in 600 B.C. Two nations grow from his posterity, the Nephites and the Lamanites, named respectively for two of his sons. The Nephites tend to be the more righteous people and the Lamanites the more wicked. About A.D. 421, the Lamanites destroy the Nephites in a great war. The Church teaches that Native Americans are descendants of the Lamanites. The *Book of Mormon* also recounts the story of an earlier people known as the Jaredites, who migrate to ancient America from the tower of Babel about 2000 B.C. It addresses the religious traditions as well as the cultural traits of each of these groups, detailing the salient features of their civilizations. The most significant of its claims is that Jesus Christ appeared to the people of the New World following His resurrection, taught them the gospel, called apostles, and established His church, just as He had done in the Old World.

Because its basic premises are historical, Mormons have expected archaeological research to support the *Book of Mormon*. Many years of intensive study by LDS archaeologists, however, have failed to substantiate its historicity. Although a few esoteric finds have been seized upon by some Latter-day Saints anxious for anything to demonstrate the merit of their belief before the world, the breadth of the evidence suggests instead an entirely different picture of pre-Columbian life in the western hemisphere. Of course, archaeology can't be expected to prove or disprove the occurrence of a certain set of events, such as those mentioned in the *Book of Mormon*, but it can reveal a context in which those events are likely or unlikely to have taken place. Reliable interpretations of New World history shouldn't be based on the esoteric artifact, but on broad patterns of civilization disclosed by the full range of archaeological research. As I began to understand these issues, my faith in the veracity of the

Book of Mormon was profoundly challenged. In light of the evidence, it did not seem possible that the *Book of Mormon* could truly be an ancient book as the Church taught.

For example, no geographical location for the Jaredite, Nephite, or Lamanite civilizations has ever been found. Among all the ruined cities and settlements studied by LDS scholars in North, South, or Central America, not one has been definitively identified with any of the numerous cities mentioned in the *Book of Mormon*.[14] This is a king-size problem right out of the gate—there can hardly be such a thing as *Book of Mormon* archaeology, when there is no actual physical location to place it in.

Furthermore, the *Book of Mormon* maintains that the Nephites and Lamanites were Semitic in origin, all derived from a small band of Jewish refugees.[15] Conversely, the archaeological record has shown that the western hemisphere was largely populated by people of Asiatic stock who crossed the Bering Strait thousands of years before the people in the *Book of Mormon* supposedly arrived.[16] Though the Nephites and Lamanites are said to have had a common language, specifically Hebrew, New World peoples spoke hundreds of languages and dialects, all unrelated to Hebrew and many unrelated to each other. There is no evidence for a widespread population of Hebrew-speaking Semites anywhere in ancient America.[17] Furthermore, the time frame given in the *Book of Mormon* is not sufficient to account for the development of such a broad range of tongues, let alone the vast numbers of people that it attributes to the Nephite and Lamanite nations.[18]

Some significant features of the culture described in the *Book of Mormon* simply did not exist in ancient America. For instance, the *Book of Mormon* contains passages indicating that the Nephites and Lamanites, as well as the more ancient Jaredites, possessed iron and steel in sufficient quantities to mass produce tools, machinery, and weapons of war.[19] The archaeological record, however, yields no evidence for a pre-Columbian ferrous industry. Detritus left in the wake of civilizations working with iron and steel is not something that can be hidden or that disintegrates with time. Ores must be mined, refined, and cast. This requires fuel, as well as furnaces and other tools and technologies that leave behind solid evidence. The smelting process produces slag that hardens into indestructible new rock forms and gets piled in heaps. The fact that none of this existed in pre-Columbian America is a huge strike against the historicity of the *Book of Mormon*.[20]

There are several other related difficulties—coinage, for example. The Nephite monetary system detailed in the *Book of Mormon* reckoned the value of its silver and gold pieces by measures of barley— the Nephites apparently operated on a barley standard.[21] There is no archaeological evidence for a system of coinage in the New World, dating from the period of time mandated by the *Book of Mormon*;[22] nor was barley grown in significant quantities in the western hemisphere at that time.[23] Other Nephite agricultural products, such as wheat and flax, mentioned numerous times in the *Book of Mormon* as "linen," are also missing from the archaeological record, while the existence of non–*Book of Mormon* plants, such as lima beans, tomatoes, and squash, finds abundant support.[24] The same lack of evidence holds true for domesticated animals mentioned in the *Book of Mormon*. Skeletal remains of cattle, sheep, swine, and horses are absent, while those of non–*Book of Mormon* animals, such as dogs and llamas, domesticated fairly early in the New World, and wild creatures such as the deer and the jaguar, are plentiful.[25] It is also striking that none of these uniquely *Book of Mormon* plants and animals are represented on indigenous art forms such as ceramics, murals, or sculptures, while, again, there is ample evidence of plants and animals not mentioned in the *Book of Mormon*.[26]

Technologies like metallurgy, coinage, and systems of agriculture and animal husbandry widespread enough to feed and transport large groups of people are not isolated activities. There are many complex skills and resources that must be gathered together—culture has to be organized to a certain degree before such things are feasible. The body of evidence for the social systems described in the *Book of Mormon* is simply nonexistent, while anywhere else in the world these technologies have developed, the evidence is there to prove it. As information shaping the understanding of pre-Columbian New World civilization has accumulated, it has pointed to a radically different kind of culture than the one detailed in the *Book of Mormon*. When all the evidences are taken together, they combine to create a large, coherent context in which the *Book of Mormon* simply does not hold up as a real historical record.

As children, LeAnn and I were taught that the Bible had been corrupted by errors and omissions on the part of careless or conniving
translators. Many "plain and precious things" were missing.[27] On
the other hand, we had been told that the *Book of Mormon* and other
LDS scriptures were free from such errors and therefore completely
trustworthy.[28] So naturally we had expected this assertion to be
borne out in the real world. We were deeply distressed to see the discrepancies mounting up.

We were also surprised to find that textual problems in the *Book
of Mormon* abound. Foremost among these difficulties are numerous anachronisms, such as references to uniquely nineteenth-
century words, phrases, and concepts that would have been familiar to Joseph Smith from the Protestant revivals of upstate New York
but meaningless to the ancient Jews.[29] The *Book of Mormon* also
contains quotations from the Bible that appear in time periods long
before they were actually composed.[30] In fact, large sections of the
King James Bible are reproduced nearly verbatim in the *Book of Mormon*. One of these is the "Sermon on the Mount," which the resur-
rected Jesus delivers to the inhabitants of the New World. With few
exceptions, the *Book of Mormon* text of the sermon slavishly follows
the King James Version, even to the point of reproducing italicized
words added by the sixteenth-century English translators.[31] These
anachronistic insertions would not have been included if Joseph
Smith had really translated the sermon from an uncorrupted, primary source, as he claimed he had.

The "Book of Abraham" is probably the most vulnerable to criticism of all the uniquely Mormon scriptures, having failed to pass a
textbook test case for Joseph Smith's inspiration and integrity as a
translator. Joseph claimed that he translated this sacred writing from
papyri found with a group of Egyptian mummies that he acquired
in 1835, stating that the papyri contained the writings of Joseph of
Egypt and the patriarch Abraham.[32] The "Book of Abraham" was
included in the Mormon canon in 1880 as part of the *Pearl of Great
Price*. In 1966, some of the original papyri, presumed to have been
destroyed in the Chicago fire, were discovered in New York's Metro-
politan Museum of Art and translated afresh, this time by Egyptian
language scholars. The new translations presented a unique opportunity to vindicate Joseph Smith and many interested Mormons

looked forward to their publication with anticipation. The new translations, however, showed that these papyri were familiar portions of the Egyptian *Book of the Dead* that had absolutely nothing to do with the "Book of Abraham." Joseph Smith's "translation" was completely fraudulent.[33]

Many arguments were advanced to soften this blow. Some LDS scholars tried to distance Joseph Smith from the papyri in various ways, contending that they must be the wrong papyri, or the wrong portions of the right papyri. Others wondered if he had simply used them to stimulate his spiritual curiosity, preparing his mind for a direct revelation unconnected to the actual texts themselves. One prominent LDS scholar even suggested that the papyri were encrypted texts, and that the *Book of the Dead* formed the basis of a code that Joseph Smith translated rather than the characters themselves.[34] All of these arguments struck me as rationalizations rather than persuasive defenses. This was especially true in light of another existing primary source, Joseph Smith's *Egyptian Alphabet and Grammar,* a notebook that displays the Egyptian characters on one side of the page along with their "translations" on the other.[35] There seemed no escaping the obvious conclusion: the "Book of Abraham" was not what the Mormon Church claimed it was.

The textual problems in the *Book of Mormon*, the *Doctrine and Covenants*, and the *Pearl of Great Price* were so grave that they severely undermined my confidence in these "standard works." If I couldn't trust them to tell me the truth, how then could I continue to trust the men who had produced and promoted them? Combined with the contradictory versions of LDS Church history, these problems formed a destructive phalanx that pounded at the walls of my faith.

Ultimately, Mormonism stands or falls with the character of Joseph Smith. A believing Latter-day Saint has to take him at his word and trust his revelations—everything that is unique to the Church filters through him. Just as one can't be a Christian without believing in Jesus, so one can't be a Mormon without believing in Joseph Smith. From childhood, LeAnn and I had been taught that he was a noble character, that he "lived great and died great in the eyes of God and his people," that he had, in fact, "done more, save Jesus only, for the salvation of men in this world, than any other man that ever lived in it" (D&C 135:3). "Praise to the man who communed with Jehovah," we sang in one of our favorite hymns, "death shall not conquer the hero again."[36] For this reason, my sense of betrayal was particularly sharp when I learned of the serious moral breaches committed by the man I had trusted as my Prophet, Seer, and Revelator.

For one thing, I learned that, throughout his life, Joseph Smith was deeply involved in the practice of magic and driven by an occult worldview. His parents gave him an early education in the working of ritual magic. His mother, Lucy Mack Smith, described "the faculty of Abrac, drawing magic circles, [and] soothsaying" as an "important interest" to the Smith family,[37] and neighbors reported that Joseph's father, Joseph Smith, Sr., used divining rods in attempting to locate buried treasure.[38] Many of young Joseph Smith's occult activities were focused in the area of "money digging," local jargon for a business arrangement wherein he was hired to find hidden caches of wealth by divination using a kind of crystal called a "seer stone."[39] The treasure hunting lore of Joseph's day was thoroughly steeped in the occult, combining remnants of the rituals and cosmology of European ceremonial magic with a sort of practical Yankee materialism. Several independent accounts of Joseph's occult adventures refer to spells, magic circles, and animal sacrifices employed to bind or appease the spirits supposedly guarding the hidden treasures.[40] As late as 1826, Joseph was tried and found guilty of being a "disorderly person" in connection with one of his money digging contracts.[41] When he attempted to join a Methodist fellowship in 1828, he was rejected on the grounds that he was a "practicing necromancer."[42]

Joseph Smith's occultism became a key feature of the fledgling Mormon Church. According to reliable accounts, he used a seer stone to find another kind of buried treasure, the "golden plates," which were said to contain the original text of the *Book of Mormon*.[43] Some of Joseph's scribes, including his wife, Emma, reported that, rather than translating the text from the plates, he dictated the *Book of Mormon* while gazing into a crystal placed in his hat.[44] A number of his early revelations were received through a seer stone.[45] Joseph's interests in hidden treasure were sanctioned by direct revelation as late as 1836.[46] Occult practices continued to be significant in the LDS Church right up to the end of his life. Much of his late occult involvement revolved around the influence of Masonry. Significant portions of the temple ceremony, introduced to an inner circle of the Church in 1842, were adapted from Masonic precedents. Many of the oaths, penalties, signs, and tokens in the temple were copied virtually verbatim from the Masonic ritual.[47] Joseph Smith died with a magical talisman in his pocket and the Masonic distress call on his lips.[48]

The link between Masonry and Mormonism was brought home rather forcibly to LeAnn and me one afternoon at a Montessori school picnic. The Masons were having their picnic at the same public park that day, and, as LeAnn and I arrived for the school festivities, we watched one of the Masons check in with a grip we recognized from the LDS temple as the first token of the Aaronic priesthood. It was rather shocking to see this handshake we had sworn with our lives to keep secret used to collect a bucket of chicken.

LeAnn's and my reaction to the issue of Joseph Smith's occultism was essentially a moral one—it was a question of right and wrong. In a world captivated by the New Age, with its attendant panoply of occult concepts and paraphernalia, moral revulsion against such things may seem quaint or intolerant; nevertheless, while people disagree on where to draw the line on moral distinctions regarding the occult, everyone draws it somewhere. Some draw it between Christianity and all occultism, others between white and black magic; some approve of horoscopes but reject Ouija boards; others like dancing naked in the moonlight but repudiate human sacrifice. Even serious occultists like the Wiccans are passionate about distinguishing themselves from the Satanists.

In our case, LeAnn and I had been taught by the Church that all occult beliefs and practices were inconsistent with the teachings of Christ—unambiguous teaching about the evils of occultism formed part of the bedrock of our moral training.[49] Dissonance was created by our discovery that Joseph Smith was into it up to his eyeballs. This knowledge put us into a moral bind that we felt most pointedly with respect to our children. How could we warn them against contemporary occult influences if we continued to uphold the teachings of a man who was so deeply involved with the same sort of things? How could we draw a persuasive line between Ouija boards and trance channeling on the one hand, and divining rods and seer stones on the other? What could we honestly teach them about the behavior of our founding prophet? Could we continue sending them to Primary and have them routinely taught misleading hagiographic stories about the foundations of our faith? These questions presented us with a double standard that we could not imagine maintaining with integrity.

The question of polygamy raised another, equally disturbing red flag. Although the LDS Church has discontinued polygamy as a practice, it has never been denied as an eternal principle.[50] In my experience polygamy was rarely discussed openly in Church meetings, but everyone who grew up Mormon nevertheless had some vague notion about it. When polygamy was mentioned at all, it was usually in the context of family heritage via inspirational profiles in courage, or held out as a heavenly hope for widowers in their second marriages. The issue had long been a sore spot with LeAnn and me because we believed profoundly in the value of an exclusive marital relationship that would grow in depth and beauty with a lifelong faithful commitment. We had a huge emotional investment in this vision.

Polygamy appeared to fly in the face of conscience and of our deepest feelings about love. It also seemed to devalue women. LeAnn particularly felt the weight of this burden and wondered if the worth of a woman was indeed only a fraction of her husband's eternal glory. We maintained an uneasy peace with the issue only because of our faith in the Church, which assured us that the practice of polygamy was subject to higher moral principles with strict rules and disciplines that distinguished it from mere licentiousness. So the sting of betrayal was great when we learned of Joseph Smith's flagrantly immoral behavior.

Secrecy and deception, the forms of dishonesty so characteristic of infidelity, were dark hallmarks of Joseph's polygamous relationships. Many of his plural wives were taken without Emma, his first wife's, knowledge or consent.[51] Joseph often deceived Emma in order to carry out trysts with other women. An 1842 letter in his own hand instructs the parents of one of his young consorts to bring her secretly to a specified location, warning them first to "find out when Emma comes," so they can avoid her. "I think she wont come tonight," he writes, "if she dont dont fail to come to night." Typically, Joseph ordered the letter burned after it was read.[52] Unfortunately, his dishonesty about polygamy carried over into the Church at large.

At many points in its history, LDS Church leaders lied publicly about its practice in order to protect the Church from perceived threats to its objectives.[53]

It was characteristic of Joseph Smith to break the very rules he had made—or received by revelation, as he claimed—and to refuse to live by the disciplines he imposed on others. History reveals that he followed a pattern of setting boundaries, exceeding them, then claiming a special dispensation and concurrently lying about it to those who were not part of his innermost circle. He behaved as if he were above the moral law that governed others.[54]

On several occasions, he made advances to women who already had husbands. Some of these women were the wives of his closest associates.[55] History documents several cases of Joseph Smith's polyandrous unions—basically concubinal privileges—with other men's wives.[56] Occasionally, he backed away from these heart-wrenching proposals, claiming they were intended to test the loyalty of his followers. In one poignant incident, he asked one of his apostles, Heber C. Kimball, to give his wife, Vilate, to him in marriage. After three days of fasting and agonizing soul searching, Heber brought Vilate to Joseph's home and placed her hand in his. In tears, Joseph told Heber his request had just been a test.[57] It was not merely a test, however, when he took Heber's fourteen-year-old daughter, Helen, as a wife not long afterward.[58]

The women Joseph Smith approached were sometimes dependent on the Church for economic support while their husbands were away on foreign missions. Coercive pressure was placed upon them to accept these overtures. Those who refused were threatened with the blackening of their characters or the loss of their eternal reward.[59] Joseph also married young girls that he had taken into his household and raised from childhood. Five of his wives were orphans or dependents, and seven had lived in his home at one time or another.[60]

Our response to this information was one of moral outrage. The man whom LeAnn and I had been raised to revere as a true prophet of God had behaved no differently than Moses David Berg, debauched leader of the Children of God, a cult I had encountered while I was in Italy. A contemporary equivalent would be David Koresh, who also demanded the sexual favors of his followers, children and adults alike. Joseph Smith's relationships with his foster children also had uncomfortable overtones of incest, which distressed and disgusted us. My family would never tolerate my behaving as Joseph Smith had done, no matter how I tried to spiritualize my actions. And yet they were wholeheartedly committed to him as a prophet. Many accounts of those drawn into the practice of polygamy indicate that they believed that whatever Joseph did, it could not be wrong, effectively making him the standard by which moral issues were decided. We, like millions of others, had staked everything on his divine calling, and he had betrayed our trust.

What were LeAnn and I to do with this information? What were we to make of the litany of faith-shattering data that we confronted? What should our response be? Should we leave the one true church, or stay and live with the dissonance, drawing what comfort we could from the weak rationalizations offered by the LDS scholarly community? On what basis should we decide?

All of the issues we encountered were linked by a common thread: they depended upon the reliability of the primary sources. Of course, we now understood that the same was true of the LDS Church's official story—there was no longer any easy retreat into orthodoxy for us. For a long time, LeAnn and I struggled hard to harmonize the Church's version of its history with the things we had read. We never accepted the allegation of any challenge to the Church's position uncritically. We chased down the references and collected copies of some of the documents, trying to confirm their authenticity and relevance as best we could. The research was sometimes exciting, like detective work. I wish I could say my motives were always pure, but I have to admit to feeling a kind of rush when I located a new source or uncovered a new fact. Mostly, however, the more LeAnn and I discovered, the more our hearts sank. Our worldview was being broken up and carted away, piece by piece. It was like finding ourselves on a movie set: the facades look real, but there are no real buildings behind them, just scaffolding propped up by supports. When the shoot is over, the set is struck. I felt as if our entire way of life was false and artificial.

The depth of our reaction to these problems grew in part from our understanding of the nature of history itself. In the postmodern world, the very notion of objective history has been challenged. Deconstructionists teach that history is unrecoverable and means only what it means to each interpreter. Even the concept of truth itself has fallen into disrepute. In redefining the word, prisoners of the zeitgeist argue for "truth rather than fact." Following this line of reasoning, why should conflicting accounts of historical events or problems with arcane passages of scripture be at all troublesome? Couldn't some kind of mythic truth be found in Mormonism even if the details of its history and sacred texts were not accurate? Why should Joseph Smith's personal life be of any concern to us?

Our response to such questions was grounded in the values of our families. LeAnn and I had been raised to believe that truth was objective and absolute. Two plus two can never equal five. Even the most confirmed postmodern deconstructionists pay tacit homage to this view: they, too, expect correct change from their purchases and look both ways before they cross the street. The problems we encountered in Mormonism were objective, not simply differences of opinion or interpretation. We couldn't ignore the tremendous body of challenging evidence that we had uncovered.

Mormonism is essentially a historical religion: it requires the actual occurrence of certain events for it to be true. It cannot stand merely as a myth with its truths couched in elaborate metaphors. In this way it is like the other historical religions, Christianity, Judaism, and Islam. Judaism depends upon the existence of a real Moses, Islam upon a real Mohammed. For Christians, the words of Paul to the Corinthians are key: "If Christ be not raised" from the dead then our faith is "vain," and "we are of all men most miserable" (1 Corinthians 15:14–19). The fact of the resurrection lies at the root of Christian faith. Just so, the truth and power of Mormonism depend upon the actuality of Joseph Smith's revelations and experiences. People don't give their lives, as some of my pioneer forebears did, for a story which they know to be a fiction. Either Mormonism is true or they were deeply deceived. If Joseph Smith did not see God and Jesus Christ in a vision, if there was no general apostasy and no actual restoration of the priesthood, if the *Book of Mormon* is not real history and the "Book of Abraham" a bogus translation, then Mormonism simply can't be true, no matter how many good feelings people may have about it. Two plus two cannot equal five; nor could all of my spiritual experiences, however overwhelming, make it so. Under the strain of this realization, LeAnn compared herself at the time to a double-jointed contortionist—one knee twisted up behind her neck, an arm behind her back, reaching around to grab the opposite heel. She felt like a spiritual pretzel, and experienced the deep ache that such a twisted life brings.

In defending the problems of Mormonism, some have adopted the deconstructionist position and argued that history can never be fully known, that there will always be contradictions deriving from the varying perceptions and biases of historians. This point is not without merit, but it does not warrant a wholesale capitulation to a featureless past; nor is it consistent with the way life works on a daily basis. I don't require full assurance of anything, let alone of my faith. I merely require a high degree of probability that the things I believe are grounded in reality. For instance, when crossing the street, I look both ways, estimate the speed and distance of the oncoming traffic, factor in my own physical capabilities, and assess the likelihood of success, all instantaneously and unconsciously. If I have a good chance of getting across without being flattened, I commit myself one hundred percent to the act, based upon the evidence observed and the resulting judgments made. I stake my life every day on the ability to make this kind of determination. To me, faith is like this. It is not so much a leap into the dark as a reasonable step off the curb and into the street, one that is warranted by the available evidence.

While I do not require one hundred percent assurance of the truth of my beliefs, I do require them to have integrity. This is another value I learned from my family. The word "integrity" means "wholeness," referring to a state of life that is consistent. Because I rely on rationality in the ordinary course of life, it should also occupy an important position where my faith is concerned. If I compartmentalize my faith by applying a different set of standards to it than I do to the issues that govern the rest of my life, I compromise my integrity and am guilty of hypocrisy. As a young man, I was taught that double standards were wrong and that hypocrisy was evil. These values seemed consistent with LDS faith at the time.

Mormonism did not prove true, however. It was as if our faith was a jigsaw puzzle in a box, with a picture on the cover showing what the puzzle was supposed to look like after it was all put together. As we assembled the puzzle, it didn't resemble the picture; the pieces didn't fit; something was terribly wrong. The testimonies of Church apologists began to ring discomfitingly in our ears like the rantings of extremists—"the earth is flat, the Holocaust never happened, and the *Book of Mormon* is true."

In the early 1980s, the LDS Church rarely responded to issues that challenged its authority unless it was compelled by negative publicity. When a response was deemed necessary, the Church public relations department donned a mask of self-protective, institutional bluster, much like a politician denying a scandal. As new information appeared and the Church reacted, by no stretch of the imagination could I characterize its posture as one that displayed confidence in the truth of its position, confidence that there was nothing to fear from honest questions or scholarly inquiry. Instead, it evidenced a siege mentality. LDS writers who published accounts at variance with the official Church story were threatened or intimidated, and pleas for sensitivity ran into stone walls. Not that these confrontations filtered down to the average Latter-day Saint. In my experience, most Mormons were not willing to investigate the historical issues beyond what they were told in church. They were sheltered by a carapace of willful ignorance that repelled any possibility of a serious challenge to the official story.

There was no one to whom LeAnn and I could talk about our concerns within a Church-sanctioned context. They were either dismissed as deriving from malicious or untrustworthy sources or they were met with a deflecting testimony. When we tried to talk with members of our study group, one of them answered, "I resolved those issues long ago. I have a testimony and that's all that counts." Sometimes I would mention my struggles to friends in an oblique manner. On the few occasions when I felt free to voice my doubts openly, I experienced tremendous relief as I crossed the border and spoke out loud about something that I thought or felt but had never before dared to say. On those occasions, that sense of freedom could be quite healing for me.

LeAnn, on the other hand, found such open speech terribly threatening. She feared that it undermined our marriage. While we were both reading the same material, the roles we played in our discussions were different: I attacked the Church and LeAnn defended it. Our home became a battleground. Sundays were horrible. I came home from Church meetings with a splitting headache. We fought and argued in front of the children. It was awful.

As the foundations of Mormonism crumbled, my moral sense became distorted and the will to resist temptation was eroded. I began to believe that if Mormonism wasn't true, nothing else was—and that meant I could do whatever I pleased. Before long, I was living as if truth were relative and tolerance, sentimental love, and good intentions were the greatest of moral imperatives. It saddened me to recognize this about myself, but this point of view was also somewhat exciting, too, because of the freedom I felt. That freedom was not without its price, however.

In the midst of this moral confusion, I had an affair. I betrayed LeAnn, the person I loved most in the whole world. She reacted with such great terror and agony that I was shocked out of the cocoon of my selfishness. I couldn't believe how stupid I'd been. I felt utterly convicted of my behavior and agonizingly sought LeAnn's forgiveness and the restoration of her trust. Before we were finished, I had to beg her, sobbing on my hands and knees, just to let me stay in our home.

It was then that LeAnn began to realize the depths of the evil in her own heart, as she lashed out to make me pay the utmost for what I'd done. She felt powerless to not want—and to not try—to hurt me as badly as I had hurt her. My betrayal helped me recognize my own weakness and propensity for sin. The horrible way LeAnn and I treated each other showed us that we were not the good people that we had thought ourselves to be. We were capable of great cruelty. We no longer had any illusions about our own perfectibility. And so we experienced the first stage of the "good news," ironically, the bad news that we were sinners.

Confronting my own capacity for evil was a blast of cold water in the face, a wake-up call that left me chastened and humbled. LeAnn and I endured the difficult process of rebuilding, and our marriage rose from the ashes. It was strange, considering my previous bouts with guilt and LDS teachings about the formal "steps of repentance," that I never felt the need to earn God's approbation. From the instant I acknowledged my sin, I felt that He was right there alongside of me, loving me and helping me get back on my feet. Somehow I knew He had forgiven me. This was my first real glimpse of unmerited grace.

I decided I would try to become active in the Church again. In order to do it by the book, I formally confessed my adultery to Church authorities and was tried for my membership before a High Council court. How dry and distant this tribunal seemed in light of the strong sense of forgiveness I already felt in the center of my being. I knew that the Church required it, however, so I accepted it as an act of obedience as well as an institutional necessity. Instead of excommunicating me, the court chose to apply a lesser form of discipline. I attended priesthood meeting the next morning where they announced my disfellowship-ment. I was to be "on probation" for a year.

After that year had passed, I was asked to teach the high school seniors in Sunday school. Although I returned to full activity in the Church, I couldn't unlearn what I had discovered in my studies. I still couldn't resolve Mormonism's historical problems with any degree of peace, so I decided to find a new way to believe in it. After all, the Church was my heritage, at the very least. Perhaps I could start there.

Because of the pain LeAnn and I had been through in our own marriage, our eyes were opened to the realization that marriage was not the "happily ever after," "for time and all eternity" fantasy that we had believed as newly married Mormons. This truth was driven home again when three of our friends' marriages dissolved. In one case, it came to light that a friend we had known since high school had been physically abusing his wife. A second couple's marriage failed because of adultery and a third through simple neglect. Trag-ically, these couples had tried for years to hold up the mask of happy Latter-day Saints, living contented lives. The abused wife had been unable to say, even to her closest friends, that her husband had been beating her since the week they had come home from the temple. The Church seemed to take sides with the husband and, a short time after their divorce, he was married in the temple to a new wife. This seemed outrageous to us. Why wasn't greater effort expended to get him some help—for his own sake as well as his wife's—to deal with the root of his problem rather than glossing it over?

In none of these cases did the Church take a position that ulti-mately contributed to healing the couples' relationships. Instead, in protecting its own policies and interests, it actually furthered the separation between the partners, usually finding fault with the wives. The Church presents itself as a positive, family-oriented institution with old-fashioned, conservative values. While there is some truth to that picture, the necessity of maintaining this image means that the Church cannot afford to allow the vulnerability of its own people to be expressed forthrightly.

Although marriage problems or failures are not the final test of a theology's truth, our own struggles and those of our close friends made us further question the practical outworking of a worldview that was supposedly preparing men and women for godhood. We realized that, practically speaking, Mormonism wasn't able to deal with these profound human tragedies. There was too much pressure to maintain the image, even while the heart was crying out in pain. I've come to believe that this was so because of the lack of grace in Mormon theology. At base, it is such a works-centered religion that the ultimate solution to one's problems is always to grit one's teeth and work harder at keeping the commandments.

In virtually every Mormon man or woman we knew with any degree of intimacy, there was a deep, underlying sense of failure to measure up. Those with a penchant for self-examination especially knew how far short they fell from doing all the Church expected of them. In the midst of our struggles, I wish someone had told us about the rest of the "good news." I wish we had known that although we had "sinned and come short of the glory of God" like everyone else, we could be washed clean and presented blameless before Him, not because of the "righteous" things we had done, but because of Christ's righteousness and his death in our behalf on the cross. No one ever told us about this gospel of grace. Most significantly, no Mormon ever did, despite the LDS Church's vaunted protestations of its Christianity. I believe this is so because the gospel isn't preached in Mormonism. It simply wasn't available for us to hear.

It eventually became clear that we could not continue to have faith in Mormonism or reasonably defend it before the world and still maintain integrity. We could not affirm Joseph Smith as God's prophet; nor could we raise our children with authentic faith while making excuses for him. We could not send our son on a mission to teach things we knew to be false; nor could we raise our daughters to derive their sense of self from a corrupt concept of priesthood authority.

Over the years, LeAnn and I had watched the emergence of a Mormon feminism that strove to establish some kind of recognized female authority within the structure of the Church. Its proponents felt the heavy hand of Church intimidation and discipline. Even on the local level, the disapproval was manifest. Once a group of women in our ward wanted to start a support group and were forbidden to do so. The leadership was afraid that their meetings would turn into gripe sessions about the Church. We simply didn't want our daughters to spend their life's energies on a spiritual Gallipoli, breaking themselves against an impenetrable line in a futile struggle for a dubious prize. This would only crush their spirits. Watching bright and articulate LDS women struggle to belong to a club that didn't want them, wasn't interested in their ideas, and didn't want anyone else to hear them either was a source of great sadness to us.

Ultimately, I felt that I would be betraying the very principles I held most deeply if I did not take a stand against Joseph Smith and the church he founded. But was there anything to stand for beyond Mormonism? Was there anything real and true that could be trusted?

10

In the juvescence of the year
Came Christ the tiger.

—T.S. Eliot, "Gerontion"[1]

*I*n Florence, Italy, the Galleria dell'Accademia that houses Michelangelo's *David* also contains a group of his unfinished works called the *Four Prisoners*. As flawless and satisfying as the *David* is, I find the *Prisoners* even more moving. Perhaps it's the turbulent motion of these captives in stone as they struggle to hurl themselves free of the surrounding marble. Perhaps it's the sense that we see them at the very moment of their liberation, the moment of new birth. Whatever the reasons, I can hardly look at them without awe welling up in my chest and tears brimming in my eyes.

In the days of our deliverance, LeAnn and I were like living "captives in stone," feeling the strokes of the hard chisel of the Almighty. All the chunks that didn't belong to the creatures he was making of us were being chipped away, one by one, by His careful hand. The New Testament calls those who belong to God His "poiema," His poems, His workmanship (Ephesians 2:10). From our perspective, it was a time of grief and loss that hurt terribly. Beneath the veneer of external career success, we were losing all the precious supports that we thought held us secure. Would there be anything left at the heart of our poor stone when the last chunks of Mormonism fell away? Would there be anything left to believe in?

Christ: the name that lay at the root of my child hope for home. Christ: the hero of my adolescent yearning for the triumph of good over evil. Christ: the forgiver of sin and redeemer of blighted years. Could He still be trusted? Would He still be there when all the coruscations of Mormonism lay in heaps around our feet?

In the wake of the chisel, there emerged the features of a deeper truth, resonating with the music and literature that had been speaking to me since childhood. A "sharpening" was taking place that acted as a kind of compass. The things that were dearest to my soul remained and were polished, honed to a point. I could hear in them the dim echoes of a single voice. It was there in the innocent expectation of *West Side Story's* Tony and in the triumph of *The Firebird's* Prince over the demon Kastchei. It was there in my grandmother's hamburgers and in the soaring beauty of her voice, interweaving with my mother's as they sang "Homing." It was there in the pages of Tolkien and C.S. Lewis, in the poems of e e cummings and Gerard Manley Hopkins. It was there at the heart of Christmas. This voice wasn't afraid of the dark: it knew the human tragedy of Sweeney Todd and the sorrow of a Knoxville summer night. It "bade me welcome" in the *Five Mystical Songs* and asked, "Know you not who bore the blame?" And, suddenly, Christ the tiger broke upon us in a riot of color and flame and seized us in His magnificent jaws.

This is how it happened.

A somewhat unorthodox Mormon friend invited LeAnn to a non-denominational Christian women's group called Bible Study Fellowship. A year passed before she finally plucked up the courage to go—Latter-day Saints are not encouraged to participate in Bible studies outside Mormonism. It was a big step, one that LeAnn knew would expose her to non-LDS perspectives; nevertheless, since the assault on our confidence in Mormonism, she had grown spiritually hungry. Our Mormon Study Group, unresponsive to issues that had become crucial to us, was no longer the source of spiritual nourishment that it once had been. LeAnn was attracted to the idea of studying the Bible with Christian women holding other points of view. She went, believing that she was strong enough to sort out what was good, ignore what was not, and still remain a Latter-day Saint. She certainly didn't think that she would be radically changed by the experience.

LeAnn hadn't bargained on finding a group of women who loved Jesus with such obvious vitality. These Christians trusted that God had faithfully preserved His Word and found daily insight and inspiration in studying it. They worshiped with a delightful passion, prayed for one another with vulnerability, and were unconcerned about denominational affiliations. They seemed to have a joy and inner peace that were missing from our lives.

The BSF course of study that year was "Acts and the Life and Letters of Paul." LeAnn had taken a class at Brigham Young University on this subject, but the concept of grace had hardly been mentioned. The index for the course syllabus did not contain a single entry on this key idea in Paul's writings. Nor had there been much discussion of Paul's frank declaration that "all have sinned and fallen short of the glory of God" (Romans 3:23). The contrast between messages was striking. Mormonism taught LeAnn that she was born innocent, a child of God with the potential to become a god herself if she worked at it hard enough. The Bible taught that her sin nature was real and that only in being saved by grace through faith in Jesus Christ could she *become* a child of God. In an excerpt from her testimony, written in 1989, LeAnn describes what happened to her:

> In Bible Study Fellowship the "good news" of the real gospel began to unfold for me; my hunger for God's Word became almost unquenchable. Each week as I carefully studied the Bible, verse by verse, chapter by chapter, in context, allowing it to say what it said apart from interpretation by Mormon prophets, I found I had been taught a false gospel. . . . And so I came before the cross of Christ, bankrupt of my own efforts to earn my way to heaven. I saw in that cross the true glory of Jesus; there He manifested both His Father's complete righteousness and His extreme love; a holiness unable to tolerate my sin and a love so endless He willingly gave his son to blot it out.

LeAnn and I talked often about the things she was learning in BSF. We read passages of Scripture aloud together and discussed them in detail. Her study spurred me to read Paul's letters on my own, straight through, in context, without mentally leaping from proof text to proof text. For the first time, I began to see that his writings were direct, well reasoned, and consistent. With LeAnn, I began to see that Paul's understanding of the gospel was radically different than the one we had been raised to believe as Mormons. Doctrines the LDS Church branded as creedal "abominations" were in fact the towering truths of biblical Christianity. The living, authentic Christ of the Bible completely eclipsed the pale, impotent Christ invented by Joseph Smith.

There was freedom in accepting the verdict of a sin nature. It was a great equalizer that formed a deeper connection with our fellow human beings as it opened our hearts to a deeper relationship with God. We were all in the same boat, struggling with the same basic problem, all needing the grace of God to transcend our human propensity for evil. We needed the imputation of Christ's righteousness to make up for a righteousness that we couldn't generate ourselves, no matter how hard we tried. Guilt for failing to measure up was swept away in the breathtaking abundance of the grace of God.

The things LeAnn and I were learning caught up, gathered together, and made sense out of so many of the important influences in our life: the books we read, the art and music we loved. My faith was also stimulated with new and unexpected intellectual vigor. In Christ, I found a solid core of objective truth rather than flaccid excuses in the face of the evidence. In Christ, I found those fundamental values of my youth upheld and nurtured, rather than rationalized in support of a renegade prophet.

As LeAnn unreservedly surrendered herself to Christ, she began to glow with new life. I could tell something had changed inside her. Still, I held back, despite the fact that initially I had been the more aggressive one in rooting out problems with the LDS Church and she the more defensive. I was convinced now that Mormonism wasn't true, but I wasn't sure where to turn next. I didn't want to be fooled again. I didn't want to buy into another set of self-deceptive illusions. I didn't want to hurt our parents, the rest of our families, or our friends. I prayed that God would allow us to remain in the Mormon Church even with our new confidence in Christ. His answer was always, "No. Follow Me." I could hear this as if it were a clear, calm voice inside my head.

Telling our children what was going on became a major concern for us. We didn't want to hurt them or to uproot their lives any more than was necessary, but we had to be honest with them and wanted intensely to share our newfound joy. One day when LeAnn was bringing the girls home from piano lessons, she was laying some of the groundwork for this discussion, contrasting Jesus and Joseph

Smith. Jerusha, always very sensitive and able to jump right to the heart of any situation, immediately grasped the implications of what her mother was saying.

With tears welling up in her eyes, she said, "Mommy, don't you believe in Joseph Smith anymore?"

LeAnn admitted, "No, honey, I don't."

Jerusha said, "But Mommy, all our families and all our friends are Mormons. They won't love us anymore." At this, LeAnn's tears began to fall as well. Then Jerusha added, "But if you tell me that this is right, I will follow you."

As parents, LeAnn and I felt an immense burden to be certain that we were making the right decision. We love our children and would rather die than do anything to harm them. We could never have left Mormonism if we hadn't been sure, in the depth of our souls, that it was the right thing to do.

In the spring of 1984, we decided to visit some local churches in search of one that was solidly grounded in biblical Christianity. This was harder than we had anticipated. We didn't have a recommendation. We hardly knew a Christian in our area, other than the members of LeAnn's Bible study, and BSF had a wise policy that discouraged any discussion of church affiliation, so we looked in the Yellow Pages. The first congregation we visited was more like a social club than a church; it seemed to be focused less on God than on community service. The sermon was delivered by a minister who used many sports analogies and talked about Jesus as if He were some kind of divine point guard. It was quite evident to us that this pastor didn't really believe that Jesus was the Son of God. The next weekend, we visited a second church and were again disappointed. LeAnn's Bible study, while never bringing up the subject of churches, had nevertheless given us a sense of what a Christ-centered community could be. We prayed we would find one.

One Sunday, we accepted the invitation of the friend who cut our hair. She thought we might enjoy her church because of its excellent music. We attended the First Evangelical Free Church of Fullerton on Mother's Day. The music was indeed excellent, but we weren't expecting Pastor Chuck Swindoll's wonderful sermon. It didn't put the mothers in the audience on a pedestal, but instead acknowledged the impossibility of their task. Chuck invited the women of the congregation to stand and asked everyone else to pray with him that God would strengthen, encourage, and enable these harried moms. Here was an authenticity we had never experienced in an LDS Mother's Day program. Tears streamed down our faces. We knew that we had found a church home.

After the service, as we were heading for our car, an associate pastor saw our red visitor ribbons, introduced himself, and asked us where we were from. We told him that we'd just left Mormonism. That raised his eyebrows. This was our first encounter with Paul Sailhamer. He offered to meet with us, to help us process the transformation we were going through and to answer our questions. We were tremendously encouraged that he was willing to do this, and we hoped against hope that we could have a "real" and honest dialogue.

Nothing better illustrates the difference between Paul Sailhamer's attitude and that of our Mormon bishop than their offices. Our bishop's office was bare except for a desk and a couple of chairs. A flow chart of church positions and pictures of the temple and the Prophet were the only wall decorations. A "triple combination," containing the *Book of Mormon,* the *Doctrine and Covenants,* and the *Pearl of Great Price,* sat on his desk. The office was clean and well organized with nothing out of place. By contrast, Paul's office was a chaos of books and papers, piled on his desk, on the floor, and overflowing from large bookcases. Here was a man who obviously took great delight in reading. Paul wasn't afraid of our questions. In fact, they didn't even seem new to him—he was familiar with multiple perspectives on the issues we raised, including some ancient heresies we thought were doctrines unique to Mormonism. Far from being the empty vessel we had been led to expect of Christian pastors by LDS leaders, Paul drew deep sustenance from his life in Christ in order to minister to us. He was compassionate and responsive and helped guide us through the next few months of transition.

When LeAnn and I began meeting with Paul, I didn't quite know how to become a Christian without joining a church. For LeAnn, conversion had been a process. She couldn't point to a day or a time, nor did she feel the need to. I felt as if I needed to do something, if only for myself, to know that I had truly been born again. We had read Sheldon Van Auken's *A Severe Mercy* and had been deeply moved by Davy's recognition of the bankruptcy of what, on the sur-

face, appeared to be a good and untroubled life. Her words had resonated deeply with our experience and articulated our need. We,
too, had felt the grief of spiritual bankruptcy. What moved us most,
however, was the power and simplicity of her surrender to Christ:
"Today, crossing from one side of the room to the other, I lumped
together all I am, all I fear, hate, love, hope; and, well, DID it. I committed my ways to God in Christ."[2] Like Davy, I felt somehow I
needed to cross from one side of a room to the other, not literally, of
course, but just to be able to say "from this moment on." Paul told
me that some people needed to build an altar, to "pile up some
stones" and point to a precise time when it happened.

My moment finally came over the Memorial Day weekend in 1984.
On May 26, LeAnn and I were out for an early morning walk, talking
about all the things that were happening to us. Suddenly, I knew it
was time—I couldn't postpone it any longer. We knelt together under
an evergreen in front of a red-brick municipal building. I prayed,
"Lord, I'm not sure what it all means right now, but I've basically made
a mess of my life trying to run it myself. Now I'm ready to trust you
exclusively and completely. From this moment on, I belong to you."

There were no bells or whistles, no fiery angels flared. I wasn't
manipulated by God with high octane emotion or an overwhelming spiritual experience such as I had known in my youth. In a curious sense this was the purest act of free will that I've ever known, as
if at that moment I could have chosen any path with absolute liberty. There was a profound quiet in my heart. Life seemed to be holding its breath. I had found "the still point of the turning world."[3]

In that silent place, I freely made my choice to follow Jesus. I have
never experienced a moment's regret for that decision, nor have I
once wanted to return to Mormonism since that day. God has honored my choice and has blessed my family beyond all that I could
have imagined, though not always in ways I would have chosen.

11

But in your hearts set apart Christ as Lord. Always be prepared to give an answer to everyone who asks you to give the reason for the hope that you have. But do this with gentleness and respect, keeping a clear conscience, so that those who speak maliciously against your good behavior in Christ may be ashamed of their slander.

—1 Peter 3:15–16 NIV

The tiny, picturesque village of Oberammergau in the Bavarian Alps is home to a world-famous theatrical production called the Passion Play. A portrayal of the final days of the life of Jesus, it celebrates the town's miraculous deliverance from the Black Plague in 1633 and is performed by residents, according to a solemn vow, once every ten years. My mother and stepfather, Jack Dawson, had seen the play and it became one of Jack's greatest dreams to take his children to Europe to share the experience. With characteristic generosity, he included me, LeAnn, my brother Rick, and his wife Lisa. Plans for this family vacation had been in the works for nearly four years. The trip was scheduled for the summer of 1984, the 250th anniversary of the play's first performance. The family was to spend a week in Paris, then tour Austria and Germany, arriving in Oberammergau in time for the Passion Play. Our children were scheduled to stay with LeAnn's parents in Salt Lake City during the time we were away.

LeAnn and I decided that we wouldn't tell our families about our decision to leave Mormonism until after we had returned from Europe. We didn't want to ruin the summer for everyone by stealing the thunder from Jack's bounteous gift. Telling our parents would be a heart-wrenching task, and we wanted to speak with them in person, at times chosen to minimize their pain as they heard what would certainly be devastating news to them.

LeAnn and I left for Europe ten days earlier than the rest of the family and traveled through Italy together. Those ten days were our honeymoon with God as well as the honeymoon LeAnn and I had never had. I felt amazing joy and peace. The burdens of Mormonism had been lifted, the conflicts resolved—I no longer had to defend the indefensible. I felt liberated! Spiritually, it was a time of great nourishment and excitement. Reading the Bible was like getting good news from home. There was a freshness and dynamism about our faith that expressed itself in sudden bursts of spontaneous delight as well as in deep conversation. LeAnn and I felt a profound sense of connection with each other and with Christians of all ages, especially as we drank in the great art and architecture that is Western civilization's legacy of faith.

We flew into Rome and subsequently traveled by train to Florence, Genova, and Milano, then on to Lugano, Switzerland, and from there to Paris. It was a trip of many hallmarks. Freed from the restrictions of the "Word of Wisdom," an LDS code of health that forbids smoking and the drinking of alcohol or caffeinated hot drinks, LeAnn and I reveled in our morning cups of coffee, the aroma of which hailed us from our pensione bed like church bells. In the evening, we drank wine with sacramental thanksgiving. In Rome, we visited St. Peter's for the first time and saw Michelangelo's poignant and glorious *Pieta*, as well as the awe-inspiring Sistine Chapel, although it was still being restored and was partially obscured. We were thrilled by Bernini and Caravaggio at the Borghese Gallery and by Michelangelo's *Moses* at San Pietro in Vincolo. In Milano, I took LeAnn to the palazzo that contained my first missionary apartment (she was suitably aghast) and the Piazza dell'Duomo where I had worked the street board nearly twelve years before.

It was Florence, however, that captured our hearts. It was uplifting just to walk through the streets and behold such glories of Tuscan architecture as the Duomo, the Giotto Campanile, and Santa Croce. The Ghiberti doors of the Baptistry eloquently told the story of Christian faith, which we were now able to appreciate without reservation. We saw the *David* and the *Four Prisoners* for the first time in the Galleria dell'Accademia. Across the street, we discovered

Fra Angelico's golden angels in the monastery of San Marco. The Uffizzi gallery was a palace of treasures. I stared at the Botticelli *Primavera* for nearly an hour before LeAnn finally touched my shoulder and awakened me from my reverie. At the sight of Caravaggio's *Sacrifice of Isaac*, we both wept, full of gratitude for the new significance that story now held for us.

After a Sabbath rest in Lugano, we met the rest of the family in Paris. The remainder of our vacation was similarly inspiring, filled with further glimpses of the divine through the works of Monet and Rodin, Mozart in Salzburg, Beethoven in Vienna, and, of course, the Passion Play. Family bonds were warm and strong, though at times I shivered with the passing shadow of the hard words I would soon have to speak to my loved ones.

Several weeks after our return from Europe, I drove alone to Mom and Jack's home in Boulder City, Nevada. My mother and I sat together and I quietly explained that I could no longer be a Mormon. We shed some tears, but there were no harsh words, no destructive emotional outbursts. She listened considerately to what I had to say, told me she was sad, and reaffirmed her love for me. For her, anger and defensiveness, along with other expressions of heartbreak and betrayal, would come later, as I knew they must, in bits and pieces. When LeAnn told her parents, it had the immediate effect of a bomb going off and was agonizingly painful for all of them. Jesus had spoken truly when He said:

> Do not think that I came to bring peace on the earth; I did not come to bring peace, but a sword. For I came to set a man against his father, and a daughter against her mother, and a daughter-in-law against her mother-in-law; and a man's enemies will be the members of his household. He who loves father or mother more than Me is not worthy of Me; and he who loves son or daughter more than Me is not worthy of Me. (Matthew 10:34–37 NASB)

LeAnn and I knew that rebuilding close relationships with our parents would take time, dedication, and love.

We began to break the news slowly to a few friends in the autumn of 1984. Members of the Study Group were among the first we told. One of them responded by asking us to write down our disagreements with LDS beliefs, specifically with reference to some articles he enclosed. It was a fair request, respectfully made, but it was a struggle to comply. Writing of this sort was new to us and our emotions were still on edge from the encounters with our parents. Still, we saw the practicality of a written explanation of our position, so we began "An Open Letter to Our Family and Friends." It soon grew to many typewritten pages (we had yet to own a computer) and became a real burden on top of our family and career responsibilities. Finally, after a couple of exhausting, all-night sessions, we delivered this letter to our friend in rough-draft form.

As news of our decision spread, either directly or by word of mouth, we encountered a kaleidoscope of responses. Christian friends, like my longtime music copyist, Ross de Roche, rejoiced outright and admitted that they had been quietly praying for us for years. We were astonished to learn that a number of Christians barely acquainted with us had also been praying, as well as some who had only heard about us through friends or because of the visibility of my career. Apparently, I was a marked man for the hound of heaven. LeAnn and I were deeply grateful for these prayers and for the depth of faith and compassion they represented.

There was also a variety of responses from our Mormon friends and family. Some were respectful and kind, as my mother had been; others lashed out in pain or anger. We were dismayed by the reaction of a few of our LDS friends, who shunned us as apostates, refusing to be associated with us. One even childishly turned her back on LeAnn at the grocery store. Others became hostile, attacking our character and demeaning the issues that were meaningful to us. Despite our best efforts to balance candor with restraint, warfare had broken out. We were subjected to name-calling and ridicule. One of those who responded to our "Open Letter" declared that it was a "silly slander, borrowed thoughtlessly" from "anti-Mormon sources," that it was "essentially baseless, naive, wearisomely common, and irritatingly familiar." Needless to say, these comments hurt deeply. Nevertheless, we persisted in attempting to dialogue and tried not to succumb to bitterness and resentment, though not always successfully. It was a difficult time.

Sensitive to the misunderstandings inherent in the responses we received to our "Open Letter," LeAnn and I felt that we had to continue working on it in order to communicate our experience with greater clarity and to document our study of the issues of Mormonism more thoroughly. We also realized that we needed time to deepen and mature in our new faith, and to let our emotions stabilize so that both the content and style of the letter could be improved. As much as it hurt, the criticism we received did demonstrate that our writing had failed to achieve the balance we had hoped it would. With the benefit of hindsight, it's clear that during the first few months following our announcement, we were raw and overly reactive, feeling the sting of rejection and responding to criticism in an aggressive and defensive manner. The character of our discourse was intense and urgent. In our minds, it was as if our loved ones had been snookered by a giant investment scam that placed their life savings at risk. We felt we had to warn them.

Eventually, this posture settled into a resolute determination. Our writing became more technical, almost academic. We felt that well-constructed arguments and thorough documentation would help us avoid the excesses of our first draft. At various stages of completion, we gave the "Open Letter" to a number of people. At first these were mainly friends and family, but soon the net widened to include others, such as Mormons in transition out of the LDS Church or Christians who wanted information about Mormonism in order to better share their own faith with Latter-day Saints. In its unfinished state, we were concerned that the letter's focus would be skewed to the historical issues that began it, and that the more personal side of the story would be left untold. Carefully drafted cover letters were included to fill out the picture. Soon mounds of correspondence began to pile up.

A kind of war was indeed being waged—a war of worldviews—and, from the LDS perspective, we had betrayed the cause and joined the other side. The history of antagonism between the LDS Church and Christianity is as old as Mormonism itself. Beginning with Joseph Smith, Mormon leaders have called the churches of Christendom "corrupt," "wicked," and "destitute of all authority," and labeled their cardinal doctrines as an "abomination" originating in the "courts of darkness."[1] Evangelical Christians believe that Mormonism is a cult, a purveyor of perverse and destructive views about God and His relationship with humanity. When LeAnn and I were growing up, the term "Christian" had a similarly negative connotation among Latter-day Saints. In recent years, however, Mormon rhetoric has softened in an effort to mainstream the LDS Church and improve its public image. It is now important to the Latter-day Saints to be perceived as Christians, and further as victims of anti-Mormon persecution, instead of aggressors in a conflict of ideas. In large part, this strategy is driven by proselyting zeal—the Church doesn't want to alienate potential converts. Regardless, Mormonism is fundamentally a breakoff from Christianity and LDS converts are still actively recruited from the membership rolls of Christian churches. Evangelicals view this incursion with alarm, as shepherds would regard wolves raiding their flock.

That two such worldviews would clash is not surprising, although some people today might find this conflict a little mystifying and in slightly bad taste. Contemporary culture seems to regard the vigorous defense of the truth of one's principles as an embarrassing, if not unforgivable, sin against the overarching law of tolerance. Anyone making distinctions between "true" and "false," "right" and "wrong," or "good" and "bad," runs the risk of appearing arrogant and judgmental, even malicious.

Nevertheless, everyone has principles, either by choice or by default, and the merit of these principles is ultimately determined, not just by how good they make us feel about ourselves, but more important, by how closely they correspond to objective reality—or in other words, to the "truth." No one intentionally believes something he or she knows to be false. We all want to think that our beliefs are grounded in reality. And that is precisely what makes ideas so dangerous and divisive. Dorothy L. Sayers said it well through her brilliant fictional detective Lord Peter Wimsey, who observed that "principles have become more dangerous than passions . . . and the first thing a principle does—if it really is a principle—is to kill somebody."[2] Principles "kill" because they are exclusive by nature and none "kill" more thoroughly than those involving issues of faith. These are the battlelines where worldviews collide.

Jesus bluntly declared, "I am the way, the truth, and the life: no man cometh unto the Father, but by me" (John 14:6), a claim that would be utterly preposterous if it were not true. Anyone who made such a statement would have to be either lying or colossally self-deceived to the point of madness, not the great moral teacher even skeptics generally acknowledge Jesus to be. If this is true, however, it means that a life apart from Jesus is a life apart from the truth, and therefore grounded in a fundamental unreality that He said would ultimately prove disastrous.

For LeAnn and me, following Jesus meant a thorough reexamination and restructuring of our worldview. It didn't happen all at once, in an instant, at conversion. The process had begun even before our faith in Mormonism was dismantled and was greatly influenced by our exposure to historic Christianity through literature and the arts. LeAnn's experience with Bible Study Fellowship was a catalyst, encouraging us both to read the Bible with new eyes. As we did, we began to learn the dynamics of a biblical worldview, and many questions regarding the nature of God and Jesus, man and salvation, Scripture and the church, had to be asked again and answered authoritatively, beyond the narrow context of Mormonism. These questions were brought into focus and articulated as we prepared our "Open Letter."

The issues we grappled with were essentially rooted in theology, not a discipline that arouses much passion in contemporary culture. For LeAnn and me, however, these issues were intensely personal—not just intellectual curiosities, but touchstones that revealed the genuineness or artificiality of the various facets of our relationship with a God who was actively engaged in rearranging our lives. For us, theology had an immediate, practical application, both in the defense of our decision to leave Mormonism and follow Christ and in our daily experience. Our prayers, thoughts, activities, and relationships were all impacted by theological concerns. In the years that followed our conversion, the study of theology continued to consume much of our spare time and breathed vitality into our intellectual life. This part of the journey was characterized by the careful, painstaking work of serious Bible study.

It was of critical importance, in approaching questions about God, that LeAnn and I have confidence in the Bible. Before we could ever be fully satisfied with the answers it offered, we had to be sure that the Bible was a trustworthy source of information, that we wouldn't be compromising our integrity by placing faith in its historicity. Given the failure of the LDS scriptures in this regard, we didn't want to be guilty of buying into a set of rationalizations and excuses for the Bible, similar to those made about the *Book of Mormon.*

Aside from the issues of Mormonism, however, the need for some objective point of reference was obvious. Without one, all questions about God are reduced to matters of personal opinion or subjective experience. This is tantamount to playing a sport without first agreeing on the rules. If God is real, however, and not just a figment of human imagination, our opinions and even our experiences are ultimately irrelevant unless they are in accord with what is really true about Him. That is why Christians give the Bible such primacy. It is the ruler by which the truth of all further claims about God are measured.

As Mormons, LeAnn and I had been taught to hold a rather ambivalent view of the Bible. Although the LDS Church affirms the Bible as the first of its four standard works and the primary witness to the divinity of Jesus Christ, it also holds that it contains the Word of God only "as far as it is translated correctly."[3] Joseph Smith taught that "many important points touching the salvation of men, had been taken from the Bible, or lost before it was compiled."[4] He also said that the Bible was correct as "it came from the pen of the original writers," but that "ignorant translators, careless transcribers, or designing and corrupt priests have committed many errors."[5] The *Book of Mormon* claims that many "plain and precious things" were removed from the Bible and mocks those who would rely on it alone (1 Nephi 13:20–29 and 2 Nephi 29:3–14).

Because of these teachings, when LeAnn and I read the Bible, we did so with the caveat that it ultimately had to be interpreted in light of the revelations unique to Mormonism. In other words, we could only have full confidence that the Bible was true where LDS leaders had affirmed that it was. Thus, their authority was effectively equal to or even superseded the authority of the Bible.[6] These significant reservations ultimately rendered the Bible insufficient as a trustworthy guide for our faith as Latter-day Saints. LeAnn and I had what Christians sometimes call a "low view" of the Bible as Scripture. We read it and quoted from it when it served to prove a point, but we rarely allowed it to challenge our basic assumptions or convict us of error. Whenever the Bible came into conflict with modern revelation, we dismissed these passages as evidence of textual corruption.

One of the most important things God did for LeAnn and me in restructuring our worldview was to change our attitude toward the Bible. This happened in two fundamental ways. On the empirical side, we discovered that the historical veracity of the Bible rested on some very solid ground indeed. We didn't have to commit intellectual suicide in order to trust it. More profoundly, though, our faith in the authority of the Bible as the Word of God increased, enabling us to submit our own wills to it in obedience. This frame of mind was not forced upon us. As Christians living under grace, LeAnn and I began to find an inner desire to order our lives according to its standards and to shape our thinking about God according to its precepts.

While no amount of material evidence can force one to faith, in the case of the Bible, we learned that there is more than sufficient evidence to warrant taking the step of faith with integrity. To believe in it is not to take a leap in the dark. LeAnn and I found support for the reliability of the Bible in two fields of empirical endeavor that had proven so disastrous to our confidence in the historicity of the *Book of Mormon*: textual studies and archaeology.

As we became better acquainted with scholarship relative to the biblical texts, we were impressed with the remarkable preservation and amazing fidelity of both Old and New Testaments. The Jewish Scriptures of the Old Testament were safeguarded as no other manuscripts have ever been. For example, during the Talmudist period, between A.D. 100 and 500, special classes of men were assigned to count each letter and syllable, every word, paragraph, and column. These scribes exercised extraordinary discipline when copying the Scriptures, and detailed regulations and rituals governed all facets of the process. All manuscripts had to be verified before they were released for use, and a textually flawed or physically defaced copy was immediately condemned. As a result of these, and other like disciplines over the centuries, the number of variant readings within the early Scriptures is amazingly small, especially considering the age and number of the manuscripts. The Dead Sea Scrolls demonstrated just how accurately the text of portions of the Old Testament had been preserved. Copies of Isaiah discovered in one of the Qumran caves "proved to be word for word identical with our standard Hebrew Bible in more than ninety-five percent of the text."[7]

We learned that there is an equally strong case for the reliability of the New Testament. According to noted scholar F. F. Bruce, "There is no body of ancient literature in the world which enjoys such a wealth of good textual attestation as the New Testament."[8] The amount of time between the original composition and the date of the earliest extant manuscripts is shorter in the case of the New Testament than with any other ancient work. And "the variant readings about which any doubt remains among textual critics of the New Testament affect no material question of historic fact or of Christian faith and practice."[9] Furthermore, practically the entire New Testament can be reconstructed from quotations in the writings of the early church fathers, indicating a high level of consistency. Evidence for the New Testament writings is "much greater than the evidence for many writings of classical authors, the authenticity of which no-one dreams of questioning. And if the New Testament were a collection of secular writings, their authenticity would generally be regarded as beyond all doubt."[10]

Along with the weight of positive support from textual studies, our view of the Bible also benefited from work in the field of archaeology. Much physical evidence has been unearthed, especially in recent years, that serves to substantiate the historicity of the biblical record. While specific finds are exhilarating, such as the recent discoveries of inscriptional references to the House of David and Caiaphas,[11] it is the authenticity of the Bible's big picture that stands in starkest contrast to the *Book of Mormon*. No one can definitively pinpoint the land of the Nephites, but the location of Israel is unquestionable, as are many of its specific topographical details that are mentioned in the Bible. No one can definitively identify a *Book of Mormon* city like Zarahemla, but schoolchildren can find Jerusalem on the map. The general cultural context revealed by archaeological research has supported the biblical record rather than undermined it.[12]

All of this information came as a great relief to LeAnn and me, especially in light of the contrast it represented with the LDS scriptures. It bolstered our faith in the Bible to realize that it had survived and transcended the most detailed sort of scrutiny for many years. While LeAnn and I are aware that there are some who disagree with this assessment and that controversial issues remain, we believe there is more than enough positive evidence to justify our confidence in the Bible. In light of textual and archaeological studies, we are persuaded that it is a compilation of authentic historical texts and satisfied that our trust in its reliability can be maintained with integrity.

This conclusion is thoroughly consistent with the position of the authors of the various books that make up the Bible. The Old Testament is written predominantly as history and the writers of the New Testament consistently appeal to the historical veracity of their experience to establish the truth of their message.[13] The most important biblical witness for the historicity of the Bible, however, is Jesus Christ Himself. Jesus often affirmed the propositional truth of the Old Testament, treating its events and characters as historic rather than mythic.[14] Those who would take Him seriously should not do otherwise.

The issue of historicity, however, differs from the issue of the authority of the Bible. One can believe that it is historically true, and still reject that it has any claim on one's life. Because the Bible rests on solid footings in the material world, however, and on the bedrock witness of Jesus and His apostles, one can approach it in faith to learn about God and to develop a real relationship with Him. This is the second way God changed our attitude about His Word. As our confidence in the reliability of the Bible as history soared, so did our confidence in its authority.

LeAnn and I feel a deep sense of gratitude for the Bible and our trust in God has deepened as we've seen how He has watched over and protected the integrity of His Word—He is a God who keeps His promises.[15] We have come to treasure the biblical passages that speak of the Scripture as the trustworthy arbiter of truth: "Thy word is a lamp unto my feet, and a light unto my path" (Psalm 119:105). It is "profitable for doctrine, for reproof, for correction, for instruction in righteousness: That the man of God may be perfect, thoroughly furnished unto all good works" (2 Timothy 3:16–17). "The word of God is quick, and powerful, and sharper than any two-edged sword, piercing even to the dividing asunder of soul and spirit, and of the joints and marrow, and is a discerner of the thoughts and intents of the heart" (Hebrews 4:12).[16] Each of these passages has been brought home to us and made personal as the Word of God has worked in our lives.

There is an important intellectual component built into our response to Scripture as well: Luke writes in the book of Acts that residents of the ancient Macedonian city of Berea were considered "more noble" because "they received the word with all readiness of mind, and searched the scriptures daily, whether those things were so" (17:10–12). This is an indication that the truths contained in the Bible can be approached through reason—they do not violate the laws of logic or rationality. The Word of God also assumes universal meaning and application, maintaining that "no prophecy of the scripture is of any private interpretation" (2 Peter 1:19–21).

God has gifted all human beings with reasoning minds, conscience and intuition, hearts that feel, moral accountability in our communities, the lessons of history, and our own experience. These qualities are to be kept in balance, however, under the authority of God's Word. If any one of these factors becomes elevated disproportionately over the others, particularly if we place them above truth that God has already revealed, we become susceptible to deception. For LeAnn and me, the Bible has become the lens through which we view our life and examine questions regarding our worldview. This is where we have taken our stand and echo the powerful words of Martin Luther: "Unless I am convicted of error by the testimony of Scripture or . . . by manifest reasoning I stand convicted by the Scriptures to which I have appealed, and my conscience is taken captive by God's word."[17]

Probably the most significant issue that the Bible can address concerns the nature and character of God. While it is undoubtedly true that we will all go to our graves with a few mistaken notions about Him, who God is, nevertheless, is a critical question that must be answered in every human life. Eventually, we *will* all answer it, one way or another, if only by default. Our thoughts, our words, and our actions all testify daily to what we really think about God. Of course, the idea that we can consciously come to terms with who God is rests on the assumption that some objective truth *can* be learned about Him. Contemporary culture seems to regard this notion as the pinnacle of arrogant presumption. If God is real, however, there must be some things that are true about Him and other things that are not. There is no escaping this fact. Even the notion that God is not real becomes an affirmation of exclusive propositional truth about Him.

Beyond the question of merely knowing *about* God, however, is that of whether we can really *know* Him in a personal sense. How can we have a real relationship with our Maker? The significance of the distinction between these two ways of knowing was driven home to me by an experience I had several years ago. When my son Jonathan was about seven-and-a-half years old, we were at the beach one day with his two older sisters. At that time, the girls were not yet teenagers. After we had been on the sand for a couple of hours, they asked to go to the snack shack to get some food. Jonathan wanted to go with them. So I said to the girls, "Okay, watch your little brother, and whatever you do, stick together."

"Sure Dad, no problem."

Off they went and, about twenty minutes later, they came walking back without Jonathan. "Where's your little brother?" I demanded.

"We thought he was right behind us," they responded, surprised at his absence. "He must have stopped to buy something else. A man gave him money for some candy."

"Oh no," I thought, "the oldest trick in the book." I dashed back to the snack shack: no Jonathan. When I scoured the immediate area, I still couldn't find him. After a few more minutes of desperate searching, I ran barefoot over a stand of iceplant (without even noticing it) to a kiosk where I talked to some security personnel. They asked me to give them a description of my son. A description of Jonathan—someone I love most in the whole world. How should I describe him: three feet tall, green eyes, blonde hair? What about his affectionate nature, the sweetness of his spirit, his silvery laughter? A physical description could never contain all of who he is, not all of who he is to me anyway. Nevertheless, without it there was no chance of security recognizing him on the beach, even if they stared right at him.

It was incredibly painful for me to describe my son. In the end, all they could say was that they would bring him back if he turned up. I walked back to the beach and sat down, utterly dejected and terrified. I couldn't think of any other alternative but to sit there and wait. If he had been abducted, he was getting farther and farther away by the minute. We might never see him again. I tried to be patient and keep up my hope, praying that somehow he would show up.

After the longest half hour of my life, he came walking back along the beach with a friendly young couple. He had taken a wrong turn at the snack shack and wandered off. They had noticed him crying and had offered to help. He did the same thing I had done, only in reverse, giving them my description, trying to remember details that would enable them to help him find his father on the beach.

At its root, this is what a theology of God is all about: finding our father on the beach. We are all lost, and we need some basic descriptive information about Him so that we can find Him. Theology is never going to tell us all that God is or all that He means to us (as though He could be wrapped up in a box), but at least it can help us recognize Him in a crowd. And in a world with so many competing views of God, finding Him in a crowd is exactly what we must do.

Addressing this issue in the course of our Bible study, LeAnn and I found and focused on four basic identifying characteristics of God that differed irreconcilably from concepts we had been taught as Mormons. As we did this, a strong and clear image of who God really is grew in our minds and in our hearts. Like a diamond displayed on black velvet, the contrast between worldviews heightened our appreciation for what is genuine.

First of all, the Bible teaches that there is only one true God. Among all that exists, He is absolutely unique. Moses declared to the congregation of Israel:

> Hear, O Israel: The Lord our God is one Lord: And thou shalt love the Lord thy God with all thine heart, and with all thy soul, and with all thy might. (Deuteronomy 6:4–5)

Known as the *shema,* this passage was fundamental to the monotheism of ancient Israel and the truth it articulates is reiterated many times throughout both Testaments.[18] Some of the most direct and powerful statements about God's uniqueness are found in the book of Isaiah:

> Ye are my witnesses, saith the Lord, and my servant whom I have chosen: that ye may know and believe me, and understand that I am he: before me there was no God formed, neither shall there be after me. I, even I, am the Lord; and beside me there is no saviour.

Thus saith the Lord the King of Israel, and his redeemer the Lord of hosts; I am the first, and I am the last; and beside me there is no God.

Fear ye not, neither be afraid: have not I told thee from that time, and have declared it? ye are even my witnesses. Is there a God beside me? yea, there is no God; I know not any. (Isaiah 43:10–11; 44:6, 8)[19]

Joseph Smith, however, taught that "in the beginning, the head of the Gods called a council of the Gods; and they came together and concocted a plan to create the world and people it."[20] More than this, he said that righteous and worthy men could eventually "ascend the throne of eternal power" and become gods themselves:

. . . and you have got to learn how to be Gods yourselves, and to be kings and priests to God, the same as all Gods have done before you, namely, by going from one small degree to another, and from a small capacity to a great one.[21]

Unless these words have been drained of their meaning, the Bible and Joseph Smith cannot both be right on this point. The two ideas are mutually exclusive. Human beings can never become gods when God Himself has declared, "before me there was no God formed, neither shall there be after me" (Isaiah 43:10).

The second concept is a corollary to the first. The Bible teaches not only that God is utterly unique, but that He is also the supreme being, the omnipotent Lord of all. There is no one equal to or higher than He. Solomon, for example, addresses Him with the words, "Lord God of Israel, there is no God like thee, in heaven above, or on earth beneath . . . behold, the heaven and heaven of heavens cannot contain thee" (1 Kings 8:23). Throughout the Bible, God is referred to as the "most High" or, in Jesus' words, "the Highest." He is morally perfect, the Almighty, and the "most just," the "only wise," and the only "good". The apostle Paul describes Him as "the blessed and only Potentate, the King of kings, and Lord of lords; who only hath immortality, dwelling in the light which no man can approach unto" (1 Timothy 6:15–16).[22]

Joseph Smith, however, advanced notions that run completely contrary to this. He believed, for instance, that God the Father also had a father.

> Where was there ever a son without a father? And where was there
> ever a father without first being a son? . . . Hence if Jesus had a Father,
> can we not believe that He had a Father also?[23]

In fact, LDS doctrine holds that there is an infinite number of gods,
similar to the generations of man, which proceed from father to
son.[24] Furthermore, God the Father earned His exaltation and earns
even greater glory as His children become gods. Joseph Smith represented Jesus as saying:

> My Father worked out his kingdom with fear and trembling, and I
> must do the same; and when I get my kingdom, I shall present it to
> my Father, so that he may obtain kingdom upon kingdom, and it will
> exalt him in glory. He will then take a higher exaltation, and I will take
> his place, and thereby become exalted myself.[25]

Obviously, if God could ever "take a higher exaltation," then He
couldn't have possessed the highest to begin with.

Third, the Bible teaches that God is eternal. He has always been
and will always be God: "Before the mountains were brought forth,
or ever thou hadst formed the earth and the world, even from everlasting to everlasting, thou art God" (Psalm 90:1–2).[26] He is self-
existent, meaning that He owes His life to nothing and to no one
else. While His dealings with us are responsive, He does not change
in His basic nature or moral will.[27]

Again, Joseph Smith taught a radically different view of God with
respect to this issue.

> God himself was once as we are now, and is an exalted man, and sits
> in yonder heavens! That is the great secret. . . . I am going to tell you
> how God came to be God. We have imagined and supposed that God
> was God from all eternity. I will refute that idea and take away the veil
> that you may see.[28]

Though the Bible clearly maintains that God is God from everlasting to everlasting, Joseph Smith wanted to "refute" this basic truth.
If God "came to be God," He cannot eternally have been God.

The fourth important aspect of God's nature that LeAnn and I
found clearly articulated in the Bible is that He is the creator of all

things.[29] This includes human beings, both body and spirit.[30] The Bible teaches that God called them into being when they did not exist (Romans 4:17, also Hebrews 11:3). He was fully able to create out of nothing by the power of His word: "For he spake, and it was done; he commanded and it stood fast" (Psalm 33:9, also 148:1–5 and 2 Peter 3:5–7).

Once again, Joseph Smith set himself against the Word of God, this time with regard to creation:

> The pure principles of element are principles which can never be destroyed; they may be organized and reorganized, but not destroyed. They had no beginning and can have no end. . . . the soul—the mind of man—the immortal spirit. Where did it come from? All learned men and doctors of divinity say that God created it in the beginning; but it is not so: the very idea lessens man in my estimation.[31]

Joseph Smith taught that element, or matter, had no creation. Despite his allegation, "learned men and doctors of divinity" didn't originate the idea that God created the soul of man in the beginning. The Bible itself reveals that God is the source of man's existence. Man did not become a "living soul" of any kind until God gave him the "breath of life" (Genesis 2:7). He even "formeth the spirit of man within him" (Zechariah 12:1). It appears that Joseph Smith preferred to "lessen" God rather than man in his estimation.

LeAnn and I found these four distinctions to be quite clear and fundamental to our relationship with God. Where the uniqueness, supremacy, eternal nature, and creativity of God are concerned, the teachings of the Bible and those of Joseph Smith are in direct opposition. In each case, Joseph Smith's ideas obfuscated the clarity of that most basic of all Christian concepts—that God is God and we are not.

In considering these issues, LeAnn and I ran headlong into an historic Christian doctrine that as Mormons we had found ridiculous: the Trinity. While the Bible plainly teaches that there is only one God, three persons are actually called God: the Father, the Son, and the Holy Spirit.[32] As we studied the relevant biblical passages, we came to believe that the early Christian Fathers' definition of "God in three persons" was the best way to articulate this paradox. Explanations that deny the Trinity distort the Word of God, either by reducing God,

Jesus, and the Holy Spirit to three aspects of a single person, or by sundering the unity of God in favor of three completely separate beings.

Joseph Smith erred according to the latter of these two extremes, insisting the Father, Son, and Holy Spirit were three separate Gods:

> I have always declared God to be a distinct personage, Jesus Christ a separate and distinct personage from God the Father, and that the Holy Ghost was a distinct personage and a Spirit: and these three constitute three distinct personages and three Gods. If this is in accordance with the New Testament, lo and behold! we have three Gods anyhow, and they are plural; and who can contradict it?[33]

The Father, the Son, and the Holy Ghost cannot be three separate and distinct gods or God would be mistaken when He says, "beside me there is no God" (Isaiah 44:6). Moreover, Joseph Smith did not limit the plurality of gods to the Father, Son, and Holy Spirit, but included the idea that men could become gods as well.

For LeAnn and me, unraveling the Mormon conception of God was like solving a case of mistaken identity. If someone had approached me the day Jonathan was lost on the beach, claiming that they had found him, but then had proceeded to describe him as four feet tall, with black hair and blue eyes, I would have known immediately that they were not talking about my son. In a similar manner, the more LeAnn and I studied the Bible, the more obvious it became that the God described by Joseph Smith was not the same as the God revealed in Scripture.

The same sort of conflict between the Bible and Mormonism can be seen regarding the identity of Jesus. Most critically, the Bible teaches that Jesus is God:

> In the beginning was the Word, and the Word was with God, and the Word was God. The same was in the beginning with God. All things were made by him; and without him was not anything made that was made. In him was life; and the life was the light of men. . . . And the Word was made flesh, and dwelt among us, (and we beheld his glory, the glory as of the only begotten of the Father,) full of grace and truth. (John 1:1–4, 14)

This passage is as moving and indisputable an affirmation of the deity of Christ as one could require. "The Word" obviously refers to Jesus because John further says He was "made flesh, and dwelt among us." John later reports that, following the resurrection, even the skeptical Thomas calls him "My Lord and my God" (John 20:28). The other apostles also affirm the deity of Jesus Christ. Matthew refers to him as "Emmanuel, which being interpreted is, God with us" (1:23). Paul instructs the Ephesian elders to "feed the church of God, which he hath purchased with his own blood" (Acts 20:28) and tells the Colossians that "in him dwelleth all the fulness of the Godhead bodily" (Colossians 2:9). To Timothy, he writes unambiguously that "God was manifest in the flesh" (1 Timothy 3:16).[34]

As Mormons, LeAnn and I had believed that Jesus, like all mortals (and devils, including Lucifer), was a spirit child of God the Father—preeminent not because He was of a different nature than ours, but rather because He was the *firstborn* son, inheritor of His Father's business along with all the rights and powers that accrue to that position. He had further distinguished Himself through the excellence of His character and works in the pre-earth life. Then, because He led a sinless life on earth and successfully accomplished the work of atonement to which He was called, He earned His own salvation and was exalted to ultimate godhood, thereby setting an example and providing the means and opportunity for our own eternal progression.[35]

As a consequence of these beliefs, Mormonism views the incarnation of Christ as rather routine—all spirit children of the Heavenly Father must necessarily take on bodies in order to advance. In contrast to this, LeAnn and I now see the incarnation as a unique and miraculous event—Almighty God made flesh—what T.S. Eliot calls "the point of intersection of the timeless with time." "Here the impossible union of spheres of existence is actual, here the past and future are conquered, and reconciled."[36]

The Bible teaches that the birth of Jesus was a miracle accomplished through the power of the Holy Spirit—a supernatural rather than a natural event. The classic Christian doctrine of the Virgin Birth comes from a careful adherence to the Scriptures regarding the incarnation.[37] Mormonism, by contrast, teaches that "Christ was begotten by an Immortal Father in the same way that mortal men are begotten by mortal fathers."[38] In other words, Jesus was con-ceived through a sexual union between God the Father and Mary, made possible because, according to LDS doctrine, God has a cor-poreal body owing to the fact that He is a glorified man. In contrast to the biblical account of the Virgin Birth, Mormonism effectively reduces "the glory of the incorruptible God into an image made like to corruptible man" (Romans 1:23). This pattern emerges in many of Joseph Smith's teachings.

Misunderstanding the identity of God and Jesus is to theology what reasoning from a faulty theorem is to mathematics—every-thing that follows is skewed. So it is in the case of Joseph Smith. Just as his ideas about the nature of the Father and Son were distorted, so he distorted another basic biblical teaching, concerning the nature of man. Few ideas are better documented in the Bible than the sin of Adam and its tragic effect on the nature of man. "Where-fore, as by one man sin entered the world and death by sin; and so death passed upon all men, for that all have sinned" (Romans 5:12).[39] Because of Adam's rebellion, we are born with a sin nature, an evil bent. David laments, "Behold, I was shapen in iniquity; and in sin did my mother conceive me" (Psalm 51:5).[40]

Sin nature manifests itself through individual acts of sin. None can escape the inevitable flowering of evil: "we are all as an unclean thing, and all our righteousnesses are as filthy rags; and we all do fade as a leaf; and our iniquities, like the wind, have taken us away" (Isaiah 64:6). Despite contemporary confidence that the person who follows his or her heart will never go wrong, the Bible teaches that "the heart is deceitful above all things, and desperately wicked: who can know it?" (Jeremiah 17:9).

Yet as Mormons, LeAnn and I were taught from childhood that "men will be punished for their own sins and not for Adam's trans-gression."[41] LDS apostle John A. Widtsoe observed that "in the true gospel of Jesus Christ there is no original sin,"[42] and President Joseph Fielding Smith stated:

> The fall of man came as a blessing in disguise, and was the means of furthering the purposes of the Lord in the progress of man, rather than a means of hindering them. . . . I never speak of the part Eve took in this fall as a sin, nor do I accuse Adam of a sin.[43]

These ideas flow directly from Joseph Smith's teachings that in order to become gods, it was necessary for men to experience mortality. Therefore, Adam's "choice" was not a sin, but rather an opportunity. Some Mormons referred to it as a fall "upward." The *Book of Mormon* infers as much: "Adam fell that men might be, and men are that they might have joy" (2 Nephi 2:25).

Once again, the Bible and Mormonism are in conflict over a fundamental issue. Yet even apart from the weight accorded sin nature in the Word of God, LeAnn and I believe the biblical view corresponds more closely to the reality of human experience. We find plenty of evidence for the truth of the Bible's tragic assessment of the root of human evil in ourselves and in the world around us. With what we have learned from our own experience and the lessons of history, nothing rings more false to us now than the artificial optimism of those who believe in the perfectibility of man through some process of evolution or self-improvement.

The apostle Paul declares that "the wages of sin is death" (Romans 6:23), referring not only to physical death, but also to spiritual death, which is eternal alienation from God and consequently all that is just, right, and good—a horrible prospect. It's not just a question of the quantity of our sin, but of its quality. Even a single sin rips the cosmic fabric and renders us guilty, deserving of spiritual death according to the justice of an utterly holy and righteous God—"For whosoever shall keep the whole law, and yet offend in one point, he is guilty of all" (James 2:10).

If this determination seems harsh, it differs not in kind, but merely by degree when compared with what every human being instinctively knows to be true. Whatever our moral code, none of us has been able to observe it perfectly. We have all crossed over the line at one time or another. Ordinarily, we let ourselves off the hook with excuses or by pretending that our actions didn't really hurt anyone. It is evident, however, that they do, often in ways that we can't see. The effects spread and amplify like ripples on a lake. The God of the Bible insists that we own every last shred of responsibility for our behaviors.

Yet this responsibility is a burden that we are not able to bear. How we can be relieved of guilt and saved from the justice we deserve for the harm we cause is still another issue on which the Bible and Mormonism differ. As Latter-day Saints, LeAnn and I were taught that "to get salvation we must not only do some things, but everything which God has commanded."[44] The third LDS Article of Faith states that "through the Atonement of Christ all mankind may be saved by obedience to the laws and ordinances of the Gospel." This effectively means that Jesus merely opens the door for individual men and women to earn, by their own good works, a life with God hereafter. Former LDS President Heber J. Grant expanded on this idea:

> If you want to know how to be saved, I can tell you: it is by keeping the commandments of God. No power on earth, no power beneath the earth, will ever prevent you or me or any Latter-day Saint from being saved, except ourselves. We are the architects of our own lives, not only of our lives here, but our lives to come in the eternity.[45]

President Spencer W. Kimball, prophet of the LDS Church at the time LeAnn and I left Mormonism, succinctly stated the Mormon perspective:

> Man can transform himself, and he must. Man has in himself the seeds of godhood, which can germinate and grow and develop. As the acorn becomes the oak, the mortal man becomes a god. It is within his power to lift himself by his very bootstraps from the plane on which he finds himself to the plane on which he should be. It may be a long, hard lift with many obstacles, but it is a real possibility.[46]

The assertion that man is a god in embryo with the ability to transform himself is the real heart of the Mormon plan of salvation. Among the innumerable good deeds required for ultimate exaltation, this plan also demands personal payment for all unrepented sins. This belief was the cause of much of the depression I experienced as a Mormon. I can barely remember all my sins, let alone repent of them. But a holy and just God remembers—He hears my idle words, knows my prideful thoughts and ulterior motives, sees the disguised selfishness that is my daily ruin. I once tried to rationalize these sins, thinking that if I just did my best, God would overlook the rest, essentially compromising His perfect righteousness to salve my conscience. But the fact is that spiritual death is the payment for all such sins and without help beyond my own feeble attempts at repentance, I am certainly lost.

The Bible's concept of salvation from sin is rooted in grace, the unmerited favor of God offered as a free gift to anyone who will take it. We receive it simply by believing Him, trusting His promises and His provision over our own resources. When LeAnn and I took God at His word and trusted the fact that Jesus really was our Savior and Lord—which meant believing that His death on the cross was the last word on our sin—we were given a spiritual rebirth in which our old nature was ruled dead and Jesus' righteousness was credited to our account. Even though we knew we would continue to fall short of His perfect holiness, we could have the confidence that, because *He* keeps *His* promises, we would go home to be with Him in heaven when life was over. This was good news! In fact, it was the best news LeAnn and I had ever heard. This is the crux of Christianity. As Latter-day Saints, we had implicitly denied Christ's sufficiency when we attempted to add our own efforts to His finished work.

Although Mormons speak of Christ as Savior, with love and reverence, they do not trust him solely or completely. Not long after LeAnn became a Christian, she was accused of trusting in Jesus too much. "Don't you tell me Jesus is enough," one Latter-day Saint warned. This is because the Mormon Jesus is ultimately unable to save those who do not keep all of His commandments. Hence, the LDS Church trains its members from childhood on to rely on a myriad of "do's and don'ts" and to focus on their obedience to the laws and ordinances taught by the Church, rather than emphasizing the liberating grace of Christ that transforms life from within. LeAnn and I know firsthand that the preponderance of LDS Church teaching is on self-reliance and the earning of exaltation through personal righteousness. Good works to that end were enjoined in numberless sacrament meetings and conferences that we attended. The absence of a strong and consistent focus on Jesus and His work is hard for most Mormons to recognize. Yet, in our experience as Latter-day Saints, if He was mentioned at all, other than at the end of talks and prayers, He was discussed primarily as an exemplar of the perfection that we were expected to imitate. In Mormonism, the cross is seen merely as the cruel instrument of Jesus' death, not as the means of human redemption.

By contrast, the Bible offers assurance to those who believe that Jesus is able to save them completely.

> For God so loved the world, that he gave his only begotten Son, that whosoever believeth in him should not perish, but have everlasting life. For God sent not his Son into the world to condemn the world; but that the world through him might be saved. He that believeth on him is not condemned: but he that believeth not is condemned already, because he hath not believed in the name of the only begotten son of God. (John 3:16–18)

> Verily, verily, I say unto you, He that heareth my word, and believeth on him that sent me, hath everlasting life, and shall not come into condemnation; but is passed from death unto life (John 5:24).

The apostle Paul, who was converted en route to killing Christians, understood just how sufficient this Jesus is:

> But God, who is rich in mercy, for his great love wherewith he loved us, even when we were dead in sins, hath quickened us together with Christ, (by grace ye are saved;) and hath raised us up together, and made us sit together in heavenly places in Christ Jesus: that in the ages to come he might shew the exceeding riches of his grace in his kindness toward us through Christ Jesus. For by grace are ye saved through faith; and that not of yourselves: it is the gift of God: not of works, lest any man should boast. For we are his workmanship, created in Christ Jesus unto good works, which God hath before ordained that we should walk in them. (Ephesians 2:4–10)[47]

Salvation is found only through the blood of Jesus Christ, shed on the cross as payment in full for our sins, not through our own good works, however impressive they may be. At the foot of His cross, Christ put an end to our fruitless attempts to make ourselves worthy before Him. LeAnn and I now trust solely in His grace for eternal life and respond to Him with obedience rooted in love and gratitude rather than in self-centered efforts to earn favor or escape punishment. Moreover, He has promised in His Word to shoulder the responsibility for the development of our personal righteousness and we are confident that "He which hath begun a good work in [us] will perform it until the day of Jesus Christ" (Philippians 1:6).

In addition to divergent ways of understanding the nature of God and Jesus, man and salvation, Mormon views also differ significantly from those of the Bible concerning the nature of the church. According to Mormonism, Christ failed to establish a church that lasted. Joseph Smith claimed that Jesus' church in Israel ended in universal apostasy, and that the form of Christianity that eventually made its way to Europe and beyond was not the true worship of God.[48] Joseph Smith claimed that he was called by God to restore the true church.[49]

The Bible doesn't allow for a universal apostasy. The New Testament contains numerous promises that guarantee the uninterrupted continuity of Christ's church. Jesus tells Peter that "the gates of hell shall not prevail against it" (Matthew 16:18). He assures the apostles that they will bring forth fruit, and that their fruit will remain (John 15:16).[50] There was no need for a restoration of the church claimed by Joseph Smith. As Paul writes to the Corinthians: "For other foundation can no man lay than that is laid, which is Jesus Christ" (1 Corinthians 3:11). The church is represented in the Bible as Christ's body—having been raised from the grave, how could it die again?

Ironically, the *Book of Mormon* recounts that Jesus failed to establish a church that lasted in the western hemisphere as well. The realization was not lost on Joseph Smith, who once boasted:

> For I will come out on the top at last. I have more to boast of than ever any man had. I am the only man that has ever been able to keep a whole church together since the days of Adam. A large majority of the whole have stood by me. Neither Paul, John, Peter, nor Jesus ever did it. I boast that no man ever did such a work as I. The followers of Jesus ran away from him; but the Latter-day Saints never ran away from me yet.[51]

Joseph Smith's claims and his assertion of a universal apostasy are deeply offensive to Christians. The Lord of the Universe does not fail. The true church of Christ is a community of faith made up of people from many cultures all over the world. It is more like an organism than an organization, and it has continued to grow as God causes it to grow, uninterrupted since He began it.

The Bible and Mormonism further differ on the related concept of the authority of the church. LDS doctrine teaches that God's authority, the priesthood, is a thing that must be physically transmitted by means of a ritual act, from one who possesses it to another who does not. According to Mormon belief, there is no other way to obtain it.[52]

In the Bible, however, God grants believers permission to exercise His authority through His Word. In fact, He has commanded this.

> And Jesus came and spake unto them, saying, All power is given unto me in heaven and in earth. Go ye therefore, and teach all nations, baptizing them in the name of the Father, and of the Son, and of the Holy Ghost: teaching them to observe all things whatsoever I have commanded you: and, lo, I am with you alway, even unto the end of the world. (Matthew 28:18–20)

In this passage, Jesus confirms that He possesses all power. Therefore He is fully able to grant authority by verbally commanding His disciples to go, teach, and baptize. This doesn't require an act of transmission, but a word of permission. Jesus designed this authority to reproduce itself among all nations as the disciples taught others to spread the gospel. He promised that He would be with them—and by extension, with us—even unto the end of the world. His apostles are still teaching us today through their words, divinely preserved in the Bible, by which we have been given authority to observe all of God's commands.

These distinctions between Mormonism and the Bible are authentic, fundamental, and mutually exclusive. They require that one choose between the two, and only one can be the final arbiter of the truth. Most Latter-day Saints, however, are unwilling to see the choice in these terms. Some contemporary LDS apologists, perhaps in an effort to make Mormonism more palatable to potential converts (or even to themselves), have attempted to downplay these disparities and incorporate into Mormonism some of the vocabulary and concepts common to evangelical Christians. The ideas inevitably undergo a radical redefinition, however, in the Mormon context. Ultimately, such efforts founder on the shoals of Joseph Smith's teachings, which are clear and inescapable.

It is Joseph Smith, not Jesus Christ, that sets Mormonism apart from the rest of the world's religions, Christian or otherwise. He is the pivotal figure in LDS faith. He is the grid through which Mormons ultimately filter their understanding of God, and therefore, in a very real sense, their relationship to the Creator depends on Joseph Smith. Despite clearcut biblical teaching that "there is one God, and one mediator between God and men, the man Christ Jesus" (1 Timothy 2:5),[53] the Mormon Church has effectively made Joseph Smith an additional mediator. Brigham Young even went so far as to say:

> Joseph Smith holds the keys of this last dispensation, and is now engaged behind the veil in the great work of the last days . . . No man or woman in this dispensation will ever enter into the celestial kingdom of God without the consent of Joseph Smith . . . He holds the keys of that kingdom for the last dispensation—the keys to rule in the spirit-world; and he rules there triumphantly . . . He was foreordained in eternity to preside over this last dispensation.[54]

This is a dangerous situation, no matter who the leader might be. God states clearly through Jeremiah that "cursed be the man that trusteth in man, and maketh flesh his arm" (17:5). Jesus warned that false prophets would come and appear to be sheep of His flock. They might even do many wonderful works in His name. Inwardly, however, they would be ravening wolves (Matthew 7:15). The apostle Paul writes that no one should marvel at this masquerade "for Satan himself is transformed into an angel of light. Therefore it is no great thing if his ministers also be transformed as the ministers of righteousness" (2 Corinthians 11:14). He exhorted the early Christians not to be moved from "the grace of Christ unto another gospel" (Galatians 1:6), even if it is preached by one who appears to be "an angel from heaven" (Galatians 1:8). Jesus said that we might know false prophets by their fruits (Matthew 7:20).

In light of the centrality of Joseph Smith, a number of Latter-day Saints have challenged LeAnn and me over the years to evaluate the truthfulness of his prophetic calling based on the fruits of the church he founded. There are many fruits one could choose to examine in testing him, but the most important of these are his teachings. If Joseph Smith was wrong about the nature of God and Jesus, man and salvation, Scripture and the church, then he cannot have been a true prophet no matter how good the church he founded might otherwise appear.

For this reason, LeAnn and I have concluded that Mormonism is not genuinely Christian, despite the fact that it claims to be. This is not to say that there are no Christians in Mormonism. At root, Christian faith is a matter of the heart, not of church affiliation—Mormons won't go to hell for their church membership any more than Baptists will go to heaven for theirs. Nevertheless, those who ultimately choose to place their confidence in the anti-biblical teachings of Joseph Smith are trusting in a treacherous fiction, and therefore placing themselves in opposition to the healing, redemptive truth that is manifest in Christ Jesus. As harsh as this assessment may sound, it is the sort of distinction that should be familiar to mainstream Latter-day Saints, who, on grounds of their own, repudiate contemporary Mormonism's heretics, the polygamists.

In some respects, Joseph Smith's false teachings are more like roots than fruits. And because the Mormon Church sprang up from a corrupt root, the fruit that it produces has been polluted. Some of that pollution was manifest in our own experience. Trying to observe all the requisites of being faithful Latter-day Saints resulted in failure and guilt followed by rigorous attempts to ratchet up the level of our obedience. Motto-infested pep talks from Church leaders urged us to "DO IT!" or to "lengthen our stride and quicken our pace." The struggle I experienced in trying to keep the Spirit with me, believing as I did then that His presence was dependent on my efforts rather than God's promise, ended in inevitable despair. There was no lasting satisfaction or peace for me in living the Mormon law. I know LeAnn and I were not the only ones to feel this way. This was an outgrowth of the so-called gospel of self-reliance that I had been taught as a Mormon and which I now know to be utterly false.

Christ put to an end to the damaging dynamics of legalistic rule-keeping in our lives. It is a joy to serve God now, not because we are earning His approbation and our own glory, but out of love for a Savior whose perfect life and willing death wrought a reconciliation with Him that we could never accomplish on our own. It is an extraordinary experience to discover each day that God is really working in us, "both to will and to do of his good pleasure" (Philippians 2:13).

After many years spent in the search for peace, LeAnn and I finally found it in God's redemptive grace. We made a radical break with our past by becoming Christians, but we also recognize the patient unfolding of God's sovereign purpose through our many diverse experiences over the years. Rather than resenting or repudiating our life as Mormons, we are learning to understand it as part of the continuum of God's overarching mercy, to see the strands of meaning that wind through it all. In emphasizing the differences between Mormonism and Christianity, I don't want to lose sight of the consistency of God's faithfulness in answering our deep desire for Him.

I believe that my spiritual experiences as a Mormon were predominantly the result of my intense yearning for God. Some of them were moments of genuine inspiration, threads of understanding that God graciously gave and patiently knit together as He drew me to Himself. Some may have been demonic. I ran into problems with my spiritual experiences because I had not been taught to submit them to the judgment of Scripture. This left me vulnerable to deception. I was dead wrong to extrapolate the truth of Mormonism from these experiences, particularly when Mormon doctrine undermined my confidence in the unique authority of the Bible, taught me to worship a false god, and made my efforts the basis of my relationship with him.

Now I know the One in whom I trust. My life is anchored by faith in the Lord Jesus Christ who loved me enough to go to the cross for my sins. My prayer is that I may love the things He loves and hate the things He hates. My heart resonates with the words of the apostle Paul, who after rehearsing all the "advantages" of his life before knowing Christ, was able to say without a tinge of regret:

But what things were gain to me, those I counted loss for Christ. Yea doubtless, and I count all things but loss for the excellency of the knowledge of Christ Jesus my Lord: for whom I have suffered the loss of all things, and do count them but dung, that I may win Christ, and be found in him, not having mine own righteousness, which is of the law, but that which is through the faith of Christ, the righteousness which is of God by faith. (Philippians 3:7–9)

12

"I've been educated," she answered, brilliant in her pause before they parted. "Twice educated, Peter. Shall I try?
Merrily, merrily shall I live now
Under the blossom that hangs on the bough
Bless me to it."
"Under the Mercy," he said, and watched her out of sight before he went to find a way to his own seat.

—Charles Williams, *Descent into Hell*[1]

*I*t's astonishing to me now that in spite of all of the intensity and effort that marked our transition out of Mormonism and our decision to follow Christ, the progress of my career never missed a beat. It's almost as if our conversion happened in some parallel universe. Looking back, I wonder where I found the time for all the reading and the correspondence, the conversations and the phone calls—the process seemed to devour aeons. And this to say nothing of the family demands LeAnn and I faced as the parents of three active young children. A lot of life was condensed into those few hinge years. Nevertheless, my career did keep growing, even through our darkest hours, and that growth increased exponentially a few months after we began telling the news of the change in our lives.

Series television work continued to put bread on the table. I was nominated for Emmy Awards for my work on *St. Elsewhere* in both 1984 and 1985. I also picked up episodes of several other series for Universal, Fox, and Warner Brothers. Early in 1985, I was hired to compose the music for two large-scale projects, a feature film called *Cry from the Mountain* and a four-hour television mini-series called *The Key to Rebecca*. In addition to holding more music than I was accustomed to writing for television programs, these "long-form" assignments would utilize larger orchestras than those with which I had worked up to that point. The dramatic and musical requirements of both scores held great promise and challenge for a young film composer, and I was chomping at the bit to tackle them.

For budgetary reasons, both *Cry from the Mountain* and *The Key to Rebecca* were slated to record in London, and their schedules overlapped in a way that placed their recording dates within a month of each other. So LeAnn and I decided to take the whole family to London for the month. We arranged to rent a flat in Chelsea, and she and the children planned to visit the sights while I worked. Complicating matters was the fact that I would have to return to Los Angeles between the recording sessions to score three episodes of *St. Elsewhere*. The rest of the family would remain in London throughout the entire month, however, despite my absence.

Cry from the Mountain was my second feature film score. What a contrast to the first! Where *Stingray* excelled in cheapness and vulgarity—if one can speak of "excelling" in such things—*Cry from the Mountain* was consistently sincere and sensitively directed. It followed a father and son on a river trip in the Alaskan wilderness, and combined scenes of great natural beauty with the suspense of a dangerous accident and the sorrow of a marriage coming unglued. It was produced by World Wide Pictures, the filmmaking division of the Billy Graham organization and it climaxed, like all of the other Billy Graham films, at a crusade where one of the film's protagonists goes forward to make a decision for Christ. The first time I saw *Cry from the Mountain* in a small screening room at the World Wide studios, I was so moved by this scene, resonating as it did with my own experience, that I wept openly in front of the producer. I felt embarrassed; though I'm a notorious soft touch at the movies, I generally keep my emotions in better check under professional circumstances. Fortunately, the producer was a Christian and understood something of what I was feeling. In fact, it created a kind of bond between us. We were to become good friends during the course of this project and remain so today.

The Key to Rebecca was an entirely different sort of challenge as far as the dramatic and musical demands of the film were concerned.

Based on a spy novel by Ken Follett, the story was set in Egypt during World War II and the score called for a heady cocktail of military suspense music, romantic themes, forties-style big band swing tunes, and ethnic Middle Eastern cues. Because I was a Christian, one of the score's principal challenges was a moral one: I was asked to compose music for a scene that featured a ménage à trois. A composer's choices are limited in such situations. You can refuse to sign onto a particular project, but once you're in the army, you can't question every order. I don't recall how much I knew about the sexual content beforehand, but, in any event, I had agreed to score the picture and now I had some decisions to make regarding how to play this scene. Fortunately, the main characters involved were the "bad guys" and the segment was shot in such a way as to emphasize their wickedness. My musical solution was to accompany the scene in horror movie fashion, with liberal dollops of dissonance peppering the harmonic language. The music had a chilling effect: the evildoers grew monstrous in their perversion. When I was finished, I felt certain that no viewer would walk away from that scene with any doubt about the cruel nature of the sin being represented. I've thought back to this experience many times when faced with similar moral dilemmas in other pictures.

From a recording standpoint, my second experience working in London was even better than the first. Once again, the English musicians played beautifully, with verve and style, and were very responsive to my conducting. It was a joy to work with them. Furthermore, living in London was a great experience for the family. LeAnn and the children wandered the halls of the National Gallery and Windsor Castle, tried brass rubbing at All Hallows Church, ate lunches in pubs, and watched snooker games and Miss Marple on the "telly." Jonathan was nipped on the finger by one of the infamous ravens at the Tower of London. Jerusha became expert in plotting our course on London's subway system, the "Tube." It was a broadening and enriching experience for all of us, and a tremendous educational opportunity for the children in particular. LeAnn and I began to see firsthand how important it was for them to have a world perspective, to recognize that our engagement with life stretches beyond the narrow dimensions of our home, our neighborhood, and our country. We wanted them to understand that being part of the human family means living in community with a vast and colorful congress of brothers and sisters, both now and in history, who nevertheless share the common ground of love and hope, fear and grief, faith and despair.

Working on *Cry from the Mountain* and *The Key to Rebecca* left me with some important realizations; and with each of these came an awareness of God's faithfulness and provision, even in the muddy details of my work. Foremost was the confidence that I could really do it—I could step up to the plate and hold my own in the big game. God saw to it that my imagination didn't flag, nor was I abandoned without musical ideas. In fact, I seemed to find greater liberty in my composition than I had experienced before. *St. Elsewhere* had prepared me for this to some degree, but in working on *Cry from the Mountain* and *The Key to Rebecca,* I felt I was taking yet another giant conceptual step forward. I also learned the meaning of stamina. Composing almost three hours of music in just over two months was a backbreaking marathon for me. Eighteen hours of writing was a routine day. I survived on Irish tea and sandwiches. By the time we returned home from England, I was completely spent. Yet God had seen me through. As hard as it had been to get up every morning and face a new array of cues to be written, He didn't let me falter or fall. Under the Mercy, I found strength in my "sea legs."

In September 1985, only a few months after completing *Cry from the Mountain* and *The Key to Rebecca,* I was contracted to score an independent feature film called *The Trip to Bountiful.* Although it was produced by my longtime friend, Sterling Van Wagenen, my employment on the project was not a fait accompli. The approval of the director was also required. I was still young and relatively unknown at the time, with only a few credits behind me. From a director's perspective, I was a risk. Had it not been for the recommendation of veteran composer Dave Grusin, I might never have secured the job. It was then I learned what a blessing it had been that Dave had been hired to write the theme for *St. Elsewhere,* even though it had seemed like a setback for me at the time not to have composed the theme myself. God had been involved in the details even then.

The Trip to Bountiful turned out to be a wonderful film with finely shaded performances, full of heart and heartbreak. Horton Foote's script was superb, a classic example of profound understatement.

Geraldine Page went on to win an Oscar for her realization of the character of Carrie Watts. I was honored to be composing music for this film and planned a score that would combine instruments normally associated with folk and country music—acoustic and steel guitars, fiddle, mandolin, accordion, tin whistle, and tack piano—with a small orchestra.

I ran into a roadblock, however, when I began working on the "main title," the opening sequence of a film during which the titles and primary credits roll. Generally, the main title is a composer's first and most important opportunity to introduce the defining musical elements of a score: the principal melody, or theme, and the musical vocabulary, the "sound" or style. Acoustic guitarist Doc Watson's arrangement of "What a Friend We Have in Jesus" had temporarily been recorded over the flashback that began the film, but we all knew something else was needed that would be more specific to the story. I knew the style I wanted to use, but I couldn't come up with the theme. Something wasn't clicking. After several frustrating days with nothing to show for my efforts, I decided to research the songs that Carrie Watts sings or hums throughout the film, to see if they might provide some source material for me or at least prod the muse.

I was told that the songs were old Baptist gospel songs, much beloved in that region of southern Texas in which the story unfolds. Other than "What a Friend We Have in Jesus," however, they were completely unfamiliar to me. I had been a Christian for only a year-and-a-half, and had never heard the others. So I called Dr. Howard Stevenson, the gracious and able music minister at our new church, the First Evangelical Free Church of Fullerton. Howie recognized "Blessed Assurance" and "Softly and Tenderly" right away. I borrowed a hymnbook, made work copies of the three songs, and laid them out on my desk, moving them around like pieces in a shell game, experimenting with arrangements of the melodies—and paying no attention to the lyrics at all.

When this meandering produced no immediate results, I threw up my hands in disgust. Sometimes I grow impatient with the incubation phase of the creative process and, on those dark days, failure to lock in quickly on an idea tends to leave me with a short fuse. This was one of those times. Just then, LeAnn walked into the converted garage I used as a studio and asked how things were going. I let my frustration fly. To her credit, she was undeterred, and, curious about the songs, asked if she could see them. She took them back into the house while I sat steaming. A few minutes later, the door burst open and LeAnn rushed back in, her face flushed with excitement. "Have you read the words to 'Softly and Tenderly?'" she demanded. I had to admit that I hadn't. "Just look at the chorus," she said with conviction. I picked up the hymn and, for the first time, read the words, "Come home, come home, ye who are weary come home. Softly and tenderly, Jesus is calling, calling, oh sinner, come home."

It was perfect, absolutely perfect. I found it hard to believe that no one else had noticed it before. I called Sterling immediately. "Have you heard the chorus to 'Softly and Tenderly'?" I asked. "No," he replied, "I haven't." "Well, listen to this," I said and read him the lyrics. "It's perfect," he laughed, amazed at the synchronicity. I played the music for him on the decrepit piano I used for work in those days. "Even better," he said, responding to the melody. And thus the main theme for *The Trip to Bountiful* was born, or rather, discovered.

Having found the song, now I had to decide whether it should be sung or performed instrumentally. I was in favor of the vocal version—I was beginning to catch a vision of how the opening sequence would look, accompanied by those simple, haunting words. Producer and director concurred, and the search for the right vocalist commenced. I had a good idea where to start looking. Soon after LeAnn and I had committed our lives to Christ, we were introduced to a genre of music that was relatively new to us: contemporary Christian music. Those first few years following our conversion were a dynamic period for this genre, and we discovered many artists who moved us with their lyrics while intriguing us with their music. We listened to Bob Bennett, Michael Card, Amy Grant, Keith Green, Mark Heard, Phil Keaggy, Rich Mullins, Twila Paris, and Randy Stonehill, as well as Christians who released records in the secular market such as The Alarm, Lone Justice, Tonio K., and Bruce Cockburn, all of whose music we first heard on Christian radio. When I needed a vocalist for *The Trip to Bountiful*, I chose to look first to this community of artists.

The first step was easy—I eliminated all the male vocalists right off the top, intuitively feeling that the singer should be female. Then I called Amy Grant, the best known performer of the group. When her management dismissed the idea out of hand, I tried to think of others who might have some crossover appeal, but the list was short. Once again, LeAnn came to the rescue. While I was stewing over the options, she suggested Cynthia Clawson, a Christian singer with a fabulous voice, a sincerity that spoke from the heart, and a taste for eclecticism in her choice of material. I called her and, to my great delight, she was willing to sing and available for the recording.

On the day of the session, I told Cynthia that my mother's maiden name was Clawson, and she asked about my family line. When she heard the name of Hiram Bradley Clawson, my great-great-grand-father, she cried out, "We're kin!" and swept me up in a giant embrace. Hiram Bradley was her great-great-grandfather's brother who had left the family and moved to Utah with the Mormons. Generations later, I had found my Christian cousin. She also asked if I knew that "Softly and Tenderly" was her signature song. I hadn't known, but somehow wasn't surprised. It was simply one more providential occurrence to be added to an already remarkable collection.

The recording session was a great success. Cynthia sang magnificently—her unaccompanied rendition of the first verse of "Softly and Tenderly" at the beginning of the film is one of its highlights. There was great camaraderie among the musicians as well, as everyone sensed they were working on something special. The music seemed to flow unhindered from their instruments with that sense of inevitability or "rightness" that all musicians recognize, although this synergy is difficult to describe to someone who hasn't felt it before. Nor has the feeling dimmed with the passage of time. No matter how often I listen to the score, my heart still hums with the pleasure of that performance.

The subsequent year, 1986, brought another new challenge. In April, I scored a feature film for Robert Young, a fine director I had met at the Sundance Film Institute. Based on the Broadway play by the same title, *Extremities* was a tough film about a tough subject: the story of a single woman, stalked and nearly raped in her own home, who manages to turn the tables on her attacker. The conflict of the second act centers on her roommates' attempts to talk her out of burying him alive in the garden. In her lust for revenge, she has become a mirror image of the evil in her assailant's heart. The violence and emotional intensity of the film wasn't gratuitous, but the movie was unrelenting in its presentation of its central issues. It didn't make the violence attractive by romanticizing it.

Accepting this assignment was a hard decision for me. I keenly felt the desire to honor God as well as my family with my music. Only a few months before, I had turned down a picture that employed graphic violence in a wanton, albeit comical way. I had found it problematic that the audience was supposed to laugh at the gore in that film. In the case of *Extremities,* however, I believed that the hearts of the producers and the director were in the right place. They were trying to make a statement about the nature of evil. The film had been shot with intelligence and restraint and the violence that was there, whether visible or implied, served the greater design. After some serious thought, prayer, and consultation with LeAnn, I decided to take the job.

Composing the score, however, was a sore trial. Six weeks of constant and intimate reviewing of very disturbing scenes took their toll on me. I was emotionally exhausted and especially vulnerable to anger and discouragement. Never since have I had much patience with those who maintain that movies are merely harmless entertainment and have no significant influence on their audiences. On a more positive note, I had the opportunity to work with Bonnie Raitt, who sang the main title song, "Stand Up to the Night." I co-wrote the song with veteran lyricist, Will Jennings, and played keyboard for the recording. Bonnie was friendly, funny, and thoroughly professional. She turned our song into something much more than it might have been in the hands of a lesser artist, and she included it on her *Nine Lives* album.

In the end, *Extremities* was not a success, either commercially or aesthetically. The marketing campaign billed it as some sort of "female Charles Bronson movie," seriously undermining the intention of the filmmakers. The screening I attended at the Sundance Institute was a disaster. Many viewers walked out, offended at the unallayed frankness of the film's brutality. Earlier in my career, I would have been devastated to witness such an exodus in response to a work for which I shared responsibility; nevertheless, the grace of God was operative even here. I felt sad that audiences hadn't understood what we were aiming for, and sad that we hadn't achieved all that we had set out to achieve, but I didn't feel guilty or ashamed of my work. I was secure with my choices; they had been my best under the circumstances. I didn't have to be perfect. Whatever mistakes I had made would eventually be revealed and corrected in God's own good time. Under the Mercy, I was learning to trust that He would draw me to greater things rather than drive me from lesser ones.

This faith has helped me to deal with the praise as well as the rejection inherent in the work of a successful film composer. *The Trip to Bountiful* and *Extremities* represent two opposite ends of that spectrum. Where *The Trip to Bountiful* is almost universally admired, *Extremities* is almost universally reviled. The grace of God, however, has taught me to look beyond the limited horizon of the reviews—whether they are good or bad, public or personal—and given me a sense of perspective and balance. These are only movies, after all. Nevertheless, such are the labors to which I've applied myself, and Hollywood the post to which I've been called to serve, and thus all my work ought to be done with as much excellence and passion as I can muster. I want to be able to see my work clearly and truthfully, for what it is, just as God, in grace, sees me, neither deceiving myself with regard to its flaws nor affecting any false modesty with respect to its strengths; but rather viewing it with affection, compassion, and an eye to improvement. Under the Mercy, I aspire to look on my own creative work, as well as that of others, with an unflinching charity.

The next few years were variations on a theme as far as my career was concerned, filled with scores for various television series and a growing list of feature films and television movies. The same basic process was repeated over and over again and it generally went something like this:

The phone rings. My agent is on the line with word of a new job opportunity. Could I send a tape with samples of my work for the producers and director to listen to? The cues should be somehow related to their picture. It's a comedy about a bunch of misfit kids who find self-esteem; or a drama about a woman in jeopardy; or a gritty parable of street life; or a story about someone with a devastating disease. Whatever the subject is, it sounds awfully familiar—but it's just different enough that none of the music I've already written for another picture quite seems to fit. "When do they need it?" I ask.

"Yesterday!" my agent laughs, a tad too heartily.

"I'll get on it right away."

I drop whatever earth-shattering work I am doing and spend a couple of hours culling the most appropriate musical segments, called cues, from my vast archive of tapes, which are organized with corresponding logs so I can locate any piece of music I might need at any time. Finally, a list of potential cues is assembled. Half of these will be thrown out as I work to create a tape order, geared for maximum aural and emotional impact, though I suspect the merit of my selections may ultimately be assessed in someone's car at the end of the day, all of my meticulous counterpoint disappearing into the perpetual hum of an automobile engine. I make the final copy of the tape and rush to the post office to mail it just before closing time.

Several days go by. The phone rings again and my agent tells me the company has lost the tape. Or perhaps they just need an extra copy. Could I make another? "No problem," I grumble. Fortunately, experience has taught me always to keep a master. I dub a new tape and send it, trying not to take this audition too personally. I remind myself of the young exec, "a pharaoh who knew not Joseph," who once asked the great Henry Mancini for an audition tape. Gentleman that he was, Mancini refrained from icily referring the executive to the multiple Mancini CDs available at the music store.

Several more days pass. The phone rings again. My agent says the producers and director want to meet me. I drive into Los Angeles through the traffic and the smog, praying for a clear head and a generous heart. I also pray for God's will, whether or not I get the job—but, to be honest, I really think I need it. "I have a big tax bill due," I remind Him. At the meeting we all talk about the movie. It will be the greatest of its genre. I nod blankly in agreement. We shake hands. They give me a videotape to watch containing the latest incarnation of the picture. After the meeting, I drive home, sometimes jotting down a musical idea that occurs to me while merging onto the freeway.

After a few more days my agent calls once more. I didn't get the job. Joe Blow of Some Obscure Rock 'n' Roll Band got it. He will improvise the score on his guitar. Oops. Rewind. That was the last time—or the last five times. Start again. This time I get the job. Cheers and huzzahs! Jigs on the kitchen floor. The next day I clear the decks of any extraneous activity or unfinished business—like sleeping—

and say goodbye to my family. I'll be quarantined downstairs now for the next few weeks, more or less, depending on the size of the project. There will be little time for anything other than offerings to the film god. Except, of course, for the work that remains from the last job that went over schedule.

I spend the next few days trying to come up with themes, melodies that seem to capture the essence of the picture. They may come slowly or quickly, but they always come—like a baby after labor. They may occur to me at some unexpected moment or in an inconvenient place: in the shower, at a restaurant, or even, incredibly, at my piano. Suddenly the theme appears inside my head. I hear it just as one hears audible sound, except that it's playing inside my skull. It may just be a fragment of melody that needs developing with the tools of my craft, or it may be deposited fully formed like a gift. I live with this theme for a few days and fine tune it if necessary. I want to make sure it's memorable without being clichéd; that it sustains interest, yet is readily accessible; that it has heart or humor, nobility or terror, a lift in just the right place—whatever emotion is called for.

Complicating this process sometimes is the presence of a "temp score," music taken temporarily from other movies to help the picture editor pace the scenes as he or she cuts them, or to provide aural lubrication for the preview screenings for the studio brass. If there is temp music on the work copy of the videotape I'm watching, it will interfere with the creative process in a major way. Just when I'm trying to come up with my own themes, I will find that I can't get someone else's out of my mind. Worse yet, a producer or director may fall in love with the temp music and insist that it be mimicked to a degree just short of copyright violation.

At any rate, once the themes are generated, they must be presented to the producers and director in a form that they, as nonmusicians, can understand. Sometimes I present my themes on a piano, playing them live, or via a cassette tape I've recorded at home. Other cases require full-blown orchestral mock-ups, performed on synthesizers. I always have several options ready. The theme presentation meeting is a harrowing time. My sensibilities are on the line. It's like the judgment of Caesar: a thumbs up means freedom, a cause for rejoicing, but a thumbs down means there are lions in my future.

Sometimes reactions are rather curious. I once wrote a theme I thought particularly beautiful. Upon hearing it, the producer complained, "I can't hum it."

This comment has always raised my hackles. I firmly believe that if you can hum a tune after hearing it once, it means you've heard it before; nevertheless, I pursued his concern. "What would make it more hummable for you?" He couldn't precisely say, but as I asked more questions, it became clear that he needed the first phrase of the melody, often called the "hook" in popular music, to repeat a few times before it went on in order to cement it in his memory. "I can do that," I said. "Is there anything else?"

"Yes," he said. "Your theme keeps going down." He emphasized this point with his hands, as if tracing the flight of an expiring pelican. "I want it to go up. In fact, I want it to go up, up, up."

"Okay. Let me work on it."

I happened to be out of town for this meeting, so I went back to my hotel room and wrote seven more themes, each one starting on a different note of the major scale, each one with an opening phrase that repeated twice more and went up each time. I took these themes in to the office the next day and played them on a piano we had rented for the occasion. "Great," the producer said. "Can we combine the first part of number one with the middle part of number three, then come back to number one to finish it?"

"Sure." The strange thing is, it turned out to be a really good theme.

A spotting session is the next important step in the process of scoring a film. This is a meeting at which the producers, the director, and I watch the picture together and pick the spots where the music will go. There will be a few disagreements before it's all over, but these will be hammered out in the course of the meeting. Ultimately, either the producer or the director has the final say, depending on the project. Generally speaking, television is a producer's medium whereas film is the province of the director. One has to know who holds the trump cards to play the game well.

Also present at the spotting session is another critical member of the team: the music editor. He or she has probably worked on the temp score already, is intimately acquainted with the picture, and will now be responsible for breaking down the scenes that have been set aside for music into "timing notes." These notes describe every detail of a scene—the start and end of every line, every cut and camera angle, every movement or pause—and are precise to a hundredth of a second. The timings are generated from a continuous time code called SMPTE, originally developed by NASA to keep track of every frame of video shot during a mission in space. In the early days of film composition, the timing notes were known as "the Bible." Nowadays both the term and the book it refers to have fallen into disrepute. But the function still betrays its origins. I will have to observe these timings precisely if I want my music to be synchronized with the picture. Even the slightest departure will cause a mismatch somewhere down the line. There's a sermon in that.

The daily grind of composing begins not long after the spotting session, when the timing notes begin to arrive at my home. From that point on, my routine is characterized by thousands of minute decisions devouring long and wearisome hours, carried out under the shadow of a looming deadline. Creativity on demand is anything but glamorous. Of course, smaller projects require less time and larger ones more. They all have one thing in common, however: there is never enough time for the volume of work. Sometimes the deadline works against the natural rhythms of the creative process, sometimes it actually spurs the imagination on to greater heights. In either case, however, there is little room for second guessing. There are plenty of interruptions, though, chiefly phone calls, which can seem as incessant and irritating as a hive of angry bees when one is in the throes of solving an especially knotty problem. Nor can one escape the demands of daily life, which, in my case, have ranged from broken water mains and power outages to a child's transportation needs or a spouse's health crisis.

Despite these distractions, the score must be written and that means making choices. There are many ways to handle a scene. Ultimately I have to choose one approach and run with it, hoping that it will fulfill the expectations of the powers that be. I start by watching the scene over and over until its particular dynamics begin to sink in. The next step is to sketch out the dramatic form. Every scene has a shape, a dramatic arc that can be plotted out and reflected in the structure of the music. Working with the timing notes, I circle those moments where significant changes occur in the development of plot or character, paying special attention to the emotional currents of the scene, as these will be most closely related to the music. Music forms an emotional bridge between the two-dimensional flickering images on the screen and the hearts of the audience, and I take very seriously my responsibility to build that bridge.

When the scene has been mapped out in this way, there may be a great number of circled "hit" points, as in a cartoon or a comedy, or there may be very few, as in a serious drama. Moving from point to point, I will build my cue with musical phrases and gestures appropriate to the moment. Before I do this, however, I work to find the proper tempo, so that the pace and speed of the music ride alongside the pace of the scene. Scenes create their own rhythms with the interplay of dialogue and movement, the motion coming from both the characters and the camera. I try to find the inner rhythms of a scene rather than superimpose a rhythm of my own on top of it. To do this, I conduct to the picture before I compose a note of music. I can tell as I move my arms whether I'm going too fast or too slow. A good tempo will soon reveal itself. However, a single tempo won't always do—one scene may contain a number of different tempi. It's easy to tell at this stage whether a picture has been well edited or not. I can feel the difference in my hands.

Finally, it's time to begin writing the sketch, the musical equivalent of an outline. The sketch may be written on any number of lines, called staves, and contains the basic musical information for the cue: the melody, harmony, or counterpoint, as well as orchestration indications, dynamics, and articulation markings. Even large orchestral gestures can be sketched on two staves that look like piano music. By the time I'm ready to begin sketching, I have already made a number of key decisions, so it's rare that I won't have some ideas brewing. But if I'm stumped, I sometimes pose some basic questions, framed as binaries: Should this music be light or dark in timbre, high or low in range, dense or spare in orchestration? Analyzing a scene in this way helps me get moving. I can also prime the pump by putting down one note, then another, then another until I have something on paper. Once there, I can work with the sketch, as a sculptor works with clay. Music has a strong visual element for me, perhaps as the result of my studying so many scores. I can often see whether it will sound good or not. Once I break the ice on a cue, the rest is grit and stamina, putting one note next to another until the sketch is finished. Music is a language and I write notes, themes, and cues just as I would write words, sentences, and paragraphs. And just like those sentences and paragraphs, the notes should combine to mean something.

What I have been describing thus far is essentially my approach to an orchestral score. The process changes, of course, when the score is electronic, utilizing synthesizers, or requires a rock 'n' roll rhythm section. Different styles dictate different approaches, though the fundamental principles remain the same. Whatever the methodology, musical ideas have to be concretized in some sort of format that can be synchronized with the picture.

A score for a feature film may contain as much as two hours of music and it may take weeks to compose. The eminent film composer John Williams once said that on a good day he could sketch two minutes of high-quality, unorchestrated symphonic music. In terms of creative output, that's a lot. I crave his consistency, but a regular schedule never seems to work for me. There is an arc to my writing routine that arises from my own creative process and can't be circumvented, no matter how hard I wish it could be. For me, the work always begins at a painfully slow pace, gathers a head of steam after a few days, and finishes in a tumultuous flurry of activity just before the deadline arrives. I often make the mistake of setting goals to write a predetermined amount of music each day so I can regularly check off my progress. Inevitably, I end up falling behind the first few days, battering myself with recriminations, then playing catch up until a day or so before the deadline, at which point I finish early.

Most of my composition work is carried out in solitude. There are, however, support personnel available to help during the process. The music editor, of course, is one. He or she can provide technical assistance in synchronizing the music with the scene. Another is the orchestrator, whose job it is to flesh out a composer's sketch by assigning the notes to instruments of the orchestra and writing them out on a full symphonic score. Most film scoring schedules are too tight to permit a composer to orchestrate his or her own sketches, although many of us in the industry are certainly capable of doing this. Finally, there is the copyist, who transfers each of the parts on the score to its own separate sheet so that it can be played by an individual musician during the recording. At its most efficient, the writing process resembles an assembly line as timing notes are passed on to the composer, who creates sketches that are sent to the orchestrator, who turns them into scores and sends these to the copyist, who produces the parts.

There is one critical element that can potentially throw a wrench into the composing process: picture changes. The precision of synchronization depends entirely on the timing of each scene remaining constant, a state that is known as "locked picture." Yet the producers and director often continue to make changes well into the composition process. Frequently, just at the moment I'm hitting my stride, the phone will ring and the music editor, very apologetically, will inform me of timing changes in scenes for which I have already written music. The consequences for me can be as serious as a complete rewrite or as simple as a couple of dropped beats. Ah, but which beats? Even the simplest of solutions robs me of precious time and focus as I strain for the finish line.

The first day of recording arrives. This is the deadline that has driven the entire schedule. If the score is for a feature film, the recording will take place over several days. If it's for a television movie, it may well take only six hours. The orchestrators and copyists have done their work and a contractor has hired the musicians. They have taken an 'A' to tune and are now sitting before me waiting. I stand before them for an instant and take a deep breath. Then I raise my arm and bring it down for the first downbeat. This is the Memorex moment. The sound of the orchestra rises to envelope me like a tide. As long as I live, I will never cease to be thrilled by that glorious mix of timbre and harmony, color and light produced by the symphony orchestra. From this moment on, throughout the recording sessions, the orchestra will sight-read enormous amounts of music, usually playing it flawlessly within one or two passes. I will conduct, simultaneously watching them, my score, and a videotape monitor, reproducing my tempi in sync with the picture as we go.

Of course, the question of what constitutes a flawless performance is a complex one. An orchestra could play every note perfectly, every dynamic and tempo indication, and yet still miss the mark. A machine can produce that kind of perfection. While technical excellence is important and a goal well worth pursuing, as a conductor I am far more concerned with the spirit of the performance. I want to hear passion and commitment in the music, love, courage, and faith. For me, an orchestra playing music is a metaphor for what it means to be human, what it means to be in community with others, and I want to sing our humanity with every phrase, even if the object is only a television program.

A conductor's role is one of leadership. He or she must bring together a large group of highly individualistic artists, get them to forget for a while about their quarrels and complaints, and unite them under one banner in the service of the music. Musicians want good leadership from a conductor. They appreciate someone who both has a vision for the music and is able to communicate that vision. Nevertheless, the role of the conductor has often been abused in the history of the art. The image of the tyrannical intimidator, ruling with fear and verbal abuse, is ubiquitous. I don't have the stomach for this kind of posturing, and furthermore, as a follower of Christ, I feel there has to be a better way. When I conduct, I try to take inspiration from the words of Jesus: "And whosoever will be chief among you, let him be your servant" (Matthew 20:27).

One of the ways I can serve is by treating my fellow musicians with genuine respect and affection. Such things are communicated best in personal ways—a warm greeting, an embrace, a word of thanks, or a quiet moment exchanging family news. Yet such personal contact is often hard, simply because of the sheer size of the ensemble. I must relate to the orchestra on a basis of one to sixty-five (or however many make up the ensemble), while they relate to me one to one. I always pray before I conduct that I won't neglect the personal expressions of our shared humanity.

Even on a Hollywood sound stage, musicians can get completely caught up in the glorious enterprise of making music, striving together for a common goal, our daily trials left at the downbeat— and sometimes music really happens. When it does, it feels like a touch of grace. Musicians take on a certain "look" when they're totally focused in the midst of a performance. I've seen hard and anxious faces transformed into angelic calm at such moments. It is like the single eye that fills the body with light.

One of the defining characteristics of film music is that it is ultimately collaborative. It is a work for hire, intended to function as counterpoint or accompaniment to the medium of film. As such, the producers and director have final authority over the music, absolute veto power, if you will. No matter how I try to prepare them beforehand, from theme presentations to mock-ups, the actual score always comes as something of a surprise to them. How could it not? Often, they are pleasantly surprised and genuinely happy with what I've done with their picture, but sometimes they are not. Even under the best of circumstances, requests for changes on the recording stage are frequent. Some changes are relatively easy to make and can be dictated from the podium. Others require overnight rewrites and will have to be recorded the following day. When the clock is ticking and salaries are mounting, you have to be quick on your feet.

The most egregious example of executive interference in my experience occurred during an electronic session. A synthesized score differs from an orchestral recording in that individual parts must be recorded one at a time instead of simultaneously. The music is built "line upon line," one sound or instrument at a time. Sometimes I begin with a provisional sound that won't even appear in the final mix, just to get the juices flowing. One morning, I was working with Stu Goldberg, a fine synthesist and composer in his own right, on just such a score. The director had asked to attend the session and I had readily agreed with the single proviso that she wouldn't make any comments until we were well into the process. I needed to be free to create. Stu and I had just called up a provisional sound for the first cue. We hadn't played more than half a bar of music when the director suddenly leaped to her feet, shouting, "It's all wrong! It's all wrong!" I don't know how I had the presence of mind to do it, but I called, "Lunch!" We then took a two-hour break, and she wasn't there when we got back. She had the last laugh, though; she just didn't use most of my music.

Once the recording is completed, the music must often be "mixed" or balanced so that all of the instruments are heard in their proper "place." This is most important in the case of popular music or electronic music that has been laid track by track. Many recording engineers are adept at recording the orchestra with a live natural balance, but even so, adjustments may need to be made. For the composer, this means another myriad of minute decisions, affecting the most delicate nuances of the score. This work is called producing, not to be confused with producing the film, although the terms are related. Just as the film's producer oversees the film, the music producer oversees the music. Most of the time, a film composer produces his or her own score and the work of producing actually begins during the recording process. Decisions must be made after every take to determine whether a cue is up to snuff or needs to be rerecorded or even rewritten.

There is one more step in the process, but it is one I try to avoid: the "dubbing" session during which all the dialogue, sound effects, and music are mixed with their final balances. Watching the producers and director make a thousand more decisions, some of which will result in my work being lost beneath squealing tires and gunshots, is a prime recipe for a migraine.

I much prefer having written to writing. After the last session, I drive home and sit for a while in a comfortable chair, dazed, listening to the pleasant, though indecipherable utterances of my family as they attempt to communicate with me. Somewhere deep inside, I relish the thought of awakening late the next morning and spending a relaxing day with them. I fall into bed and sleep more peacefully than I have for weeks. True to my best hope, the sun has risen high in the sky before I regain consciousness again. It must be ten o'clock. I hoist my legs over the side of the bed and yawn contentedly. The phone rings. My agent is on the line . . .

The final episode of *St. Elsewhere* aired in the spring of 1988. It had enjoyed a great run: six years and 136 episodes, all with my scores excepting the pilot. Although the show still had a loyal following, the producers felt it was time to hang up our spurs and end on a high note, which we did, quite literally. The closing episode called for an operatic aria to be heard coming from a sound system in one of the doctor's offices. We didn't want to pay a hefty licensing fee for the use of an existing recording, so I hired my mother to sing Puccini's glorious aria, "La Canzone di Doretta" from *La Rondine*. As a child, I often heard her practicing this aria late at night, while I lay in my bed on the edge of sleep. She sang with transcendent sweetness then, and she did so now as I conducted an orchestra composed of some of the finest musicians in Los Angeles to accompany her. Something beautiful had come full circle for me.

LeAnn and I wondered how we were going to make up the hole that the loss of *St. Elsewhere* left in our budget. It had been the only long-term steady paycheck we had ever known. Our worries were short-lived, however, as new opportunities were quick in coming. When the next fall television season began, I was the composer for three new series. Two of them lasted only half a season, but the third, a situation comedy called *Coach*, became a hit and continues its successful run to this day. *Coach* has been a great job. It has provided steady employment while still leaving me ample time to pursue other opportunities, and I've been able to work with good people in an atmosphere of mutual respect. On the occasion of our hundredth episode, the executive producer Barry Kemp summed up what it meant to have a hit series. He said it meant that families would be able to buy homes, have children, or send children to college. He viewed the show's success primarily in terms of the benefits it provided for its people. I was deeply impressed, knowing firsthand that these were not hollow words. I have been the beneficiary of the blessings of his success as well as the leadership style that his attitude reveals.

In the late eighties, I began to develop a relationship with Walt Disney Pictures. It began, as so many opportunities do in my line of work, with a friendship. I had worked with a talented singer and songwriter named Chris Montan during my years on *St. Elsewhere*. Now he was head of the music department at Disney. Chris knew and liked my music and recommended me for a number of films. The first project for which I was hired was the animated musical, *Oliver and Company*. The score featured six songs of widely disparate styles that had been written by six different sets of songwriters. My job was to weave these diverse themes together into a dramatic underscore. It was a mammoth job. Even the orchestra was enormous, consisting of ninety-two musicians. From the perspective of the conductor's podium, the sound was awe-inspiring.

Oliver and Company was a success and led to Disney hiring me to conduct their next animated film musical, *The Little Mermaid*. Because both songs and score for this film had been written by Alan Menken, my duties were limited to wielding the baton. This was great fun, however, and the movie and its score were a stellar success, further cementing my relationship with the company. Success breeds success, in Hollywood as elsewhere, and I worked for Disney again in 1992, composing the underscore for *Newsies*, a live-action film musical for which Alan had also written the songs. Since that time, I have continued to work for Disney with some regularity. In 1994, I composed the music for *D2: The Mighty Ducks,* followed by *Heavyweights.* That year I also wrote the score for *Bye Bye Love,* a picture for Twentieth Century Fox. Late in 1995, I scored *D3,* the third installment in the Mighty Ducks series, again for Disney.

To date, I have written the music for a dozen feature films, two dozen TV movies, and over 450 episodes of series television. As a conductor, I have recorded scores for composers Rachel Portman, Danny Elfman, Marc Shaiman, and Mark Isham, as well as conducting and co-producing a new recording of the classic *Cinderella* score for Disney. In the course of my career, I have had the opportunity to conduct orchestras in some of the greatest cities of the world: New York, London, Toronto, and Prague. My composing opportunities have extended also to the theater. I have written incidental music for fine productions of plays by Harold Pinter, Simon Gray, and Sam Shepherd, as well as classic plays by Shakespeare and Chekhov, at respected venues such as the Matrix Theater in Los Angeles and the South Coast Repertory Theater. I have had the privilege of collaborating with many fine producers, directors, actors, and actresses.

When working on films, however, I don't usually meet the actors whose performances I have been accompanying until the cast and crew screening. A film composer's work takes place primarily during post-production, after nearly everyone else has already finished their work. The real stars in my firmament are those with whom I work on a regular basis: the musicians of Los Angeles. I never tire of hearing them apply their brilliant artistry, born of years of dedicated practice, to the special demands of my music. Nor can I say enough about the other soldiers—the music editors, orchestrators, copyists, and contractors—all highly competent and supportive professionals who labor tirelessly to make my scores sound their best. I owe a good deal of my success to them and thank God for the blessing it is to know and work with each of them.

I've seen many changes in the business during the twenty years I've been working in Hollywood. Some are due to advancements in technology. When I began my career, there was no videotape to work with at home—I had to rely on the timing notes and my memory of the picture as I had seen it at the spotting session. There was no time code and no MIDI interface to synchronize synthesizers with computers. Synthesizers themselves were still primitive and there was no such thing as a fully electronic score. Soundtracks were still released on LPs—CDs and the digital realm were still in the development stages. The emergence of these technologies has had a profound impact on the process of film composition. It is now entirely possible to compose, perform, and record a score at home.

Unfortunately, one of the most significant changes that has occurred is the steady chipping away of the amount of time allowed for composition. Similar advances in the technology of film editing have made it possible for producers to make changes later in the process, thus delaying the finality of locked picture. Moreover, most films are now screened several times for preview audiences and altered based on their feedback. The auteur has given way to the pollster.

The greatest change, however, has been within me. When I committed myself to Christ, it meant I was no longer slave to the things that drive this world. It is a singular experience to be a Christian in Hollywood. Despite the many good and honorable men and women with whom I've worked, I sometimes feel as if I'm greasing the wheels on the train to hell. The entertainment industry's contribution to the decline in culture occurs not only through the presence of vulgarizing elements in films and television (the usual suspects being coarse language, graphic violence, and promiscuous sex), but through the creation of an illusory worldview. Even if all cursing, killing, and nudity were removed from the movies, this skewed worldview would still remain, embodied in the industry's fascination with street wisdom, machismo, and sexual entitlement.

The point of view of a film is more important to me than the presence of specific offensive elements. I give a film wide latitude if it seeks to tell the truth about our humanity, the consequences of sin, and the redemption of love. While no film or television program will ever fully reflect my way of looking at the world as a Christian, I try to choose projects that aren't wholly antithetical to it. In making such decisions I am answerable not only to God, but also to my family. I always ask myself what my children will think of my participation in a given project. Ultimately, it is the Holy Spirit who convicts of sin, and I trust that my choices will become more refined as I pursue my career under the Mercy.

Profane language, violence, and sex are representative of the more obvious points of tension between my faith and the prevailing culture. A more subtle issue is the conflict between the pursuit of success and a grace-based worldview in which accomplishments are understood as gifts from God. I have not found a final resolution to this dichotomy. Perhaps I don't believe there really can be such a thing, at least in this world. These two warring value systems will always inhabit the same territory under an uneasy truce. Nevertheless, I have learned more than I knew when I started to explore the frontiers of this country.

Under the Mercy, I have greater freedom to make mistakes and take risks. I can take authentic delight in the success of my colleagues without feeling threatened. And there is protection against the temptation to idolize celebrities. We Americans have an unhealthy attitude toward those who impress us with their success or their skill or their insight. For us, they become a strange sort of scapegoat. First, we load them up with the responsibility of living out our fantasies of wealth or sex, knowledge or power; then, when they show signs of the inevitable strain of maintaining such illusions, we pile on our moral recriminations and drive them out of the camp. This is true of pastors as well as pop stars, pundits as well as politicians. Grace beckons us to a better way, neither trivializing the sin nor devaluing the sinner.

There are two forms of currency in Hollywood: money and respect. Both confer power, although each in a different way. Most Hollywood films are driven by one or the other. The lure of money is self-explanatory in our materialistic culture, but the nature of respect requires some amplification. Respect can take the form of admiration or fear, but in either case, it increases the power of the party with the upper hand. While there's nothing innately wrong with making a good living or with attaining the recognition of one's peers, when the lust for either takes over and becomes addictive, it can devour life rather than nourish it. The grace of God has had a profound impact on me where these issues are concerned.

Under His mercy, God has cooled the fever of my ambition, and liberated me from the craving for cash and kudos. I have learned there is another currency, more valuable and life-giving than these: the good will of God. This idea is best summed up for me by Eric Liddel in the film *Chariots of Fire:* "When I run I feel His pleasure." I have found this to be true. When I run as God made me to run, in the paths of His good will, I too feel His pleasure, and it is immeasurably sweet. Having once rested in the embrace of my Father's arms, hearing Him utter the words I have ached to hear—"Well done, my son"—nothing else could satisfy as deeply or as thoroughly. Growing in this relationship is what I aspire to above all. I still need to make a living and still want to achieve excellence in my work, but I try to trust God for these provisions. I know that even the circumstances of my employment are in His hands. He holds the reins of my life, not a studio executive or a producer, not even I myself.

13

Welcome, all wonders in one sight!
Eternity shut in a span.
Summer in winter, day in night
Heaven in earth, and God in man.

—Richard Crashaw, *Welcome All Wonders*

*A*lthough it was becoming more and more difficult for me to carve out time in the midst of my burgeoning film and television career, I remained dedicated to what I considered my primary vocation: the composition of concert and chamber music. In pragmatic terms, that meant trying to fit the pieces that I wanted to write in the cracks between projects for hire. The first chamber work I completed after becoming a Christian in 1984 was called *Inside Passage*. It was commissioned by a studio trombonist I worked with for a college trombone ensemble he directed.

The title was taken from a Sierra Club desk calendar that contained a beautiful photograph of Alaska's Inside Passage, taken from the ocean looking shoreward, with a brilliant, yellow-white sun hovering over the far horizon, warmly illuminating the dark, rippled water in the foreground. This evocative image breathed life into my imagination, its name not only a reminder of the staggering grandeur of creation but also a metaphor for my inward spiritual journey. Although I didn't realize it when I composed the piece, it formed the other side of a parenthesis that began with *Rebirth*, written during my freshman year in college. Like *Rebirth*, *Inside Passage* features a trombone soloist playing the principal theme, sometimes striving with the ensemble, sometimes soaring above it, moving in and out of the tensions manifest in the work's dissonance and rhythm, achieving resolution through a chorale and ending on a definitive major chord. While *Rebirth* finished heroically, however, *Inside Passage* ends in contemplation, with a sigh of peace.

I didn't write another concert or chamber work for nearly two years. Despite my best intentions, an increasingly demanding schedule simply wouldn't permit it. These were the years of *St. Elsewhere, Cry from the Mountain* and *The Key to Rebecca, The Trip to Bountiful* and *Extremities.* In the midst of my success, I sometimes despaired of ever being able to compose anything other than music for hire again. I ached for unencumbered time in which to develop some fully realized pieces of my own. As soon as I had finished *Extremities* in the spring of 1986, I leapt immediately into the composition of a short anthem, *Christ Is Alive!,* for our church choir and orchestra. Our music minister, Howie Stevenson, had encouraged me to write something for the choir and had referred me to the vivid text by the English hymnodist, Brian Wren, which I set in suitably celebratory, somewhat cinematic fashion. Howie premiered *Christ Is Alive!* at the First Evangelical Free Church of Fullerton on Easter Sunday in 1986. I rejoiced in having a part in ministering through music to our community of faith.

During the months my vocation had been put on hold, I began to sense the need for another teacher, a mentor who would be able to hear and understand my "voice" and help me raise the level of my expression and technique. LeAnn and I, along with some dear friends, Bill and Janice Rossen, had been praying together about this for some time when, not long after the premiere of *Christ Is Alive!,* I learned about Thomas Pasatieri.

Tom had a brilliant career as a composer in the concert music field. Beginning as a child prodigy on the piano, he had gone on to write seventeen operas and had been nominated six times for the Pulitzer Prize. He was probably best known for his oeuvre of over five hundred art songs, an exquisite contribution to the legacy of music for the solo human voice. Tom was personally acquainted with many of the giants of twentieth-century American music—Aaron Copland, Samuel Barber, and Gian Carlo Menotti—as well as many of the country's finest singers and instrumentalists. He had most recently served as artistic director of the Atlanta Opera Company. Now he was living in Los Angeles, working as an orchestrator for some of film's busiest composers.

On the recommendation of a colleague, I went to see him and asked if I could study with him. At first, he tried to talk me out of it. He told me that we would have to start at the beginning again with species counterpoint, and that it would be the hardest work I had ever done. He didn't want to waste his time with anyone who was less than totally dedicated. When that warning didn't dissuade me, he asked, "Why do you want to do this? There are hundreds of composers who would love to have a career like yours—why isn't that enough?"

"Because it isn't enough," I responded, with genuine passion. "I have to compose, whether you help me or not."

Satisfied with the seriousness of my intent, Tom agreed to take me on as a student. In an interesting counter-twist, I began to hire Tom to orchestrate my film scores. If either of us had possessed a different sort of ego, this arrangement could never have worked. As it was, however, our collaboration flourished in an atmosphere of friendship and mutual respect. Tom brought a masterful technique and a brilliant sense of color to his orchestrations and I learned a great deal as we worked together apart from my lessons. However, my prayers for a mentor were answered most directly in the hours we devoted to my counterpoint exercises and concert works. Tom proved to be a gifted teacher, helping me speak more clearly and profoundly with my own voice, rather than imposing his own on me. The effort I put into my studies was soon to yield the harvest of new works for which I had hoped.

Diminutiae, a set of four inventions for two violins, was the first piece I composed under Tom's tutelage in 1986, and it bore the unmistakable imprint of my renewed studies in counterpoint. While the Bach Inventions were its direct antecedent, *Diminutiae* differed from them in that it employed a starker, more contemporary musical vocabulary and made an intensely dramatic, almost operatic statement, despite the diminutive size of its two-person ensemble. The following year, 1987, produced two new compositions, *Shout for Joy to the Lord,* a setting of a portion of Psalm 98 for high voice and piano, and *The Growing Season,* a thorny, single-movement work for strings. Both of these pieces were also highly dramatic and contrapuntal in character, with wide variations in dynamics and lines made of jutting rhythms that fenced gleefully with one another. These sorts of stylistic touches were becoming signature elements of my style.

The Growing Season was originally composed for string quartet and later adapted for a larger string ensemble. It opens introspectively with a long, wistful line in the high register of the violin, accompanied in the lower strings by lush, acrid harmonies, like the sun on a steamy patch of dew-soaked earth. Out of this, a fiercely rhythmic secondary theme emerges. These two themes intertwine and grow until, finally, the first theme returns for a spare and philosophic conclusion.

Shout for Joy also ends philosophically. After a dance-like treatment of the greater part of the text, accenting colorful phrases such as "let the rivers clap their hands, let the mountains sing together for joy" (Psalm 98:8 NIV) the primary rhythmic figure subsides into a quiet ostinato over which the singer chants: "For he comes to judge the earth, he will judge the world in righteousness and the peoples with equity" (Psalm 98:9 NIV), finally almost whispering, "Shout, shout for joy to the Lord." This bittersweet treatment of the concept of judgment is something I thought a lot about as I was composing the piece and is a good example of how I hope my music can illuminate a theological concept. The final judgment is sweet in that it means the end of evil and injustice, but bitter in that there will be what Jesus described as "weeping and gnashing of teeth" (Matthew 25:30 NIV). Any exultation one would take in the former thought must be tempered by a sober recognition of the latter.

The process of composing a concert or chamber work differs in significant ways from that of writing a score for a film, but there are some similarities. Both kinds of composition obviously start with pitches and durations of sound, the alphabet of the language of music that must be worked into themes and harmonies, rhythms and structures, and developed sequentially over time in ways common to all composition. In fact, writing either kind of music is like sculpting time. Whether a piece is to be a work for film or for the concert hall, it requires creating some type of form. Practically speaking, this means making a map or outline to plot the course and trace the shape of the piece. In composing a cue for a movie, this outline is fused to the timings of a dramatic scene. Where film music is collaborative, however, existing essentially as counterpoint to the work of the actors and the director, concert music is most often, as Tom is fond of saying, like "creating the world from the ground up."

The collaborative nature of film music highlights what are perhaps the two most important distinctions between film scores and concert or chamber compositions. The first and most obvious distinction has to do with the function of the music. Film scores are written primarily for commercial purposes in a popular entertainment medium. As such, musical integrity is easily trumped by the box office. Producers, directors, executives—and their relatives—may dictate the content of a score based on prevailing trends in the marketplace, rather than trust the dramatic sensibilities of a composer. Responsibility for the final product can therefore be somewhat ambiguous: one can never be sure whether a particular dramatic or musical decision was made by the composer or requested by the producer. While it would be extremely naive to suppose that comparable situations don't arise in the concert music world, especially where commissions are involved, for the most part a concert composer is free to make his or her own artistic determinations and the work ultimately represents the composer's craft and taste alone.

The second and more significant of the distinctions between film and concert music concerns the content of the work. Where the character of a film composer's discourse is largely limited by the aspirations of the movie for which he or she is writing (though there are many notable examples of brilliant scores that have utterly transcended their films), the concert music composer's ideas can range as far as the frontiers of his or her own imagination. Because film music, in most cases, is designed to accompany other sounds, to say nothing of the visual images, it must, of necessity, be of a simpler character than music that demands the full focus of the listener. Concert and chamber music offer more opportunity for a composer to speak deeply and at length, without interruption, from the inner resources of his or her own soul. This is what I hope to achieve when I compose for the concert or recital hall, and the fierce desire to do so is what keeps me engaged in this pursuit even to the point of personal sacrifice.

At first glance, these contrasts between film and concert music may seem to give ammunition to the notorious prejudice against film scores that often infects the concert world. It must be pointed out, however, that the extent of a composer's liberty is no guarantee of the value of his or her work. Historically, great composers have often performed spectacularly within imposed limitations, including collaborations with artists working in other disciplines such as the theater or dance, while lesser writers have made a hash of their unlimited freedom. I prefer to look at film music and concert music simply as different, though related, art forms, each with its own merits and pitfalls. The critical difference lies in how well the composer exploits whatever medium he or she is working in, judged on its own terms.

In the year that followed my writing of *Shout for Joy to the Lord* and *The Growing Season,* the work I was doing with Tom blossomed significantly as I wrote my most ambitious composition to date, an Easter choral symphony entitled *A Paschal Feast.* Commissioned by the Southern Nevada Musical Arts Society, an amateur choral group with which my mother often sang as a soloist, this new work was, according to the contract, to be approximately twenty-five minutes in length, "of medium difficulty," and "somewhat conservative in harmony." The premiere was scheduled for the Musical Arts Society's Silver Anniversary Concert, which was to be held on March 20, 1988. I was very excited about the commission and the musical opportunities it promised. *Christ Is Alive!* had given me a brief glimpse of new possibilities for my choral writing and I was anxious to explore this territory further.

I have always had a particular affection for vocal music. The human voice is a powerful, vulnerable, perilous, sensitive, maddening, and heartbreaking instrument, a heaven-bound exhalation of the first breath with which God inspired man. Even the spoken word rides on its own mysterious rhythms, in an aural landscape colored by subtle shadings of pitch and timbre. The range of vocal music that I enjoy has yet to know its boundaries, but in the midst of this variety, I especially love the English boys' choir tradition. The purity of treble voices without vibrato is a harbinger of the divine for me, and its sound was echoing in my ear as I pondered what I should write in response to the commission.

Apart from the sound of the singing voice itself, there is a second facet of vocal music that I love equally: the unique marriage it makes of music and words. In the pantheon of the arts, poetry is nearly as important to me as music. So when I set out to compose a vocal work, the choice of a text is critical to me. My goal is always to illuminate the words—as the monks of the Middle Ages illuminated their manuscripts—so that the audience better understands the poem after hearing it with my music. To achieve this, I try to let the natural accents and rhythms of the words, as they sound when spoken, dictate the rhythms of the music.

A Paschal Feast germinated from a single seminal idea. From the start, I wanted to set texts with an Easter theme. When the time arrived to begin work, I had already collected a number of poems and scriptural passages I thought might be appropriate. I made work copies of these and taped them up on the wall of my studio where I could look at them every day and move them around in different configurations. I also began to pray about these texts, joined in my prayers by LeAnn and the Rossens. Slowly—and this is the part I am most impatient with because it's like watching grass grow—I began to winnow out the options. Each time I eliminated a poem, I would remove it from the wall and reconfigure the others. As the process developed, a form began to emerge. The poems were finally reduced to four: "New Readings" and "He hath abolished the old drouth" by Gerard Manley Hopkins, "Still Falls the Rain" by Dame Edith Sitwell, and "A Better Resurrection" by Christina Rosetti. I noticed that all of these contained images of food or nourishment of some kind.

For instance, "New Readings" describes:

> How soldiers platting thorns around Christ's Head
> Grapes grew and drops of wine were shed.

A few lines later, the idea is developed further, completing the reference to the Eucharist:

> From wastes of rock he brings
> Food for five thousand: on the thorns He shed
> Grains from His drooping Head.[1]

"Still Falls the Rain," written during the 1940 air raids over Britain, is a meditation on evil, and its images reflect a lack of nourishment. Jesus is "the Starved Man hung upon the cross." In another place, the poem speaks of His healing blood as life to the soul:

> It flows from the Brow we nailed upon the tree
> Deep to the dying, to the thirsting heart[2]

241

"A Better Resurrection" continues in a dark and parched mode, though focused not on corporate evil, but rather on a sense of personal hollowness:

> My life is like a broken bowl,
> A broken bowl that cannot hold
> One drop of water for my soul
> Or cordial in the searching cold.

Yet there is a turning point as the poem concludes:

> Cast in the fire the perished thing
> Melt and remould it, till it be
> A royal cup for him, my King
> O Jesus, drink of me.[3]

The fourth poem, "He hath abolished the old drouth," rejoices in a glorious picture of plenty in the context of a reconciled community:

> We meet together, you and I
> Meet in one acre of one land,
> And I will turn my looks to you,
> And you shall meet me with reply,
> We shall be sheaved with one band
> In harvest and in garnering,
> When heavenly vales so thick shall stand
> With corn that they shall laugh and sing.[4]

I didn't know *A Paschal Feast* would be a symphony until I had organized these four poems in the order they appear above, with the brighter two in the first and fourth positions and the darker two as the interior movements. I placed "A Better Resurrection" in the third position because I felt its key turning point provided a better lead into the fourth movement. Something was still missing, however. In particular, "New Readings" lacked the strong opening statement that I wanted for the first movement. At this point, my love for liturgy came into play. On the surface, liturgical forms interest me because they combine three prominent threads of my own experience: faith, music, and the theater. On a deeper level, though, the forms resonate with me spiritually because they take the celebrant on a sacred journey.

As I pored over the poems, it occurred to me that the order I had chosen had a liturgical quality to it, that the listener did indeed travel on a sort of spiritual journey from praise to the dark night of the soul, through confession and sacramental absolution to praise again. Early in the process, I had considered using scriptural excerpts for portions of the text, as they were gathered in the Easter services of the Book of Common Prayer. When the liturgical connection became clear to me, I was able to fold these sections in place around the poems. I decided that the biblical passages should be declaimed rather than sung to add to the atmosphere of liturgical worship. The symphony now began with an alleluia and ended with an amen. I also now knew what its title should be: *A Paschal Feast,* for Christ, the Passover Lamb, who nourishes us with His body and blood and whose resurrection is celebrated as a high and holy feast day of the church.

From a musical standpoint, composing *A Paschal Feast* was a complex and difficult task, something like planning the strategy for a battle. The forces required were large. On the choral side, the symphony employed two soloists, a soprano and a baritone, a mixed chorus, and a narrator. The orchestra was made up of two flutes, two oboes, two clarinets, and two bassoons; four French horns, two trumpets, and two bass trombones; three percussionists, harp, piano, and strings. Balancing these elements was an ever present concern, necessary in terms of the size of the sound, so that the orchestra wouldn't overpower the singers or the textures become monotonous. Balance was also important, however, where the pacing was concerned, so that the "tale" of the journey unfolded naturally, with a sense of inevitability, appropriate weight and color falling on the most important words. Writing a symphony also requires the talents of a storyteller.

A Paschal Feast contains several sections that received my special attention. The alleluia that opens the first movement takes the form of a rather somber introit scored almost programmatically to suggest the spacious, incense-filled environment of a great cathedral. By turns, the women and the men enter as if they were walking in procession down opposite sides of the nave and taking their places in the choir. I imagined some smiling, others solemn, all moving forward together, in step with the music, bonded in their faith. This is a beautiful image to me and I tried to hint at it in the opening moments of the symphony. Later in the first movement, the narrator, quoting from the Book of Common Prayer, announces the good news:

> Christ is risen from the dead, and become the first fruits of them that slept. For since by man came death, by man came also the resurrection of the dead. For as in Adam all die, even so in Christ shall all be made alive.

To give these words greater significance, I decided to treat them counterintuitively: I instructed the narrator to whisper them over hushed strings and muted horns. After the final word falls, he suddenly shouts "alleluia" at the top of his lungs and the chorus takes up the praises to the end.

The second movement opens with a moody quartet featuring timpani, suspended cymbals, and two solo 'celli, giving way to ghostly, chant-like choral repetitions of the title phrase "still falls the rain." It also features a stylized middle section that incorporates references to medieval music at a point in the poem where a fragment of an old English text is quoted. The chorus in this section breaks down to six solo singers, three men and three women. The third movement, on the other hand, requires no singers other than the soprano soloist, and was written with my mother's voice in mind. The amen that concludes the symphony is a fugue of Handelian propulsion and character, yet it employs a twentieth-century vocabulary. Each of these sections demanded a great deal of thought, both in coming up with the idea and in its execution and I spent many long hours still as a statue, listening to the alternatives in my mind and considering the consequences of my decisions.

In order to finish *A Paschal Feast*, I couldn't write between film and television projects alone. I had to find a way to compose it simultaneously with the demands of my career. To accomplish this, I got up two hours earlier each morning to compose, before my day of work for hire began. Three months before the deadline, a hole opened up in my schedule and I worked eighteen- to twenty-hour days exclusively on the symphony. Nor was I the only one to make sacrifices. The emotional toll on my family was great as I spent time, energy, and focus that might have gone to them on *A Paschal Feast*.

Composing it was the hardest thing I ever had to do musically, but the satisfaction I felt when it was completed was immense. It was done! I had finished my first symphony!

The premiere of *A Paschal Feast* was a celebration. The chorus, under their director Doug Peterson, had worked extremely hard on the music and performed it passionately and well, as did my mother and the fine baritone soloist, George Skipworth. The orchestra, made up of Las Vegas professionals, displayed an artistry and commitment one doesn't normally associate with that venue. I was the guest conductor. Several friends came in from out of town for the premiere, including Tom, who finally witnessed the fruit of his long labors in advising and encouraging me over the course of the writing. I felt energized and profoundly happy—and I wondered what would happen next.

The following five years saw another explosion of growth in my film and television career and, as was the case in the period between 1984 and 1986, I didn't write any new concert works. This was again a source of deep frustration for me. It occurred to me this time, however, that occasional stretches of fallow time might actually be normative rather than aberrant where my concert music composition was concerned, at least as long as I was still active in Hollywood. I tried to reconcile myself to this reality, to see it as a time to enrich the soil of my imagination, though I dreamed of the day when I could spend a greater percentage of my time on works that were more expressive of my vocation.

Not that those years were entirely devoid of activity. Two more of my works received new performances in 1988: a suite based on my score for *The Key to Rebecca* was performed by the Utah Symphony, and my *Five Songs for Flute and French Horn* was recorded and released on Crystal Records. A talented and dedicated Christian conductor in New York, Robert Davis, took an interest in my concert music in 1990. At the Fort Washington Collegiate Church, he led his orchestra in a performance of a suite of music from *St. Elsewhere* and later performed *Christ Is Alive!* on Easter Sunday, premiering *Shout for Joy to the Lord* a few weeks afterward. *October Overtures* was also performed again that year, this time by the Beach Cities Symphony in southern California. *The Growing Season* was premiered at a Pacific Composers Forum concert and broadcast on

KUSC radio in 1991. During Easter season the following year, *Christ Is Alive!* was performed at London's Royal Albert Hall by the All Souls Choir and Orchestra under the direction of Noel Tredinnick.

These events are representative of the ways in which the career of a concert music composer develops: through commissions and premieres, repeat performances and recordings. Networking and a good reputation are critical factors in this field, as they are in other endeavors. Aside from these basic points of commonality, however, my path has often diverged from that of other concert music composers. Unlike many of these composers, I don't teach at a university, nor have I ever sought to exploit the system of government and corporate grants. There is a downside to these choices. It is harder to build a reputation as a "serious" composer without the prestige of important positions or subsidies. Nevertheless, there are also benefits. My success in the film music business has actually created interest in my concert works, and some of my commissions have come from fellow musicians working in the studios. Perhaps more significantly, my career has given me the freedom to be my own patron. That means I can grow artistically in my own way and in my own time, apart from the dictates and politics of the contemporary concert music scene, which can sometimes be every bit as oppressive as those of Hollywood.

The time spent away from concert composing must have done me good, because 1993 proved to be a banner year for concert and chamber works. I wrote three new pieces, comprising nearly an hour of music, all in response to commissions. The first of these was called *Water Walker* and was commissioned through a program of the Pacific Composers Forum for the Debussy Trio, a fine chamber ensemble consisting of flute, harp, and viola. It was premiered in Los Angeles in March.

Water Walker is essentially an abstract piece of music, more impressionistic than programmatic. There were, however, a few recurring intuitive images that floated through my mind during the composition process, finally tossing up on the beach and suggesting the title. One was an impression of the cool white winter sun easing below the western horizon off the seaside California town of Corona del Mar, silhouetting seabirds like acrobats diving and dancing over the shining green curl of the waves. Another was a picture of Jesus, calmly traversing the whitecaps on the wind-buffeted Sea of Galilee to catch up with the boat bearing His dumbfounded friends. A third was the image of the apostle Peter, clambering out of the boat to meet him, and actually making it a few steps across the water before losing his confidence and starting to go down. "Why did you doubt?" says Jesus as he hoists him back up. I can't answer Jesus' question any better than Peter could. I suppose *Water Walker* was born of the same restless ambiguity, a mixture of the faith that drew Peter from the boat and the doubt that nearly drowned him.

The second work I composed in 1993, *The Ancient of Days,* is a dramatic music narrative based on the seventh chapter of Daniel. It was commissioned by the Westminster Brass and scored for brass quintet, organ, percussion, and a narrator. I became interested in setting the chapter to music while studying the book of Daniel as part of a men's Bible study organized through my church. As I settled into the text, I found myself identifying strongly with Daniel. In a sense, we were both "fish out of water." The film and television industry is an environment that at best marginalizes Christian faith, and at worst can be actively hostile to it. Yet I have a leadership role in my field and must work with large groups of musicians and collaborate with producers and directors who hold many differing worldviews.

Daniel was transplanted from his own Hebraic culture into the life of the aristocratic ruling class in Babylon. He charted a precarious course as a trusted counselor to at least three different regimes in two antagonistic empires. As a devout follower of Yahweh, he surely must have felt the tension between his life and faith and the prevailing paganism of Babylonian society. His was a difficult journey through minefields of political intrigue, religious competition, and moral decline. Yet somehow he kept his balance and even flourished. It's in this context that Daniel had his great apocalyptic vision recorded in chapter seven.

The Ancient of Days begins with a simple, stately theme modeled after the great hymns of the Protestant tradition. It gives the listener a touchstone or reference point, as preparation for the turbulent images to come. At the second statement of the theme, however, shifting dissonances in the organ and broken military rhythms on the snare drum suggest a culture in decline, like Daniel's and our own. This sort of treatment highlights one of the salient features of

The Ancient of Days: it is very specifically programmatic, using a technique called "word painting" that colors the literary images with musical effects intended to bring the images to life between the listeners' ears, a sort of sonic hologram.

The music that describes the opening of the vision is dreamlike, punctuated by trumpet calls that hint at the violent nature of the things Daniel is about to see. The listener knows that this will be no pastoral idyll, but a fierce and terrifying nightmare. The piece unfolds in earnest as winds whip up the sea in a tempestuous section, orchestrated for the full ensemble. Out of the sea arise four great beasts, each characterized by its own particular music. These beasts have a cinematic quality to them—overblown, sometimes almost comically puffed up in their self-importance.

The first beast is like a lion with eagle's wings. Many Bible scholars believe that this animal represents the Babylonian Empire under King Nebuchadnezzar. My primary metaphor for this music was found in stone friezes at the British Museum that depict the Babylonian lion hunts. In a vulgar show of manliness, Babylonian kings would release hundreds of lions into an arena, chase them about in chariots, and slaughter them with arrows and spears. With this in mind, the music takes the form of a garish, bloody hunt. Daniel watches this beast until its wings are plucked and a man's heart is given to it. This is descriptive of Nebuchadnezzar's conversion and the restoration of his kingdom after his seven years of insanity. I addressed this transformation musically with a brief reprise of the opening hymn tune, reminding the listener that God is in charge even where the mighty kings of Babylon were concerned.

The second beast is like a bear, generally interpreted to symbolize the Medo-Persian Empire that came into power after the Babylonians. I used the trombone, tuba, and timpani to depict this huge, lumbering creature gnawing on its feast of ribs. The third beast is like a leopard with wings, usually thought to represent Alexander the Great and the Greek Empire. The primary musical image is one of fierce speed, representing the force and swiftness of Alexander's conquests. This relentless energy is portrayed by the trumpets, using a technique called double-tonguing that allows the trumpeters to play in very quick staccato rhythms, and accompanied by the xylophone.

The fourth beast is more terrible than the other three, traditionally signifying an evil leader, commonly known as the Anti-Christ, who will appear on the scene in the last days to dominate the world. Musically, this section begins with an arrogant initial statement that eventually turns into a fugue that never quite gets off the ground. It sinks under the weight of its own turbulent sonorities, finally yielding to a militaristic march theme that describes the war that this beast will wage against the followers of God. The beast theme and warlike elements return repeatedly throughout this section until the music degenerates into complete chaos through a compositional technique called aleatory or "chance" music, which involves free improvisation on the part of the musicians. This builds to a fever pitch and suddenly ends as God, the Ancient of Days, arrives to deal with the beasts.

The Ancient of Days is identified with traditional musical forms: primarily, a fugue derived from the fourth phrase of the primary theme that suggests divine order and inevitability. But overwhelming power is present also, described in the climactic moment as the beasts are judged and destroyed. Finally, the Son of Man, whom Christians identify as Jesus, appears to receive His rightful kingdom, accompanied by a quiet and straightforward statement of the hymn tune in its purest form, which grows gradually to a triumphant finish.

The Ancient of Days was premiered in October by the Westminster Brass at a Ligonier Ministries conference in San Diego, California. Ligonier Ministries is theologian R.C. Sproul's teaching ministry, and R.C. narrated the text for this performance with great passion and conviction, his husky voice savoring each word like a sip of vintage wine. The Westminster Brass played with courage, excellence, and understanding. There was a deaf interpreter on hand for the conference and during the performance of my piece, she not only signed the text, but also spontaneously created the sound and drama of the music with her gestures, almost like an improvised dance. Watching her recreate my piece was one of the highlights of the evening for me.

Every composer wants his work to have some impact on the listener. I had hoped that *The Ancient of Days* would create a sonorous landscape that would encourage the audience to imagine and experience some of the sensations and emotions that Daniel may have experienced during his deeply disturbing and inspiring vision. This apparently happened, at least for some listeners. Bible scholar John Sailhamer used the *The Ancient of Days* in classes devoted to the study of Daniel's vision and found that discussions following a hearing of the piece opened new doors to the students' imaginations, enabling them to penetrate the difficult text with greater depth and appreciation. I could not have asked for more. My gratitude to God was profound.

In spite of all these successes, He still had one more gift in store for me in 1993, a Christmas gift. The third and largest of my compositions that year was called *Welcome All Wonders: A Christmas Celebration.* Commissioned by the Utah Chamber Artists, *Welcome All Wonders* is a five-movement "cantata" for chorus and orchestra, based on five texts, two by Renaissance poets and three by contemporary writers. In thirty minutes, *Welcome All Wonders* expresses the heart of my faith with more clarity and emotion than anything else I have ever written.

The commission came about through Liz Sorenson, a friend of LeAnn's since the fifth grade and someone I had known since junior high school. Liz sang with the Utah Chamber Artists. Her husband Jim served as its president. The artistic director was a talented conductor and pianist named Barlow Bradford. Barlow had formed the Utah Chamber Artists and developed them into a first-rate choral and instrumental ensemble that presented several concerts a year. Their focus was on sophisticated repertoire, which they performed with a high degree of excellence and spirit. Liz introduced me to Barlow, and the eventual fruit of our meeting was a commission for me to compose a multimovement Christmas work, perhaps a large-scale cantata or oratorio, which they could premiere at the Utah Chamber Artists' Christmas concert the following year.

To prepare for the commission, I flew to Salt Lake with LeAnn to hear the ensemble in performance. I wanted to get their sound into my head, and I couldn't have chosen a better occasion. That evening, the Utah Chamber Artists were performing an extraordinarily beautiful and difficult a capella work, the original Russian version of the Rachmaninoff *Vespers,* in the Utah State Capitol Rotunda. The sound in that large marble-paneled space was not unlike the sonorities produced by a choir in a European cathedral. The music was transcendent and the voices were wonderful, well-trained, and expertly conducted. Thrilled and inspired, I couldn't wait to hear them perform my music.

With that haunting and glorious sound reverberating in my mind, I set out to choose the texts. I wasn't the least interested in snowmen or reindeer, not even in the warmth of the Yuletide hearth. Christmas is about Christ, and I wanted to select poems that would focus on Him. Nevertheless, I felt a certain caution about doing so. The special meaning that Christmas had held for me from childhood had changed focus, had been amplified and deepened since my conversion. While the Utah Chamber Artists was not an LDS organization, I knew that there were a number of Mormons who were part of the ensemble. I wasn't afraid to treat ideas that stretched or challenged, but I did not want to make a statement that would be pointlessly offensive and I prayed to find the right balance.

As I had done in writing *A Paschal Feast,* I taped poems on the wall of my studio. Initially, there were seventeen poems that I moved about in different configurations, searching for some combination that would make sense. I was eventually able to narrow these down to five texts that I organized as follows: "Welcome All Wonders," by seventeenth-century English poet, Richard Crashaw; "Christmas Mourning," by Vassar Miller, an American woman writing in the twentieth century; "The Nativity of Christ," by English Renaissance poet Robert Southwell; and "Good Is the Flesh" and "Christmas now" by Brian Wren, the contemporary English hymnodist who wrote the text I set for *Christ Is Alive!* These poems were extremely poignant and resonant for me. I felt that, through them, I would be able to say what lay at the center of my heart, directly and passionately. The poems were rich and complex with gorgeous and evocative imagery, but the most profound thread that wove them all together was the paradox of the incarnation of Christ.

"God made flesh" is the centerpiece of Christmas. It combines mirth and mystery, power and powerlessness, glory and tragedy in a single, blessed event. Paradox is part of the holiday's appeal. Since deciding to follow Jesus, I have reveled in my relationship with a God who defies tidy mortal explanations. The poem I set for the first movement, "Welcome All Wonders," begins with an unabashed declaration of the heart of the matter:

> Welcome, all Wonders in one sight!
> Eternity shut in a span
> Summer in winter, day in night
> Heaven in earth, and God in man.[5]

In four short lines, these bold paradoxes are sown like bright star-seeds in the dark firmament of the mind: eternity is caged in mortal flesh, a blaze of summer ignites in winter, day is born into night, heaven stoops to earth. These images are gathered in one as God in Christ becomes man.

The paradoxes of Christmas find even more outlandish expression in the third poem, "The Nativity of Christ:"

> Behold, the father is his daughter's son,
> The bird that built the nest is hatched therein,
> The old of years an hour hath not outrun,
> Eternal life to live doth now begin,
> The Word is dumb, the mirth of heaven doth weep,
> Might feeble is and force doth faintly creep.[6]

This sort of poetic imagery has always appealed to me. Robert Southwell, the author of "The Nativity of Christ," made the words fairly dance on the page. Initially, when I considered the musical setting for these words, I had in mind a majestic, hymn-like treatment, but the laughter that spilled from this poem ultimately inspired me to set it with a much brighter, more rhythmic, and colorful music, full of delight in its clashing, cascading images.

The notion of paradox is further continued in the other poems. The fourth, "Good Is the Flesh," celebrates the human side of the incarnation. There is a poignant sweetness that invests even the simplest experiences of life, which God blesses and the poem celebrates:

> Good is the flesh that the Word has become
>   good is the birthing, the milk in the breast,
>   good is the feeding, caressing and rest,
>   good is the body for knowing the world,
> Good is the flesh that the Word has become.
>
> Good is the body for knowing the world,
>   sensing the sunlight, the tug of the ground,

feeling, perceiving, within and around,
good is the body, from cradle to grave,
Good is the flesh that the Word has become.

Good is the body, from cradle to grave,
growing and aging, arousing, impaired,
happy in clothing, or lovingly bared,
good is the pleasure of God in our flesh,
Good is the flesh that the Word has become.

Good is the pleasure of God in our flesh,
longing in all, as in Jesus to dwell,
glad of embracing and tasting and smell,
good is the body, for good and for God,
Good is the flesh that the Word has become.[7]

Rather than creating a false dichotomy between God and mortal flesh, the incarnation celebrates their union. The good Christmas news is not a Gnostic message of ethereal spirituality with its corresponding denigration of the body, but an affirmation of the marriage of spirit and flesh, a complete integration of the two in the person of Jesus. I don't have much patience for the ephemeral, bloodless spiritism of the New Age. I want a faith that is as true on earth as it is in heaven, that pulses with the life that God has poured into both.

The paradox of the fifth poem, "Christmas now," can be seen in the birth of a joyful and triumphant new song, proceeding from two unlikely sources: the cradle, where a helpless infant lies, and the cross, a cruel instrument of death. Whether evil takes a political or a religious form, it is ultimately defeated by Christ's "helpless love."

Child, when Herod wakes,
and hate or exploitation
swing their dripping swords,
from your cross and cradle
    sing a new song.

Child, when Caesar's laws
choke love or strangle freedom
calling darkness light,
from your cross and cradle
    sing a new song.

> Child, when Caiaphas
> sends truth to crucifixion
> to protect his prayers,
> from your cross and cradle
>   sing a new song.
>
> Child, your helpless love
> brings death and resurrection;
> joyfully we come
> to your cross and cradle
>   with a new song -
>   Alleluia! Alleluia![8]

The tragic truth of our humanity is that evil is not found only in the hearts of a few spectacular monsters, like Herod or Caesar, Hitler or Stalin. Evil dwells within each one of us, a fact that God has gone to extraordinary lengths to address. The working out of the relationship between sin and redemption has defined the tragedy and the glory that is human history. "The Nativity of Christ" declares:

> Man altered was by sin from man to beast;
> Beast's food is hay, hay is all mortal flesh.
> Now God is flesh and lies in manger pressed
> As hay, the brutest sinner to refresh.
> O happy field wherein this fodder grew,
> Whose taste doth us from beasts to men renew.[9]

However, it is not only in the joyful and loving image of the cradle that God's redemption is seen and understood, but in the fist-clenching injustice and agony of the cross. *Welcome All Wonders'* second poem, "Christmas Mourning," contains perhaps the most powerful and moving expression of this profound paradox, that Christ had to die in order that we might live. He was hoisted onto that cross to pay for the evil that existed in *our* hearts, not in His. I know of no more poignant articulation of this great exchange than "Christmas Mourning."

> On Christmas day I weep
> Good Friday to rejoice.
> I watch the Child asleep.
> Does he half-dream the choice
> The Man must make and keep?

At Christmastime I sigh
For my good Friday hope
Outflung the Child's arms lie
To span in their brief scope
The death the Man must die.

Come Christmastide I groan
To hear Good Friday's pealing.
The Man, racked to the bone,
Has made His hurt my healing,
Has made my ache His own.

Slay me, pierced to the core
With Christmas penitence
So I who, new-born, soar
To that Child's innocence,
May wound the Man no more.[10]

Yet even in the midst of the sorrow and the penitence, God has provided for a Christmas joy that wells up from within like a sudden stream of laughter. This paradox is captured in "The Nativity of Christ."

Gift better than Himself God does not know;
Gift better than his God no man can see.
This gift doth here the giver given bestow;
Gift to this gift let each receiver be.
God is my gift, himself he freely gave me;
God's gift am I, and none but God shall have me.[11]

Throughout the process of choosing these texts, I spent long stretches of time developing thematic material for each of them. I like composing away from an instrument—I don't want my ideas to be limited by what I can play, and I did much of the thematic work for *Welcome All Wonders* on the beach at Corona del Mar. I had gotten into the habit of writing at the beach while composing *Water Walker.* The seaside images that filled my gaze at Corona del Mar had provided some of the inspiration for that work. Now the sea played an even more definitive role. Some days I would sit on the sand for hours and spin out melodies that almost seemed to rise from the voice of the ocean itself. There was a flow to my writing there. The rhythms of the waves became part of *Welcome All Wonders,* even the shouts of children and the cries of their mothers cautioning them to be careful in the surf. The laughter, the smell of sweat, the heat rising from the sand—it is all wrapped up in the music.

Another important musical influence came from my travels in Europe. Whenever there, I spend much of my time in museums, absorbing the work of great artists, or soaking up the sights, sounds, and smells of the cathedrals. I am inspired and refreshed by my contact with painting, sculpture, and architecture. Early on in my adult life, I developed a taste for fine art, especially the painting of Monet and Van Gogh. After my conversion, however, I found that I felt connected to artists of earlier generations. I saw those of the Renaissance and Middle Ages with new eyes because I now shared their faith and desire to express the passion for God in a creative medium. Much of the great art of Western civilization is anchored in the story of Jesus. I tried to capture some of the flavor of my experiences with this art in *Welcome All Wonders* through the use of colorful orchestration, contrapuntal devices, and harmonic structures, such as chords built on seconds and fourths, which I find reminiscent of medieval and Renaissance music.

As with *A Paschal Feast*, finishing *Welcome All Wonders* on time involved working very hard, missing a lot of sleep, and neglecting my family. When it was finally done, I dedicated the work to LeAnn, each movement for a different aspect of her character—her tears, her faith, her joy, her love, and her fire—each one of these qualities a way that she has been a blessing in my life.

Welcome All Wonders was premiered on December 11, 1993, at Abravanel Hall in Salt Lake City. Barlow Bradford conducted the Utah Chamber Artists chorus and orchestra in the performance. It's hard to describe my feelings that evening as this work that meant so much to me was performed in my hometown. I felt an enormous sense of gratitude that my decision to leave Mormonism had not made this night impossible. Many people I knew and loved came to the concert, some that I hadn't seen since high school. We were all mixed together there in the audience: LDS friends; Christian friends; LeAnn and the girls; my mother, my brother, my father, uncles, aunts, and cousins. We all sat there together as the music washed over us like a wave. It was the culmination of a cherished dream, a vision of how

I hope with all my heart heaven will look, each one of us under the Mercy, assembled to worship and to welcome all wonders.

Since that night, opportunities in the concert music field have continued to proliferate. Early in 1994, I arranged a suite of five Christmas carols, entitled *In Dulci Jubilo,* which was commissioned and recorded by the Philadelphia Brass. Also that year, a recording of the premiere performance of *Welcome All Wonders* was broadcast nationwide over NPR-affiliated stations on the syndicated choral music program, *First Art.* In 1995, *Welcome All Wonders* was recorded by the Utah Chamber Artists on the Bonneville Classics label. I was asked to produce the album and the recording sessions were a great delight—Barlow and the Utah Chamber Artists performed the music beautifully. The album included a new Christmas piece called *Shepherd Story* that I wrote especially for the CD.

So where do I go from here? Of course, I'd like to see more performances of my existing concert and chamber works. I compose to communicate, not just to express myself, and that requires an audience. Currently, I promote my own work through my publishing company, Plough Down Sillion Music, which I hope will continue to grow over the next few years. For the future, I dream of writing a cycle of symphonies and a couple of operas, as well as more choral and orchestral music, art songs, and chamber compositions for various instrumental groupings. I would like to contribute new sacred works to the body of Christian church music. Finding more time to write is a big part of this dream. My concert works represent the purest synthesis of my music and my deepest-held beliefs. I experience the birthing and parenting of these compositions as the fulfillment of who God made me to be, and "when I run, I feel His pleasure."

Further Up and Further In

It was the Unicorn who summed up what everyone was feeling. He stamped his right fore-hoof on the ground and neighed and then cried: "I have come home at last! This is my real country! I belong here. This is the land I have been looking for all my life, though I never knew it till now. The reason why we loved the old Narnia is that it sometimes looked a little like this. Bree-hee-hee! Come further up, come further in!"

—C.S. Lewis, *The Last Battle*[1]

In The Last Battle, the masterful and stirring conclusion to his children's tales, the *Chronicles of Narnia,* C.S. Lewis describes the apocalypse of his imaginary country. The end begins when Narnia, long a secure land of freedom and prosperity, is deceived and overrun by its enemies. As the title suggests, the story culminates in a fierce battle that takes place at night in front of a stable on a hill. In the heat of the fighting, Lewis's protagonists, among them two English children, are forced through the stable door. On the other side, they expect to meet a swift and ruthless death at the hands of a sword-wielding assassin. Instead they suddenly find themselves in a peaceful, verdant countryside, under a deep blue sky on a sunlit morning poised at the brink of summer—Aslan's country. Aslan! the great golden lion, ruler and protector of Narnia, Son of the Emperor-over-sea, the Christ of the *Chronicles.*

As the children begin to explore their new environment, they soon recognize familiar Narnian landmarks. This discovery is puzzling until it dawns on them that Aslan's country is the real Narnia, of which the old one had been only a shadow. This new Narnia is somehow richer and deeper, more redolent with joy than the one they had known. With a deep sense of satisfaction, they realize that this is where they belong—they have finally come home. The cry rings out, "Further up and further in!" and the children join a great company of pilgrims moving forward into the new land.

Although Lewis was ultimately writing about heaven in this portion of his allegory, this passage is in some measure descriptive of what conversion was like for LeAnn and me. Following Christ was less like arriving at a destination than crossing the border into a beautiful new country—the country of grace—with its wide landscape spread out before us, just waiting to be explored. From the time of that crossing-over, the adventure has been sweet: we have experienced the kinship of love and the awe of worship in our community of faith; our minds have been sharpened with the iron of the Word of God; and we have felt ourselves deepen spiritually through prayer and acts of service. Nevertheless, the journey has not been without pain. We have also been tried, stretched, and wounded, and had an illuminating spotlight trained upon our sins. In short, there has not been an inch of our life that has not been invaded by God's overpowering grace, either with rich joy or profound disquiet. We, too, have heard the cry, "Further up and further in!"

The country of grace has its own topography. How shall I describe it? Its contours are revealed in the everyday details of my life. Living in grace means waking in the morning with God's praise on my lips, looking forward to what He has in store instead of wondering how I might disappoint Him today, instead of wondering how I might disappoint anyone—including myself—today. It means having confidence in the promise that He who began a good work in me will carry it forward to completion, that my inevitable missteps and ill-spoken words will be washed away like so much flotsam in the healing tide of His love. It means there is no place to fall but into His arms. It means that I will never walk alone.

Living in grace means being drawn to the good, not driven from the evil. It means standing firmly on principle, yet leaving judgment in the hands of Him who is intimately acquainted with each extenuating circumstance. It means embracing the downtrodden and disease-ridden, while at the same time rejoicing with those whom God has prospered and honoring those who work steadily and hard in the service of their families and communities. Grace converts ordinary meetings into divine appointments, transforms work into vocation and obligation into mission, invests the tedious with passion and purpose, and renders food and drink in the company of fellow travelers exquisite and sacramental. This is what my life is like on my best days.

On my worst days, I slip back into old habits, old patterns of thought where fear and pride, lust and ambition wait like drugs seeking a vein. In the country of grace, the sun soon sets on such days; their power to torment is short-lived, and any residue of shame is soon swept aside as easily as a pile of dry leaves. Living in grace means being fully engaged with life, looking squarely, with unflinching charity, into the face of the truth without excuses or false modesty.

When LeAnn and I told our Mormon bishop that we were leaving the Church, he predicted that our lives would soon become empty husks. Like so many other Latter-day Saints, he really believed that there is no life after Mormonism. Nor was his assessment the only negative one to which LeAnn and I were exposed as we contemplated the prospect of finding a Christian community with which to worship. Popular cultural caricatures of evangelical Christians were even worse than my bishop's bleak view: they were ignorant fundamentalists steeped in dogmatic superstition, or moralistic spoilsports who wanted to compel everyone to see the world in their own censorious terms, or joyless hypocrites driven by a guilt-ridden obsession to keep others from taking any pleasure in life. These exaggerated stereotypes were light years removed from the realities of Christian faith and experience at the First Evangelical Free Church of Fullerton. The rich banquet LeAnn and I have enjoyed since our association with that body of believers demonstrates how terribly mistaken these perceptions truly are.

Soon after we began attending the Evangelical Free Church in 1984, LeAnn and I began to blossom and thrive spiritually in its nourishing atmosphere. Church services were lively, interesting, and often moving, a sharp contrast with the blandness of the Mormon services to which we were accustomed. Our pastor, Chuck Swindoll, was an expressive speaker and his sermons had genuine substance. It was a rare Sunday when our hearts weren't pricked by a deep sense of gratitude at the freshness of God's mercy. We were so happy to find a church where we could raise our children without twisting faith into a defense of the indefensible, a place where Christ was consistently central and parishioners were authentic and open, vulnerable in their humanity even as they sought the will of God.

Even my aesthetic needs were nurtured in our new surroundings. Under the direction of our music minister, Howie Stevenson, our church enjoyed an outstanding variety of music, from the historic hymns and anthems to contemporary songs of praise, accompanied by all sorts of instruments from pipe organ to drums and electric guitars. A number of fine vocal and orchestral or chamber ensembles could be drawn from the congregation and they were regularly employed in the worship services. Sometimes great works of Christian faith, such as the Brahms *German Requiem* or the Haydn *Creation,* were performed in special evening concerts by the church choir and orchestra. LeAnn and I began learning how to worship from Howie and those who served with him. Losing ourselves in the delicious abandonment of praise to God was a fresh and moving experience for us. It was a form of expression we had never known as Mormons, and we were like children soaking up every gesture and nuance.

We joined a Sunday school class, an adult fellowship called Joint Heirs after the apostle Paul's term for those who share in the inheritance of God's family, and the people we met there took us in immediately. In fact, only a few weeks prior to our first visit, the class had concluded a series of studies on Mormonism, so they were uniquely prepared to welcome us, as well as being exceedingly curious about how our LDS experience squared with the information they had been absorbing. The Joint Heirs struck us as exceptionally loving, thoughtful, and fair-minded people. Perhaps we can be forgiven for the fact that this came as something of a shock to us. Although we had genuinely been born again, LeAnn and I still carried vestiges of the assumptions that had motivated our bishop's dire prediction, and we had wondered upon leaving Mormonism whether we would ever find another community of faith with bonds as strong and as deep.

We soon came to feel that the Joint Heirs were more like an extended family than a church group. In part, this was due to a string of heart-wrenching events. Within a single month, three of the women in the class delivered profoundly premature babies, two of whom died almost immediately. The child who lived was the son of Ken and Jeanie Johnson—among the first Joint Heirs to befriend LeAnn and me—and they named him Bjorn.

As Jeanie went into labor, one of the doctors recommended she have an abortion, telling her that their unborn child was not "viable." With extraordinary courage and faith, she and Ken said no. A procedure was eventually scheduled to deliver the baby and the Joint Heirs began to pray. At this point, the doctors feared for Jeanie's life because of multiple complications. By the grace of God, the delivery was successful and both Jeanie and Bjorn survived, though Bjorn, at only 24 weeks' gestation, was in critical condition and had to be taken to the neonatal intensive care unit. He weighed less than one-and-a-half pounds.

In the months that followed, LeAnn and I visited Jeanie and Bjorn at the hospital, as did many others from the class. Bjorn was so tiny that he could be cradled in the palm of Ken's hand—his legs weren't much larger than the tubes that carried his intravenous fluids—but he was a fighter! Jeanie sat with her son's hand curled around her little finger for hours on end, singing to him, praying over him, telling him that she loved him and that he could make it.

He slowly grew stronger and bigger, and after 4 1/2 months was well enough to leave the hospital, weighing 4 1/2 pounds. There was celebration in Joint Heirs the first Sunday that Ken and Jeanie brought him to church. Bjorn's homecoming marked the end of our season of grief.

These experiences in the valley of the shadow of death were defining ones for the Joint Heirs. Our families were knit together in a profound way through the shared suffering of those months. LeAnn and I no longer had any lingering questions about the depth of Christian fellowship. On the material plane, in a noodle-for-noodle comparison with the Mormons, the Joint Heirs could be counted on to deliver just as many casseroles to those who were sick or otherwise in need. In contrast to our experience as Latter-day Saints, though, we found that they were also willing to stand by those who struggled with doubt or sin. Accountability in our class grew organically out of our relationships, rather than artificially through an imposed authoritarian hierarchy. There was less emphasis on uniformity and more room for individual differences. LeAnn and I were relieved to discover that other men and women in the group wrestled with thorny spiritual issues and asked tough questions of their faith just as we did. We began to learn what it meant to live in community in "the body of Christ."

One important way that this community was built and maintained spiritually was through "conversational prayer," speaking to God by taking turns praying within a single continuous supplication. This approach differed significantly from Mormon group prayers, which were always voiced by one person using formalized language including archaic terms such as "thee" and "thou." Conversational prayer allowed for more humanity, more vulnerability, and authentic personal expression, just as any real conversation between people in a genuine relationship does. God was as real to us as LeAnn and I were to one another, and talking with Him without affectation helped define and shape our new spirituality.

While Joint Heirs provided the majority of our most intimate friendships, we also formed close relationships with our pastoral staff and in the church body at large. Opportunities for fellowship could be found before and after the main services in the sanctuary as well as through a variety of church-sponsored outreach programs, seminars, and activities. One of the best of these was held at the Forest Home Christian Conference Center in the San Bernardino mountains. Every year the church contracted for a week there and offered a program featuring speakers, reliable child care, recreational activities, and three family-style meals a day. Children from nine to eleven years of age went to their own camp where they slept in teepees, hiked, swam, studied the Bible, and did crafts. There were also separate camping facilities and programs for the junior high and high school age groups.

It was a great week in terms of getting away from the pressures of work and home maintenance, but the best things about it were the worship, the good humor, the friendships, and the teaching. Howie Stevenson and his wife Marilyn led the music, which was as rousing as aerobic exercise one moment and peaceful as the surface of a lake on a windless day the next. They consistently kept the primacy of Jesus in focus during these deeply fulfilling times of worship. But not all of our camp activities were carried out in an atmosphere of seriousness. Laughter abounded everywhere: pure, unforced, cleansing laughter like water spilling over stones.

Everything was more informal at camp than it was down the hill in the suburbs. It was delightful to see the pastoral staff let down their hair, dress in shorts and t-shirts, and make outrageous jokes. This contributed to a healthy balance in the relationship between our congregation and the church leadership. Along with the fun, there was nourishment for the spiritually hungry. Chuck Swindoll usually shared the teaching duties with a guest speaker and the messages were full of quality content that sunk deep into the bedrock of our spiritual life. We always came away from camp enlivened and enlightened. Forest Home became an annual tradition in the Redford family.

After more than a year of association with the First Evangelical Free Church of Fullerton, LeAnn and I felt that it was time to take care of some unfinished business with the Mormon Church. Late in 1985, we asked that our names be removed from LDS membership records. There were several reasons for taking this step. We wanted to make a statement, to reinforce the finality of our decision to leave Mormonism in terms that LDS Church authority would recognize. As long as we were still on the rolls, we would continue to be included on LDS mailing lists and contacted by Church representatives, such as priesthood home teachers and Relief Society visiting teachers, all charged with the duty of maintaining the official lines of communication. Unless we put a stop to it, this institutional penchant for keeping track of everyone would follow our children into adulthood, no matter where in the world they chose to live. We also felt uncomfortable knowing that we continued to be numbered among the Latter-day Saints in the annual growth reports which they trumpeted to the media. The bottom line was that we wanted closure with our former faith and felt secure enough with our new one to pursue a formal separation.

In order to process our request, LDS policy required that a Church court, made up of the stake president, his councilors, and the twelve members of the stake high council, be convened. LeAnn and I appeared before this court in person so that we could witness about the things that God had done in our lives. We sent a copy of our "Open Letter" to each of the high councilmen in advance to inform them of the reasons for our leaving. Our daughter Jessica, then nine years old and a baptized member of the Church herself, insisted on being there with us. She looked so small and determined before the assembled stake leaders as they sat facing us in a semicircle, all dressed in crisp business suits.

We were allowed to make a short statement. I referred them to the materials I had sent and added a few personal words of amplification. LeAnn spoke eloquently of our commitment to Christ and the liberating power of His grace in our lives. Although the men listened politely, it appeared that only one had even bothered to skim our "Open Letter." Then, without much discussion, they honored our request to disassociate. According to Church dictates, the stake president formally stripped us of all our Mormon blessings, such as the priesthood and the privilege of temple attendance. He told us that we no longer had a right to the guiding influence of the Holy Ghost. Finally, he informed us we could continue to tithe if we so desired, but only through a third party.

LeAnn and I received this ruling with a variety of emotions. LeAnn was jubilant, having communicated the message she had felt called to deliver. I was sad that the historical, scriptural, and spiritual issues we found so significant had elicited no response from the council, not even a single probing question. The absence of genuine dialogue or curiosity made the proceedings seem weirdly automated, almost surreal. We were also amazed at the institutional arrogance of a church that presumed to control the Spirit of God, whose comings and goings Jesus compared to the wind that blows where it will, beyond the grasp of human authority. The policy on tithing struck us as ludicrous, like something out of a late-night comedy sketch, and we had to restrain a strong desire to giggle when this arrangement was suggested to us. Ultimately, we were relieved and satisfied with the outcome of the meeting. We left the court with our hearts at peace, believing that we had done the right thing, and it was good to get the experience behind us.

The following year, LeAnn and I decided to become members of the First Evangelical Free Church of Fullerton. There was no particular reason for our waiting so long to do this—we just hadn't felt any urgency about the matter. The Evangelical Free Church doesn't emphasize formal association as the Mormons do; there is no sense that members are somehow more faithful than nonmembers. Lack of membership didn't impede our opportunities to participate in church activities, other than in certain leadership and teaching positions. When we finally did decide to join, we found that this experience also contrasted with the process of becoming a Mormon. For one thing, joining the Evangelical Free Church didn't involve baptism, as entrance into the LDS Church does. Instead, we attended a class intended to familiarize applicants for membership with the church's statement of faith. Then we met with a deacon who heard the story of our decision to follow Christ. Afterward, we were accepted. Everything was quite straightforward without undue weight being placed on affiliation over faith.

A few years later, in May 1989, LeAnn and I were baptized as a public testimony that we had received Jesus Christ as our Savior and Lord. It had taken us five years to get to the water. In part, this was due to impediments as prosaic as the logistics of scheduling. More important, however, we had felt no pressing need to be baptized right away. This choice was expressive of our new understanding of the ordinance. As Mormons, we had been taught that baptism was the gateway into the "one true church." Further, we were told it was the primary ordinance of salvation—we couldn't ultimately enter the celestial kingdom without it. In the country of grace, however, no such work was required for one to cross that border. We wanted to be baptized, and did it as an act of obedience, not as a way of earning God's approbation. It was the outward expression of an inward reality: our relationship with Jesus. In retrospect, the delay actually underscored this new facet of our faith in a way that an immediate baptism may not have done.

Opportunities for service at the Fullerton Evangelical Free Church were numerous and wide-ranging. Many of the ministries grew organically from the passion and sense of vocation felt by individuals responding to the work of God in their own lives. In one instance, the mother of a handicapped child established an outreach to other handicapped children and their parents. In another case, a man who suffered from multiple sclerosis formed a support group for others with the disease. These ministries were welcomed and fully integrated at the Evangelical Free Church since its organizational structure was not as rigidly defined as that of the LDS Church.

I gravitated to the music ministry immediately and enjoyed playing guitar and piano, singing, and writing arrangements for various worship services. As I learned how to worship myself, I began to lead others. Often, LeAnn and I did this as a couple, weaving music, prayer, and scriptural readings together into a unified program. Our love for liturgy influenced the structure of these programs as we tried to make each one a unique spiritual journey in its own right. It was especially fulfilling to share these programs with our friends in Joint Heirs. In addition to service in the field of music, both of us enjoyed performing with the church's readers' theater group. We were also often asked to tell the story of our conversion, and we occasionally volunteered to teach on the subject of Mormonism. LeAnn also taught in the children's Sunday school and the Pioneer Girls, the church's counterpart to the Girl Scouts. We counted it a blessing to develop friendships with and contribute to the financial support of a number of missionaries, both in the United States and overseas.

Evangelism is a high priority at our church, which sponsors many who hear the call of God to serve full-time. Sometimes our global vision provides for unique cross-cultural connections. In August 1990, for example, the church arranged for a group of visiting Russian engineers to spend a Sunday with the Joint Heirs. We attended church together, then two of the engineers, Leonid and Viktor, joined us and a few other families from the class at our house to swim in the pool, barbecue chicken, and talk about our differences and similarities. We all had a grand time. Leonid spoke English very well and entertained us with many jokes and stories. Viktor sat for a long time with one of the children on his knees, describing how he loved and missed his grandson. There was something exquisitely moving about this experience—a reconciliation of worldviews that transcended our own small context. It made us wish that all those divided by politics, race, culture, and religion could come together once in a while to share meals and stories and time with children.

People frequently asked LeAnn and me to join them as they met with Mormon friends or neighbors to share their faith. Sometimes the church or a parachurch organization referred us to people who had called seeking information. A few of the Latter-day Saints with whom we met acted threatened and hostile. One young woman who came to our home with her Christian boyfriend stormed out in the middle of the discussion, slamming our front door behind her. Others, however, wanted us to help them find their way out of the LDS Church and into a new relationship with the Lord.

We didn't seek this kind of work as a formal ministry. God simply sent people to us, and when He did, we tried to respond in the best way that we could, with love, understanding, and integrity. We also developed our own study materials to aid us in the process. These were based on the work we had originally done with the "Open Letter," as well as the Bible study we had undertaken as we further assimilated the distinctions between the teachings of Mormonism and the Bible. Gradually, our work in the area of Mormonism evolved to include a group of interested people who met at the church on a regular basis to study the issues, talk about ways to improve our approach to Mormons, and pray for those Latter-day Saints with whom we had relationships. This group stayed together for several years before new seasons of life drew us to other avenues of service. We counted it a privilege to stand for Jesus Christ in whatever arena God chose to place us.

Because of this ministry, I was contacted by Scott McKinney, then the associate pastor of a neighboring congregation, the Cypress Evangelical Free Church, and invited to share my story and make a presentation about Mormonism to his church. Not long thereafter, Scott accepted a call to pastor the Orem Evangelical Free Church in Utah, not far north of the Brigham Young University campus. Scott and his wife, Sara, came to LeAnn and me for background on Mormonism and help in preparing for their life in the mostly LDS community of Orem. We became close friends in the process.

In the early days of his pastorate, Scott invited us several times to minister through music and our testimony at the Orem church. We fell in love with many of the dear people there and came to feel that this church was a second home to us. This relationship led to a unique mission opportunity that the Fullerton church sponsored at our instigation. By 1991, the Orem church had grown significantly and needed more space in which to meet. LeAnn and I volunteered to organize a team from southern California to help them accomplish this.

We were delighted at the diversity of people that responded when we announced this short-term mission in the church bulletin. We had anticipated hearing from single young men, but a number of retired couples also indicated interest and a few parents wanted to make it a family affair and take their children. We welcomed them all and the team was ultimately comprised of thirty-six adults and seven children, including our son, Jonathan. The mission plan was expanded to include helping the Orem church run a Christian day camp for children called Vacation Bible School. Some of our group were interested in working on banners for the Orem church sanctuary. We even had an artist on the team who designed the layouts. We lacked a construction foreman, however, so we mobilized a prayer effort and, within a few weeks, one literally showed up at our front door one evening.

In August 1991, after months of preparation, the team finally left for Utah. The experience was something like an old-fashioned barn raising. The men of the two churches worked hard together with a good will and succeeded in building six new classrooms. Vacation Bible School ran smoothly and attracted children from the community as well as the church. Some of them made commitments to Christ. The banners turned out beautifully and lifted the heart as well as the eye. Friendships grew between members of the team and the Orem church families that housed them. The joy we experienced in the priceless fellowship we found there transcended the long hours and hard work. I felt a sense of complete freedom in serving God there. Each morning I rose without expectations and prayed to be His man wherever He might lead me that day. I floated like a feather on His breath.

There is one more important aspect of my experience in Christian community that needs mentioning and it has to do specifically with my art. Not long after committing my life to Christ, I began to hunger for relationship with other professional Christian artists who shared the experience of His grace. God answered my prayer in many ways, but never more forthrightly than in October 1990, when a fresh wind blew through the familiar routines of my career. I was asked to conduct a concert in Anaheim for the gospel singer, Michael Card. He was appearing there with a small orchestra and needed someone to contract the musicians and conduct the arrangements of his songs. Mike and I recognized one another as kindred spirits right away. There was an immediate ease in our conversation and a harmony that derived from our mutual experiences, both spiritual and professional. The men in his backup band were also gifted musicians and interesting people, and a tangible sense of brotherhood bonded us all.

The concert was a delightful and touching time for me. Mike's songs were well-crafted and inspiring, with lyrics that were unusually thoughtful and perceptive. He played both guitar and piano beautifully, and his arrangements were sensitively written. One of Mike's songs in particular, "Joy in the Journey," resonated with me deeply. For LeAnn and me, it has become a kind of anthem.

There is a joy in the journey,
there's a light we can love on the way.
There is a wonder and wildness to life,
and freedom for those who obey.[2]

After the concert, Mike hired me to arrange and conduct his forthcoming Christmas album, *The Promise,* set to record in London the following May. The sessions were distinguished by the same sense of "rightness" I had experienced while recording *The Trip to Bountiful.* The musicians played superbly and the recording came off without a hitch under the expert supervision of Mike's producer, Phil Naish. We were all delighted with the results and rejoiced in the way the project had come together. One of the songs, "We Will Find Him," hadn't been scheduled for an orchestral arrangement, but while we were there, Phil decided that it could benefit from some strings. He asked me if I could quickly throw something together. While the musicians took their break, Phil and I went into the studio, sat at the piano, and quickly wrote out the arrangement, which we then Xeroxed and presented to the musicians when the break was over. They played it beautifully and we kept the tracks for the album.

The songs from *The Promise* were woven together to form a Christmas program, and for the next two Christmases, Mike hired me to conduct *The Promise* in concerts in the United States and abroad. In 1991, we performed in Philadelphia and in Chicago at the Moody Bible Institute in a concert that was broadcast live on Christian radio. Soon afterward, we premiered *The Promise* in Northern Ireland and in England.

The concert in Northern Ireland was booked in a town outside Belfast, called Carrickfergus. It was an extraordinary experience for me to ride through the streets of Belfast alongside armored cars with soldiers sitting atop them, guns trained at street level. I asked David, the man whose family Mike and I were staying with, if living with the political unrest was a great source of stress to him. How close did the violence come to his own family and friends? After explaining that his life was not consumed with concerns about the situation, he asked me where I lived. When I told him Los Angeles, he ticked off a list of perils—drive-by shootings, gang slayings, freeway ambushes, child abductions, earthquakes, fires, and race riots—all things that were associated in his mind with my home. He shook his head and said, "I can't imagine living there." This observation gave me pause.

That afternoon, David drove us up to a war memorial on a beautiful green sward that overlooked the inlet of Carrickfergus. As I stood there drinking in the vista of slate gray water and emerald green landscape, I felt as if I had come another full circle, given all the years that I'd loved the music of Ireland. The ruins of a monastery could be seen on the hills on the other side of the inlet. For three hundred years, generations of monks had prayed unceasingly there for the salvation of Ireland. It was the dream of Mike's Irish promoter, Hyndman Milliken—as earthy and as spiritually sensitive a man as I have ever met—to begin that tradition of prayer again. His vision led ultimately to one of Mike's most evocative songs, "The Greening of Belfast," which I can never hear without remembering that day in the hills above Carrickfergus.

That night, we played in a large cultural hall to an audience of both Protestants and Catholics who had gathered to praise God through Mike's music. Many of his songs were well known to the crowd. It was haunting to stand backstage during his solo set, hearing Mike's voice from the speakers and the answering voices of all those Protestants and Catholics within the hall, singing together in glorious unity. When I try to imagine the essentially abstract concept of world peace, I see that concert in my mind's eye and hear those voices ringing in my ears.

Following the concert in Belfast, we flew to England. There we performed in Manchester before taking the train to London, where we recorded the arrangements for five more of Mike's songs for the third album in his Old Testament trilogy, *The Word: Recapturing the Imagination*. Since then, I have conducted for Mike several times, performing *The Promise* live in Dallas, Washington, D.C., Philadelphia, Nashville, and Los Angeles. I recently collaborated with him again on *Unveiled Hope*, an album based on the book of Revelation.

Mike has become a treasured friend, one of the remarkable men I have met along the way, and working with him has been one of the joys of my journey.

My work for Mike eventually led to other opportunities in the Christian music field. In 1992, Phil Naish asked me to compose a "Prologue" for Steven Curtis Chapman's album, *The Great Adventure*. A sincere and engaging young man with a winsome gift as a songwriter and performer, Steven Curtis is one of the most popular artists in contemporary Christian music. Phil described what they were looking for as "the opening theme for a motion picture—without the movie." I composed the music and flew to Nashville to record it. Steven Curtis's face shone with delight when the orchestra began to play, and he spent a good part of the session sitting on the floor in the room with the musicians listening live rather than in the booth through the monitors. *The Great Adventure* eventually earned a Gold Record for sales exceeding five hundred thousand copies, and won a Grammy for Best Pop Gospel Album. LeAnn and I saw him perform not long after the record was released. The concert began with my "Prologue," played at the volume of a jet taking off. It was a thrilling moment.

Phil Naish and I have become good friends in the course of our working together. He is a gifted musician and producer who strives for excellence, yet is pragmatic and supportive under pressure. It's always a pleasure to conduct when he's overseeing things in the booth. We collaborated again last year on Steve Green's Christmas album, *The First Noël,* for which I arranged and orchestrated two medleys of traditional carols and a hymn, "Come, Thou Long Expected Jesus," as well as adding strings to a new song, "Rose of Bethlehem." The high point of this experience for me was conducting the orchestra and "accompanying" Steve as he sight-read the arrangements with precision and heart. He has a strong and clear voice, which is reflective of his character. With Steve, what you see is what you get—a man truly zealous for God.

All of these shared experiences—the prayer and the labor, the laughter and the grief, the worship and the word, the music and the friendship—all are gathered together and grounded in the love of Jesus. He is the context in which they have meaning and cumulative force, defining for LeAnn and for me what it means to dwell in community. In contrast to our bishop's warning, we found that there is "life after Mormonism," abundant, joyful life in the country of grace, without the frowning thunderhead of a bean-counting God lurking over the horizon. I know there are Latter-day Saints all over the world who have lost faith in their church, yet feel resigned, unable to move, because they are afraid that "if Mormonism isn't true, then nothing is." I wish they could know about the grace LeAnn and I have found in Jesus. I, too, was afraid that nothing could ever replace the strong ties that once held me to the faith of my fathers—until I met Him. He is the way, the truth, and the life, and there are no limitations on His love. The cross settled that question forever.

Whatever I left behind in leaving Mormonism has been restored to me a hundredfold in the country of grace. Each of the primary themes of my life has sounded with new and more profound meaning under the Mercy, my counterpoint finding its truest expression as it joins the cantus firmus that is Jesus. I have already spoken of my faith and my music. One theme yet remains to be addressed, the oldest one with the deepest roots: the theme of family. How has the love of Christ varied that melody?

First and foremost, I continue to love and respect my family. In fact, my appreciation for them has grown as I have matured in my faith. I honor my parents and admire the courage of my progenitors. My mother has remained close. LeAnn and I speak regularly with her by telephone, and she goes out of her way to be with us on holidays or for our children's significant events. She knows each of her grandchildren intimately. As a parent, I now recognize how much of herself she has poured into our lives, and I am deeply grateful for her love and the many sacrifices she made in my behalf.

My brother Rick is a good man, a devoted husband, and a loving father to his children. He has also been a loyal friend to me, a staunch supporter quick to celebrate my successes or to speak proudly of me to his friends and colleagues. My father and I also communicate by telephone and get together whenever I'm in Salt Lake City. It's a treat when Rick and I happen to be there at the same time, and the three of us, like battle-scarred musketeers, can share a meal together.

Though I don't see as much of my uncles, aunts, and cousins as I did while growing up, I harbor great affection for each of them and delight in the moments when our paths cross. I am especially grateful to my Aunt Sue and Uncle Gene for caring so tirelessly for my beloved grandmother in her declining years. These family ties are of great value to me, while conversations that touch on religious issues can be painful, we are people who care for one another despite our differences.

While I was young, my relationship to family was that of a child, looking up to my parents and the other adults in my life, and looking back to the legacy of my pioneer forebears. My family showed me how life was to be lived and every voice in this chorus was LDS. Today, Mormonism is far behind me. I am in midlife and a shift in my perspective on family has occurred. Now I have children of my own who look up to me. At this point in my life, when I hear the word "family," I think first of LeAnn, and of Jessica, Jerusha, Jonathan, and Ian. What will be the legacy I leave for them?

There are four significant events that illustrate God's gracious work in our family and point to the inheritance of Christian faith that belongs to my children. The first has to do with the establishment of our family home. By 1986, the year I scored *Extremities* and began studying with Tom Pasatieri, and the year LeAnn and I joined the Fullerton Evangelical Free Church, our growing family and career needed more space. We felt that it was time to move to a larger home. LeAnn and I began looking in January and soon fell in love with a house in the canyon-riven hills northeast of Whittier. It was situated on an acre-and-a-half of land covered with fruit and avocado trees and looked like a cabin, with interiors in warm woods of various hues. There was plenty of room for my office and studio. The price was more than we wanted to pay, but we consulted with our accountant, prayed about it, and waited for the outcome patiently. Then God opened the doors in a rather spectacular way. Our current home sold for our asking price before the sign even went up and a mortgage lender gave us a "jumbo loan" (two words that should never appear together). We were able to buy the house and move in on April 16.

I had been carrying around deep feelings of loss and rootlessness ever since my grandparents had sold their house on the avenues in Salt Lake City, the home where the family had gathered for swimming parties, hamburgers on the porch, and evenings of music. Recovering my own "family home" and making one for my children was a goal of great importance to me. When we moved into the new house, LeAnn and I walked slowly through every room and prayed, dedicating each one to the Lord and asking for His benediction on the life that would unfold within. Not long afterward, we threw a house-warming party at which a violin and harp duo, comprised of two of our friends from recording studios in Los Angeles, christened the house for future musical soirées with a performance that bubbled with joy like the champagne we served. Following the lead of our Joint Heirs friends, LeAnn and I began to invite small groups over for evenings of Bible study, prayer, communion, and worship. I felt that the music and the prayers hovered like angels around the large wooden beams that traversed the ceiling of our living room. Our new home has become a place of blessing to me. My roots have sunk deep and are flourishing there.

As significant as our moving was, there was a second, even bigger event that occurred in 1986. In June of that year, we found out that LeAnn was pregnant with our fourth child. The circumstances of our discovering this were extraordinary. For some time, LeAnn and I had been feeling that our family was complete. We had thought and prayed about this issue quite seriously. Deliberately contemplating not having more children was a big step for us, all the more so because of the residual effects of LDS proscriptions against limiting families. LeAnn and I found that some aspects of Mormonism still had the power to rise up occasionally and affect us viscerally even when we knew better spiritually and intellectually.

At a certain point, we decided to take the necessary steps to insure that we wouldn't have any more children, and LeAnn made an appointment to have a tubal ligation. The night before the surgery, we knelt together to pray. LeAnn modeled her prayer on that of the Virgin Mary, "Behold, the handmaid of the Lord; be it unto me according to thy word." We asked God to make it unmistakably clear if He wanted to contravene our plans.

The following morning, I dropped LeAnn off at the front door of the hospital and went to park the car. Walking down the corridor to meet her again in the admitting room, I was taken aback when she stepped into the hallway first and faced me, looking ashen. "I have good news and bad news," she said.

"What's the bad news?" I inquired innocently.

"I can't have the surgery today," she said, waiting anxiously for my reaction.

"Why not?"

"Because I'm pregnant," she answered. The doctor had called while I was still parking, and had told her that her final blood test had turned up positive. "The good news is that God is sending us another child."

I fell against the wall in shock, then burst into astonished laughter. There was no point in getting upset, especially not after our prayers of the previous night. God had certainly made His will in the matter unmistakably clear and we knew it!

We were both overtaken with a spontaneous joy that only grew as the months progressed, despite the rigors of the pregnancy. LeAnn and I both felt that this was to be a very special child. As the end of the year approached, I was hired to score a TV movie, a western called *Independence.* Budget considerations mandated that it be recorded out of town, and in light of a previous successful experience in Toronto, I booked the studio there again. My contract required that I handle the project as a package deal, which meant that I was given a lump sum, out of which I would be responsible to pay for the recording costs as well as my own fee. The sessions were scheduled just prior to Christmas, in time for me to get back for the holiday with my family.

Ten days before I was to leave, and only seven months into her pregnancy, LeAnn's water broke unexpectedly following a women's Bible study she was attending. She drove herself to the hospital, where she was admitted and was told that she wouldn't be able to leave until the baby was born. This obviously threw an enormous hitch into our plans. What was God doing? Would LeAnn and our providential baby be alright? And what was I going to do? Because of my contract, it would be devastating financially if I didn't show up in Toronto as scheduled.

As soon as LeAnn's condition became known, our Joint Heirs family stepped in, helping with meals and transportation—anything I needed to maintain the children's routines. One young couple volunteered to come and stay with them while I was out of town. With this support system in place, I could leave with a clear conscience, although intuitively, I felt that LeAnn was going to have the baby while I was away. The morning I left, I visited her in the hospital and caught a glimpse, via sonogram, of our child.

Our second son was born December 18. LeAnn's labor and delivery were the hardest she had yet endured. In the early morning hours, she turned to Psalm 22 and God calmed her fears for the baby with these words:

> Yet thou art he who didst bring me forth from the womb; thou didst make me trust when upon my mother's breasts. Upon thee I was cast from birth. Thou hast been my God from my mother's womb. (Psalm 22:9–10, NASB)

It was the first day of recording for the *Independence* score. I learned of the baby's arrival on the orchestra's first break—LeAnn had called the studio manager with the news. When I walked back to the podium, somewhat dazed, to begin the second hour of work, I was welcomed with applause and a cigar.

LeAnn and I named our son Ian James. He weighed four pounds, eight ounces when he came into the world. Because he was eight weeks early, he had to stay in an incubator at the hospital for several days. We took the other children with us and visited him every day and had a little Christmas celebration with him there. We were able to bring him home on the twenty-eighth, a tiny and precious gift from God.

As is true in the life of any family, not all of our experiences were celebratory. Some tried us to the limits of our trust in God. In the summer of 1988, LeAnn experienced some serious health problems, beginning with an onset of numbness in her fingers and hands, later complicated by chronic pain in her lower arms, neck, and back. Despite a battery of tests and physical therapy treatments, doctors were unable to either diagnose her condition or to bring her any relief. Treatments with a chiropractor helped some, and the symptoms eventually subsided, leaving behind a sense of disquiet in our minds. LeAnn had a history of some unusual health problems: sudden weakness, dizziness, numbness in her extremities, and an intermittent sensation of "pins and needles." These symptoms had occurred off and on since Jonathan was little, but never anything as severe as those that summer. Was this incident a manifestation of a deeper chronic condition of some kind? One of the doctors seemed to believe that it was psychosomatic, an inference at which LeAnn and I both bristled. She wasn't crazy—something was going on. We just didn't know what.

When LeAnn experienced another unexplained incident of numbness, dizziness, and double-vision the following February, a good friend recommended that she see a neurologist, who promptly ordered an MRI scan. A few days later, he spoke with me by telephone: "I would like you and LeAnn to come to my office together as soon as possible," he said. At those words, a wave of fear rose in my stomach that remained until our appointment.

As we sat together in the doctor's office, our life was changed dramatically and irreversibly within a few seconds of time. He informed us that LeAnn had multiple sclerosis, a serious and progressive disease of the central nervous system. We knew of a woman from LeAnn's Salt Lake neighborhood who had M.S. She was wheelchair-bound and couldn't perform normal bodily functions without help. Her husband had abandoned her and their eight children. "Oh God," I thought, spitting out my prayer silently through clenched teeth. "Oh God, not that. Please. Not that." I clutched LeAnn's hand with desperate impotence. She grasped mine with the specter of her neighbor's tragic life tearing at her heart.

We listened, stunned and numb, to the doctor's information. The diagnosis had put a name to the strange symptoms LeAnn had experienced for the past nine years. It gave us some relief, at least, to know that she wasn't crazy. The doctor told us her case was probably mild, and that her prognosis was good, for the time being. He recommended that she avoid exposure to colds and flu, stress and heat, and gave her instructions regarding diet and rest. Afterward, LeAnn and I walked out to our Vanagon, took a deep breath, and prayed together for strength to meet this overwhelming and unwanted challenge. We had only a few minutes alone—there were children to be picked up from school, deadlines to be met, and all the usual obligations of what had been our life.

Somehow, through the grace of God, LeAnn and I were able to find a measure of peace in the days that followed. Characteristically, LeAnn bought books and checked out materials from the library to learn all she could about the disease. I tried to keep up with her quest for information, but I had no stamina for the task. Every time I tried to read about it, I felt as if I were shut in a giant plastic sandwich bag, losing oxygen by the second. I did manage to stick with it long enough to learn the basics, however.

M.S. is a neurological disease. Doctors think it is probably caused by a virus, contracted early in life, which lies dormant in the body, mutating and altering the immune system. Years later, certain T-cells begin to attack the central nervous system, damaging the myelin that surrounds and insulates the nerve fibers in the spinal cord and the white matter of the brain. The disease also renders the body unable to repair the damage properly and scars or spots of plaque called "sclerosi" are formed. This causes the nerves to "short out" from time to time, causing pain, numbness, and/or loss of control at various related points in the body. In the most severe cases, M.S. results in complete disability, although there are milder forms of the disease. There is no known cure for M.S. and, at the time of LeAnn's diagnosis, there were only a few effective medications to treat the worst symptoms.

As we came to grips with her M.S., LeAnn and I didn't feel bitter or abandoned by God—not that we didn't experience these emotions, but we didn't let them define the terms of our response to the disease. We still had much for which to be grateful. LeAnn didn't appear to have a chronic-progressive case of the disease. In all probability, she would not end up in a wheelchair, although apart from God's miraculous intervention, she would have to endure an ongoing cycle of exacerbations and remissions for the rest of her life. There was some permanent damage to her nerves, and she would have to learn to cope with daily symptoms, particularly with overwhelming fatigue. LeAnn actually found reason to praise God for the answer to what had been lurking behind her peculiar health problems. Trusting Him took on a whole new dimension for us.

The situation soon degenerated further, however. The first serious episode after LeAnn's diagnosis began with severe pain in her left optic nerve. Over three days, she became so weak and dizzy that she couldn't walk or keep her food down. The doctor put her in the hospital and began a course of massive intravenous steroid therapy. This treatment halted the downward spiral of disability, but also brought on some unpleasant side effects, such as sleeplessness, exhaustion, and weight gain.

For the next few years, LeAnn's health was fragile. She coped as best she could with the demands of family life and her outlook was basically positive, but we never knew when she might get sick again. We prayed constantly for healing and tried to be at peace with whatever happened.

Then, in the spring of 1993, LeAnn experienced another attack of M.S. that lasted for several weeks, forcing her to undergo another hospitalization and regimen of steroid treatments. With this new exacerbation of the disease, the cumulative stress and fear that grew from her condition finally started getting to me. I was afraid she was going downhill, entering the chronic-progressive stage of the disease that would ultimately leave her completely disabled like her childhood neighbor. I didn't think I could bear it if that happened. I began to doubt God—not so much His power to heal her, but His goodness if He chose not to. These tensions made it hard for me to work and raised troubling issues in our marriage, bringing on what is commonly called a midlife crisis. My symptoms had been building for some time. I had probably entered the rapids of midlife the day LeAnn was diagnosed with multiple sclerosis, although I wasn't conscious of it at the time.

In popular terms, a "midlife crisis" refers to a season of life in which men and women typically have affairs, desert their families, and blow off their jobs, more or less destroying whatever they have worked to build throughout the first half of their lives in an attempt to find some fresh new thing to revitalize the second half. These are often acts of desperation, misguided attempts to shore up crumbling coping mechanisms, or to create the secular equivalent of a spiritual renewal. By the grace of God, none of this tragic behavior happened in my case. Still, the course of my midlife journey took me awfully close to the edge of the abyss, and forced me to travel an arduous path, marked by hard lessons and painful emotions.

Even in the midst of my midlife crisis, much was still right with my life, and I knew it. Knowing that didn't keep me from feeling distress and grief, however, as the emotions swept over me like a dark and turbulent storm. Sometimes I felt trapped in my life, as if there weren't air enough for me to breathe. There were also days when I was overtaken by a sense of resignation and mourned the loss of my dreams. It was strange that I should feel this way, with so many of my objectives well on the way to being achieved. Despite this fact, I felt "let down" and seriously began to wonder if my success was all that it was cracked up to be. My heart dreaded the fate of the man in Stephen Crane's cynical poem:

> A man saw a ball of gold in the sky;
> He climbed for it,
> And eventually he achieved it -
> It was clay.

> Now this is the strange part:
> When the man went to the earth
> And looked again,
> Lo, there was the ball of gold.
> Now this is the strange part:
> It was a ball of gold.
> Ay, by the heavens, it was a ball of gold.[3]

This was a different sort of depression than I had experienced as a Mormon. For one thing, I was able to be open and honest about it, both with myself and with my Christian friends. They were completely supportive, put up with my bouts of melancholy, and didn't desert me when I descended into narcissistic fits of self-analysis, pulling the scabs off every tiny wound. Nor did God desert me, even when I sometimes railed at Him, like the psalmist, in my prayers. During this time, I had no question about my relationship with God. He had wiped out any lingering existential despair when I committed my life to Him, and I never again experienced that awful sense of the ground opening up beneath me or the hellish feeling of hollowness that had plagued my pre-Christian years. God had swallowed all of that up in the miracle of His grace. While there were times when I struggled with the playback of old tapes, berating myself with well-rehearsed accusations, the heart had gone out of it. I knew the old tapes simply weren't true and I couldn't believe them anymore.

As LeAnn and I fought for stability in the wake of her most recent M.S. attack, our relationship suffered. By turns, we grew distant or spoke injuriously to one another. There were few respites for relaxed time or intimate talks together. Our prayer life degenerated into routine recitation. At the peak of this difficult time, I was faced with a terrible temptation that arose one afternoon early in June 1993 over lunch with a woman I had met in the course of my work. Both she and I were simultaneously struck with a powerful feeling of kinship and attraction. Neither of us said anything about it at the time, but a couple of days later, during a follow-up phone conversation, she broached the subject: "Did you feel anything unusual at lunch the other day?" she asked. I had to admit that I had. It was as simple as that. A door suddenly swung open, and sin was crouching there, a beast with my own face, waiting for my permission to devour everything that meant anything to me.

I wish I could say that I didn't pursue the relationship, that I put a stop to it then and there, but I didn't. We talked on the phone almost daily for two weeks. She was also married and we both were aware of the stakes of our deepening bond, but it was so hard to give up the promise of that unexpected "revelation." I should have known better—I should have been well past the days of being deceived by this sort of impression; nevertheless, I was still susceptible.

Despite this weakness, however, I was a genuinely different person than I had been before I gave my life to Christ. Under the Mercy, my relationships with God, LeAnn, my children, and my friends ultimately proved dearer to me than the temptation. His kindness led me to repentance and brought me to my senses before it was too late.

The first step I took was to decide that I had to define and set some strict boundaries, and I met with the woman a second time in order to do so. At that stage, I still hoped that we could remain friends and colleagues. As it turned out, it was the last time I ever saw her. LeAnn had intuitively become suspicious of our growing relationship. When she finally demanded to know if there was something going on, I told her the truth. My confession hit her extremely hard. It reawakened the memory of old terrors and LeAnn was both badly wounded and volcanic with anger. She forbade me to have any further contact with the woman or else I would face divorce.

When I saw how terribly I had hurt LeAnn, I felt devastated and foolish. I was also defensive and angry, resenting the restriction and her threat. I believed, however mistakenly, that I had this friendship under control. LeAnn and I fought horribly for two days. My former unfaithfulness was a continuous goad and I wondered in my darkest moments if, in spite of the grace of God, some deep-seated flaw in my character made this a scene that we would be condemned to play again and again throughout our life together.

As the crisis reached a critical mass, we sought counseling together. Despite our mistakes, in the deepest places of our hearts, LeAnn and I both wanted our marriage to flourish. We didn't want to turn our children into orphans of divorce. We wanted to grow old and enjoy our grandchildren together, but we had a lot of hard work ahead of us. Fortunately, LeAnn had already been working with a fine family therapist who attended our church and we committed together to work with him.

Late in June, on his recommendation, we attended a codependency recovery clinic called The Meadows in Wickenburg, Arizona. This was an extremely valuable experience for us. I learned how influences from my early years made me particularly vulnerable to feelings like the one that precipitated the present crisis in our marriage: the loss of my father when my parents divorced; the exaggerated sense of empowerment I received from my mother and grandmother, reinforced by the Mormon doctrine that men might become gods; and the family history of polygamy. LeAnn also learned about issues in her own life that caused her to react with such terror.

God used this week in Arizona to help restore our marriage in a powerful way. What began as the most horrible month we had experienced in years ended in healing. When our time at The Meadows was over, LeAnn and I celebrated with a fabulous dinner at a restaurant in Phoenix. Our relaxed and loving conversation was even better than the food. The following month, LeAnn came up with a brilliant gift for my fortieth birthday: a full-size swing set, reminiscent of the one she and I had enjoyed so many times at the school in the foothills above her childhood home, the place where we had shared our dreams as teenagers. Now we could swing high together and watch the sunset over the trees in our own backyard. In September, we commemorated our nineteenth anniversary, rejoicing that we had survived another major test of our commitment to one another.

Though great strides were made toward the restoration of our relationship at The Meadows and in the weeks that followed, the healing process would still take time. For the next several months, LeAnn and I continued working with our therapist to clear away debris left in the wake of our brush with disaster, and to sort through the issues that had brought it about. Self deception dwells at the root of every sin and no one is undeceived in an instant. So we applied ourselves to the task of renewing our love, and, when we were at last able to step back and regard the road we had traveled, we realized we were wiser and our marriage stronger than before.

I am abashed when I consider how close I came to making a ruinous mistake, and so grateful that God preserved our marriage. LeAnn is the great love of my life. She is my best friend, my sister in spirit, my "partner in crime," my gentle-fierce lover, and the good mother of my children. She is smart and beautiful; warm, witty, and deep; soulful and sensitive; competent and honest to a fault. She has been loyal and faithful to me in my darkest hours, even when I, in my weakness, have idolized or betrayed her. She is my dearest companion, the one with whom I most enjoy spending time, sharing the jokes, the sidelong glances, and the arcane allusions that only we can understand. We are bound together by a thousand tiny threads. I love her profoundly and passionately, with all of my heart, and I honor her unswerving devotion to our life. I can say, without being falsely modest, that I do not deserve her, yet this too is the grace of God. And in Him, we have found a deep current of joy together.

Not only did God renew our marriage, but He also demonstrated His faithfulness by saving me from professional burn-out. During this period, I had seriously considered leaving the film composing business, downscaling, moving away from Los Angeles and pursuing a new career. I had considered a couple of real options, but in each case God made His will clear: "No," He said. "Stay at your post. Do the work I have given you until I tell you otherwise."

In retrospect, 1993 was an incredibly important year. Although the enemy of my soul tried to undermine both my marriage and my work, God was faithful to preserve both. I think I understand now part of the reason for the enemy's attack and God's overpowering grace in 1993: it was the year I composed *Water Walker, The Ancient of Days,* and *Welcome All Wonders.*

God was also faithful in answering our prayers concerning LeAnn's disease. In the autumn of 1993, LeAnn and I were excited to hear that the FDA had approved a new drug therapy for M.S. called Betaseron. It was a genetically engineered form of interferon that might help manage the present symptoms of the disease and prevent further decline, although it could not reverse already existing effects. Distribution of Betaseron would be handled by lottery in order to avoid discrimination. It was very expensive, but we learned that our insurance would cover most of the cost.

LeAnn entered the lottery and we anticipated her turn with hopeful hearts. The following April, she began the treatments, which required a subcutaneous injection every other night. After experiencing several weeks of flu-like symptoms while her body acclimated itself to the drug, she woke one morning, filled with enthusiasm for some project she wanted to accomplish that day. I hadn't seen her that energized for years. She was more like her old self again. It turned out that LeAnn was one of the fortunate fifteen percent with whose body chemistry Betaseron worked beautifully. Her increased sense of energy became the norm and the drug forestalled the onset of further exacerbations.

LeAnn's improved health meant we could host more special gatherings at our home. In 1994, two couples were married in our living room and wedding vows were added to the songs and prayers lingering around our ceiling. LeAnn and I celebrated our twentieth anniversary in September, praising God for amazing grace and joy in the journey. He had been there through it all, helping me negotiate my midlife rapids and take up the obligations of work and family again with a renewed freshness and sense of purpose.

I believe that God has a purpose for midlife. It keeps us from getting stale, from relying on habit and routine in our work and our relationships. It compels us to reassess our choices and our motives and to deal with long-buried issues and presents an opportunity to lay down tired old assumptions and take up imaginative new solutions. A midlife crisis doesn't have to be destructive. For those attached to a nurturing community, accountable to friends and family, and connected to God by the umbilical of faith, it can be a season of authentic personal renewal.

These four events—the establishment of our family home, the circumstances of Ian's birth, the diagnosis of LeAnn's multiple sclerosis, and my midlife crisis—were major turning points for my family in the late eighties and early nineties. Each one became an occasion for God to demonstrate His faithfulness. The primary lesson that I hope my children will learn from these episodes is that God can be trusted, even when things look most bleak, even when we are weak or foolish or follow after sin in a nose dive for some shiny object. His grace is truly sufficient, but He acts in His own time and usually in ways that we can't predict.

My children are mostly grown up now. At this writing, both girls are getting ready to graduate from college—Jessica from USC in philosophy, and Jerusha from Rice with a double major in German and history. Jonathan will also graduate this spring from Sunny Hills High School. He's interested in pursuing a career in theater and film. Ian is thriving as LeAnn schools him at home. I love my children with all my heart. I am proud of each one and deeply grateful for the good choices they have made in building constructive lives.

Each of our children have made professions of faith, the older three at church and Ian while riding in the car with me two days after his seventh birthday. His prayer to receive Jesus as his Savior and Lord was heartbreakingly earnest and direct, and it was a privilege to share this hallowed moment with him. So far, our three eldest have also followed Christ in baptism. Jessica chose to be baptized in the pool in our backyard, along with other members of her youth group, just a few months after our own baptism. Later, Rusha was baptized in the surf at Corona del Mar by her youth group leader. Jonathan was also baptized at Corona del Mar. We had finished reading *The Lord of the Rings* aloud to Ian that evening, just before meeting Jonathan and his youth group on the beach. I cherish the memory of that night: the deep orange sun sinking low over the ocean, Tolkien's true and beautiful words sounding in our ears, Jonathan's clear-eyed testimony, and the echoing voice of the sea as he went under the waves. God has been good to us.

At our church, our children have been able to participate in many fine youth activities that have undergirded their faith. They sang in choirs and performed in musicals, played handbells and worshiped with their peers, learned from the Bible and enjoyed camp at Forest Home. One of the activities we found particularly gratifying was the opportunity for them to join others of their age group in short-term missions in villages across the border in Mexico. While there, they played with the children and taught them the basics of Christian faith. It was an eye-opening experience, to be with those who lack so many of the material things we enjoy. Yet our children could recognize their shared humanity and the universal need for redemption.

Over the years, I have learned to be a father under the Mercy, to offer grace to my children as I have received it from my Father in heaven. Fatherhood has not been easy, and I have made more than my share of mistakes along the way, but I have improved steadily. It has been wonderful to move from "enforcer" to "confidant" as my dear ones have matured. Still, it's hard to leave the earlier stages of our relationship behind. Whenever I began to feel that I had them all figured out, I would discover that they had already moved on. I fell in love with my children at each stage of their lives and mourned the loss of the person they had been as they turned into someone new. I hope in heaven, when there is no more linear time, that I will have all of each one of them back again to love once more. At this stage, they are, for the most part, past the point of childhood instruction. What I had to teach cognitively, I've already told them a hundred times over. I hope that the "incarnational" truth of our faith, as LeAnn and I live it out from day to day under the Mercy, will continue to speak to them, perhaps even louder than before.

A father's legacy is not solely transferred through his words or at the turning points of life. In fact, the ongoing, day-to-day character of his relationships may be even more important in the long run. There are so many things LeAnn and I share with our children that define the quality of our life together. We love reading aloud, cheering for the Los Angeles Lakers, and taking vacations together. Music is a strong point of connection. Each of the children has taken the requisite piano lessons, of course, and they continue to sing and play other instruments, but it goes deeper than that. We love to worship through music together and even enjoy some of the same popular music. One of the best parts of a long drive or the clean-up after a Thanksgiving or Christmas dinner is singing along with the Beatles, Simon and Garfunkel, or James Taylor.

Musical theater is likewise a shared passion and we have enjoyed family excursions to Frank Loesser's *The Most Happy Fella,* Stephen Sondheim's *Into the Woods,* and Rodgers and Hammerstein's *Carousel.* We have also watched each of our children create their own roles: Jessica starring in high school productions of *Cabaret* and *Once Upon a Mattress;* Jerusha choreographing and performing in *West Side Story* and *Little Shop of Horrors* at Rice; Jonathan bringing down the house as Nicely Nicely Johnson in *Guys and Dolls,* Will

Parker in *Oklahoma,* or Tony in *West Side Story;* even Ian, making an auspicious debut with his home schooling co-op in a performance of my own musical, *Don't Count Your Chickens Until They Cry Wolf.*

From the first trip to London while I was working on *Cry from the Mountain* and *The Key to Rebecca,* family vacations have become focal points in communicating our legacy to the children. Because our love for art and music is a central part of that legacy, LeAnn and I have wanted to share our experiences in Europe with them. In 1992, we were able to spend a month there with our daughters. The boys stayed home with friends from the church, while we traipsed across four countries, taking in all the culture we possibly could. It was a wonderful bonding time for the four of us. Each day seemed to hold new treasures.

In Paris, LeAnn and I felt a deep sense of fulfillment as we watched our daughters' eyes flame with their first glimpse of the Louvre's noble *Winged Victory,* Notre Dame, Van Gogh's paintings at the Musée d'Orsay, and Monet's enormous water lily canvasses at the Orangerie. My heart seemed too small to hold the pleasure I took in Jessica's awed response to the elegant alchemy of counter-tenor, recorder, and portative organ that transformed the air on the night of a concert of medieval music in the Saint-Chapelle, the chapel's brilliantly hued stained glass windows darkening slowly as the sun set. But there were light-hearted moments as well, like the rollicking ferry ride we took on the Seine late one night in the pouring rain.

We linked up with a short-term mission team from our church in Seville, Spain—the girls and I were slated to sing for a church planting conference there. LeAnn was taken ill, however, and had to spend most of the week in bed. We felt discouraged and out of sync, but there was a lesson even in this. While joy in sharing our faith is part of the legacy LeAnn and I hope to pass on to our children, they also need to know that it is hard, and that there will be opposition, both materially and spiritually, to any opportunity we may have to do it. Perhaps even worse, some experiences may simply seem flat and uninspiring, leaving us to trust that God will somehow weave a blessing from our efforts anyway.

The time we spent in Italy was the highlight of our trip. In Milano, I took Jessie and Rusha on a nostalgic tour of my former missionary haunts. Their reaction was short on the pity I had hoped to elicit with their exposure to my old digs. All was forgiven, however, in Florence.

It was profoundly satisfying for LeAnn and me to introduce the girls to the God-soaked art and architecture we loved there: the majestic Duomo and Campanile, the Baptistry with its beautiful doors, the Uffizi and the Accademia, Fra Angelico in the cells of San Marco, and Michelangelo at San Lorenzo. So much of what we value in Western civilization finds expression in Florence. The very air hums with the glory of it. We hated to leave, but moved on to Rome to witness the profound sadness of the Coliseum, the splendors of St. Peter's and the Sistine Chapel, and the art of Bernini and Caravaggio at the Borghese.

We rode a train through the Dolomites of northern Italy to conclude our vacation in Munich. While there, we took a day trip to the Zugspitze, the highest mountain in Germany. We went to the top via a funicular that seemed to defy the laws of physics as it soared nearly vertically with little visible means of support. The view of the opaque blue waters of the Eidersee below and the surrounding postcard-perfect villages was spectacular. The girls and I climbed the perilous path to the cross planted at the summit, where Rusha lost an earring and wisely chose not to go after it.

One of the most moving experiences of the trip was an afternoon spent at the Dachau concentration camp, where we were forcibly reminded of the dark side of our humanity, an important balance after so many days of witnessing the highest and best of what human beings may achieve. A haunting wake of the grotesque evil that was perpetrated there nearly crushes the soul. It is hard to avoid the reality of sin nature at Dachau.

While in Rome, we received word that my stepfather Jack had been taken seriously ill while on vacation with my mother in British Columbia. When we arrived at the Frankfurt airport for our return flight home, we had an emergency message to call the family and were told that he had died in a hospital there. We were filled with grief—Jack had loved us as if we were his own children, and we would miss him terribly. Telling the boys when we returned home was especially hard and we all shed many tears.

In the intervening years, the long-term impact of this European trip has been manifest in both my daughters' lives. They feel at home in the wider world and confident of their abilities to make their way in it. In 1995, Jessica studied abroad in Florence for six months, living with an Italian family and traveling all over Europe on the weekends and afterward. Rusha joined her there on her spring break and the two of them enjoyed Florence once again. Happy is the man whose children dwell together in unity! Last summer Jessie worked in Israel on an archaeological dig at Megiddo. I hope to take Jonathan to Europe on a father–son backpacking trip before his college commitments make it impossible.

I thank God for the love of my family and for the resources to develop these connections between us. I never want to take these things for granted or forget that most of the people in the world don't have such privileges. I don't really understand why we have them. I believe that they are not ours to be hoarded, but to be enjoyed as gifts of grace and passed on without reservation in the form of blessings to others.

For the future, I look forward to knowing my children as adults. They are fine people and excellent company—I cherish the time I have to spend with them here on earth. I trust by the grace of God that someday I will see them in heaven where there are no more heartaches and no more goodbyes. I want to bless my grandchildren with the kind of love that my grandparents showed me. I want my children to have a vibrant, dynamic relationship with Jesus that provides both an immovable rock on which to build their lives and the freedom in His grace to soar, to risk, and even to fail. I hope their souls are quick to be moved by God's handiwork, manifest in the wild majesty of nature or disguised in the face of a stranger. My wish for them is that the deep places in their hearts will ever delight in His praise. I pray that they won't have to suffer for these things, but I know that such gifts are only treasured with tears.

There are also darker truths I want my children to know about what it means to be fully human. I want them to know about the anger that reaches down like roots and wraps itself around the heart until the heart cannot beat without it; about how anger must be schooled if one is to survive in this fallen world, as wise as a serpent; about the fierce thirst to reverse the flow of rivers of injustice or cruelty; and about the grief lying still and cold as a subterranean sea, filled with the salt tears of all the wars, all the struggles to cling to life in the harsh lands, all the injuries and the daily death of dreams. How do I tell them about these things? They are lessons that cannot be heard with the ears. They must be absorbed through the skin.

They seep into the bloodstream like nourishment—or toxins—and lodge in the viscera.

In my forty-three years of life on this sad, splendid planet, I've learned that people must come to know the truth by themselves, not because the truth is fluid, but because we are. The truth will not compel anyone to believe, even when it stares them in the face. Embracing it must be a choice, an act of the will. I want my children to love the truth and to pursue it, even when it hurts or makes them afraid. I want them to have a healthy skepticism, to "prove all things" and "hold fast that which is good" (1 Thessalonians 5:21), but in so doing, I hope that they don't banish the ineffable and the miraculous from their lives. Only God knows where their journeys will take them, and LeAnn and I trust Him alone for that. We have no agenda for their church affiliations or career objectives, indeed no stake in any human institution. Christ is the center of our life now. He is the way, the truth, and the life for us. I pray that He will be for them as well.

God has been good to me, far beyond my power to ask or even imagine. The worst part of me still waits for the other shoe to drop, still fears that God's goodness is so far removed from my notion of goodness that it sometimes appears to be cruel or arbitrary. This world seems so utterly lost sometimes, it makes me wonder if He is truly in charge. But the best part of me trusts that He is and looks to Him with shining eyes, just as my own son's eyes shine sometimes when he looks to me, and believes that there is protection and hope in his father's arms.

Coda: The Road Goes Ever On

The Road goes ever on and on
Down from the door where it began.
Now far ahead the Road has gone,
And I must follow, if I can,
Pursuing it with eager feet,
Until it joins some larger way
Where many paths and errands meet.
And whither then? I cannot say.

—J.R.R. Tolkien, *The Fellowship of the Ring*[1]

Sometimes the sky is constructed with a careless architecture: cloud castles heave effortless as the tide, birds carve their reckless geometry across the heavens. God creates with a terrifying ease. At such moments we are offered a glimpse of the world beyond this world, a world of fleshier flesh and richer blood, a resurrection world to which Christ's improbable rise points like a sextant—the North Star of the north star. Each glimpse is a moment of sheer grace. And the proper response is to fall on our knees.

LeAnn and I had such a glimpse in 1996 on a trip to Israel and Jordan with a tour group led by Howie and Marilyn Stevenson. It was our first time in the Holy Land, and it was an extraordinary pilgrimage for us. Places that were only dots on a map sprang to vivid life. There were so many poignant moments: sunrise over the Sea of Galilee, the ruins of cities the Romans thought would last forever, the Jezreel Valley spread out like a quilt, a lingering sadness over Masada, the lush greenery of the Golan Heights, and an opportunity to share the story of our decision for Christ at Caesarea Phillipi, near the headwaters of the Jordan where Jesus had asked his disciples, "Who do men say that I am?" Everywhere we saw reminders of the reality of biblical history. It really happened in someone's neighborhood, in someone's hometown. We couldn't help but contrast this with the unanchored fantasy of the *Book of Mormon*.

The most transcendent of our experiences, however, occurred in Jerusalem, the last place we visited on the tour. Our first view of the city was breathtaking. The bus crested the Mount of Olives and there it was before us, gleaming white in the setting sun like a vision. Our guide chose that moment to bid us a heartfelt "welcome home." We arrived at the hotel about 5:30 P.M. on a Friday afternoon. Some of us had hoped to be at the Western Wall when the Sabbath began at 6:00, but it was late and we were all tired from the day's journey. There would scarcely be time to stow our bags. LeAnn and I looked at one another and wondered, "Should we still try to go?" Of course, we had to go in the end. How many times would we be in Jerusalem for Shabat?

We took a cab to the Old City and passed on foot through the security checkpoints to enter the square that fans out from the Western Wall, the oldest remaining portion of Herod's temple. Orthodox Jews were already there, bowing and praying in front of the huge white stones. LeAnn and I stood still for a while, transfixed. The imminence of sacred history was palpable, electric in the air. The hair stood up on our necks. The reality of a God made flesh seemed inevitable here.

Suddenly we heard the sound of singing, coming from behind us. We looked up and saw a group of perhaps 120 young men, marching, six abreast arm in arm, down the steps from the Jewish Quarter. They were singing with a fierce joy and as they drew nearer, their march seemed like a dance. They danced and sang their way through the square and down a ramp leading to a large space before the Wall where they began to pray. The sound washed over us like waves. The voices of several cantors rose above the sea of prayers, soaring and intertwining with cacophonous abandon.

There were swallows overhead, wheeling in ovals and diving headlong into niches between the stones of the temple wall where their nests were crammed. The swallows were singing too, their voices like flutes above the cantors, whose voices were trumpets above the violas and 'celli of the prayers. It was a symphony, brave and clean and strong. The stones themselves may well have been crying out. And I knew myself to be in the presence of a God who is so much greater and older and stronger than my categories, whose love runs deeper and longer than my imagination can ever embrace.

And so the journey continues; the road goes ever on. How should I bring an end to a story that doesn't yet have an ending? Perhaps it is best to close with a sense of expectation. There are still many paths that lie before me and I know that some of them won't be easy. I didn't lose all doubt when I became a Christian, nor did I become inured to suffering or immune to sin. With my life in the hands of the Water Walker, I know the journey will not always be calm, but He has promised that I will reach my destination, and that it will be good, better than I could ever hope for.

> Still round the corner there may wait
> A new road or a secret gate;
> And though I oft have passed them by,
> A day will come at last when I
> Shall take the hidden paths that run
> West of the Moon, East of the Sun.[2]

Soli Deo Gloria

Credits and Discography

Credits

CONCERT WORKS

HE IS RISEN INDEED! (1997)
  An Easter anthem for choir and orchestra
SHEPHERD STORY (1995)
  A Christmas narrative based on Luke 2 for chorus and orchestra
IN DULCI JUBILO (1994)
  A suite of five Christmas carols for brass quintet
WELCOME ALL WONDERS: A CHRISTMAS CELEBRATION (1993)
  A Christmas cantata for chorus and orchestra
THE ANCIENT OF DAYS (1993)
  A dramatic music narrative based on Daniel 7 for brass quintet, organ,
  percussion, and a speaker
WATER WALKER (1993)
  A trio for flute, viola, and harp
ST. ELSEWHERE (1990)
  A suite from scores for the 1982–88 television series
A PASCHAL FEAST (1988)
  An Easter choral symphony
THE KEY TO REBECCA (1988)
  A suite from the score for the 1985 television mini-series
THE GROWING SEASON (1987)
  A string quartet (also arranged for string ensemble)
SHOUT FOR JOY TO THE LORD (1987)
  A psalm setting for high voice with piano accompaniment
DIMINUTIAE (1986)
  An unaccompanied duo for violins
CHRIST IS ALIVE! (1986)
  An Easter anthem for choir and orchestra
INSIDE PASSAGE (1984)
  A single-movement work for solo trombone, trombone choir, and percussion
CLEMENTINA'S CACTUS (1983)
  A ballet for children based on the book by Ezra Jack Keats
FIVE SONGS FOR FLUTE AND FRENCH HORN (1982)
  An unaccompanied duo

DREAM DANCES (1982)
A duo for violin and harp
OCTOBER OVERTURES (1980)
A divertimento for orchestra
VALSE TRISTE (1980)
An unaccompanied duo for 'celli
FIVE SONNETS (1976)
A song cycle to poems by e e cummings for soprano with piano accompaniment

FEATURE FILMS

D3: THE MIGHTY DUCKS (1996)	Walt Disney Pictures
A KID IN KING ARTHUR'S COURT (1995)	Walt Disney Pictures
BYE BYE LOVE (1995)	20th Century Fox
HEAVYWEIGHTS (1995)	Walt Disney Pictures
D2: THE MIGHTY DUCKS (1994)	Walt Disney Pictures
NEWSIES (1992)	Walt Disney Pictures
OLIVER AND COMPANY (1988)	Walt Disney Pictures
EXTREMITIES (1986)	Atlantic
THE TRIP TO BOUNTIFUL (1985)	Island Pictures
CRY FROM THE MOUNTAIN (1985)	World Wide Pictures
STINGRAY (1978)	AVCO Embassy

MOVIES FOR TELEVISION

TWO VOICES (1997)	Lifetime
FOR THE CHILDREN: THE IRVINE FERTILITY SCANDAL (1996)	Lifetime
NAOMI AND WYNONNA: LOVE CAN BUILD A BRIDGE (1995)	NBC
IS THERE LIFE OUT THERE? (1994)	CBS
ONE MORE MOUNTAIN (1994)	ABC
AND THEN THERE WAS ONE (1993)	Lifetime
FOR THEIR OWN GOOD (1992)	ABC
KISS OF A KILLER (1992)	ABC
LOCKED UP: A MOTHER'S RAGE (1991)	CBS
STOP AT NOTHING (1990)	Lifetime
CONAGHER (1990)	TNT
WEB OF DECEIT (1990)	USA
A SON'S PROMISE (1990)	ABC
BREAKING POINT (1989)	TNT
SAVE THE DOG (1988)	Disney
THE LONG JOURNEY HOME (1987)	CBS
DANGEROUS AFFECTION (1987)	NBC
INDEPENDENCE (1987)	NBC
EASY PREY (1986)	ABC
ALEX: THE LIFE OF A CHILD (1986)	ABC
THE KEY TO REBECCA (4 hour Mini-series)(1985)	OPT
GOING FOR THE GOLD: THE BILL JOHNSON STORY (1985)	CBS

HELEN KELLER: THE MIRACLE CONTINUES (1983)	OPT
HAPPY ENDINGS (1983)	NBC
HONEY BOY (1982)	NBC
THE LONG SUMMER OF GEORGE ADAMS (1981)	NBC

EPISODIC TELEVISION

COACH (1988-97)	ABC
ADVENTURES FROM THE BOOK OF VIRTUES (1996-97)	PBS
7TH HEAVEN (1996)	WB
MURDER SHE WROTE (1994)	CBS
THE ROAD HOME (1994)	CBS
DELTA (1992-93)	ABC
CAPITOL CRITTERS (1992)	ABC
HOMEFIRES (1992)	NBC
PRINCESSES (1991)	CBS
COCONUT DOWNS (1991)	ABC
THE ASTRONOMERS (1991)	PBS
DAD'S A DOG (1990)	ABC
CAPITAL NEWS (1989-90)	ABC
CAMP CALIFORNIA (1989)	ABC
FAMILY TIES (1989)	NBC
ANNIE McGUIRE (1988-89)	CBS
COMING OF AGE (1988-89)	CBS
ST. ELSEWHERE (1982-88)	NBC
Emmy Nominations 1984 and 1985	
THE TWILIGHT ZONE (1986)	CBS
THE CITY (1986)	ABC
BEST TIMES (1984)	NBC
COVER UP (1984)	CBS
HAWAIIAN HEAT (1984)	ABC
AUTOMAN (1984)	ABC
WHIZ KIDS (1984)	CBS
TRAUMA CENTER (1983)	ABC
CUTTER TO HOUSTON (1983)	CBS
VOYAGERS (1983)	NBC
BLISS (1983)(Pilot)	NBC
TUCKER'S WITCH (1982)	CBS
KNOT'S LANDING (1982)	CBS
KING'S CROSSING (1982)	ABC
BRET MAVERICK (1981-82)	NBC
FAME (1981)	NBC
AMERICAN DREAM (1981)	ABC
240-ROBERT (1979)	ABC
THE DOOLEY BROTHERS (1979)	CBS
YOUNG GUY CHRISTIAN (1978)	ABC
JAMES AT 16 (1978)	NBC
JAMES AT 15 (1977)	NBC
STARSKY AND HUTCH (1977, 1979)	ABC

THEATRE

THE SEAGULL (1994) Anton Chekhov	Matrix Theater (Los Angeles, CA)
DIARIES OF ADAM AND EVE (1988) Mark Twain, adapted by David Birney	Plaza Theater (Dallas, TX)
BURIED CHILD (1986) Sam Shepard	South Coast Repertory Theater (Costa Mesa, CA)
THE COMMON PURSUIT (1986) Simon Gray	Matrix Theater (Los Angeles, CA)
ORPHANS (World Premiere)(1983) Lyle Kessler	Matrix Theater (Los Angeles, CA)
EMINENT DOMAIN (1983) Percy Granger	Matrix Theater (Los Angeles, CA)
BETRAYAL (1982) Harold Pinter	Matrix Theater (Los Angeles, CA)
A MIDSUMMER NIGHT'S DREAM (1981)	Oxnard Civic Auditorium (Oxnard, CA)
MACBETH (1981) Sherwood Shakespeare Festival	

MUSICAL THEATRE

I BELIEVE IN MAKE BELIEVE (1977) Carol Lynn Pearson	Sundance Summer Theatre (Provo Canyon, UT)
DON'T COUNT YOUR CHICKENS UNTIL THEY CRY WOLF (1976) Carol Lynn Pearson	Sundance Summer Theatre (Provo Canyon, UT)

OTHER COMPOSITIONS

PRELUDE (1997)
From the album *Unveiled Hope* by Michael Card
Music by Scott Brasher and J.A.C. Redford

REPRISE (1997)
From the album *Unveiled Hope* by Michael Card
Music by Michael Card and J.A.C. Redford

THE CONSCIENCE OF THE KING (1995)
From the album *A Kid in King Arthur's Court*
Music by J.A.C. Redford

PRELUDE: THE ANCIENT FAITH (1993)
From the album *The Ancient Faith* by Michael Card
Music by Michael Card and J.A.C. Redford

PROLOGUE: THE GREAT ADVENTURE (1992)
From the album *The Great Adventure* by Steven Curtis Chapman
Music by J.A.C. Redford

LOVE AND DESIRE (1989)
From *Love and Desire*, an album of love poems read by David Birney, Jane Lapotaire,
   Lee Remick, Robert Stephens, and Michael York
Incidental music by J.A.C. Redford

STAND UP TO THE NIGHT (1986)
From the motion picture *Extremities* and the Bonnie Raitt album *Nine Lives*
Lyrics by Will Jennings
Music by J.A.C. Redford and Richard Kerr

CONDUCTING

A PYROMANIAC'S LOVE STORY (1995)	Hollywood Pictures
Rachel Portman, Composer	
BLACK BEAUTY (1994)	Warner Bros.
Danny Elfman, Composer	
THE NIGHTMARE BEFORE CHRISTMAS (1993)	Touchstone Pictures
Danny Elfman, Composer	
THE JOY LUCK CLUB (1993)	Hollywood Pictures
Rachel Portman, Composer	
HEART AND SOULS (1993)	Universal
Marc Shaiman, Composer	
BENNY AND JOON (1993)	MGM
Rachel Portman, Composer	
BILLY BATHGATE (1991)	Touchstone Pictures
Mark Isham, Composer	
THE LITTLE MERMAID (1989)	Walt Disney Pictures
Songs by Howard Ashman and Alan Menken	
Music by Alan Menken	

DISCOGRAPHY

CONCERT WORKS

WELCOME ALL WONDERS (1995)   Bonneville Classics BCD 9501-2
   Utah Chamber Artists
    "Welcome All Wonders" and "Shepherd Story" composed and co-produced by
    J.A.C. Redford.

CHRISTMAS (1994)   Philadelphia Brass
   Philadelphia Brass
    A suite of Christmas carols "In Dulci Jubilo" arranged by J.A.C. Redford.

IS THIS THE WAY TO CARNEGIE HALL? (1988)   Crystal S350
   Calvin Smith, Horn and John Barcellona, Flute
    "Five Songs for Flute and French Horn" composed by J.A.C. Redford.

FEATURE FILM SOUNDTRACKS

THE TRIP TO BOUNTIFUL (1997)   Plough Down Sillion Music PDS 101
   Original Motion Picture Soundtrack
    Original underscore composed, arranged, conducted, and produced by J.A.C.
    Redford.

D3: THE MIGHTY DUCKS (1996)   Hollywood Records HR-62019-2
   Original Motion Picture Soundtrack
    Original underscore composed, conducted, and produced by J.A.C. Redford.

A KID IN KING ARTHUR'S COURT (1995)   Walt Disney Records 60885-7
   Original Motion Picture Soundtrack
    Original underscore composed, conducted, and produced by J.A.C. Redford,
    including "The Conscience of the King," performed by Liona Boyd.

BYE BYE LOVE (1995)   Giant Records 9 24609-2
   Original Soundtrack Album
    Underscore cue "The Main Thing" composed, conducted, and produced by J.A.C.
    Redford.

D2: THE MIGHTY DUCKS (1994)   Hollywood Records HR-61603-2
   Songs from the Motion Picture
    Original underscore composed, conducted, and produced by J.A.C. Redford.

NEWSIES (1992)   Walt Disney Records 60832-2
   Original Motion Picture Soundtrack
    Original underscore composed, conducted, and produced by J.A.C. Redford.

OLIVER AND COMPANY (1988 and 1996)   Walt Disney Records 60890-7
   Original Motion Picture Soundtrack
    Instrumental score composed, conducted, and produced by J.A.C. Redford.

TELEVISION SOUNDTRACKS

INDEPENDENCE (1996)   Prometheus Records PCD 139
Original Television Soundtrack
Music composed, conducted, and produced by J.A.C. Redford.

THE KEY TO REBECCA (1993)   Prometheus Records PCD 123
Original Television Soundtrack
Music composed, conducted, and produced by J.A.C. Redford.

THE ASTRONOMERS (1991)   Intrada MAF 7018D
Original Television Soundtrack
Music composed and produced by J.A.C. Redford.

OTHER RECORDINGS

UNVEILED HOPE (1997)   Myrrh 7014605607
Michael Card
"Prelude" composed by Scott Brasher and J.A.C. Redford and "Reprise" composed
by Michael Card and J.A.C. Redford, both conducted by J.A.C. Redford.

THE ANCIENT FAITH (1993)   Sparrow Records SPD 1377
Michael Card
"Prelude: The Ancient Faith" composed by Michael Card and J.A.C. Redford and
conducted by J.A.C. Redford.

THE GREAT ADVENTURE (1992)   Sparrow Records SPD 1328
Steven Curtis Chapman
"Prologue: The Great Adventure" composed and conducted by J.A.C. Redford.
1993 Grammy Award winner in Best Pop Gospel Album category.

LOVE AND DESIRE (1989)   Dove Books on Tape 40670
An anthology of great love poems read by David Birney, Jane Lapotaire, Lee Remick,
Robert Stephens, and Michael York.
Incidental music composed, conducted, and produced by J.A.C. Redford.

NINE LIVES (1986)   Warner Bros. Records 9 25486-1
Bonnie Raitt
"Stand Up to the Night" (title song from the motion picture EXTREMITIES)
Lyrics by Will Jennings. Music by J.A.C. Redford and Richard Kerr.

ARRANGING

UNVEILED HOPE (1997)   Myrrh 7014605607
Michael Card
"Holy, Holy, Holy," Hallelujah," and "The New Jerusalem" arranged and conducted
by J.A.C. Redford.

THE FIRST NOEL (1996)   Sparrow Records SPD 1585
Steve Green
"It Came Upon the Midnight Clear/Angels We Have Heard on High/O Come, All Ye
Faithful," "Come, Thou Long-Expected Jesus," "Away in a Manger/O Little Town of
Bethlehem," and "Rose of Bethlehem" arranged and conducted by J.A.C. Redford.

IT IS WELL WITH MY SOUL (1993)   The Bible Study Hour
Westminster Brass
"It Is Well With My Soul" arranged by J.A.C. Redford.

THE GREAT ADVENTURE (1992)   Sparrow Records SPD 1328
Steven Curtis Chapman
"Go There With You" arranged and conducted by J.A.C. Redford.
1993 Grammy Award winner in Best Pop Gospel Album category.

THE WORD: RECAPTURING THE IMAGINATION (1992)   Sparrow Records SPD 1321
Michael Card
"The Prophet," "Then They Will Know," "Song of Gomer," and "The Kingdom"
arranged and conducted by J.A.C. Redford. "Will You Not Listen" arranged by J.A.C.
Redford.

HE IS MY STRENGTH (1991)   AMM/CD-103
Steve Amerson
"Hymn of Praise," "He Must Be Love," "I Will Follow," and "God Is There" arranged
and conducted by J.A.C. Redford.

THE PROMISE (1991)   Sparrow Records SPD 1296
Michael Card
"The Promise (Overture)," "Unto Us A Son Is Given," "What Her Heart
Remembered," "Joseph's Song," Vicit Agnus Noster," "Shepherd's Watch," "Jacob's
Star," "We Will Find Him," "Thou The Promise," and "Immanuel" arranged and
conducted by J.A.C. Redford.

IMMORTAL (1986)   Dayspring Records 7-01414557-6
Cynthia Clawson
"Softly and Tenderly" (title song from the motion picture THE TRIP TO
BOUNTIFUL) arranged and conducted by J.A.C. Redford.

CONDUCTING

CINDERELLA (1995)   Walt Disney Records 60886-2
Walt Disney Records presents the music of Cinderella
Oliver Wallace and Paul J. Smith, Composers
    Score conducted and co-produced by J.A.C. Redford

A PYROMANIAC'S LOVE STORY (1995)   Varese Sarabande VSD-5620
Original Motion Picture Soundtrack
Rachel Portman, Composer
    Conducted by J.A.C. Redford

BLACK BEAUTY (1994)   Giant Records 9 24568-2
  Original Soundtrack
  Danny Elfman, Composer
  Conducted by J.A.C. Redford

NIGHTMARE BEFORE CHRISTMAS (1993)   Walt Disney Records 60855-7
  Original Motion Picture Soundtrack
  Danny Elfman, Composer
  Dramatic underscore conducted by J.A.C. Redford

THE JOY LUCK CLUB (1993)   Hollywood Records HR-61561-2
  Original Motion Picture Soundtrack
  Rachel Portman, Composer
  Conducted by J.A.C. Redford

HEART AND SOULS (1993)   MCA MCAD-10919
  Music from the Motion Picture Soundtrack
  Marc Shaiman, Composer
  "Main Title" and "Julia's Farewell" conducted by J.A.C. Redford

BENNY AND JOON (1993)   Milan 73138/35644-2
  Original Motion Picture Soundtrack
  Rachel Portman, Composer
  Conducted by J.A.C. Redford

THE LITTLE MERMAID (1988)   Walt Disney Records CD-018
  Original Motion Picture Soundtrack
  Songs by Howard Ashman and Alan Menken, Music by Alan Menken
  Conducted by J.A.C. Redford

  1990 Grammy Award winner in both Song for Motion Picture and Recording for
  Children categories.

For more information, contact J.A.C. Redford at www.jacredford.com

Texts of Concert Works

five sonnets

i thank You God for most this amazing

i thank You God for most this amazing day:
for the leaping greenly spirits of trees
and a blue true dream of sky;
and for everything which is natural
which is infinite which is yes

(i who have died am alive again today,
and this is the sun's birthday;
this is the birth day of life
and of love and wings:
and of the gay great happening illimitably earth)

how should tasting touching hearing
seeing breathing any lifted from the no of all nothing
human merely being doubt unimaginable You
(now the ears of my ears awake
and now the eyes of my eyes are opened)

when serpents bargain for the right to squirm

when serpents bargain for the right to squirm
and the sun strikes to gain a living wage—
when thorns regard their roses with alarm
and rainbows are insured against old age—

when every thrush may sing no new moon in
if all screech owls have not okayed his voice—
and any wave signs on the dotted line
or else an ocean is compelled to close

when the oak begs permission
of the birch to make an acorn
valleys accuse their mountains of having altitude
and march denounces april as a saboteur

then we'll believe in that incredible
unanimal mankind (and not until)

so many selves (so many fiends and gods)

so many selves (so many fiends and gods
each greedier than every) is a man
(so easily one in another hides;
yet man can, being all, escape from none)

so huge a tumult is the simplest wish:
so pitiless a massacre the hope most innocent
(so deep's the mind of flesh and so awake
what waking calls asleep)

so never is most lonely man alone
(his briefest breathing lives some planet's year,
his longest life's a heartbeat of some sun;
his least unmotion roams the youngest star)

how should a fool that calls him "I" presume
to comprehend not numerable whom?

all ignorance toboggans into know

all ignorance toboggans into know
and trudges up to ignorance again:
but winter's not forever, even snow melts;
and if spring should spoil the game, what then?

all history's a winter sport or three:
but were it five, I'd still insist
that all history is too small for even me;
for me and you, exceedingly too small.

Swoop (shrill collective myth)
into thy grave
merely to toil the scale to shrillerness
per every madge and mabel dick and dave

tomorrow is our permanent address
and there they'll scarcely find us
(if they do, we'll move away still further:
into now

your homecoming will be my homecoming

your homecoming will be my homecoming—
my selves go with you, only i remain;
a shadow phantom effigy or seeming
(an almost someone always who's no one)

a noone who, till their and your returning,
spends the forever of his loneliness
dreaming their eyes have opened to your morning
feeling their stars have risen through your skies:

so, in how merciful love's own name,
linger no more than selfless i can quite endure
the absence of that moment when a stranger
takes in his arms my very life who's your—

when all fears hopes beliefs doubts disappear.
Everywhere and joy's perfect wholeness we're

e e cummings (1894–1962)

Christ Is Alive!

Christ is alive! Let Christians sing.
　　His cross stands empty to the sky.
Let streets and homes with praises ring.
　　His love in death shall never die.
Christ is alive! No longer bound
　　to distant years in Palestine
he comes to claim the here and now
　　and conquer every place and time.

Not throned above, remotely high,
　　untouched, unmoved by human pains
but daily, in the midst of life,
　　our Savior with the Father reigns.

In every insult, rift, and war
　　where color, scorn or wealth divide,
he suffers still, yet loves the more,
　　and lives, though ever crucified.

Christ is alive! His Spirit burns
　　through this and every future age,
till all creation lives and learns
　　his joy, his justice, love and praise.

Brian Wren (1936–)

Shout for Joy to the Lord

Shout for joy to the Lord
All the earth
Burst into jubilant song with music
make music to the Lord with the harp and the sound of singing
with trumpets and the blast of the ram's horn
Shout for joy before the Lord the King.

Let the sea resound and ev'rything in it
The world and all who live in it
Let the rivers clap their hands
Let the mountains sing for joy
Let them sing before the Lord
Shout for joy to the Lord.

For He comes to judge the world
He will judge the world in righteousness
And the people with equity.
Shout for joy to the Lord.

Psalm 98:4–9 NIV

A Paschal Feast

I. New Readings

Alleluia.
Christ our Passover is sacrificed for us,
    therefore let us keep the feast,
Not with old leaven,
neither with the leaven of malice and wickedness,
    but with the unleavened bread of sincerity and truth. Alleluia.

Christ being raised from the dead dieth no more;
    death hath no more dominion over him.

For in that he died, he died unto sin once;
    but in that he liveth, he liveth unto God.
Likewise reckon ye also yourselves to be dead indeed unto sin,
    but alive unto God through Jesus Christ our Lord. Alleluia.

                                        From the Book of Common Prayer

New Readings

    Although the letter said
On thistles that men look not grapes to gather,
    I read the story rather
How soldiers platting thorns around CHRIST'S Head
    Grapes grew and drops of wine were shed.

    Though when the sower sowed,
The winged fowls took part, part fell in thorn
    And never turned to corn,
Part found no root upon the flinty road,—
    CHRIST at all hazards fruit hath shewed.

    From wastes of rock He brings
Food for five thousand: on the thorns He shed
    Grains from His drooping Head;
And would not have that legion of winged things
    Bear Him to heaven on easeful wings.

                                        Gerard Manley Hopkins (1844–1889)

Christ is risen from the dead,
  and become the first fruits of them that slept.
For since by man came death,
  by man came also the resurrection of the dead.
For as in Adam all die,
  even so in Christ shall all be made alive. Alleluia.

From the Book of Common Prayer

II. Still Falls the Rain

Still Falls the Rain
  The Raids, 1940. Night and Dawn

Still falls the Rain—
Dark as the world of man, black as our loss—
Blind as the nineteen hundred and forty nails
Upon the Cross.

Still falls the Rain
With a sound like the pulse of the heart that is changed to the ham-
  mer-beat
In the Potter's Field, and the sound of the impious feet

On the Tomb:
    Still falls the Rain
In the Field of Blood where the small hopes breed and the human
  brain
Nurtures its greed, that worm with the brow of Cain.

Still falls the Rain
At the feet of the Starved Man hung upon the Cross.
Christ that each day, each night, nails there, have mercy on us—
On Dives and on Lazarus:
Under the Rain the sore and the gold are as one.

Still falls the Rain—
Still falls the Blood from the Starved Man's wounded Side:
He bears in His Heart all wounds,—those of the light that died,
The last faint spark
In the self-murdered heart, the wounds of the sad uncomprehend-
  ing dark,
The wounds of the baited bear,—
The blind and weeping bear whom the keepers beat
On his helpless flesh . . . the tears of the hunted hare.

Still falls the Rain—
Then—O Ile leape up to my God: who pulles me doune—
See, see where Christ's blood streames in the firmament:

It flows from the Brow we nailed upon the tree
Deep to the dying, to the thirsting heart
That holds the fires of the world,—dark-smirched with pain
As Caesar's laurel crown.

Then sounds the voice of One who like the heart of man
Was once a child who among beasts has lain—
'Still do I love, still shed my innocent light, my Blood, for thee.'

Dame Edith Sitwell (1887–1964)

III. A Better Resurrection

A Better Resurrection

I have no wit, no words, no tears;
   My heart within me like a stone
Is numbed too much for hopes or fears.
   Look right, look left, I dwell alone;
I lift mine eyes but dimmed with grief
   No everlasting hills I see;
My life is in the falling leaf:
   O Jesus, quicken me.

My life is like a faded leaf,
   My harvest dwindled to a husk:
Truly my life is void and brief
   And tedious in the barren dusk;
My life is like a frozen thing,
   No bud nor greenness can I see;
Yet rise it shall—the sap of Spring;
   O Jesus, rise in me.

My life is like a broken bowl,
   A broken bowl that cannot hold
One drop of water for my soul
   Or cordial in the searching cold;

Cast in the fire the perished thing;
  Melt and remould it, till it be
A royal cup for him, my King:
  O Jesus, drink of me.

Christina Rosetti (1830–1894)

IV. He hath abolished the old drouth

He hath abolished the old drouth,
And rivers run where all was dry,
The field is sopp'd with merciful dew.
He hath put a new song in my mouth,
The words are old, the purport new,
And taught my lips to quote this word
That I shall live, I shall not die,
But I shall when the shocks are stored
See the salvation of the Lord.

We meet together, you and I,
Meet in one acre of one land,
And I will turn my looks to you,
And you shall meet me with reply,
We shall be sheaved with one band
In harvest and in garnering,
When heavenly vales so thick shall stand
With corn that they shall laugh and sing.

Gerard Manley Hopkins (1844–1889)

O God, who for our redemption didst give thine only-begotten Son
to the death of the cross, and by his glorious resurrection hast
delivered us from the power of our enemy: Grant us so to die daily
to sin, that we may evermore live with him in the joy of his resurrection; through the same thy Son Christ our Lord, who liveth and
reigneth with thee and the Holy Spirit, one God, now and for ever.
Amen.

From the Book of Common Prayer

Welcome All Wonders: A Christmas Celebration

I. Welcome All Wonders

Welcome, all wonders in one sight!
    Eternity shut in a span.
Summer in winter, day in night.
    Heaven in earth, and God in man.
Great little one! whose all-embracing birth
    Lifts earth to heaven, stoops heaven to earth.

Welcome, though nor to gold nor silk.
    To more than Caesar's birthright is;
Two sister-seas of virgin-milk,
    With many a rarely-tempered kiss
That breathes at once both maid and mother,
    Warms in the one, cools in the other.

Welcome, though not to those gay flies.
    Guilded in the beams of earthly kings;
Slippery souls in smiling eyes;
    But to poor shepherds, home-spun things,
Whose wealth's their flock, whose wit, to be
    Well read in their simplicity.

Yet when young April's husband showers
    Shall bless the fruitful Maia's bed
We'll bring the first-born of her flowers
    To kiss thy feet and crown thy head.
To thee, dread Lamb! whose love must keep
    The shepherds, more than they the sheep.

To thee, meek Majesty! soft King
    Of simple graces and sweet loves.
Each of us his lamb will bring
    Each his pair of silver doves;
Till burnt at last in fire of Thy fair eyes,
    Ourselves become our own best sacrifice.

Richard Crashaw (1613–1659)

II. Christmas Mourning

On Christmas Day I weep
Good Friday to rejoice.
I watch the Child asleep.
Does He half dream the choice
The Man must make and keep?

At Christmastime I sigh
For my Good Friday hope.
Outflung the Child's arms lie
To span in their brief scope
The death the Man must die.

Come Christmastide I groan
To hear Good Friday's pealing.
The Man, racked to the bone,
Has made His hurt my healing,
Has made my ache His own.

Slay me, pierced to the core
With Christmas penitence
So I who, new-born, soar
To that Child's innocence,
May wound the Man no more.

Vassar Miller (1924–   )

III. The Nativity of Christ

Behold the father is his daughter's son,
The bird that built the nest is hatched therein,
The old of years an hour hath not outrun,
Eternal life to live doth now begin,
The Word is dumb, the mirth of heaven doth weep,
Might feeble is, and force doth faintly creep.

O dying souls, behold your living spring;
O dazzled eyes, behold your sun of grace;
Dull ears, attend what word this Word doth bring;
Up, heavy hearts, with joy your joy embrace.
From death, from dark, from deafness, from despairs,
This life, this light, this Word, this joy repairs.

Gift better than himself God doth not know;
Gift better than his God no man can see.
This gift doth here the giver given bestow;
Gift to this gift let each receiver be.
God is my gift, himself he freely gave me;
God's gift am I, and none but God shall have me.

Man altered was by sin from man to beast;
Beast's food is hay, hay is all mortal flesh.
Now God is flesh and lies in manger pressed
As hay, the brutest sinner to refresh.
O happy field wherein this fodder grew,
Whose taste doth us from beasts to men renew.

Robert Southwell (1561–1595)

IV. Good is the Flesh

Good is the flesh that the Word has become,
  good is the birthing, the milk in the breast,
  good is the feeding, caressing and rest,
  good is the body for knowing the world,
Good is the flesh that the Word has become.

Good is the body for knowing the world,
  sensing the sunlight, the tug of the ground,
  feeling, perceiving, within and around,
  good is the body, from cradle to grave,
Good is the flesh that the Word has become.

Good is the body, from cradle to grave,
  growing and ageing, arousing, impaired,
  happy in clothing, or lovingly bared,
  good is the pleasure of God in our flesh,
Good is the flesh that the Word has become.

Good is the pleasure of God in our flesh,
  longing in all, as in Jesus, to dwell,
  glad of embracing, and tasting, and smell,
  good is the body, for good and for God,
Good is the flesh that the Word has become.

Brian Wren (1936–)

V. Christmas now

Child, when Herod wakes,
  and hate or exploitation
  swing their dripping swords,
  from your cross and cradle
    sing a new song.

Child, when Caesar's laws
  choke love or strangle freedom,
  calling darkness light,
  from your cross and cradle
    sing a new song

Child, when Caiaphas
  sends truth to crucifixion
  to protect his prayers,
  from your cross and cradle
    sing a new song.

Child, your helpless love
  brings death and resurrection:
  joyfully we come to your cross and cradle
    with a new song—
        Alleluia! Alleluia!

Brian Wren (1936–)

Shepherd Story

And there were shepherds abiding in the field,
Keeping watch over their flock by night.
And for these shepherds, the hope that night would yield
Short hours untroubled until first light.
Crisp was the air and damp the ground,
The restless sheep encamped around,
And from the stars, a welcome glow
That smiles on shepherds far below.

And suddenly on this night,
This particular night of nights,
An angel of the Lord appeared before them
And the glory of the Lord blazed around them
And they were sore afraid.
And the angel said unto them:

Fear not, for behold, I bring you good tidings of great joy
Which shall be for all people.

For today in the city of David
There has been born for you a Savior
Who is Christ, the Lord.

And this will be a sign for you:
You will find a baby wrapped in cloths
And lying in a manger.

And suddenly, there was with the angel
A multitude of the heavenly host,
Praising God, and saying:

Glory to God in the highest,
Glory to God on high.
Glory to God in the highest,
Glory to God on high.
And on earth, peace, peace to men of good will,
And on earth, peace to men of good will.
Glory to God in the highest
And on earth, peace to men on whom his favor rests.

When the angels had left them and gone into heaven,
The shepherds said to one another,

"Let's go to Bethlehem and see this thing
Which the Lord has told us about".

So they came with haste and found Mary and Joseph
And the baby lying in a manger.
And when they had seen him they spread the word
Telling all they had heard about this child.

Glory to God in the highest,
Glory to God on high.
Glory to God in the highest,
Glory to God on high.
And on earth, peace, peace to men of good will,
And on earth, peace to men of good will.
Glory to God in the highest,
Glory to God, glory to God,
Glory to God on high!

And all who heard it wondered,
And all who heard it were amazed,
And all who heard it were astonished
At what the shepherds said.

And the shepherds returned, praising God
For all they had heard and seen.
And the shepherds returned, glorifying God
For it all had been just as was told them.

Glory to God in the highest,
Glory to God on high.
Glory to God in the highest,
Glory to God on high.
And on earth, peace, peace to men of good will,
And on earth, peace to men of good will.
Glory to God in the highest,
Glory to God, glory to God,
Glory to God on high!

J.A.C. Redford (1953–)
Text and adaptation

Overture

1. Frederick Buechner, _The Sacred Journey_ (San Francisco: Harper & Row, 1982), pp. 3 and 6.

2. T.S. Eliot, "Gerontion," _The Complete Poems and Plays 1909–1950_ (San Diego: Harcourt Brace Jovanovich, 1971), p. 21.

Chapter 1: _Of Godly Parents_

1. "History of Robert Eckersall Redford," compiled by Mary R. Stoddard (unpublished family record), p. 1.

2. Ibid., p. 3.

3. See _Improvement Era_, Vol. XXXII, No. 11 (September 1929), pp. 881–886 (Part 1) and _Improvement Era_, Vol. XXXII, No. 12 (October 1929), pp. 972–980 (Part 2).

4. Richard S. Van Wagoner, _Mormon Polygamy: A History_ (Salt Lake City: Signature Books, 1986), pp. 120–121.

5. "History of Robert Eckersall Redford," compiled by Mary R. Stoddard (unpublished family record), pp. 5–6.

6. Ibid., p. 7.

Chapter 2: _I Am a Child of God_

1. Naomi W. Randall and Mildred T. Pettit, "I Am a Child of God," _Sing with Me_ (Salt Lake City: Deseret Book Company, 1974), p. B–76.

2. "Something's Coming," from _West Side Story_, music by Leonard Bernstein and lyrics by Stephen Sondheim (New York: G. Schirmer, Inc. and Chappell & Co., Inc., 1957 and 1959).

3. Blessing and confirmation given to J.A.C. Redford by Dr. Thomas A. Clawson, Jr., Sunday, August 6, 1961, as transcribed by Patricia C. Redford (unpublished family record).

Chapter 3: _A Time of Innocence_

1. Frederick Buechner, _The Sacred Journey_ (San Francisco: Harper & Row, 1982), p. 58.

Chapter 4: _Your Young Men Shall See Visions_

1. "Homing," words by Arthur L. Salmon and music by Teresa del Riego (New York: Chappell & Co., Inc., 1927).

2. Orson Pratt, _Orson Pratt's Works_ (Salt Lake City: Deseret News Press, 1945), p. 31.

3. Patriarchal Blessing given to J.A.C. Redford by John A. Buehner, May 26, 1970 (unpublished family record).

4. *Teachings of the Prophet Joseph Smith,* Joseph Fielding Smith, editor (Salt Lake City: Deseret News Press, 1956), p. 150.

Chapter 5: *The Glory of God Is Intelligence*

1. Rainer Maria Rilke, *Letters to a Young Poet* (New York: W.W. Norton & Company, Inc., 1962), p. 29.

Chapter 7: *For Time and All Eternity*

1. First Presidency (David O. McKay, Hugh B. Brown, N. Eldon Tanner), letter to stake presidents, bishops, and mission presidents, April 14, 1969, as cited in *Living Prophets for a Living Church,* published for the use of college students in the Church educational system, pp. 126–127.

2. George Herbert (1593–1633), "Love," as published in *Eerdmans Book of Christian Poetry,* compiled by Pat Alexander (Grand Rapids: Eerdmans, 1981), p. 27. Recording: Ralph Vaughn-Williams (1872–1958), *Five Mystical Songs* (1911), as performed by John Shirley-Quirk, baritone, the Choir of King's College, Cambridge, and the English Chamber Orchestra, conducted by Sir David Willcocks (EMI Records CDM 7 69949 2).

3. James Agee, *Knoxville: Summer of 1915,* adapted by Samuel Barber. Recording: Samuel Barber (1910–1981), *Knoxville: Summer of 1915* (1947), as performed by Eleanor Steber, soprano, and the Dumbarton Oaks Orchestra, conducted by William Strickland (Sony Masterworks MPK 46727).

Chapter 8: *Higher Positions*

1. Shakespeare, *Julius Caesar* II.i.21–22.
2. "History of Robert Eckersall Redford," compiled by Mary R. Stoddard (unpublished family record), p. 5.
3. See the following passages:
   Book of Mormon:
   —1 Nephi 12:20–23 "a dark, and loathsome, and a filthy people"
   —2 Nephi 5:20–24 "a skin of blackness"
   —2 Nephi 30:3–6 "a white and delightsome people" *(Note:* This verse was altered in 1981 editions to read "a *pure* and delightsome people")
   —Jacob 3:5–9 "their skins will be whiter than yours"
   —Alma 3:6–10 "a curse upon them"
   —3 Nephi 2:14–15 "their skin became white"
   —Mormon 5:14–15 "a dark, a filthy, and a loathsome people"
   Contrast these passages with 2 Nephi 26:32–33.
   Pearl of Great Price:
   —Moses 7:21–22 "for the seed of Cain were black" (compare 5:16–41).
   —Moses 7:8 "a blackness came upon all the children of Canaan" (compare v. 12).
   —Abraham 1:21–27 "being of that lineage by which he could not have the right of Priesthood" (compare 2:9–11).

4. Bruce R. McConkie, "Negroes," from *Mormon Doctrine* (Salt Lake City: Bookcraft, 1958), pp. 476–477. See also "Cain," p. 102; "Caste System," pp. 107–108; "Ham," p. 314; and "Races of Men," pp. 553–554. Compare with Brigham Young, *Journal of Discourses* (Liverpool: F.D. Richards, 1855, photo reprint, 1966), Vol. VII, pp. 290–291.

5. Bruce R. McConkie, "All Are Alike Unto God," Book of Mormon Symposium, BYU, August 18, 1978. See *Doctrine and Covenants*, Official Declaration–2, for the text of the First Presidency letter "extending priesthood and temple blessings to all worthy male members of the Church."

6. Carol Lynn Pearson, "Optical Illusion," from *The Growing Season* (Salt Lake City: Bookcraft, 1976), p. 10.

Chapter 9: *Things Fall Apart*

1. William Butler Yeats, "The Second Coming," as published in *The Rag and Bone Shop of the Heart*, Robert Bly, James Hillman, and Michael Meade, editors (New York: Harper Collins, 1992), p. 216.

2. Shakespeare, *King Lear* IV.i.36.

3. *Pearl of Great Price: Joseph Smith—History* 1:19 (5–20).

4. Gordon B. Hinckley, "The Cornerstones of Our Faith," *Ensign*, November 1984, p. 52.

5. Compare "History, 1832" with "History, 1838" in *The Personal Writings of Joseph Smith*, compiled and edited by Dean C. Jessee (Salt Lake City: Deseret Book, 1984), pp. 4–6 and pp. 196–200. For the canonized version of the 1838 history, see *Pearl of Great Price: Joseph Smith—History*.

For discussion of the problems associated with the First Vision, see:

—James B. Allen, "The Significance of Joseph Smith's 'First Vision' in Mormon Thought," *Dialogue: A Journal of Mormon Thought* 1:3 (Fall 1966).

—James B. Allen, "Emergence of a Fundamental: The Expanding Role of Joseph Smith's First Vision in Mormon Religious Thought," *Journal of Mormon History* Vol. VII (1980).

—Marvin Hill, "The First Vision Controversy: A Critique and Reconciliation," *Dialogue: A Journal of Mormon Thought* 15:2 (Summer 1982).

—Lawrence Foster, "First Visions: Personal Observations on Joseph Smith's Religious Experience," *Sunstone* 8:5 (September/October 1983).

For a Mormon defense of the canonized version, see:

—Milton V. Backman, Jr., "Joseph Smith's Recitals of the First Vision," *Ensign*, January 1985.

6. See "Roundtable: The Question of the Palmyra Revival," *Dialogue* 4:1 (Spring 1969). Contributions include: Wesley P. Walters, "New Light on Mormon Origins from the Palmyra Revival" (a critique of the canonized version); Richard L. Bushman, "The First Vision Story Revived" (an LDS response); and Wesley P. Walters, "A Reply to Dr. Bushman." See also Milton V. Backman, Jr., *Joseph Smith's First Vision: The First Vision in Its Historical Context*, 2nd edition (Salt Lake City: Bookcraft, 1980), for a Mormon defense; and Wesley P. Walters, "Joseph Smith's First Vision Story Revisited," *Journal of Pastoral Practice* 4 (1980), pp. 92–109, for a rebuttal. Compare H. Michael Marquardt and Wesley P. Walters, *Inventing Mormonism* (Salt Lake City: Signature Books, 1994), pp. 15–41 (also pp. 1–13), and D. Michael Quinn, *Early Mormonism and the Magic World View* (Salt Lake City: Signature Books, 1987), p. 113, note 1.

7. *Pearl of Great Price: Joseph Smith—History* 1:70 and 72 (66–75), and *Doctrine and Covenants* 27:12 (5–14), and 128:20.

8. *History of the Church* (Salt Lake City: Deseret Book, 1978), Vol. I, pp. 40–42 (footnote by B.H. Roberts).

9. *History of the Church* (Salt Lake City: Deseret Book, 1978), Vol. I, pp. 175–176.

10. The reference appears in the writings of John Whitmer, John Corrill, Ezra Booth, and Lyman Wright, for instance, all of whom attended the June 1831 conference. See *From*

Historian to Dissident: The Book of John Whitmer, edited by Bruce N. Westergren (Salt Lake City: Signature Books, 1995), pp. 69–71; Gregory A. Prince, *Power from on High: The Development of the Mormon Priesthood* (Salt Lake City: Signature Books, 1995), pp. 17–20; and D. Michael Quinn, *The Mormon Hierarchy: Origins of Power* (Salt Lake City: Signature Books in association with Smith Research Associates, 1994), pp. 27–32 (14–32). Compare Brigham Young, *Journal of Discourses* (Liverpool: F. D. Richards, 1855, photo reprint, 1966), Vol. X, p. 303, and George A. Smith, *Journal of Discourses* (Liverpool: F. D. Richards, 1855, photo reprint, 1966), Vol. XI, p. 4.

The writing of John Whitmer's history was enjoined in *Doctrine and Covenants* 47 and 69. The position of the LDS Church regarding the June 1831 conference is that the ordinations mentioned refer specifically to the office of high priest rather than to the Melchizedek or High Priesthood itself. With the exception of Quinn, the works cited above simply reiterate this position with no explanation or substantiation. Drawing his conclusions from admittedly circumstantial and anecdotal evidence, Quinn suggests a date of July 1830 for the restoration of the Melchizedek priesthood, but this too is subsequent to the organization of the Church in April 1830 and thus also contravenes the official story. See Quinn, pp. 24–26 (14–26) and Richard Bushman, *Joseph Smith and the Beginnings of Mormonism* (Urbana and Chicago: University of Illinois Press, 1984), p. 163.

11. For two examples, compare *Doctrine and Covenants* 7 with *Book of Commandments* VI (the reference to "keys" in this passage was inserted after its first publication), or *Doctrine and Covenants* 27 with *Book of Commandments* XXVIII (the references to the visits of John the Baptist and the apostles, Peter, James, and John, are missing from the earlier version). See D. Michael Quinn, *The Mormon Hierarchy: Origins of Power* (Salt Lake City: Signature Books in association with Smith Research Associates, 1994), pp. 30–31.

12. David Whitmer, *An Address to All Believers in Christ* (Richmond, Missouri: David Whitmer, 1887), photographic reprint, pp. 49, 56–57.

13. See Robert Lindsey, *A Gathering of Saints* (New York: Simon and Schuster, 1988), Steven Naifeh and Gregory White Smith, *The Mormon Murders* (New York: Onyx, 1988), or Linda Sillitoe and Allen Roberts, *Salamander* (Salt Lake City: Signature Books, 1988).

14. See Dee F. Green, "Book of Mormon Archaeology: The Myths and the Alternatives," *Dialogue: A Journal of Mormon Thought* 4:2 (Summer 1969), pp. 77–78; and Michael D. Coe, "Mormon Archaeology: An Outsider View," *Dialogue: A Journal of Mormon Thought* 8:2 (Summer 1973), pp. 41–42, 46.

For the traditional LDS position on *Book of Mormon* geography, see:

—*Pearl of Great Price: Joseph Smith—History* 1:34.

—*Doctrine and Covenants* 28:8–9 and 57:4.

—*The Personal Writings of Joseph Smith,* compiled and edited by Dean C. Jessee (Salt Lake City: Deseret Book, 1984), pp. 215 and 273.

—*History of the Church* (Salt Lake City: Deseret Book, 1978), Vol. I, p. 315 and Vol. 2, pp. 79–80.

—*B.H. Roberts: Studies of the Book of Mormon,* Brigham D. Madsen, editor (Urbana and Chicago: Illinois University Press, 1985), pp. 277–278.

—Joseph Fielding Smith, *Doctrines of Salvation* (Salt Lake City: Bookcraft, 1956), Vol. III, pp. 232–243.

For the geographical model currently favored by Mormon scholars associated with FARMS, see:

—John L. Sorenson, "Digging into the Book of Mormon: Our Changing Understanding of Ancient America and Its Scripture," *The Ensign* (September 1984).

—John L. Sorenson, *An Ancient American Setting for the Book of Mormon* (Salt Lake City: Deseret Book and FARMS, 1985), pp. 28–32 and 46–48 (1–48).
Critiques of this model include:
—Deanne G. Matheny, "Does the Shoe Fit? A Critique of the Limited Tehuántepec Geography," from *New Approaches to the Book of Mormon: Explorations in Critical Methodology*, Brent Lee Metcalfe, editor (Salt Lake City: Signature Books, 1993), pp. 269–281 and 310–320 (269–328).
—Raymond T. Matheny, "Book of Mormon Archaeology," Sunstone Symposium #6, Salt Lake Sheraton Hotel, August 25, 1984 (transcript, 1984, in the David J. Buerger Collection, Manuscript 622, Box 33, Fd 17, Manuscripts Division, J. Willard Marriott Library, University of Utah, Salt Lake City, Utah), pp. 19–21 and 30-32 (19-34).
—George D. Smith, "'Is There Any Way to Escape These Difficulties?': The Book of Mormon Studies of B.H. Roberts," *Dialogue: A Journal of Mormon Thought* 17:2 (Summer 1984), pp. 95 and 103–104 (94–111).
—Stan Larson, *Quest for the Gold Plates* (Salt Lake City: Freethinker Press, 1996), pp. 175–268.

15. For some of the many references, see *Book of Mormon*: Title Page, 1 Nephi 1:1-4, 5:14, and 6:2, 2 Nephi 3:4 and 30:4, Jacob 2:25, Alma 10:3 and 46:23-24, and 3 Nephi 10:17. See also *History of the Church* (Salt Lake City: Deseret Book, 1978), Vol. I, p. 315 and *The Personal Writings of Joseph Smith*, compiled and edited by Dean C. Jessee (Salt Lake City: Deseret Book, 1984), pp. 76, 215, and 273. Compare George D. Smith, "'Is There Any Way to Escape These Difficulties?': The Book of Mormon Studies of B.H. Roberts," *Dialogue: A Journal of Mormon Thought* 17:2 (Summer 1984), p. 104.

16. See Smithsonian Institution, Department of Anthropology, "Statement Regarding the Book of Mormon" (1996), #2; Dee F. Green, "Book of Mormon Archaeology: The Myths and the Alternatives," *Dialogue: A Journal of Mormon Thought* 4:2 (Summer 1969), p. 78; George D. Smith, "'Is There Any Way to Escape These Difficulties?': The Book of Mormon Studies of B.H. Roberts," *Dialogue: A Journal of Mormon Thought* 17:2 (Summer 1984), p. 102; Dan Vogel, *Indian Origins and the Book of Mormon* (Salt Lake City: Signature Books, 1986), pp. 51–52; and *B.H. Roberts: Studies of the Book of Mormon*, Brigham D. Madsen, editor (Urbana and Chicago: Illinois University Press, 1985), pp. 127 and 134 (116–143). The fact is even conceded (with some qualifications) by John L. Sorenson, *An Ancient American Setting for the Book of Mormon* (Salt Lake City: Deseret Book and FARMS, 1985), p. 87 (83–90).

17. Smithsonian Institution, Department of Anthropology, "Statement Regarding the Book of Mormon" (1996), #6–8.

18. John C. Kunich, "Multiply Exceedingly: Book of Mormon Population Sizes," from *New Approaches to the Book of Mormon*, Brent Lee Metcalfe, editor (Salt Lake City: Signature Books, 1993), pp. 231–267. See also *B.H. Roberts: Studies of the Book of Mormon*, Brigham D. Madsen, editor (Urbana and Chicago: Illinois University Press, 1985), pp. 63–94; and John L. Sorenson, "Digging into the Book of Mormon: Our Changing Understanding of Ancient America and Its Scripture," *The Ensign* (September 1984), p. 29.

19. *Book of Mormon*: 2 Nephi 5:15, Jarom 1:8, Mosiah 11: 3 and 8, Alma 27: 29, Ether 7:9a and 10:22–23.

20. Smithsonian Institution, Department of Anthropology, "Statement Regarding the Book of Mormon" (1996), #5; Deanne G. Matheny, "Does the Shoe Fit? A Critique of the Limited Tehuántepec Geography," from *New Approaches to the Book of Mormon: Explorations in Critical Methodology*, Brent Lee Metcalfe, editor (Salt Lake City: Signature Books, 1993), pp. 283–297; and Raymond T. Matheny, "Book of Mormon Archaeology," Sunstone

Symposium #6, Salt Lake Sheraton Hotel, August 25, 1984 (transcript, 1984, in the David J. Buerger Collection, Manuscript 622, Box 33, Fd 17, Manuscripts Division, J. Willard Marriott Library, University of Utah, Salt Lake City, Utah), pp. 22–25. See also Stan Larson, *Quest for the Gold Plates* (Salt Lake City: Freethinker Press, 1996), pp. 195–204 and 246–257; and *B.H. Roberts: Studies of the Book of Mormon*, Brigham D. Madsen, editor (Urbana and Chicago: Illinois University Press, 1985), pp. 107–112.

21. *Book of Mormon*: Alma 11:7 and 15 (1–19). Compare Mosiah 7:22 and 9:9.

22. Raymond T. Matheny, "Book of Mormon Archaeology," Sunstone Symposium #6, Salt Lake Sheraton Hotel, August 25, 1984 (transcript, 1984, in the David J. Buerger Collection, Manuscript 622, Box 33, Fd 17, Manuscripts Division, J. Willard Marriott Library, University of Utah, Salt Lake City, Utah), p. 25.

23. Smithsonian Institution, Department of Anthropology, "Statement Regarding the Book of Mormon" (1996), #4; Deanne G. Matheny, "Does the Shoe Fit? A Critique of the Limited Tehuántepec Geography," from *New Approaches to the Book of Mormon: Explorations in Critical Methodology*, Brent Lee Metcalfe, editor (Salt Lake City: Signature Books, 1993), p. 302; and Raymond T. Matheny, "Book of Mormon Archaeology," Sunstone Symposium #6, Salt Lake Sheraton Hotel, August 25, 1984 (transcript, 1984, in the David J. Buerger Collection, Manuscript 622, Box 33, Fd 17, Manuscripts Division, J. Willard Marriott Library, University of Utah, Salt Lake City, Utah), p. 28. See also Stan Larson, *Quest for the Gold Plates* (Salt Lake City: Freethinker Press, 1996), p. 181. The few esoteric discoveries of what appear to be small quantities of domesticated North American barleys are inappropriate to confirm the existence of Old World-style barley at the level of use and during time periods reported by the Book of Mormon.

24. *Book of Mormon*: 1 Nephi 18: 24–25. Wheat is mentioned specifically in Mosiah 9:9, linen in Mosiah 10:5, Alma 1:29 and 4:6, and Helaman 6:13. The earlier Jaredites are also said to have had linen in Ether 9:17 and 10:24. For critiques, see the Smithsonian Institution, Department of Anthropology, "Statement Regarding the Book of Mormon" (1996), #4; Deanne G. Matheny, "Does the Shoe Fit? A Critique of the Limited Tehuántepec Geography," from *New Approaches to the Book of Mormon: Explorations in Critical Methodology*, Brent Lee Metcalfe, editor (Salt Lake City: Signature Books, 1993), pp. 300–302; and Ray T. Matheny, "Book of Mormon Archaeology," Sunstone Symposium #6, Salt Lake Sheraton Hotel, August 25, 1984 (transcript, 1984, in the David J. Buerger Collection, Manuscript 622, Box 33, Fd 17, Manuscripts Division, J. Willard Marriott Library, University of Utah, Salt Lake City, Utah), pp. 27–29. See also Stan Larson, *Quest for the Gold Plates* (Salt Lake City: Freethinker Press, 1996), pp. 179–181 and 238–239.

25. *Book of Mormon*: 1 Nephi 18:25, Enos 1:21, Alma 18:7–9, 3 Nephi 3:22, 4:4, and 6:1, as well as numerous references to flocks, herds, firstlings, fatlings, and other terms related to animal husbandry. The earlier Jaredites are also said to have domesticated Old World animals in Ether 9:17–19. For critiques, see the Smithsonian Institution, Department of Anthropology, "Statement Regarding the Book of Mormon" (1996), #4; Deanne G. Matheny, "Does the Shoe Fit? A Critique of the Limited Tehuántepec Geography," from *New Approaches to the Book of Mormon: Explorations in Critical Methodology*, Brent Lee Metcalfe, editor (Salt Lake City: Signature Books, 1993), pp. 302–310; Raymond T. Matheny, "Book of Mormon Archaeology," Sunstone Symposium #6, Salt Lake Sheraton Hotel, August 25, 1984 (transcript, 1984, in the David J. Buerger Collection, Manuscript 622, Box 33, Fd 17, Manuscripts Division, J. Willard Marriott Library, University of Utah, Salt Lake City, Utah), pp. 29–30; and J. Henry Ibarquen, as cited in George D. Smith, "'Is There Any Way to Escape These Difficulties?': The Book of Mormon Studies of B.H. Roberts," *Dialogue: A Journal of Mormon Thought* 17:2 (Summer 1984), p. 106, footnote 42. See also

Stan Larson, *Quest for the Gold Plates* (Salt Lake City: Freethinker Press, 1996), pp. 182–194 and 240–246; and *B.H. Roberts: Studies of the Book of Mormon*, Brigham D. Madsen, editor (Urbana and Chicago: Illinois University Press, 1985), pp. 95–107.

26. Stan Larson, *Quest for the Gold Plates* (Salt Lake City: Freethinker Press, 1996), pp. 239, 246, and 257.

27. *Pearl of Great Price*: Articles of Faith 8; *History of the Church* (Salt Lake City: Deseret Book, 1978), Vol. I, p. 245 and Vol. VI, p. 57; LDS Bible Dictionary, Holy Bible (Salt Lake City: The Church of Jesus Christ of Latter-day Saints, 1979), p. 624; and *Book of Mormon*: 1 Nephi 13:26–40 (20–42).

28. *Pearl of Great Price*: Articles of Faith 8; *History of the Church* (Salt Lake City: Deseret Book, 1978), Vol. IV, p. 461; and *Doctrine and Covenants* 17:6.

29. Mark Thomas, "Revival Language in the Book of Mormon," *Sunstone* 8:3 (May–June 1983); H. Michael Marquardt, "Early Nineteenth Century Events Reflected in the Book of Mormon," *The Journal of Pastoral Practice*, Vol. III, No. 1, pp. 114–136; *B.H. Roberts: Studies of the Book of Mormon*, Brigham D. Madsen, editor (Urbana and Chicago: Illinois University Press, 1985), pp. 308–310 (284–316); and Susan Curtis, "Early Nineteenth-Century America and the Book of Mormon," from *The Word of God*, edited by Dan Vogel (Salt Lake City: Signature Books, 1990), pp. 81–96.

30. H. Michael Marquardt, "The Use of the Bible in the Book of Mormon," *The Journal of Pastoral Practice*, Vol. II, No. 2, pp. 95–136.

31. Stan Larson, "The Historicity of the Matthean Sermon on the Mount in 3 Nephi," from *New Approaches to the Book of Mormon: Explorations in Critical Methodology*, Brent Lee Metcalfe, editor (Salt Lake City: Signature Books, 1993), pp. 115–163.

32. *History of the Church* (Salt Lake City: Deseret Book, 1978), Vol. II, pp. 235–236 and 350–351.

33. "The Facsimile Found: The Recovery of Joseph Smith's Papyrus Manuscripts," *Dialogue: A Journal of Mormon Thought* 2:4 (Winter 1967); Klaus Baer, "The Breathing Permit of Hôr: A Translation of the Apparent Source of the Book of Abraham," *Dialogue: A Journal of Mormon Thought* 3:2 (Autumn 1968), pp. 109–134; Edward H. Ashment, "The Facsimiles of the Book of Abraham: A Reappraisal," with H.W. Nibley, "The Facsimiles of the Book of Abraham: A Response (to E.H. Ashment)," *Sunstone* 4:5–6 (December 1979), pp. 33–51; Edward H. Ashment, "Reducing Dissonance: The Book of Abraham as a Case Study," from *The Word of God*, edited by Dan Vogel (Salt Lake City: Signature Books, 1990), pp. 221–235; and Charles M. Larson, *By His Own Hand Upon Papyrus: A New Look at the Joseph Smith Papyri* (Grand Rapids, Michigan: Institute for Religious Research, revised edition, 1992), pp. 9–87 and 100–111.

34. Charles M. Larson, *By His Own Hand Upon Papyrus: A New Look at the Joseph Smith Papyri* (Grand Rapids, Michigan: Institute for Religious Research, revised edition, 1992), pp. 114–166; and Stan Larson, *Quest for the Gold Plates* (Salt Lake City: Freethinker Press, 1996), pp. 112–118.

35. *History of the Church* (Salt Lake City: Deseret Book, 1978), Vol. II, pp. 238, 318, and 320; Charles M. Larson, *By His Own Hand Upon Papyrus: A New Look at the Joseph Smith Papyri* (Grand Rapids, Michigan: Institute for Religious Research, revised edition, 1992), pp. 88–99; Klaus Baer, "The Breathing Permit of Hôr: A Translation of the Apparent Source of the Book of Abraham," *Dialogue: A Journal of Mormon Thought* 3:2 (Autumn 1968), pp. 126–133; and Stan Larson, *Quest for the Gold Plates* (Salt Lake City: Freethinker Press, 1996), pp. 104–108.

36. William W. Phelps, "Praise to the Man," *Hymns* (Salt Lake City: Deseret Book for The Church of Jesus Christ of Latter-day Saints, 1973), #147.

37. Lucy Mack Smith, "History" (draft), as cited in D. Michael Quinn, *Early Mormonism and the Magic World View* (Salt Lake City: Signature Books, 1987), pp. 54–56; Richard Bushman, *Joseph Smith and the Beginnings of Mormonism* (Urbana and Chicago: University of Illinois Press, 1984), pp. 72–73; Ronald W. Walker, "Joseph Smith: The Palmyra Seer," *BYU Studies* 24:4 (Fall 1984), p. 464; and John E. Thompson, "The Facultie of Abrac: Masonic Claims and Mormon Beginnings," *The Philalethes* 35:6 (December 1982), pp. 9 and 15. For broader context, see D. Michael Quinn, *Early Mormonism and the Magic World View* (Salt Lake City: Signature Books, 1987), pp. ix–x and 1–21.

38. Regarding Joseph Smith, Senior's use of the divining rod, see the affidavit of Peter Ingersoll, from Eber D. Howe, *Mormonism Unvailed*, as cited and discussed in Rodger I. Anderson, *Joseph Smith's New York Reputation Reexamined* (Salt Lake City: Signature Books, 1990), pp. 134–138, with 55–58 and 61–62 (note 37); and D. Michael Quinn, *Early Mormonism and the Magic World View* (Salt Lake City: Signature Books, 1987), pp. 28–36. See also Ronald W. Walker, "Joseph Smith: The Palmyra Seer," *BYU Studies* 24:4 (Fall 1984), p. 464; Richard Howard, Restoration Scriptures (Independence, Missouri: Herald Publishing House, 1969), pp. 211–212; and Barnes Frisbie, *The History of Middletown Vermont* (Published by request of the citizens of Middletown, 1867, republished in a Bicentennial Edition, Middletown Springs Historical Society, 1975), pp. 62–63 (43–64). Compare Ronald W. Walker, "The Persisting Idea of American Treasure Hunting," *BYU Studies* 24:4 (Fall 1984), pp. 440–442. Oliver Cowdery's use of the divining rod was sanctioned by Joseph Smith in an April 1829 revelation, first published as Book of Commandments VII, and currently as *Doctrine and Covenants* 8 (in which the original references to the "rod of nature" have been altered to the "gift of Aaron"). The rod continued to be used as a medium of revelation by later Church leaders, such as Heber C. Kimball and Brigham Young, who apparently used a rod to point out where the Salt Lake Temple should be built. See D. Michael Quinn, "Latter-day Saint Prayer Circles," *BYU Studies* 19:1 (Fall 1978), pp. 82–83; D. Michael Quinn, *Early Mormonism and the Magic World View* (Salt Lake City: Signature Books, 1987), pp. 204–206; and Stanley B. Kimball, *Heber C. Kimball: Mormon Patriarch and Pioneer* (Urbana, Chicago, and London: University of Illinois Press, 1981), pp. 248–249.

39. Richard Van Wagoner and Steve Walker, "Joseph Smith: The Gift of Seeing," *Dialogue: A Journal of Mormon Thought* 15:2 (Summer 1982), pp. 54–56; D. Michael Quinn, *Early Mormonism and the Magic World View* (Salt Lake City: Signature Books, 1987), pp. 36–52 (also 195–204); and the affidavits of Joseph Capron, Willard Chase, Isaac Hale, and William Stafford, from Eber D. Howe, *Mormonism Unvailed*, as cited and discussed in Rodger I. Anderson, *Joseph Smith's New York Reputation Reexamined* (Salt Lake City: Signature Books, 1990), pp. 118–119 with 32–33 (Capron), pp. 120–126 with 43–48 (Chase), pp. 126–129 (Hale), and pp. 143–146 with 48–55 (Stafford). For more discussion of these affidavits, see Marvin S. Hill, "Money Digging Folklore and the Beginnings of Mormonism: An Interpretive Suggestion," *BYU Studies* 24:4 (Fall 1984), pp. 477–482; and Rodger I. Anderson, *Joseph Smith's New York Reputation Reexamined* (Salt Lake City: Signature Books, 1990), pp. 113–116. See also Donna Hill, *Joseph Smith: The First Mormon* (Midvale, Utah: Signature Books, 1977), pp. 61–67; and Richard Bushman, *Joseph Smith and the Beginnings of Mormonism* (Urbana and Chicago: University of Illinois Press, 1984), pp. 74–76. Compare Ronald W. Walker, "The Persisting Idea of American Treasure Hunting," *BYU Studies* 24:4 (Fall 1984), pp. 442 (429–459); D. Michael Quinn, *Early Mormonism and the Magic World View* (Salt Lake City: Signature Books, 1987), pp. 21–26; *Dale Morgan on Early Mormonism*, John Phillip Walker, editor (Salt Lake City: Signature Books,

1986), pp. 227–243; and Ronald W. Walker, "Joseph Smith: The Palmyra Seer," *BYU Studies* 24:4 (Fall 1984), pp. 463–464.

40. See the affidavit of William Stafford, from Eber D. Howe, *Mormonism Unvailed*, as cited and discussed in Rodger I. Anderson, *Joseph Smith's New York Reputation Reexamined* (Salt Lake City: Signature Books, 1990), pp. 143–146 with 48–55; H. Michael Marquardt and Wesley P. Walters, *Inventing Mormonism* (Salt Lake City: Signature Books, 1994), pp. 70, 180–181; D. Michael Quinn, *Early Mormonism and the Magic World View* (Salt Lake City: Signature Books, 1987), pp. 53–111; and Donna Hill, *Joseph Smith: The First Mormon* (Midvale, Utah: Signature Books, 1977), pp. 65–66. Compare Francis W. Kirkham, *A New Witness for Christ in America* (Independence, Missouri: Zion's Printing and Publishing Co., 1942), Vol. I, p. 292, and Ronald W. Walker, "The Persisting Idea of American Treasure Hunting," *BYU Studies* 24:4 (Fall 1984), p. 445.

41. H. Michael Marquardt and Wesley P. Walters, *Inventing Mormonism* (Salt Lake City: Signature Books, 1994), pp. 70–75. Compare Lucy Mack Smith, *History of Joseph Smith by His Mother, Lucy Mack Smith*, edited by Preston Nibley (Salt Lake City: Bookcraft, 1958), pp. 91–92, with Articles of Agreement, November 1, 1825, as cited in Francis W. Kirkham, *A New Witness for Christ in America* (Independence, Missouri: Zion's Printing and Publishing Co., 1942), Vol. I, pp. 493–494. See also *Dale Morgan on Early Mormonism*, John Phillip Walker, editor (Salt Lake City: Signature Books, 1986), pp. 321–339; and D. Michael Quinn, *Early Mormonism and the Magic World View* (Salt Lake City: Signature Books, 1987), pp. 44–46.

42. Linda King Newell and Valeen Tippetts Avery, *Mormon Enigma: Emma Hale Smith* (Garden City, New York: Doubleday and Company, 1984), p. 25. It is curious that in 1828 Joseph Smith would seek fellowship with a church, having been forbidden in his First Vision to "join with any of them." See *Pearl of Great Price: Joseph Smith—History* 1:19, 20 and 26.

43. Richard Van Wagoner and Steve Walker, "Joseph Smith: The Gift of Seeing," *Dialogue: A Journal of Mormon Thought* 15:2 (Summer 1982), pp. 56–57; H. Michael Marquardt and Wesley P. Walters, *Inventing Mormonism* (Salt Lake City: Signature Books, 1994), pp. 89–103; and the affidavit of Isaac Hale, from Eber D. Howe, *Mormonism Unvailed*, as cited and discussed in Rodger I. Anderson, *Joseph Smith's New York Reputation Reexamined* (Salt Lake City: Signature Books, 1990), pp. 126–129. Compare D. Michael Quinn, *Early Mormonism and the Magic World View* (Salt Lake City: Signature Books, 1987), pp. 112–143. Judge Hosea Stout recorded in his journal that "President [Brigham] Young exhibited the Seer's stone with which The Prophet Joseph discovered the plates of the Book of Mormon" at a meeting of the Board of Regents of the University of Deseret on February 25, 1856. See *On the Mormon Frontier, The Diary of Hosea Stout, Volume Two 1848–1861*, edited by Juanita Brooks (Utah State Historical Society, University of Utah Press, reprint edition 1982), p. 593.

44. Richard Van Wagoner and Steve Walker, "Joseph Smith: The Gift of Seeing," *Dialogue: A Journal of Mormon Thought* 15:2 (Summer 1982), pp. 49–54; H. Michael Marquardt and Wesley P. Walters, *Inventing Mormonism* (Salt Lake City: Signature Books, 1994), pp. 103–106; D. Michael Quinn, *Early Mormonism and the Magic World View* (Salt Lake City: Signature Books, 1987), pp. 143–149; and James E. Lancaster, "The Translation of the Book of Mormon," from *The Word of God*, edited by Dan Vogel (Salt Lake City: Signature Books, 1990), pp. 97–112. See also David Whitmer, *An Address to All Believers in Christ* (Richmond, Missouri: David Whitmer, 1887), photographic reprint, p. 12; Lawrence Foster, *Religion and Sexuality* (New York and Oxford: Oxford University Press, 1981), pp.

295–297; and Scott C. Dunn, "Spirit Writing: Another Look at the Book of Mormon," *Sunstone* 10:6 (June 1985), pp. 17–26.

45. Richard Van Wagoner and Steve Walker, "Joseph Smith: The Gift of Seeing," *Dialogue: A Journal of Mormon Thought* 15:2 (Summer 1982), pp. 57–63; and David Whitmer, *An Address to All Believers in Christ* (Richmond, Missouri: David Whitmer, 1887), photographic reprint, p. 31.

46. *Doctrine and Covenants* 111:4. Compare with *The Personal Writings of Joseph Smith*, compiled and edited by Dean C. Jessee (Salt Lake City: Deseret Book, 1984), pp. 349–350; and D. Michael Quinn, *Early Mormonism and the Magic World View* (Salt Lake City: Signature Books, 1987), pp. 206–211. See also *The Personal Writings of Joseph Smith*, compiled and edited by Dean C. Jessee (Salt Lake City: Deseret Book, 1984), pp. 358–359.

47. Reed C. Durham, "Is There No Help for the Widow's Son?" (Nauvoo, Illinois: Martin Publishing Company, 1980, photographic reprint), p. 17. For illustrations, see William Morgan, *Illustrations of Masonry* (Printed for the proprietor, 1827, reprint Chicago: Ezra A. Cook Publications), pp. 104–110; Edmond Ronayne, *Ronayne's Handbook of Freemasonry* (Chicago: Ezra A. Cook, 1950), pp. 16–17 (with 69–70), 26–27 (with 122–123), 33–34 (with 170–173), 74–75, 126–127, 140–142, 176–177, 208–209, 211–212, 215–217, and 229; or Malcolm C. Duncan, *Duncan's Masonic Ritual and Monitor* (New York: David McKay Company), pp. 17–18, 66–67, and 121.

48. Reed C. Durham, "Is There No Help for the Widow's Son?" (Nauvoo, Illinois: Martin Publishing Company, 1980, photographic reprint), pp. 22–23 and 28; and D. Michael Quinn, *Early Mormonism and the Magic World View* (Salt Lake City: Signature Books, 1987), pp. 65–77. For illustrations of the Jupiter talisman, see Francis Barrett, *The Magus* (London: Printed for Lackington, Allen, and Co., Temple of the Muses, Finsbury Square, 1801, photographic reprint Secaucus, New Jersey: The Citadel Press, 1967), p. 143 (facing) and p. 174 (facing), Fig. 1, No. 2; or D. Michael Quinn, *Early Mormonism and the Magic World View* (Salt Lake City: Signature Books, 1987), figures 27–36.

49. Bruce R. McConkie, "Magic," from *Mormon Doctrine* (Salt Lake City: Bookcraft, 1958), pp. 421–422. See also "Occultism," p. 490, and "Sorcery," p. 675. Compare Joseph F. Smith, *Gospel Doctrine* (Salt Lake City: Deseret Book, 1920), Chapter 21, pp. 470–473.

50. Richard S. Van Wagoner, *Mormon Polygamy: A History* (Salt Lake City: Signature Books, 1986), p. v (iii–vi). Compare *Doctrine and Covenants* 132:1–6 and Official Declaration–1.

51. Linda King Newell and Valeen Tippetts Avery, *Mormon Enigma: Emma Hale Smith* (Garden City, New York: Doubleday and Company, 1984), pp. 95, 98–99, 132–137 and 147.

52. Lawrence Foster, *Religion and Sexuality* (New York and Oxford: Oxford University Press, 1981), p. 155.

53. D. Michael Quinn, "LDS Church Authority and New Plural Marriages, 1890–1904," *Dialogue: A Journal of Mormon Thought* 18:1 (Spring 1985), pp. 19–23, 46, and 95–98. See also Lawrence Foster, *Religion and Sexuality* (New York and Oxford: Oxford University Press, 1981), pp. 133–134 with 137–139; George D. Smith, "Nauvoo Roots of Mormon Polygamy, 1841–46: A Preliminary Demographic Report," *Dialogue: A Journal of Mormon Thought* 27:1 (Spring 1994), p. 12; and Richard S. Van Wagoner, *Mormon Polygamy: A History* (Salt Lake City: Signature Books, 1986), p. 35.

54. Richard S. Van Wagoner, *Mormon Polygamy: A History* (Salt Lake City: Signature Books, 1986), pp. 4, 6, 12–13, and 18–20. See also note 53.

55. Richard S. Van Wagoner, *Mormon Polygamy: A History* (Salt Lake City: Signature Books, 1986), pp. 27–35 (with pp. 99–100), 37-38, and Lawrence Foster, *Religion and Sexuality* (New York and Oxford: Oxford University Press, 1981), pp. 159–160. Compare Linda

King Newell and Valeen Tippetts Avery, *Mormon Enigma: Emma Hale Smith* (Garden City, New York: Doubleday and Company, 1984), p. 177.

56. Richard S. Van Wagoner, *Mormon Polygamy: A History* (Salt Lake City: Signature Books, 1986), pp. 38–43 or "Mormon Polyandry in Nauvoo," *Dialogue: A Journal of Mormon Thought* 18:3 (Fall 1985), pp. 76–81. See also George D. Smith, "Nauvoo Roots of Mormon Polygamy, 1841–46: A Preliminary Demographic Report," *Dialogue: A Journal of Mormon Thought* 27:1 (Spring 1994), pp. 10–11. Compare *Doctrine and Covenants* 132:1 and 37–39 with Lawrence Foster, *Religion and Sexuality* (New York and Oxford: Oxford University Press, 1981), p. 173.

57. Stanley B. Kimball, *Heber C. Kimball: Mormon Patriarch and Pioneer* (Urbana, Chicago, and London: University of Illinois Press, 1981), p. 93.

58. Linda King Newell and Valeen Tippetts Avery, *Mormon Enigma: Emma Hale Smith* (Garden City, New York: Doubleday and Company, 1984), pp. 146–147.

59. Lawrence Foster, *Religion and Sexuality* (New York and Oxford: Oxford University Press, 1981), pp. 151–153. Compare *Doctrine and Covenants* 132:1–6, 54, 64–65; and Linda King Newell and Valeen Tippetts Avery, *Mormon Enigma: Emma Hale Smith* (Garden City, New York: Doubleday and Company, 1984), pp. 100–101 (with p. 65) and 146.

60. Lawrence Foster, *Religion and Sexuality* (New York and Oxford: Oxford University Press, 1981), pp. 151–153; and Linda King Newell and Valeen Tippetts Avery, *Mormon Enigma: Emma Hale Smith* (Garden City, New York: Doubleday and Company, 1984), pp. 89, 137–139, 142–144, and 146–147. See also George D. Smith, "Nauvoo Roots of Mormon Polygamy, 1841–46: A Preliminary Demographic Report," *Dialogue: A Journal of Mormon Thought* 27:1 (Spring 1994), pp. 7 and 10.

Chapter 10: *Christ the Tiger*

1. T.S. Eliot, "Gerontion," *The Complete Poems and Plays 1909–1950* (San Diego: Harcourt Brace Jovanovich, 1971), p. 21.

2. Sheldon Van Auken, *A Severe Mercy* (San Francisco: Harper & Row, 1977), pp. 94–96 (also 67–68).

3. T.S. Eliot, "Burnt Norton," from *Four Quartets*, published in *The Complete Poems and Plays 1909–1950* (San Diego: Harcourt Brace Jovanovich, 1971), p. 119 (117–122)

Chapter 11: *Reason for the Hope*

1. *Pearl of Great Price: Joseph Smith—History* 1:18–20; Book of Mormon: 1 Nephi 13:5–9 and 14:9–13; *Doctrine and Covenants* 1:15–16 and 112:23; Orson Pratt, "Baptism for the Remission of Sins," *The Seer* Vol. II, No. 4 (April 1854), p. 255; Bruce R. McConkie, "Salvation" and "Salvation by Grace," from *Mormon Doctrine* (Salt Lake City: Bookcraft, 1958), pp. 603 and 604; "What the Mormons Think of Christ," pamphlet (The Church of Jesus Christ of Latter-day Saints, 1982), pp. 19–20; and Bruce R. McConkie, "What Think Ye of Salvation by Grace?" BYU Devotional, January 10, 1984, transcript, pp. 1–5.

2. Dorothy Sayers, *Gaudy Night* (New York: Avon Books, 1968), pp. 278–279.

3. *Pearl of Great Price*: Articles of Faith 8.

4. *Teachings of the Prophet Joseph Smith*, Joseph Fielding Smith, editor (Salt Lake City: Deseret News Press, 1956), pp. 10–11; or *History of the Church* (Salt Lake City: Deseret Book, 1978), Vol. I, p. 245. See also LDS Bible Dictionary, Holy Bible (Salt Lake City: The Church of Jesus Christ of Latter-day Saints, 1979), p. 624.

5. *Teachings of the Prophet Joseph Smith*, Joseph Fielding Smith, editor (Salt Lake City: Deseret News Press, 1956), p. 327; or *History of the Church* (Salt Lake City: Deseret Book,

1978), Vol. VI, p. 57. See also LDS Bible Dictionary, Holy Bible (Salt Lake City: The Church of Jesus Christ of Latter-day Saints, 1979), p. 624; and Orson Pratt, "Questions and Answers on Doctrine," *The Seer* Vol. II, No. 2 (April 1854), p. 213.

6. LDS Bible Dictionary, Holy Bible (Salt Lake City: The Church of Jesus Christ of Latter-day Saints, 1979), pp. 623–624; and James E. Talmage, *Articles of Faith* (Salt Lake City: The Church of Jesus Christ of Latter-day Saints, 1949), Chapter 1, p. 7, and Chapter 13, pp. 236–237. Compare *Pearl of Great Price: Joseph Smith—History* 1:12. See also *Doctrine and Covenants* 68:4; Joseph Fielding Smith, *Doctrines of Salvation* (Salt Lake City: Bookcraft, 1956), Vol. I, p. 186; Brigham Young, *Journal of Discourses* (Liverpool: F.D. Richards, 1855, photo reprint, 1966), Vol. XIII, p. 264; and Wilford Woodruff, as quoted by Ezra Taft Benson, "Fourteen Fundamentals in Following the Prophets," BYU Devotional, February 26, 1980, press copy, pp. 3–4.

7. Gleason L. Archer, Jr., *A Survey of Old Testament Introduction* (Chicago: Moody Press, 1964), p. 19. See also F. F. Bruce, *Second Thoughts on the Dead Sea Scrolls* (Grand Rapids, Michigan: Eerdmans, 1980), pp. 61–69; Millar Burrows, *The Dead Sea Scrolls*, as included in *Burrows on the Dead Sea Scrolls* (Grand Rapids, Michigan: Baker, 1978), pp. 303–304; and Richard N. Ostling, "Secrets of the Dead Sea Scrolls," *Time*, August 14, 1989, pp. 71–72.

8. F. F. Bruce, *The Books and the Parchments* (Westwood: Revell, 1963), p. 178.

9. F. F. Bruce, *The New Testament Documents: Are They Reliable?* (Downers Grove, Illinois: InterVarsity Press, 1983), pp. 19–20.

10. Ibid., p. 15.

11. The first ancient extra-biblical reference to the "House of David" was found in 1993 at Tel Dan. See "'David' Found at Dan," *Biblical Archaeology Review* Vol. XX, No. 2 (March/April 1994), pp. 26–39; André Lemaire, "'House of David'" Restored in Moabite Inscription," *Biblical Archaeology Review* Vol. XX, No. 3 (May/June 1994), pp. 30–37; Philip R. Davies, "'House of David'" Built on Sand," *Biblical Archaeology Review* Vol. XX, No. 4 (July/August 1994), pp. 54–55; Anson Rainey, The "House of David' and the House of the Deconstructionists," *Biblical Archaeology Review* Vol. XX, No. 6 (November/December 1994), p. 47; David Noel Freedman and Jeffrey C. Geoghegan, "'House of David' Is There!" *Biblical Archaeology Review* Vol. XXI, No. 2 (March/April 1995), pp. 78–79; and "Is This Man a Biblical Archaeologist?" *Biblical Archaeology Review* Vol. XXII, No. 4 (July/August 1996), pp. 34–36.

A tomb inscribed with the name of Caiaphas, the High Priest who presided at the trial of Jesus, was unearthed in 1990. See Zvi Greenhut, "Burial Cave of the Caiaphas Family," and Ronny Reich, "Caiaphas Name Inscribed on Bone Boxes," *Biblical Archaeology Review* Vol. XVIII, No. 5 (September/October 1992), pp. 28–44 and 76.

The biblical story of the Israelite assault on Jericho has similarly received new support from archaeological studies in recent years. See "Score One for the Bible," *Time*, March 5, 1990; Bryant Wood, "Did the Israelites Conquer Jericho?" *Biblical Archaeology Review* Vol. XVI, No. 2 (March/April 1990), pp. 44–58; Piotr Bienkowski, "Jericho Was Destroyed in the Middle Bronze Age, Not the Late Bronze Age" *Biblical Archaeology Review* Vol. XVI, No. 5 (September/October 1990), pp. 45–46; and Bryant Wood, "Dating Jericho's Destruction: Bienkowski Is Wrong on All Counts," *Biblical Archaeology Review* Vol. XVI, No. 5 (September/October 1990), pp. 45–49 and 68–69.

12. For general information on archaeology and biblical historicity from a Christian perspective, see Edwin Yamauchi, *The Stones and the Scriptures* (Grand Rapids, Michigan: Baker, 1972); F. F. Bruce, *Israel and the Nations* (Grand Rapids, Michigan: Eerdmans, 1969); Clifford A. Wilson, *Rocks, Relics, and Biblical Reliability* (Grand Rapids, Michigan: Zondervan, 1977); D. J. Wiseman, "Archaeology and the Old Testament," and Edwin

Yamauchi, "Archaeology and the New Testament," from *The Expositor's Bible Commentary,* Frank E. Gaebelein, general editor (Grand Rapids, Michigan: Zondervan, 1979), Vol. I, pp. 309–335 and pp. 647–669, with references. See also "Is the Bible Right After All?" *Biblical Archaeology Review* 22:5 (September/October 1996), pp. 34–37.

13. Luke opens his gospel, for instance, with a statement that assumes the objective historicity of the events to which his companions, the apostles, were "eyewitnesses" (Luke 1:1–4). In his introduction to the book of Acts, he speaks of the "many infallible proofs" that undergird the resurrection of Jesus (Acts 1:1–3). The apostle John left his personal eyewitness testimony for the world, saying, "That which was from the beginning, which we have heard, which we have seen with our eyes, which we have looked upon, and our hands have handled, of the Word of life; . . . that which we have seen and heard declare we unto you" (1 John 1:1–3). Peter appealed to the common knowledge of the specifics of Jesus' life and ministry in his address on the Day of Pentecost, reminding his listeners that Jesus was "a man approved of God among you by miracles and wonders and signs, which God did by him in the midst of you, as ye yourselves also know" (Acts 2:22). The apostle Paul made a similar appeal in his defense before Agrippa, saying "the king knoweth of these things . . . none of these things are hidden from him; for this thing was not done in a corner" (Acts 26:24–26). Paul also took pains to list the witnesses of the resurrection, noting that most were still living at the time of his writing and could easily corroborate his testimony (1 Cor. 15:3–8). See J.P. Moreland, *Scaling the Secular City* (Grand Rapids, Michigan: Baker Book House, 1987), pp. 133–157.

14. Some of the biblical events and characters Jesus treated as historical are the creation (Matt. 19:4–5), the murder of Abel (Matt. 23:35), Noah and the flood (Matt. 24:38-39 and Luke 17:27), the destruction of Sodom and the turning of Lot's wife into a pillar of salt (Luke 17:28–29, compare Matt. 10:15), the patriarchs, Abraham, Isaac, and Jacob (Matt. 8:11), King David (Matt. 12:3–4), the prophets Elijah and Elisha (Luke 4:25–27), the miraculous provision of manna (John 6:49), and the story of the prophet Jonah and the whale (Matt. 12:40).

Moreover, Jesus validated the scriptural canon as it was constituted in His day (Luke 24:27 and 44–45). His use of these writings is illuminating. For example, He successfully resisted the temptations of Satan by quoting from Scripture (Matt. 4:1–11). In doing so, He emphasized the necessity of reliance on the Word of God (Matt. 4:4), inferring its trustworthiness. He spoke of the authority of the Law and the Prophets, and their total fulfillment, even down to the smallest details (Matt. 5:17–18) and confidently proclaimed Himself to be the fulfillment of Scripture (John 5:39–40, also Matt. 21:42, 26:56). He authoritatively referred to Scripture in answering the questions that were put to Him (Luke 10:25–28), and chided His contemporaries for their misunderstanding of Scripture (Matt. 22:29), inferring that a propositional truth existed that judged their interpretations.

Furthermore, Jesus made special preparations for the eventual writing of the New Testament. He knew His words were going to be preserved (Matt. 24:35) and personally commissioned His apostles to be the eyewitnesses of His life and ministry (John 1:1–4 and 19:35, also 21:24 and 2 Peter 1:16). When a new apostle was chosen, it was on the basis of this objective experience rather than a subjective profession of faith (Acts 1:21–22 and Heb. 2:3). He gifted the apostles with special authority (Matt. 10:40 and Eph. 2:19–20) and inspiration for the task of passing on the story accurately (John 14:25–26 and 16:12–13, compare 1 Cor. 2:12–13 and Gal. 1:11–12). It is evident that they were conscious of their unique position—they exercised the authority Christ had given them and expected the churches to acknowledge it as well, both when they were physically present and in their writings (1 Cor. 2:12–13, 14:37, Gal. 1:8–9, Col. 4:16, Thess. 2:13, 5:27, 1 John 4:6, and Rev. 1:3).

15. See *Ps. 12:6–7, 119:89–90, 160, Isa. 40:8* (compare 1 Peter 1:23–25), *55:8–11,* Matt. 5:17–18, *24:35,* and Luke 24:27, 44–45.

16. See also *Deut. 8:3* (compare Job 23:12 and Matt. 4:4), *Isa. 8:20,* Matt. 22:29, *John 8:31–32* (compare 15:3), *20:30–31* (compare 5:39–40), *1 Cor. 4:6, 2 Peter 1:20–21* (compare 3:15–16), and *1 John 5:13.* Compare *Prov. 30:5–6,* Deut. 4:1–2, and Rev. 22:18–19.

17. Martin Luther, as cited in *Eerdmans Handbook of the History of Christianity* (Grand Rapids, Michigan: Eerdmans, 1977), p. 364.

18. See also Deut. 4:35, 39, 32:39, 1 Sam. 2:2, 2 Sam. 7:22 (also 1 Chron. 17:20), 1 Kings 8:60, 2 Kings 19:19, *Mark 12:28–34, John 17:3,* Rom. 3:29–30, *1 Cor. 8:4–6* (compare with Ps. 96:4–5 and 1 Cor. 10:14–21), *Eph. 4:4–6, 1 Tim. 1:17,* 2:5–6 (also Gal. 3:20), James 2:19, Jude 4, 25.

19. See also *Isa. 37:* 16, 20, 45:5–7, 18–19, *21–22,* and 46:9–10.

20. *Teachings of the Prophet Joseph Smith,* Joseph Fielding Smith, editor (Salt Lake City: Deseret News Press, 1956), p. 349; or *History of the Church* (Salt Lake City: Deseret Book, 1978), Vol. VI, p. 308; also reprinted as part of the series, "Classics in Mormon Thought," *The Ensign* (April 1971), p. 17. Compare with *Pearl of Great Price: Abraham 4–5.* See also *Teachings of the Prophet Joseph Smith,* Joseph Fielding Smith, editor (Salt Lake City: Deseret News Press, 1956), p. 370–371; or *History of the Church* (Salt Lake City: Deseret Book, 1978), Vol. VI, pp. 474–475.

21. *Teachings of the Prophet Joseph Smith,* Joseph Fielding Smith, editor (Salt Lake City: Deseret News Press, 1956), pp. 346–347; or *History of the Church* (Salt Lake City: Deseret Book, 1978), Vol. VI, p. 306; also reprinted as part of the series, "Classics in Mormon Thought," *The Ensign* (April 1971), p. 16. See also *Doctrine and Covenants* 76:50–59, 92–95, 84:33–39, 88:107, 132:16–17, 19–20 and 37; *Teachings of the Prophet Joseph Smith,* Joseph Fielding Smith, editor (Salt Lake City: Deseret News Press, 1956), pp. 370–371, or *History of the Church* (Salt Lake City: Deseret Book, 1978), Vol. VI, pp. 474–475, and Bruce R. McConkie, "Plurality of Gods," from *Mormon Doctrine* (Salt Lake City: Bookcraft, 1958), p. 521. Compare with references under note 44.

22. God is the Supreme Being: *1 Chron. 29:10–13, Isa. 40:18–31,* 55:8–9. There is "none like" Him: Exod. 8:8–10, 9:13–16, 15:11, 2 Sam. 7:22 (also 1 Chron. 17:20), Ps. 35:10, 71:19, 86:8, 89:8, and Micah 7:18. God is "above the heavens": Deut. 10:14, 33:26, 1 Kings 8:23, 27 (also 2 Chron. 6:14, 18), 2 Chron. 2:5–6, Neh. 9:5–6, *Ps. 8:1,* 57:5, 11, 68:33, 108:5, and 113:4–5, also *Jer.* 10:6–7 and *23:23–24.* God is the "most high": *Gen. 14:18–20,* Deut. 32:7–8, 2 Sam. 22:14, *Ps. 7:17,* 9:2, 21:7, 46:4, 47:2, 50:14, 56:2, 57:2, 73:11, 77:10, 78:17, 56, 82:6, 83:18, 91:1, 9, 92:1, 8, 107:11, Isa. 14:14, Lam. 3:35, 38, Dan. 3:26, 4:17, 24–25, 32, 34, 5:18, 21, 7:18, 22, 25, 27, Hos. 7:16, 11:7, Acts 7:48, and Heb. 6:18, also 7:1 (compare Mark 5:6–7, Luke 8:28, and Acts 16:16–18 with James 2:19). God is "the highest": *Luke* 1:32, 35, 76, *2:14,* 6:35, Pss. 18:13, and 87:5. God is morally perfect, the most "holy" and "most just," the "only wise," and the only "good": 1 Sam. 2:2, Job 34:10–17, *Mark 10:17–18* or Luke 18:18–19, also Rom. 16:27, 1 Tim. 1:17, *Jude 25,* and Rev. 15:4.

23. *Teachings of the Prophet Joseph Smith,* Joseph Fielding Smith, editor (Salt Lake City: Deseret News Press, 1956), p. 373; or *History of the Church* (Salt Lake City: Deseret Book, 1978), Vol. VI, p. 476.

24. See Orson Pratt, "The Pre-Existence of Man," *The Seer* Vol. I, No. 9 (April 1854), p. 132; and James E. Talmage, *Articles of Faith* (Salt Lake City: The Church of Jesus Christ of Latter-day Saints, 1949), Chapter 23, p. 430. Compare Bruce R. McConkie, "Eternal Progression," from *Mormon Doctrine* (Salt Lake City: Bookcraft, 1958), pp. 220–221.

25. *Teachings of the Prophet Joseph Smith,* Joseph Fielding Smith, editor (Salt Lake City: Deseret News Press, 1956), pp. 347–348; or *History of the Church* (Salt Lake City: Deseret Book, 1978), Vol. VI, p. 306; also reprinted as part of the series, "Classics in Mormon Thought," *The Ensign* (April 1971), p. 16. Also, compare *Doctrine and Covenants* 76:92 and 137:1–3 with 130:10–11.

26. See also *Ps.* 41:13, *93:2, 106:48,* Is. 63:16, and Hab. 1:12. God is "the first" and "the last": *Isa.* 41:4, 44:6, and *48:12.*

27. God is self-existent: *Exod. 3:14–15.* He does not change: *Ps. 102:25–27* (also Isa. 51:6), Mal. 3:6, and *James 1:16–17.* He is not a "man": *Num. 23:19, Ps. 50:21,* and Hos. 11:9 (compare Deut. 4:15–16 and *Rom. 1:22–23*).

28. *Teachings of the Prophet Joseph Smith,* Joseph Fielding Smith, editor (Salt Lake City: Deseret News Press, 1956), pp. 345–346; or *History of the Church* (Salt Lake City: Deseret Book, 1978), Vol. VI, p. 305; also reprinted as part of the series, "Classics in Mormon Thought," *The Ensign* (April 1971), pp. 15–16. See also James E. Talmage, *Articles of Faith* (Salt Lake City: The Church of Jesus Christ of Latter-day Saints, 1949), Chapter 23, p. 430; Milton R. Hunter, *The Gospel Through the Ages* (Salt Lake City: Stevens and Wallis, 1945), Chapter 17, pp. 114–115; and Bruce R. McConkie, "Man of Holiness," from *Mormon Doctrine* (Salt Lake City: Bookcraft, 1958), p. 424. Compare with references listed under note 23.

29. God created all things, including the heavens and the earth: Gen. 1:1–2:1, 2:4, Exod. 20:11, 31:17, 2 Kings 19:15, 1 Chron. 16:26, 2 Chron. 2:12, *Neh. 9:5–6,* Job 9:1–9, chapters 38–41, *Pss.* 8:3–4, 89:11–12, 95:3–6, *96:4-5,* 102:25, 104:1–35, 115:15, 121:1–2, 124:8, 134:3, 136:5–9, 146:5–6, Prov. 26:10, Isa. 37:16, 40:12–14, 18–28, 42:5, 44:24, 45:7, 12, 18, Jer. 32:17, 51:15, Jonah 1:9, Acts 4:24, 14:15, Rev. 4:11, and 14:7. Compare *Jer. 10:10–13.*

30. God created man, body and spirit: *Gen. 2:7,* Deut. 4:32, 32:18, Job 4:15, 10:8–9, 31:15, 32:8, 22, 33:4–6, 35:10, 36:3, *Pss.* 8:1–9, *33:15–16,* 94:9, 95:6–7, 100:3, *103:13–16,* 119:73, *139:13–16,* Prov. 22:2, Eccles. 12:1, *Isa. 42:5,* 43:1, 5–7, 44:2, 21, 24, 45:9–12, 49:5, 51:13, 54:5, *57:16,* Jer. 1:5, 27:5, Hos. 8:14, *Amos 4:13, Zech. 12:1,* Mal. 2:10, Mark 10:6, *Acts 17:24–26,* Rom. 1:25, 9:20–23, and 1 Tim. 2:13.

31. *Teachings of the Prophet Joseph Smith,* Joseph Fielding Smith, editor (Salt Lake City: Deseret News Press, 1956), pp. 351–352; or *History of the Church* (Salt Lake City: Deseret Book, 1978), Vol. VI, pp. 308–309; also reprinted as part of the series, "Classics in Mormon Thought," *The Ensign* (April 1971), p. 17. Compare *Doctrine and Covenants* 93:33, 131:7–8, Pearl of Great Price: Abraham 3:24, and 4:1. See also Bruce R. McConkie, "Creation" and "Elements," from *Mormon Doctrine* (Salt Lake City: Bookcraft, 1958), pp. 156 and 202. On the eternal self-existence of man, see *Doctrine and Covenants* 93:29, *Pearl of Great Price:* Abraham 3:4–5, *Teachings of the Prophet Joseph Smith,* Joseph Fielding Smith, editor (Salt Lake City: Deseret News Press, 1956), pp. 352–354; or *History of the Church* (Salt Lake City: Deseret Book, 1978), Vol. VI, pp. 310–312; also reprinted as part of the series, "Classics in Mormon Thought," *The Ensign* (May 1971), pp. 13–14. Compare *History of the Church* (Salt Lake City: Deseret Book, 1978), Vol. III, p. 387; Brigham Young, as cited in *Journal of Discourses* (Liverpool: F.D. Richards, 1855, photo reprint, 1966), Vol. 1, p. 50; and Heber J. Grant, as cited in *Latter-day Prophets Speak,* edited by Daniel H. Ludlow (Salt Lake City: Bookcraft, 1969), p. 4.

32. There is only one God: *Deut. 6:4, Isa. 43:10–11, 44:6, 8,* and the references listed under notes 16–17. The Father is God (2 Cor. 1:3, Eph. 1:3, Col. 1:2–3, and 1 Peter 1:3), a Spirit (*John 1:18, 4:24,* Col. 1:15, *1 Tim.* 1:17, *6:15–16,* and Heb. 11:27). The Son is God (*Matt. 1:23, John 1:1–4, 20:26–29, Acts 20:28, Col. 2:8–10, 1 Tim. 3:16,* along with references listed under note 32), incarnate (John 1:14). The Holy Spirit is God (*Acts 5:3–4* and *2 Cor.*

3:17). Trinitarian passages include *Matt. 28:19*, John 14:16–18, 26, 15:26, *Rom. 8:9–11, 1 Cor. 12:4–6, 2 Cor. 13:14*, Eph. 1:17, 2:18, 3:14–19, Heb. 9:14, and 1 Peter 1:2.

33. *Teachings of the Prophet Joseph Smith*, Joseph Fielding Smith, editor (Salt Lake City: Deseret News Press, 1956), p. 370 (369–376); or *History of the Church* (Salt Lake City: Deseret Book, 1978), Vol. VI, p. 474 (473–479). See also James E. Talmage, *Jesus the Christ* (Salt Lake City: Deseret Book Company, 1962), Chapter 4, pp. 32–33; and Joseph F. Smith, as cited in *Latter-day Prophets Speak*, edited by Daniel H. Ludlow (Salt Lake City: Bookcraft, 1969), p. 273. For references to the LDS teaching that God has a material body, see *Doctrine and Covenants* 130:3 and 22 (compare 129:1–3); *Pearl of Great Price*: Moses 6:9; and *Teachings of the Prophet Joseph Smith*, Joseph Fielding Smith, editor (Salt Lake City: Deseret News Press, 1956), p. 181. Compare Bruce R. McConkie, "First Vision," from *Mormon Doctrine* (Salt Lake City: Bookcraft, 1958), p. 265.

34. See also *Isa. 9:6*, Dan. 7:13–14, Micah 5:2, *John 10:30, 12:37–41 (with Isa. 6:1–10), 14:8–11*, 17:5, 1 Cor. 10:1–4, Eph. 4:9–10, *Phil. 2:6–11, Col. 1:15–19* (with Eph. 3:9), *Heb. 1:1–4*, 8–12, 7:26, 13:8, Rev. 1:8, 11, 17, 17:14, 19:11–16, 21:6, and 22:13. The apostle John writes that Jesus, in a heated exchange with his enemies, declared that "Before Abraham was, I am" (John 8:56–59), thus applying to Himself the sacred name by which the God of Abraham, Isaac, and Jacob had revealed Himself to Moses. Jesus' monotheistic audience had no trouble understanding the meaning of His declaration and promptly picked up rocks to stone Him for blasphemy, or, as it is described in another passage, "making himself equal with God" (John 5:18).

35. See *Pearl of Great Price*: Abraham 3:22–28; *Doctrine and Covenants* 93:11–14; Bruce R. McConkie, "Christ," from *Mormon Doctrine* (Salt Lake City: Bookcraft, 1958), p. 121; Milton R. Hunter, *The Gospel Through the Ages* (Salt Lake City: Stevens and Wallis, 1945), Chapter 3, p. 15; and Joseph F. Smith, as cited in *Latter-day Prophets Speak*, edited by Daniel H. Ludlow (Salt Lake City: Bookcraft, 1969), p. 281.

36. T.S. Eliot, "The Dry Salvages," from *Four Quartets*, published in The *Complete Poems and Plays 1909–1950* (San Diego: Harcourt Brace Jovanovich, 1971), p. 136 (130–137)

37. See Matt. 1:18–23 (compare Isa. 7:14) and Luke 1:26–38.

38. Bruce R. McConkie, "Only Begotten Son" and "Son of God," from *Mormon Doctrine* (Salt Lake City: Bookcraft, 1958), pp. 494 and 670; James E. Talmage, *Jesus the Christ* (Salt Lake City: Deseret Book Company, 1962), Chapter 7, p. 81; Joseph Fielding Smith, *Doctrines of Salvation* (Salt Lake City: Bookcraft, 1956), Vol. I, p. 19; and Brigham Young, *Journal of Discourses* (Liverpool: F.D. Richards, 1855, photo reprint, 1966), Vol. I, pp. 50–51; Vol. IV, p. 218; and Vol. VIII, p. 115.

39. See also Ps. 143:1–2, Eccles. 9:1–3, *Isa. 53:6, Mark 10:17–18, Rom. 3:10–11* (also Ps. 14:2–3), and 5:18–19. Compare Matt. 9:12–13 and Acts 17:29–30.

40. See also Gen. 8:21, Ps. 58:3, Prov. 22:15, Hos. 6:6–7, Matt. 7:11 (also Luke 11:13), John 8:39–44, and Eph. 2:1–3.

41. Pearl of Great Price: Articles of Faith 2. See also *Book of Mormon*: 2 Nephi 2:22–25 (with *Doctrine and Covenants* 93:38–39; and Bruce R. McConkie, "Original Sin Theory," from *Mormon Doctrine* (Salt Lake City: Bookcraft, 1958), p. 497.

42. John A. Widstoe, *Evidences and Reconciliations* (Salt Lake City: Bookcraft, 1960), p. 195.

43. Joseph Fielding Smith, *Doctrines of Salvation* (Salt Lake City: Bookcraft, 1956), Vol. I, p. 114. See also James E. Talmage, *Jesus the Christ* (Salt Lake City: Deseret Book Company, 1962), Chapter 3, pp. 65 and 70; and John A. Widstoe, *Evidences and Reconciliations* (Salt Lake City: Bookcraft, 1960), pp. 192–195. Compare *Pearl of Great Price*: Moses 5:10–11.

44. *Teachings of the Prophet Joseph Smith,* Joseph Fielding Smith, editor (Salt Lake City: Deseret News Press, 1956), p. 332; or *History of the Church* (Salt Lake City: Deseret Book, 1978), Vol. VI, p. 223. See also *Book of Mormon:* 2 Nephi 25:23, Mosiah 4:6–8, and 3 Nephi 27:13–22; *Doctrine and Covenants* 14:7, 76:52, 130:20–21, 132:5, and 138:1–4; "What the Mormons Think of Christ," pamphlet (The Church of Jesus Christ of Latter-day Saints, 1982), pp. 18–20; and Spencer W. Kimball, "Jesus of Nazareth," from *The Ensign* (December 1984).

45. Heber J. Grant, as cited in *Latter-day Prophets Speak,* edited by Daniel H. Ludlow (Salt Lake City: Bookcraft, 1969), p. 139.

46. Spencer W. Kimball, "The Abundant Life," from *The Ensign* (October 1985), pp. 5–6. See also Joseph F. Smith, as cited in *Latter-day Prophets Speak,* edited by Daniel H. Ludlow (Salt Lake City: Bookcraft, 1969), p. 73; Bruce R. McConkie, "Godhood," from *Mormon Doctrine* (Salt Lake City: Bookcraft, 1958), p. 294; Charles W. Penrose, as cited in Milton R. Hunter, *The Gospel Through the Ages* (Salt Lake City: Stevens and Wallis, 1945), Chapter 16, p. 107; Brigham Young, *Journal of Discourses* (Liverpool: F.D. Richards, 1855, photo reprint, 1966), Vol. XX, p. 5; and Joseph F. Smith, *Gospel Doctrine* (Salt Lake City: Deseret Book, 1920), Chapter 24, p. 543. Compare *Pearl of Great Price:* Moses 1:39.

47. Regarding salvation by the grace of God, see also *Luke 15:11–32, 18:9–14,* John 4:10, 14:6, 17:3, Acts 15:10–11, *Rom. 3:19–6:23, 8:1–4, 31–39, 11:6,* 2 Cor. 5:17–6:2, Col.2:13–15, 1 Tim. 1:15–16, 2 Tim. 1:7–10, *Titus 3:3–8,* James 1:16–18, and 1 John 4:9–11. Additional references indicating that the grace of God is a gift to all who believe include *John* 3:36, 5:24, *6:27–29,* 11:25–26, 20:29–31, Acts 13:38–39, *Romans 10:1–13, Gal.2:16–3:29, 5:1–6,* 1 John 5:1–5, and 10–13. John 6:37–40 and 10:27–29 show that this gift is eternal, that it won't be taken away.

For the Mormon view of grace, see LDS Bible Dictionary, Holy Bible (Salt Lake City: The Church of Jesus Christ of Latter-day Saints, 1979), p. 697.

48. See *Pearl of Great Price:* Joseph Smith-History 1:18–19; *Doctrine and Covenants* 123:7–8; James E. Talmage, *The Great Apostasy* (Salt Lake City: Deseret News Press, 1968), Preface, p. iii; James E. Talmage, *Articles of Faith* (Salt Lake City: The Church of Jesus Christ of Latter-day Saints, 1949), Chapter 11, pp. 203–204; Bruce R. McConkie, "Apostasy," from *Mormon Doctrine* (Salt Lake City: Bookcraft, 1958), pp. 41–42; Orson Pratt, "Baptism for the Remission of Sins," *The Seer* Vol. II, No. 4 (April 1854), p. 255; Joseph Fielding Smith, *Doctrines of Salvation* (Salt Lake City: Bookcraft, 1956), Vol. I, p. 188.

49. See *Doctrine and Covenants* 21:1–6. Compare *Book of Mormon:* 2 Nephi 3.

50. See also Dan. 2:44, Matt. 28:20, John 14:16, Acts 1:8, Eph. 3:20–21, and Jude 3.

51. *History of the Church* (Salt Lake City: Deseret Book, 1978), Vol. VI, pp. 408-409.

52. *Pearl of Great Price:* Articles of Faith 5. See also James E. Talmage, *Articles of Faith* (Salt Lake City: The Church of Jesus Christ of Latter-day Saints, 1949), Chapter 10, p. 189.

53. See also Acts 4:10–12. Compare John 6:35, 8:12, 10:7–9, 11 and 14, 11:25–26, 14:6, 15:1–2.

54. Brigham Young, *Journal of Discourses* (Liverpool: F.D. Richards, 1855, photo reprint, 1966), Vol. VII, pp. 289–290; also cited in *Relief Society Courses of Study 1985* (Salt Lake City: The Church of Jesus Christ of Latter-day Saints, 1984), p. 40. See also *Doctrine and Covenants* 135:3; Brigham Young, *Journal of Discourses* (Liverpool: F.D. Richards, 1855, photo reprint, 1966), Vol. IX, p. 312; William W. Phelps, "Praise to the Man" (#147), and John Taylor, "The Seer, Joseph, The Seer" (#296), from *Hymns* (Salt Lake City: Deseret Book for The Church of Jesus Christ of Latter-day Saints, 1973). In fact, Mormonism teaches that all worthy Latter-day Saints become "saviors." See *Doctrine and Covenants* 103:9–10 (also 86:11); *Teachings of the Prophet Joseph Smith,* Joseph Fielding Smith, edi-

tor (Salt Lake City: Deseret News Press, 1956), p. 357; or *History of the Church* (Salt Lake City: Deseret Book, 1978), Vol. VI, pp. 313–314; also reprinted as part of the series, "Classics in Mormon Thought," *The Ensign* (April 1971), p. 15; Joseph F. Smith, *Gospel Doctrine* (Salt Lake City: Deseret Book, 1920), Chapter 24, p. 556; and *Teachings of the Prophet Joseph Smith*, Joseph Fielding Smith, editor (Salt Lake City: Deseret News Press, 1956), p. 330; or *History of the Church* (Salt Lake City: Deseret Book, 1978), Vol. VI, p. 184.

Chapter 12: *Music under the Mercy*

1. Charles Williams, *Descent into Hell* (Grand Rapids, Michigan: Eerdmans, 1972), p. 178.

Chapter 13: *Welcome All Wonders*

For complete versions of the poems in this chapter, see Appendix 2.

1. Gerard Manley Hopkins (1844–1889), "New Readings," from *The Poems of Gerard Manley Hopkins*, edited by W.H. Gardner and N.H. MacKenzie (London: Oxford University Press, 1967), p. 18.

2. Dame Edith Sitwell (1887–1964), "Still Falls the Rain," as published in *Eerdmans Book of Christian Poetry*, compiled by Pat Alexander (Grand Rapids: Eerdmans, 1981), pp. 90–91.

3. Christina Rosetti (1830–1894), "A Better Resurrection," as published in *Eerdmans Book of Christian Poetry*, compiled by Pat Alexander (Grand Rapids: Eerdmans, 1981), p. 62.

4. Gerard Manley Hopkins (1844-1889), "He hath abolished the old drouth," from *The Poems of Gerard Manley Hopkins*, edited by W.H. Gardner and N.H. MacKenzie (London: Oxford University Press, 1967), pp. 18–19.

5. Richard Crashaw (1613–1649), "Welcome All Wonders," from *Sacred Poems in Two English Versions* [information pending], p. 83.

6. Robert Southwell (1561–1595), "The Nativity of Christ," as published in *Eerdmans Book of Christian Poetry*, compiled by Pat Alexander (Grand Rapids: Eerdmans, 1981), p. 19.

7. Brian Wren, "Good Is the Flesh," from *Bring Many Names* (Carol Stream, Illinois: Hope Publishing Company, 1989), #16.

8. Brian Wren, "Christmas Now," from *Faith Looking Forward* (Carol Stream, Illinois: Hope Publishing Company, 1983), #13.

9. Robert Southwell (1561–1595), "The Nativity of Christ," as published in *Eerdmans Book of Christian Poetry*, compiled by Pat Alexander (Grand Rapids: Eerdmans, 1981), p. 19.

10. Vassar Miller, "Christmas Mourning," from *If I Had Wheels or Love: Collected Poems of Vassar Miller* (Dallas: Southern Methodist University Press, 1991), p. 11.

11. Robert Southwell (1561–1595), "The Nativity of Christ," as published in *Eerdmans Book of Christian Poetry*, compiled by Pat Alexander (Grand Rapids: Eerdmans, 1981), p. 19.

Chapter 14: *Further Up and Further In*

1. C. S. Lewis, *The Last Battle* (New York: Macmillan Publishing Company, 1988), p. 162.

2. Michael Card, "Joy in the Journey," from *The Life* (1988) (Sparrow 1171).

3. Stephen Crane, "A Man Saw a Ball of Gold in the Sky," from *Outlooks through Literature* (Scott, Foresman and Company, 1964), p. 248.

Coda

1. J. R. R. Tolkien, "The Road Goes Ever On and On," from *The Fellowship of the Ring* (Boston: Houghton Mifflin Company, 1965), p. 44.

2. J.R.R. Tolkien, *The Return of the King* (Boston: Houghton Mifflin Company, 1965), p. 308.